Justice Lies in the District

Number Forty-six
The Centennial Series of the Association of Former Students,
Texas A&M University

Justice
LIES IN THE DISTRICT

The U.S. District Court, Southern District of Texas, 1902–1960

Charles L. Zelden

Texas A&M University Press
College Station

First edition

The paper used in this book meets the minimum requirements
of the American National Standard for Permanence
of Paper for Printed Library Materials, Z39.48-1984.
Binding materials have been chosen for durability.
∞

Library of Congress Cataloging-in-Publication Data

Zelden, Charles L., 1963–
Justice lies in the District : the U.S. District Court, Southern District of Texas, 1902–1960 / Charles L. Zelden. – 1st ed.
p. cm. – (The Centennial series of the Association of Former Students, Texas A&M University ; no. 46)
Includes bibliographical references and index.
ISBN 0-89096-520-X (cloth : alk. paper)
1. United States. District Court (Texas : Southern District)–History. 2. District courts–Texas–Gulf Region. I. Title. II. Series.
KF8755.T48Z45 1993
347.764'02–dc20
[347.64072] 92-31903
CIP

Justice lies in the District, [litigants] either get it there or they don't get it at all.

–Anonymous federal district judge

•

[W]hile infinite justice has its seat in the bosom of God, . . . finite justice, as administered under human law, has its seat in the breast of man, and its declaration and administration had been subject to and distorted by his passions . . . his will [and] . . . his needs.

–Joseph C. Hutcheson, Jr.

Contents

Illustrations

TABLES

Acknowledgments

It is a truism that no endeavor the size and complexity of a historical monograph is done alone. In my case this is especially true. I am beholden to a large number of individuals who shared their time and knowledge with me as I undertook the research and writing of this book.

First I must thank Dr. Harold Hyman. A true mentor in all the meanings of the word, Dr. Hyman's influence shapes not only this work, but my very abilities as a historian. Without his patient training, I would never have become the scholar I am today. I will be forever grateful for the time and effort he has put into teaching me the historian's craft.

Next I wish to thank the various members of the Rice University Graduate Legal/Constitution History Seminar, all of whom read and commented on all or part of the manuscript: Ken De Ville, Ray Winter, Jim Schmidt, Jim Peterson, Chris Meakin, Nick Malavis, Lloyd Kelly, Pat Tidwell, Ginger Frost, Brian Dirck, James Holmes, Matt Taylor, and Mat Moten. I am especially indebted to three of these individuals for sharing parts of their own research with me: James Holmes, former Rice undergraduate, whose work on the Texas federal courts in the nineteenth century proved key to my understanding of that period; Pat Tidwell, who expanded my understanding of James V. Allred; and Lloyd Kelly, whose work on state prisoner suits, though it does not have a direct bearing on this book, gave me an essential comparative foundation from which to work.

Further thanks go to the history faculty at the University of Texas at Arlington, especially David Narrett, Ron Zabory, and Bob Fairbanks. Their collegiality and advice proved extremely useful as I went through the sometimes painful process of publication.

I would also like to thank the judges of the Southern District Court. It was they who originated the idea of a history of the court and who funded the majority of my research. Their willingness to answer my questions and aid my investigation by providing primary research materials and their unselfish commitment to producing a serious work of historical scholarship were essential to the successful completion of the book. Provided throughout the project with copies of the chapters, they focused all their comments on clarifying technical legal matters. At no time did they pressure me to change my analysis of the court, even where that analysis produced conclusions that were critical of the court or its personnel. For this restraint and commitment I am grateful.

Additional funding for the book was provided by the law firms of Vinson and Elkins and of Joe Jamail and by the Rice University History Department. I am obliged to each for their support.

Numerous other individuals and institutions facilitated the completion of this work. Barbara Rust and the staff at the National Archives, Southwest Region, an underused resource for historians, provided essential help in locating and accessing the records of the Southern District, as did the staff at the National Archives in Washington, D.C. Ching-Cheng C. Ting and the staff of the Southern District of Texas Library provided similar services. So too did Mary Mapps, Buddy Cariker, and Jesse Clark of the Clerk's Office of the Southern District Court. The librarians of Rice University's Fondren Library and of the Houston Metropolitan Research Center of the Houston Public Library were also helpful in finding necessary sources of information. Waller T. Burns III, T. Everton Kennerly, and Joseph C. Hutcheson III provided access to family papers. Judge Lynn N. Hughes, Judge Norman W. Black, Judge David Hittner, Dr. John B. Boles, Dr. Chandler Davidson, Dr. Ira Gruber, Dr. Martin Wiener, Dr. Mark Leff, Irene Zisek, Sandy Pérez, Nancy Parker, Connie Killebrew, and Thelda Chamblis all provided needed encouragement and help.

Of Rick Stetter and the rest of the staff of Texas A&M University Press I can not say enough. Their willingness to work with me on this project was both encouraging and helpful. They have made the sometimes painful process of revision and editing a pleasant experience.

Last, I would like to thank all those who quietly put up with me during the many years I worked on this project: Matt Marks, Paula Burch, David and Heidi Needleman, Kathleen Gajewski, Pat Lawinger, Robert Schmunk, Loy Anderson, Cary Jensen, Brad and Jenny Cohen, Lee Walzer, Zeke and Catherine Leventhal-Arnold, my parents, Janice and Jerome Zelden, my sister, Renee Novit, and last, but not least, my wife Lynn, to whom this book is lovingly dedicated.

Justice Lies in the District

Introduction

I

The Constitution says little about the lower federal courts. Article III, Section 1 declares that "the judicial Power of the United States, shall be vested in one supreme court, and in such inferior courts as the Congress may from time to time ordain and establish." In addition, it grants the judges of these courts life tenure "during good behaviour" and requires that their compensation "shall not be diminished during their continuance in office."

This brevity was deliberate. Most delegates to the Constitutional Convention assumed that a national judiciary with a Supreme Court as its apex was essential to the success of the new government, but they could not agree on the need for a lower federal judiciary. Some delegates held that inferior federal courts were necessary to ensure uniform decisions, to protect the interests of the national government, and to provide a bias-free forum for out-of-state litigants. Others held that inferior federal courts would be an unnecessary and costly duplication of state courts.

Unable to agree, the convention compromised and left the decision to Congress, which found the problem equally difficult. Of seventy-nine constitutional amendments proposed by state ratifying conventions, sixteen called for changes in the judiciary article. Most asked for the elimination or restriction of Congress's powers to create inferior federal tribunals. Not only would these courts be redundant and expensive, anti-Federalists argued, but they would swallow up state courts to the detriment of individual liberties. As the minority faction in the Pennsylvania convention explained: "An inhabitant of Pittsburgh, on a charge of crime committed on the banks of the Ohio, may be obliged to defend himself at the side of the Delaware, and so vice versa."[1]

Faced with such intense opposition, the Federalist party, which controlled the first Congress and wanted a strong lower federal judiciary, compromised. The resulting Judiciary Act of 1789—which one historian has described as "an instrument of reconciliation . . . to quiet still smoldering resentments"—created two levels of federal trial courts, each with limited jurisdiction and subject to various local and regional controls.[2] Of particular significance and effect was Section 34, which ruled that "the laws of the several States, except where the Constitution, treaties or statutes of the United States shall otherwise require or provide, shall be regarded as rules of decision in trials at common law in the Courts of the United States." The result was a decentralized federal judicial system whose foundation was "lodged . . . squarely in the states."[3]

Historians have used the tension between local and national concerns inherent in this decentralized system to explain the actions—or, in some cases, the inactions—of the lower federal courts.[4] For example, Mary K. Bonsteel Tachau, in her path-breaking history of the first twenty years of the District Court of Kentucky, explains its growth into one of the federal system's busiest tribunals as the direct result of its support of "the perceptions and priorities of those who lived in the West" over "those who worked in the nation's capital." Initially distrusted by those it sought to serve, the Kentucky federal court "proved its usefulness" to local residents by "protecting the people [of Kentucky] from the consequences of ignoring unpopular federal statutes." Its increasing case load was the result.[5]

This focus on competing local and national priorities has proven a productive line of inquiry. The image of federal courts torn between serving national priorities and local needs is convincing and, further, ties neatly into general historical trends on certain divisive effects of federalism; however, it explains only some of the forces shaping the lower federal judiciary. By emphasizing tensions between local and national forces, it underplays economic and social groups whose differing needs placed conflicting demands on the lower federal courts. As a result, this body of useful scholarship produces descriptions of the federal court system that, taken together, seem contradictory; one scholar's "local" federal judiciary is another's "national" tribunal.

A comparison of two of the best works on the lower federal courts points out some of the problems. Writing on the institutional development of the lower federal judiciary in the nineteenth century, Kermit Hall sees local interests as the dominant force shaping these courts. Even the Civil War and Reconstruction did not change the court's "administrative decentralization and individuality." "The traditional concept of embedding federal district courts in the local constituencies they served," Hall argues, "made them as potentially responsive to local interests as to the dictates of national authority promulgating a program of reconstruction." Congress significantly enlarged the jurisdictions of the federal courts in the 1860s and 1870s, which greatly increased the dockets of these courts. Still, few if any changes were made to "modify court structure or [to] provide additional resources" to clear the expanded dockets. This institutional rigidity impeded all efforts to nationalize the federal court system, Hall concludes. Threatened by local resistance to change, deluged by a "flood of litigation," and hampered by inadequate resources, the federal court system "collapsed under local pressures" after the Civil War and continued to "bend to local considerations." Only the structural reforms of the twentieth century changed this pattern.[6]

Conversely, Tony Freyer, describes interactions between the lower federal courts and business interests in the nineteenth and early twentieth centuries as responses primarily to national, not local, needs. "Until fairly late in the nation's history, the federal system created uncertainty over rules governing business," he notes. Members of the business community turned to the federal courts, properly confident that these courts would provide for certainty in interstate business.[7]

Both Hall and Freyer are essentially correct in their analyses.[8] Why, then, the seeming contradictions? The same federal judges whom Freyer describes as serving the needs of interstate capitalism, Hall suggests had strong links to local communities often known for their anticorporate attitude. Where Freyer sees independent federal courts applying a powerful nationalizing ideology, Hall perceives decentralized courts bowing to local norms and values. The answer is that competition between local and national interests was not the only factor shaping the actions of the lower federal courts. Federalism was an important element in these tensions. Equally significant, however, was disagreement about whether these courts should focus on issues of public or private law.

Public law embraces areas in which "the state has a direct interest." Private law encompasses "disputes in which the interests of individuals, rather than the state, are involved."[9] As courts of general jurisdiction, the lower federal courts hear issues involving both public and private law. As courts of public law, they implement federal laws and regulations, define public rights and duties, and balance the needs of the nation with the rights of individuals. As courts of private law, they resolve such "mundane, though socially important questions, . . . as debtor-creditor relations, accidental liability, property transfer and other matters of private right."[10]

Where case loads are small and the demands on lower federal courts are limited, few tensions arise over these dual functions. When business increases and dockets become crowded, however, conflicts develop rapidly about how the court's time and energies should be spent. Faced with packed dockets, litigants, lawyers, and judges begin to choose between the two functions, selecting some cases to press for a quick decision and allowing others to languish. These decisions determine the actions and, ultimately, the wider social, economic, and political impact of the relevant lower federal court.

II

For the nation's first century, demands on the lower federal courts were small. Public and private cases coexisted peacefully on the dockets.[11] This changed with the Civil War. Although, as Hall has shown, the institutional structures of the lower federal courts remained little changed by that conflict, their powers and jurisdictions were greatly enlarged. In an "anti-institutional age," the "traditional and inexpensive" lower federal courts became the favored bureaucratic agency for enforcing new legislation.[12] Congress and the president expanded the jurisdiction of the federal courts to include a mix of military and nonmilitary matters, including confiscation, emancipation, disloyalty, military governments, Reconstruction, and bankruptcy. Congress also enhanced the right of litigants to remove certain kinds of cases from state to federal court. The Judiciary Act of 1789 had limited removals, but the Habeas Corpus Act of 1863 afforded federal officers protection from civil and criminal actions arising out of official acts by permitting removal of such suits to federal court. The 1866 Civil Rights Act (and, later, the 1871 Enforcement Act) granted similar removal rights to private litigants. The Separable Controversies Act of 1866 expanded this access, allowing nonresident parties to split their case and bring their part of the case into federal court under diversity of citizenship. One year later, the Local Prejudice Act increased access even more, authorizing any party in a state case to remove suit if "he has reason to . . . believe that, from prejudice or local influence, he will not be able to obtain justice in a state court." Finally, the Jurisdiction and Removal Act of 1875 gave the lower federal courts original and removal jurisdiction "as broad as the Constitution authorized" by permitting any party in a case to remove, authorizing removal of the whole suit if the actual controversy was between diverse parties, allowing for removal on diversity even where one of the parties involved lived in the forum state, and permitting removal of all federal question suits.[13]

This expanded jurisdiction altered the balance of judicial federalism and swelled demands on the lower federal courts. The national government now had the authority to respond to a wide range of public and private actions within the states, though it often hesitated to use this authority. Since the 1880s, however, the national government's regulatory presence has grown, and with it the lower federal courts' public law functions.

In addition to expanding the federal courts' public law functions, enlarged federal jurisdictions also encouraged private litigants, especially new interstate corporations, to use the lower federal courts. Exploiting a growing national market full of opportunities and uncertainties, business leaders used this expanded access to national courts to solve a host of economic and political problems growing out of the federal legal system.[14] An explosion of private law litigation thus joined that generated by public actions. As a result, by 1900 lower federal court dockets were more than double their size in 1860, and no end to this growth was in sight.[15]

This growth in case load caused problems for the federal courts. Unless changed, the present system was doomed to collapse under its own weight. Legislators and jurists, in turn, understood that something had to be done to shrink federal court dockets. The question was, which type of law—public or private – should be retained and which diminished in setting the federal courts' jurisdiction?

Debate quickly grew over which type of law deserved priority on federal dockets. Nationally, this debate centered on efforts by politicians and liberal legal writers to reverse the effects of the so-called *Swift* doctrine. Supreme Court justice Joseph Story's decision in *Swift v. Tyson* (1842) permitted federal judges to apply discretion freely in determining procedures and rules of decision in common law litigation, "irrespective of state court decisions," where no conflicting state law existed. While state statutes had to be followed, state court interpretations of their meanings did not. "Federal judges were free to determine for themselves the common-law rules governing private litigation" and to develop a federal common law favorable to the interests and needs of interstate business.[16]

Of limited effect prior to the Civil War, *Swift*'s reach rapidly expanded with the expansion of federal court jurisdiction in the 1860s and 1870s. Expanded jurisdiction increased access to the lower federal courts. The independent and mostly probusiness decisions of federal judges made under *Swift*'s grant of common law powers gave business a reason to use this expanded jurisdiction. Combined, these factors drew a growing number of private suits into the federal courts.

As the effects of this expansion in private suits became apparent, southern and western advocates objected to the federal courts spending so much of their limited time on private corporate cases. For example, Congressman David Culberson of Texas was troubled because "[i]n almost all the States of the Union the [U.S.] Circuit Courts are over worked and are unable to determine the business before them with that deliberation, patience, and research which becomes a judicial tribunal." On average, it took three years for a case to be concluded. "Such delay [was] not only vexatious, and expensive to litigants, but [was] tantamount to a denial of justice." Culberson blamed this unhappy situation on the rapid increase in private, mostly corporate, removal litigation. "In nine hundred and ninety-nine cases out of every thousand removed into the circuit courts . . . from state courts," Culberson asserted, "there is not the semblance, even, of an element of Federal jurisdiction involved." Cases of this sort were clogging federal dockets, leading to increasing delays and thus permitting "the greatest frauds to be practiced upon the legitimate jurisdiction of these courts."[17]

The solution, Culberson argued, was to limit the access of corporations to the federal courts. He incorporated these views into a series of unsuccessful bills, from 1877 to his retirement in 1896. He proposed that for purposes of jurisdiction all corporations be treated as local to the states in which they did business and hence unable to remove suits to federal courts on diversity. In addition, Culberson called for raising the amount necessary for diversity jurisdiction to two thousand dollars. These proposals would have prohibited most federal diversity suits, thus diminishing the private part of the federal courts' dockets and, presumably, freeing time for issues of public importance.[18]

Numerous legal scholars echoed Culberson's indictments of the lower federal courts' inefficiency. A writer in the *Central Law Journal* noted in 1884 the link between corporate removal cases and delays and inefficiency in the federal court system. Five years later, William M. Meigs, a commentator on the federal court system, reemphasized this point, arguing that the delays and injustices of the federal court system resulted directly from the large number of removal cases docketed, cases that Meigs felt were more properly placed in the state courts. At first only a vocal minority among legal professionals, these critics were ultimately joined by others, including Felix Frankfurter and James Landis, whose 1927 *Business of the Supreme Court* was intended, in part, as a critique of the *Swift* doctrine's influence on the growth of federal court dockets. By the 1930s this view had become dominant among legal academics.[19]

Assembled in opposition to this growing body of opinion, a diverse group of lawyers, politicians, and business leaders defended the extension of federal judges' discretion in private cases as necessary, proper, and useful. While the federal courts were inefficient and slow, the state courts were worse and created great uncertainty for interstate business. Each state's laws and regulations were enforced by its own courts. The "exasperating uncertainty" of these different proceedings made the conduct of business difficult, and sometimes impossible. "It is a fact of everyday observation," wrote Daniel M. Chamberlain, prominent New York City attorney and former governor of South Carolina, in 1889, "that a resident of one State may have property or commercial interests at the same time in several different states. He may also at the same time have agents making sales, contracts, and collections in several other states." This resulted in the "pecuniary interests" of this individual being "subject . . . [to] many separate jurisdictions and to many discordant decisions of courts and rules of law." In such a system, "some anomalies . . . inconveniences . . . conflicts . . . even some abuses" were inevitable.[20]

Most business leaders and their lawyers viewed the federal courts as protecting their interests. William Howard Taft frequently noted that "no single element—and I want to emphasize this because I don't think it is always thought of—no single element in our governmental structure has done so much to secure capital for the legitimate development of enterprises throughout the West and South as the existence of federal courts there, with a jurisdiction to hear diverse citizenship cases." A 1928 American Bar Association report seconded this view. "Without federal protection," it argued, the nation's financial structure would collapse. "When nonresident investors learn that they must in an emergency depend on the state courts to protect their interests, the confidence which has for generations been based upon the security afforded by the right to resort to the federal courts will be seriously impaired; and a serious blow will be directed at the financial structure which has been built up in a long course of years. . . . contractions of investments and loans . . . [and] increases in the rates of interests" would be the result.[21]

At various times, Congress sought to limit the federal courts' private dockets, but without much success. The 1887 Judiciary Act prohibited most removals on the basis of local prejudice. The 1891 Judiciary Act created a middle level of appellate courts, the circuit courts of appeals, to handle private appeals and thus free the Supreme Court's dockets for public issues. And the 1925 Judiciary Act strictly limited all appeals from the circuit court of appeals to the Supreme Court as a matter of right. Only the 1887 act successfully cleared federal court dockets, however, and it was so badly written that its effect was minimal.

Nor did the federal courts themselves—until the Supreme Court's 1938 repudiation of *Swift* in *Erie RR Co. v. Tompkins*—seek to limit the procedural independence that encouraged large private case loads. By this time, however, new federal statutes and the hardened tradition of business seeking justice in the federal courts worked against significant reductions.[22]

Disagreements over the work of the lower federal courts also occurred at the local level. As with the national debate, conflict centered on the causes of crowded federal dockets. At this level, however, the focus was on the specific work load of a single federal court. This fact gave the local debates a different tone from those at the national level. Those arguing for a particular local agenda had a large personal stake in the outcomes of the debates. Participants included local politicians and civic reformers, business leaders, and attorneys. Each had specific needs, wants, and goals, which the actions of the local federal court could affect positively or negatively. Rather than policy considerations, disputes at this level became contests between competing interests over particular legal, political, social, and economic issues and results; the arguments each side made, in turn, focused on specific issues and cases.

This specificity underlay the considerable influence that debate within individual courts had on the actions and impacts of the federal court system. By linking arguments about priorities to specific cases, this focus mandated that decisions for or against a particular agenda would be made. Unlike members of Congress, federal judges could rarely ignore problems created by overcrowded dockets. Every decision, opinion, or order, every case, whether moved up on the docket or settled administratively, reflected choices made by jurists between competing demands for judicial action. Sworn to uphold the law and to fulfill the duties of their courts as set by Congress and the Supreme Court, federal judges sat in the center of a storm. All arguments for or against a particular agenda were aimed at them and, ultimately, it was their choices that would shape their courts' actions.[23]

The agenda a particular judge chose depended on many factors. Foremost was his personal background.[24] From what social and economic class did the judge come? Did he have personal or professional links with either side of the dispute? Were his political leanings conservative or liberal? In what ways did he view the historical role of the law and of the courts? The decisions of other judges, especially those from appellate courts, were also important. No judge likes to have decisions overturned. Few feel comfortable taking positions wildly different from those of peers. An agenda widely accepted elsewhere makes it easier for a judge to move in its direction. Finally, pressures were placed on judges by public opinion. No judge likes to make unpopular decisions. As Circuit Judge John R. Brown noted in relation to the problems posed by school desegregation and other civil rights issues: "lifetime tenure insulates judges from anxiety over worldly cares for body and home and family. But it does not protect them from the unconscious urge for the approbation of their fellow-man, and fellow-man most often means those of like interests and backgrounds, business and professional experience and predilections, and even prejudices."[25]

Whatever agenda a judge finally selected and for whatever reasons, this choice shaped the response of his court to demands for justice. A district in which public issues enjoyed priority was likely to be a different place from that in which private matters had the nod. Whichever way a judge decided, segments of the population were going to have their needs, interests, and goals ignored or served in some way. Every win caused a loss. The agenda a judge followed, therefore, involved more than just the outcome of the cases before the court; it also involved the future of the district and of the nation.

Viewed from this public/private perspective, the history of the lower federal courts since the 1880s is the story of competition between the supporters of two agendas for the operation of the lower federal courts—one agenda counting public law as these tribunals' primary function, the other arguing private law as more important. Involving both national and local participants, this contest shaped not only the decisions of these courts but the processes by which decisions were made.

Which agenda has proven to be the most convincing to federal judges? Each has made his or her own settlement on this issue. As Frankfurter and Landis noted, we have a "hierarchy of courts, not of judges."[26] Most historical analyses imply that federal judges supported private agendas; however, examples abound of judges making opposite choices, or stressing both public and private law at different times.

III

What follows is an attempt to document the choices made for one lower federal district court, the Southern District Court of Texas (hereafter the Southern District Court or the court), to examine in detail the actions and functions served by this court over a sixty-year period, and to see which agenda dominated its efforts. The youngest of Texas' four district courts, the Southern District Court, came into being in 1902 in response to a growing case load crisis in the state. Serving a rapidly developing region, one including the growing Houston metropolis, the new court quickly faced a large, complex, and expanding case load. By 1931 it ranked as the largest single-judge court in the nation. Thirty years later it had four judges and was among the ten busiest federal district courts. In 1990, at the time of this writing, the Southern District has thirteen judges (with five more about to be nominated) and is one of the four largest and busiest district courts in the nation.

While its relative youth and rapid growth distinguish the Southern District Court from other district courts, they also make this court a viable subject for a study. The court's fast growth throws into sharp relief trends that might have remained obscure in a more stable court. In fewer than one hundred years, Southeast Texas evolved from a neocolonial agricultural economy into a mixed industrial-agricultural-extractive one, with its economy centered in Houston, now the fourth-largest city in the country. As part of the South, Texas society endured radical social, demographic, and political changes at a speed that meant that Southeast Texas experienced extremely high stresses and pressures from growth. The Southern District Court faced challenges similar to those of other courts, but much more intense.

This study emphasizes the period 1902 to 1960, for this was a time of remarkable continuity in the court's history. From its inception through the 1950s, the court's judges consistently applied a private agenda in setting their priorities and in making their judicial decisions. Their goal was the promotion of Southeast Texas' economic, social, and political development through private means. To achieve this goal, the judges chose to support, stabilize, and regulate local and national businesses and markets.

These regional development imperatives were in conflict with a public agenda stressing the enforcement of federal social and economic regulations. (Civil rights would not be a significant issue before the 1960s.) This public agenda grew in intensity and scope as the century progressed. Of little consequence in 1902, by 1960 this agenda's pressure on the court would be impossible to ignore. Prior to 1960, however, where private and public needs differed, the court subordinated the public to the private, most often by minimizing its duties as the enforcement arm of the federal government to the benefit of private development. Occasionally, it simply ignored its public duties entirely in the service of its private agenda. Only the two world wars changed this pattern, and then for but a short time.

The source of this private agenda's strength and endurance was threefold. First, a great demand for the court's private services issued from local business. Given the unsettled, fluid state of the Texas economy for much of the century, business leaders in the region longed for ways to foster certainty in their marketplace dealings. Seeking to avoid costly mistakes, they searched for ways to clarify their rights and responsibilities, their liabilities and assets. One method involved reorganizing corporate structures and merging into large regional entities. Another involved seeking "friendly" federal and state regulations. One of the most adaptable methods of protecting one's position, however, was to turn to the federal courts for help.[27]

This is exactly what members of the business community did in increasing numbers. They saw the court as a useful and adaptable tool with which to promote and stabilize growth within the district. As a court of law, the Southern

District could ascertain the legal relationships between business associates; as an equity court, it could protect and reorganize a failed company free from the pressures of creditors. The list of services useful to local and national businesses operating in Southeast Texas could go on and on. If business leaders did not know of the court's potential in this regard, their lawyers did. The result was to make use of the court an important part of doing business in Texas.

The second explanation for the private agenda's hold on the court lies in Southeast Texas' race relations. Work by a number of historians on the urban South has noted many occasions on which southerners rejected public works that would have benefited the whole community rather than extend access to minority groups. In the case of Houston, Harold Platt has shown how such concerns shaped the growth (or, in some cases, the lack of growth) of the city's streetcar system and electrical services.[28] It is therefore quite likely that such concerns had a similar effect in fostering the judges' and business community's emphasis on private control over regional development–creating, if you will, a hidden agenda within the more open private one. Just how important this factor was in shaping the region's private emphasis is, however, open to question. Little concrete proof of the impact of racism can be found in the court's records. Throughout the sixty years covered by this study, few minorities came before the court in anything but criminal matters. Here the judges exhibited a paternalism that, while hinting at the existence of deep-seated racial biases, does not provide clear answers as to what role such biases played in shaping the judges' actions on civil matters. Still, while the exact impact of the region's racial biases on the court's private emphasis remains unquantifiable, their existence as a deep and perhaps unconscious source of judicial motivation is undeniable.

The third and most important reason for the private agenda's strength was the general acceptance of this business vision by the judges of the court as a result of their backgrounds. The seven judges who served in the court between 1902 and 1960 came from the same political, social, and economic class as the state's business community. All called Houston, the economic and social center of the district, home. Six of the seven served as corporate attorneys for at least part of their careers, five making this category of law the foundation of their practice. All seven held what would today be considered a conservative view of the law, one that stressed protection of private property from excessive public regulation but that also stressed public duties of the holders of private property. Socially, politically, and ideologically drawn toward a private agenda for their court, the judges' very conceptions of right and wrong and of proper action thus developed along lines similar to those exhibited by most business leaders and their lawyer allies.[29]

Combined, then, these three factors led each of these judges to view the private economic development of Southeast Texas as a priority for their court, to see the needs of the civil side of the docket as the most important concern before him as a judge.

The judges' active support of Texas business interests did not mean, however, that they were subservient to any particular interests or consciously followed some blueprint of cultural or social hegemony. Howard Zinn has noted that those "who postulate [the existence of] 'power elites' are right for the most part, . . . but they often overestimate self-consciousness and confidence as characteristics of those elites." This was especially the case in Texas, where, as George Green has shown, class consciousness hardly existed in the state's political establishment.[30] The judges' primary goal was to do their duty as federal judges as best they could. An independent agent, the court freely took actions that affected individual business interests. Most cases pitted one business against another. The court's choice to help one business usually harmed another. As result of its ideological underpinnings, the court often held individual businesses to standards of practice that directly constrained their operations.

The court's emphasis on private development carried wide ramifications for individual and corporate litigants and for the entire region. Booming business and investment growth had social costs as well as economic benefits. "Houstonians paid a price for the low taxes and laissez-faire government associated with a good business climate," notes sociologist Joe Feagin. Writing on the city's business elite's successful manipulation of local government to provide a low-tax, probusiness environment, Feagin notes how these social costs, though similar to those paid by other quickly growing regions, were especially high in Southeast Texas. The choice of "private urban development without intelligent planning in the larger public interest" by the city's elite "create[d] huge social costs for city residents, . . . [with the] poorest Houstonians often bearing the heaviest burden." Among these costs were "major poverty, homelessness, minority displacement, subsidence, flooding, water pollution, toxic waste, sewage, and street maintenance problems." This was the downside of the private agenda's victory, always present, but often hidden by the more visible, and welcomed, economic benefits of growth.[31]

The court's emphasis on private matters began to change around 1960. Civil rights advocates, asserting a need for favorable judicial interpretations and the expansion of federal government programs under Presidents Kennedy and Johnson, were transforming both American society and the type of cases coming before the federal courts. More public cases were filed. These cases were larger, more complex, and limiting for lower federal jurists because they were supported by Supreme Court directives. The Southern District's judges were reluctant at first to change their priorities. But higher court directives, changing judicial personnel, and the realities of a docket crowded with important public cases forced change. By the 1970s a public agenda dominated the court's actions and priorities. Even the economic downturn of the 1980s could not change the dominance this public agenda had on the court's priorities.[32]

These were changes for the future, however. During the Southern District Court's first sixty years, it was private economic concerns that exclusively shaped its priorities. Despite Southeast Texas' significant economic and social transformations—transformations that the court itself had helped bring about—and the growing force of the public agenda, the court's priorities changed little during these years as the judges fought to promote regional growth and development through the creation, support, and regulation of regional business interests. Only external pressure would break this agenda's hold on the court, and then only with great difficulty.

1. Federal Justice in a Frontier State

THE FEDERAL COURTS IN NINETEENTH-CENTURY TEXAS

I

The congressional act of December 29, 1845, that made Texas a state also created a single judicial district over the entire state. Texas was to be served by a single judge holding court in Galveston and at "such other times and places . . . as the said judge may order." Along with its powers as a district court, the District of Texas was also granted those of a circuit court, allowing the district's judge to hear and decide all federal cases in Texas. Appeals from this court went directly to the Supreme Court.[1]

This grant of additional jurisdiction to the district court was not unprecedented. In the past, when district courts were organized in geographically remote places that were difficult for circuit-riding Supreme Court justices to reach, the new courts were granted concurrent circuit powers. Such had been the case in Kentucky during its first years of statehood in the 1790s and early 1800s.[2]

The effect of this grant was significant. It made the already-potent Texas District Court an even more powerful institution. With its expanded powers, the new district court heard all federal issues litigated in the state. Given the unsettled condition of the frontier region, these federal issues included many cases of local importance. The decision of this court would shape these issues.

One of the most troubling of these issues involved the legitimacy of Texas land titles. Land-rich but money-poor, Texas in the 1840s and early 1850s did not have a money economy; rather, wealth was judged in terms of land ownership.[3] In order to attract settlers, Texas literally gave land away. Depending on when settlers came to Texas, they were entitled to anywhere from 640 to 4,000 acres. All that a settler had to do to get this land was apply to a board of local commissioners in the relevant county. If the claim was valid, the commissioners issued certificates for land to be taken out of the public domain. The grantee then engaged a "locator" to find and survey the plot. The survey notes were certified and sent to the state land office, which issued a patent to the land.[4]

Simple in theory, in practice the system proved unwieldy and created overlapping and conflicting claims to the public domain. Mexico, the Republic of

Texas, and now the state of Texas had all issued land grants. Which of these, if any, took precedence when they conflicted was unknown. Doubts about the legitimacy of many of these grants added to the confusion. Excessive speculation and outright fraud had resulted in the issuance of patents granting land far in excess of the amounts allowed by law. Traveling boards were set up by the state to rule on the validity of these patents, and where fraud was discovered, the state repudiated them. Many of these voided patents were owned by out-of-state investors, however, who had purchased what they thought were genuine certificates. (The certificates had, in fact, been valid when purchased.) These investors were unwilling to give up their claims to the land. As a result, millions of acres of the Texas public domain had "unquiet" titles, requiring lengthy litigation to work out who was the legitimate owner.[5]

Most of this litigation lodged in the state courts, but the issue was brought before the new federal district court as well. Out-of-state investors, especially those losing their state cases, were likely to turn to the federal courts under diversity jurisdiction, especially if the district judge was known to hold a particular position on the issue.

A related issue likely to come before the new court was interstate debt. Most Texans came to the state seeking a better life; many were fleeing failure and debt in their old states. In order to encourage immigration, and also as a result of a deep-seated distrust of out-of-state creditors, Texas had liberal debtor laws. No one's homestead could be taken away for debt nor were debts acquired elsewhere considered valid after a few years. The federal court with its diversity powers was a new forum in which these debt claims could be heard, one uncontrolled by the local electorate and hence a potential threat to these debtor laws.[6]

Selecting the court's first judge was thus an important issue for Texans. The state's two U.S. senators, Sam Houston and Thomas Rusk, supported different candidates for the job. Houston's was A. B. Shelby of San Augustine, a district judge during the Republic. Rusk supported James Webb, a former territorial judge in Florida and attorney general under the Republic. Each received endorsements from leading Texas politicians. Webb in particular was highly regarded, receiving the support of sixty-five of the state's eighty-two legislators. The problem was that neither Houston nor Rusk, political opponents for years, would accept the other's candidate for the job. Since the negative vote of even one of a state's senators was usually enough to defeat the nomination of a judge, a compromise candidate was needed.[7]

John C. Watrous, a Houston lawyer, was born and reared in Connecticut. He moved to Knoxville, Tennessee, in 1828, read law with Colonel John Williams, and became a close acquaintance of young congressman James K. Polk. On completing his apprenticeship, Watrous moved to Alabama, where he practiced law and dabbled in local politics. Hurt by the depression of 1837, he moved with his brother to Texas, settling in the Republic's capital, Houston. Watrous became very successful as a lawyer who specialized in land title cases. For a time he served as attorney general of the Republic of Texas. Resigning his post in the face of political pressure, Watrous returned to private practice, again specializing in land title and debt cases.[8]

Even before Texas gained statehood, Watrous had initiated efforts to "go upon the bench if I can procure the appointment." To further his case, he and his supporters organized petitions testifying to the "general satisfaction to the bar" if Watrous would be named judge. With the impasse over the other candidates for the job, his familiarity with the land grant problem, and his friendship with President Polk, Watrous seemed the perfect compromise candidate.[9] He was thus named to the bench on May 29, 1846.

Watrous's familiarity with the issues surrounding land titles and interstate debt proved his, and ultimately his court's, undoing. Though the court's docket was initially quite small, taking on average no more than two or three months a year to clear, the issues involved in the land and debt cases that came before it created a politically explosive mixture that soon ignited.[10]

Even before annexation, cases had been pending before the Supreme Court of the Republic testing the validity of a series of grants made by the state of Coahuila and Texas in 1834 and 1835. These lands, known as the "littoral and border leagues," encompassed almost five million acres along the lower Texas Gulf Coast and the U.S.-Mexican border. The convention that declared Texas independence had also, in order to "protect" the public domain from unjust and fraudulent claims made under Mexican rule, ruled the littoral and border grants invalid. These lands, the convention argued, had been fraudulently acquired in violation of Mexican law. Not only had the Mexican government disapproved the grants, but fraud had resulted in the ownership of these grants by a small number of persons. That the land was acquired by private owners despite this opposition was clearly in violation of the Mexican Constitution of 1824.[11]

In 1841 the Texas Congress ruled that all persons claiming lands acquired by Mexican grant within the border and littoral sections had one year to bring suit against the state to determine the validity of their claims. After this date further claims under the Mexican grants would be barred forever. One year later, the government declared all unclaimed land as public domain and began distributing it to settlers claiming titles from the Republic of Texas. As far as the state was concerned, the issue was settled.

Not everyone agreed. Many of the Mexican grants were owned by northern speculators who had been unable to bring suit prior to the 1842 cutoff date. Hoping that the courts would sustain their title to this land despite the Texas Congress's rule, they brought suit in the Republic's courts. With the imposition of statehood, the speculators refiled in the new state courts, which proved similarly unwilling to validate these grants, especially as the Republic had made later grants to other settlers. Only where a Mexican grant had been approved by the Mexican executive prior to independence would the state courts rule in the claimant's favor.[12]

Stymied in the state courts, the northern speculators turned to the federal court. Here their luck changed. Watrous's background in the land grant process had been largely as an attorney for absentee speculators, though he had also dealt with the general issue as attorney general. In the late 1830s he had successfully forced the land office of the Republic to issue a patent granting all of Galveston Island west of the City of Galveston to Edward Hall and Levi Jones. In the year before he became judge, Watrous acted as chief counsel to the New York and Texas Land and Immigration Company, an unincorporated joint-stock company organized to speculate in Texas lands.[13]

Arguing that the state Supreme Court had not definitively settled the issue of the border and littoral lands, the judge utilized his own opinion in deciding these cases. In sixty suits he sustained the speculators' titles.[14] The Texas Supreme Court, however, continued to hold the titles invalid. In 1855 this court ruled that these grants were valid only if approved by the Mexican national government; four years later, it emphatically noted that the "series of decisions of this court, settling the construction of the local law upon which the titles to real property largely depend, must be regarded as emphatically the law of the state; and should be binding upon this, and every other court in which these titles may be drawn in question." With such a strong statement of the law by the state supreme court, Watrous was forced to accept that his views on the subject were not definitive. In the mid-1850s the judge began to change his stance, ruling against holders of the Mexican grants.[15]

Despite the switch, Watrous's actions in these cases were very unpopular with most Texans. As one contemporary lawyer put it, the judge's land decisions "produced a great deal of excitement against him," especially among the small holders of Texas, who feared that the title to their lands would be lost to "alien" speculators holding previously invalid Mexican grants. They feared that Watrous was "an alien at heart and an enemy to everything Texas [*sic*]." The judge was attacked as a "fiend [come] to sit in judgement upon us . . . without one feeling in common with the people, whose homes have been established here in days of fearful peril."[16]

The judge's continuing connections with the New York and Texas Land and Immigration Company added to the feelings against the court. On his appointment as federal judge, Watrous had resigned his position as the company's general counsel; however, he retained the stock with which he had been paid for his past legal services. The land company held Republic and state land certificates entitling it to more than two million acres of the public domain. The state land office ruled many of these certificates "fraudulent" because their original holder had failed to fulfill all of the requirements for receiving a grant. Questions remained as to whether the land office's rejection was conclusive, however. In late 1846 and early 1847, the land company, in a strategy worked out by Watrous when he was general counsel, filed three test cases, two in state court and the third in Watrous's court, to prove the title to this land. The two state cases were soon lost. The judge had transferred the federal case to district court for the Southern District of Louisiana, where the opposite resulted. The Supreme Court ultimately agreed with the state courts, ruling against the land company.[17]

Watrous had nothing to do with the transferred case and was ultimately on the losing side, but many Texans blamed him for the favorable result in the Louisiana case. They distrusted his ties to the land company and felt that he had dictated and directed the federal lawsuit, using his judicial authority to further the case. As they saw it, Watrous was using his position as a federal judge for private gain.[18]

Another land case initiated at this time added to the conviction that the Texas federal court was biased in favor of alien speculators and that Watrous was profiting from his position. In July, 1850, Watrous, his brother, and a mutual friend joined with John Lapsley to purchase the patents to a sixty thousand–acre grant in Northeast Texas, the La Vega Grant. Watrous was to retain a one-quarter share of the land. On January 11, 1851, Lapsley and his attorney filed suit in both state and federal courts to prove their title and to remove a number of squatters. The hope was that the state court would decide the issue and that Watrous would not have to become involved in the case as judge. In November, 1851, the state courts ruled in favor of the speculators, but the inconclusive decision left important legal points unresolved for the federal court to decide. At this point, the judge disclosed his ties to the plaintiffs and ordered the case transferred to New Orleans, where the district court ruled in favor of the Watrous group, a decision affirmed by the Supreme Court in February, 1858.[19]

Finally, Watrous's private speculations had succeeded and forced local residents off the land to the benefit of speculators. Though the judge's only official action in this case was to transfer it to another court, his opponents argued that his very involvement in the case meant that an important local issue was decided by an out-of-state jury. Of what use was a local federal court if significant issues had to be decided elsewhere? Where was the justice in this? What was Texas to do?

The judge's decisions on debt cases forced his enemies into action. An 1841 "Statute on Barring Causes of Action on Written Contracts" provided relief to debtors by providing a short statute of limitations for debt. Following the state policy of "treat[ing] the immigrant debtor with marked favor," the state courts interpreted this law as providing relief for debts made not only inside, but outside of Texas as well. Defendants who were Texas residents at the time a case was filed were protected by the statute. Drawing on practices prevalent in other states, Watrous disagreed. He ruled that the statute began to operate only from the time the defendant entered Texas. Debts legitimately incurred in other states remained valid, if not forever, then for a longer time than provided for by the state statute.[20]

This policy immediately affected many Texans, a number of whom were politically powerful. State Senator Phil Cuny, an immigrant from Louisiana, had failed to pay for slaves that he subsequently brought into Texas. One of the first suits filed in the new district court was a suit against Cuny for the price of these slaves. Though Cuny had been in Texas long enough that the state statute of limitations applied, Watrous ruled that he still owed the money.[21]

Decisions of this sort, though legally defensible, were politically dangerous. Within months of the court's opening, the Texas legislature, under the prompting of Cuny and others whom Watrous had forced to pay debts, passed a resolution demanding that Watrous resign. In Cuny's words, the resolution argued that Watrous's positions on land and debt cases showed a "prejudice and injustice towards the rights of the state and divers of its citizens," posing, as a result, a great threat to property in Texas.[22]

Watrous refused to resign, as he saw nothing improper in his actions. Undeterred by his defense of his positions, the judge's opponents pushed their case. Between 1846 and 1860 four attempts were made to impeach him. All were initiated by individuals who had either personally lost a case in the judge's court or been associated with someone who had. Their arguments for impeachment, however, rested on the judge's allegedly improper behavior in land cases and his general operation of the court.[23]

The first attempt came in January, 1852, on a petition by William Alexander, a Galveston attorney who had lost a number of land and debt cases before Watrous. The issue was immediately sent to the House Judiciary Committee, which held hearings that spring. The investigation focused largely on the judge's ties to the New York and Texas Land and Immigration Company. Finding no evidence of wrongdoing, the committee reported against impeachment in early 1853.[24]

The second attempt came in 1857. Initiated by Jacob Mussina and Eliphas Spencer, both of whom had also lost major land cases in the district court, the proceedings in this case were *ex parte*. Watrous was never called on to defend his actions; rather, the committee re-evaluated the proceedings from the first investigation. This time, the committee voted in favor of impeachment. The full house, however, failed to act on the report and the impeachment effort failed.[25]

Encouraged by their near victory, Mussina and Spencer resubmitted their memorials the next year. Full hearings were held from December, 1857, to December, 1858. Watrous was allowed to cross-examine all witnesses and to present a defense. Unable to agree on a recommendation for the house, the committee produced two minority reports, one for and one against impeachment. On December 15, 1856, the full house, by a vote of 112 to 87, refused to impeach Watrous.[26]

In March, 1860, Watrous's enemies made a last attempt to force him from the bench. Under pressure from Texas politicians, the Judiciary Committee, in an *ex parte* proceeding, recommended for impeachment. Preoccupied with the sectional crisis, the house ignored the report. When Texas seceded, the issue became moot.[27]

Judge Watrous's political difficulties were symptomatic of the general problems faced by the Texas District Court before the Civil War. Viewed as an "alien" institution, part of an interfering federal government, the court was distrusted by most Texans.[28] More so than other parts of the federal government, the Texas District Court affected Texas society, politics, and economy. It could be argued that the court's goal in protecting the interests of out-of-state land speculators and creditors was to assure the speedy development of Texas through the infusion of desperately needed capital. This is likely how Watrous saw his efforts. Few Texans in the first years of statehood, however, viewed the court's actions in this way. In "serving" the interests of northern speculators and creditors, the court seemed untrustworthy to many Texans. It seemed an institution created to help "foreigners" swindle "real" Texans out of their inheritance.

As the years passed, however, Texas developed in ways that required even greater intervention by the federal courts – intervention that a growing segment of the state's population came not only to accept but to demand. Though still largely an agricultural frontier community in the 1850s, Texas' commercial and industrial assets were extensive and growing. Increasing population, the end of Indian problems, and the railroad's expansion of trade networks were slowly pushing the economy away from subsistence agriculture, at least in some sections. Cotton, sugar, and lumber became major items of trade, helping Houston, Galveston, Austin, and Dallas to develop.[29] Diversification had come to the state's economy, and the railroads, merchants, and bankers that came with this economic expansion turned to the federal court to litigate their problems. By 1857 the growing commercial business within the state was enough to justify the creation of a second district incorporating the western half of the state. Freed from the divisive struggles over land grants, and with prosperity slowly entering the state, the federal courts in Texas quickly expanded their traditional efforts and attitudes toward land titles to meet the challenges posed by the new areas of growth.

II

This move toward an expanded private law role for the federal courts in Texas, just starting as the 1850s closed, was derailed for a time by the Civil War. Texas' two federal judges, Watrous and Thomas Duval, opted for the Union when Texas seceded, the only southern federal judges to do so. Both judges spent the war in the North. Their courtrooms did not remain abandoned for long, however.

One of the first acts of the Confederate Congress following secession was to organize a judicial system. On March 16, 1861, it passed "an Act to Establish the Judicial Courts of the Confederate States of America." It created a two-tiered judicial system, with a Supreme Court above and district courts below. Both levels were granted exclusive jurisdiction to all cases affecting ambassadors and other public ministers and consuls, admiralty issues, controversies in which the Confederate States were a party, controversies between two or more states, and cases between citizens claiming lands under grants from different states. In response to state rights concerns, diversity jurisdiction involving citizens of different states was not allowed, nor was a distinction drawn between equity and law actions.[30]

In addition, the district courts were required to enforce any unexecuted judgments or decrees made by U.S. courts prior to secession and to transfer all undecided cases from the defunct U.S. district court dockets to their own. Since the great majority of the U.S. district judges remained at their posts after secession, the transition from federal to Confederate courts caused little disruption in most districts.[31]

Judges Watrous and Duval left the state in April, 1861. One month later, state district judge Thomas J. Devine of San Antonio was named judge of the Western District and William Pinckney Hill, a lawyer from Marshall, Texas, was named to the Eastern District bench. Both opened their courts by late 1861.[32]

From the beginning their dockets were full. As with other southern courts, Texas' presecession cases were transferred to the new courts' dockets—in the Western District, the first new case filed under the Confederate system was numbered 711; the first 710 cases were carried over from the old dockets. None of these cases ever came to trial, however. From their first day of operation the new courts were too busy dealing with the needs of a wartime society to take time to litigate general private cases.[33] Of the some five thousand cases filed in the two Texas districts, well over 90 percent dealt with a single action: sequestration.[34]

A wartime measure, sequestration involved the confiscation of "enemy alien" property. On August 30, 1861, the Provisional Confederate Congress passed an act sequestering "all . . . lands, tenements and hereditaments, goods and chattels, rights and credits within these Confederate States . . . possessed, or enjoyed by or for any alien enemy." The law was to be implemented by special receivers appointed by the district courts. The receiver's job was to find, catalog, confiscate, and eventually sell all enemy alien property. This included not only land and personal goods owned by northerners, but also all debts owed by southerners to enemy aliens, which were now to be paid to the Confederate government. In order to assure the success of sequestration, Confederate citizens were required to "speedily . . . give information to the officers charged with the execution of this law" concerning alien property. Failure to inform a receiver of such property was a misdemeanor, punishable by a five thousand dollar fine and six months in jail. The offender was also civilly liable for double the value of the withheld property.[35]

Three types of sequestration cases were filed in Texas. The earliest ones involved debts owed by southerners to northern merchants. With Texas' cash-poor environment, most of the state's merchants operated on credit from the North. Realizing this fact, the sequestration receivers elicited from the state's merchants information about their debts. Sending out thousands of interrogatories– a legal questionnaire aimed, in this case, at determining the nature of a merchant's creditors–the receivers built up a list of debts owed to northern merchants totaling over two million dollars. When the two Confederate district courts opened their January, 1862, terms, the receivers filed sequestration actions against these debts. If the creditor proved to be an enemy alien, and in most cases this was the case, the court sequestered the debt, ordering the merchant to pay it to the receiver as if it were to be paid to the creditor.[36]

These suits were followed by actions against the real and personal property of northern residents. Northerners owned large segments of the state's unimproved lands. The interrogatories sent out by the receivers had also included questions about land ownership, both the respondent's own lands and those of neighbors. The returns were informative. In one four-county receivership district, over 250,000 acres of land were owned by foreigners; another district included over 100,000 foreign-owned acres. These lands were then sequestered and sold at auction, usually for a fraction of their actual value.

Sequestration actions were also commenced against cattle, goats, horses, sheep, wagons, and even slaves owned by northerners. Less common than actions against land, these suits followed procedures similar to those used in land condemnations. Once proved to be an enemy alien asset, the property was advertised for auction and sold to the highest bidder. The money was then transferred to the Confederate Treasury and the case closed.[37]

The final sequestration process involved the property of southern unionists who fled the South. Though most Texans supported secession, a sizable minority–perhaps as much as one-third–remained either neutral or loyal to the Union. This group included northern emigrés who found old loyalties stronger than new, the mostly Hispanic inhabitants of the Lower Rio Grande Valley, and much of the state's German population. Many were forced to flee for their lives in the face of Confederate repression. This made their property liable to confiscation under the Sequestration Act. *In rem* suits were instigated against the property and publicized in local newspapers. When no owner came forward showing cause why the suit should be ended (it was a given that the exiled owner would not respond), the property was sequestered and sold at auction.[38]

A small number of actions arose in response to other war issues, especially prize cases and treason. These primarily arose as a result of the Confederate recapture of Galveston Island from Union forces in January, 1863, in which the rebels took five Union ships. Three months later admiralty proceedings in the Eastern District Court condemned these ships as lawful prizes of war. Later, the Confederates seized eight additional Union ships and condemned them as prizes.[39] At the same time, indictments for treason were issued against several Galveston residents who had remained on the island during Union occupation. Judge Hill, however, did not feel that the defendants' actions were treasonous and quashed one treason indictment and indefinitely postponed the others.

In 1865 both of Texas' Confederate district courts closed their doors, having heard at best a handful of non-war-related cases. Unlike in the North, where federal economic litigation continued unabated,[40] the Texas Confederate district courts never had a chance to operate beyond the constraints of the war, to construct a new judicial framework for the region. Their efforts were but an interlude in the evolution of the federal courts in Texas.

III

On June 19, 1865, General Gordon Granger entered Galveston and raised the Union flag over the federal courthouse. Soon after, Judges Watrous and Duval returned to the state and reorganized their courts. In May, 1866, they opened their summer terms and began the difficult job of reconstruction.

There was a lot for the courts to do. Many prewar cases were reopened and litigated. Added to these were cases arising from the war's economic and legal effects. On July 17, 1862, Congress had ruled all legal actions of the Confederacy null and void, including transfers of property under sequestration. Following Appomattox, those who had had their property or debts sequestered filed suit for their return, and creditors filed foreclosure suits for unpaid debts.[41]

Social and political reconstruction added more cases to the docket, though the numbers filed were lower than conditions in the state might have generated. The Civil War amendments to the Constitution officially freed slaves and granted them equal rights of citizenship. Southern white obstructionism, however, limited the gains made by freed slaves. In 1866 the Texas legislature passed a series of "Black Codes" defining the status of the newly freed slaves. These codes defined white employers as "masters" and black employees as "servants," prohibited blacks from serving on juries, banned interracial marriage, and required separate public accommodations for the two races. Though repealed under Reconstruction, the ideas and policies implicit in these Black Codes were continued informally by local officials and private individuals into the 1880s and beyond.

Few civil rights cases were filed before 1870, however. Confusion as to the meaning of the civil rights law and opposition from President Andrew Johnson were two reasons for such inaction. It took an exceptional federal attorney who was willing to make a personal "study of the legal authorities," like Benjamin Bristow of Kentucky, to act without detailed instructions from Washington. Even when specific instructions were given in 1875, they were so procedurally vague as to how the U.S. attorneys were to proceed that confusion continued to hamper enforcement efforts.[42]

Local opposition to the laws added to the difficulties faced in prosecuting civil rights violations. Both Texas federal judges supported civil rights legislation. In 1875, for instance, Judge Amos Morrill, who had replaced Judge Watrous in the Eastern District of Texas in 1870, told the grand jury that "all persons have a legal right to have board and lodgings at inns, transportation on steamers, railroads or stages, and entrance in theaters" under the law. Where such access was denied, the judge concluded, the law had been broken and the violator should be punished. Moved by this interpretation, the grand jury indicted the manager of the Tremont Opera House in Galveston, who had refused to seat two black women in the parquet of the theater. The judge assessed him the maximum penalty, a five hundred dollar fine.[43]

Too often, however, the grand jury failed to indict under the law. In 1873 Morrill wrote that securing jurists that would convict for civil rights violations was a recurring problem in his court. "Jurors drawn at random from the list of voters . . . would not be convinced that any man had violated the revenue acts or the enforcement acts by any testimony," he wrote. Even having the marshal selectively choose jurors from among those known to support the law proved no answer. Intimidation and violence were often enough to sway the jury or keep a case out of court.[44]

As a result, few criminal civil rights cases were filed in Texas. In the Eastern District, through 1900, only 122 actions were listed by the attorney general as civil rights, enforcement, or voting cases. In the Western District, only 90 such cases were filed.[45]

Similar results occurred when blacks tried to obtain their rights through civil means. A lack of detailed information on the contents of civil rights laws as well as local opposition kept civil litigation rates down. The Civil Rights acts of 1866 and 1875 and the Enforcement acts of 1870 and 1871 included procedures for the civil protection of basic rights. This included extending federal jurisdiction to such cases and expanding the right to remove these cases from state to federal court. As originally envisioned, most civil rights cases were to be civil, not criminal, brought by blacks on their own initiative through the window provided by extended federal jurisdiction. Little effort was made to publicize to lawyers or the public the provisions of these laws, however. In 1874 the various provisions of the civil rights acts were broken up in the *Revised Statutes*, but they were not indexed under "civil rights." This made it difficult for lawyers to find the law.[46]

Still, some blacks did try, only to come away unsatisfied. Though most plaintiffs won their cases, the legal precedent set by these cases proved antithetical to the wider interests of blacks. Rather than removing social, economic, and political barriers, the courts allowed and even extended them. In a series of transportation discrimination suits heard in the 1870s and 1880s, the federal courts ruled that separate-but-equal facilities for blacks and whites were an acceptable interpretation of the equal access requirement of the Reconstruction acts—as long as the separate facilities were truly equal. Where separate facilities were not available or were unequal, laws requiring such facilities were invalid. What constituted an "equal" facility, however, was defined in terms of reasonableness (they did not have to be exactly the same), thus diluting the doctrine.

Texas was a leader in this process. In 1877 an information (or indictment) was filed in the Western District alleging that W. E. Dodge and other officials of the Houston and Texas Central Railroad, "with unlawful intent and purpose," denied Milly Anderson admission into a ladies' car solely on the grounds of her race. Following a Texas law ordering the separation of the races on transportation facilities, the railroad forced Anderson to ride in the second-class car, despite the fact that she had purchased a first-class ticket.

Noting that the "right of passing from one place to another" was "one of the most valued of all those enjoyed by . . . United States citizens," Judge Duval ruled in favor of the plaintiff. "A railway employee who refuses a female passenger with a first-class ticket entry into the only car appropriated for the accommodation of ladies alone, solely because she is of African descent, is guilty under the civil rights law of 1875," he noted to the jury. This held true even if the employee acted under orders from a superior. Common carriers, the judge went on to explain, had a responsibility to "transport every passenger, who paid the fare demanded of him, with equal accommodations and comfort." Exceptions did exist in the applications of this rule, however. "Persons who refuse to conform to reasonable regulations on the part of the carrier, or who for good reason are not fit associates for other passengers, may be refused passage." "Mere race" was not a justifiable reason for discrimination. Duval then went on to suggest that had separate-but-equal accommodations been provided for the plaintiff, there would have been no cause for prosecution: "If the jury believe from the evidence that there were two cars on this occasion, and that they were equally used and appropriated for the carriage of ladies and gentlemen who had first class tickets without distinction of race or color, and that they afforded the same advantages, comforts and conveniences, and enjoyment; and if they further believe under such circumstances, that the defendants, while denying Milly Anderson entrance into the one, gave her passage into the other, then they would not be liable to this prosecution, and the jury should return a verdict of not guilty." The only caution he placed on the jury was that the two cars had to be "truly equal" in condition.[47]

This "separate but equal doctrine" became an accepted rule. Where a plaintiff could show that no equal accommodations were provided, the Texas federal courts would sustain the suit and award damages. If, however, a separate rail car or room was provided, they favored the defendant. In 1896 the United States Supreme Court sustained separate-but-equal facilities in the Louisiana case of *Plessy v. Ferguson*.

Similar results occurred from blacks' efforts to overturn Texas' 1858 antimiscegenation statute. It prohibited interracial marriage as a felony punishable by two to five years' incarceration. In 1877 Lou Brown, a white woman, was indicted in state court for marrying a black man. The case was removed to the Western District and Judge Duval ruled the statute "obsolete and inoperative," for it directly contradicted the Thirteenth, Fourteenth, and Fifteenth amendments by punishing only one race, whites. If, however, the statute had punished both races equally, it would have been a different matter. "Marriage between the two races is wholly abhorrent to my sense of fitness and propriety, and

I presume it would be no violation of the laws or the Constitution of the United States–in as much as marriage is but a civil contract to be regulated by the laws of the several states–were the state of Texas now to pass a law forbidding such marriages under penalties extending to both races alike."[48]

By the 1890s blacks no longer brought civil rights cases before the Texas federal courts. Expanded federal jurisdiction proved inadequate to integrate newly freed blacks into southern society. Judges refused to use the new powers Congress granted their courts to these ends. Rather, in the three decades after 1870, they applied these powers in inventive ways toward the job of economic reconstruction.

The Civil War eroded Texas' economy. In 1861 the state had 468 miles of railroad track; by war's end the condition of this track had so deteriorated that the state comptroller concluded that the railroads had ceased to exist "as living organized bodies." Agriculture also declined. Many of the state's farmers had returned to subsistence farming to feed themselves. Others had given up and moved. Times were as bad for the state's merchants and artisans, who, hit by inflation and halts in trade, were without goods to sell or to build with. Conditions were so bad by 1865 that the frontier, for the first time in American history, actually retreated eastward by over two hundred miles.[49]

Efforts to rebuild began soon after Appomattox but quickly ran into difficulties. Many Texans continued to distrust outside investors. They opposed efforts by various Republican administrations to restructure Texas society along northern lines. Utilizing the power of the ballot, white Texans pushed for laws and regulations that promoted the interests of local economic groups such as farmers at the expense of northern capital. Only partially reorganized into a peacetime form and also subject to popular election, the state courts either refused to help out-of-state investors or actively supported obstructing efforts.[50]

Freed of the need to run for office, and having close ties to both the Republican party and the North, the judges of the Texas federal courts favored outside investment. They saw such investment as Texas' road to development and sought to apply expanded diversity and equity powers to protect these investments. As the only courts in the state friendly to outside litigants, the Texas district courts soon had a large number of economic cases placed on their dockets, as multistate business turned to the federal courts for protection from local interference. At first only a small part of the Texas federal courts' dockets, by the 1880s corporate cases formed a majority of civil cases.[51]

These economic suits gave the Texas federal courts the opportunity to foster its vision for the state's future. In the face of often-intense disapproval, the Texas federal courts–along with other sympathetic individuals and institutions–worked to tie the state to the national market and to bring in industry and commerce. Reassured by this court protection, external investors increased their activity and a period of unprecedented growth began for Texas.

At the center of this investment were the railroads, the nation's first large interstate corporations. Railroads provided the only viable means of bulk transportation in Texas, a necessity if the state were to grow. The state legislature granted land freely to subsidize railroad building. By the end of the century, thousands of miles of track crisscrossed the state.[52]

Many social, economic, and political problems accompanied this growth. Texans who needed the services provided by the railroads disliked and feared the dependency this situation created. Most of the state's railroads were owned by out-of-state investors whose primary interest was making money.[53] As one observer put it: "railroad owners were like many other people. Having the power to charge what they pleased, they were never overly modest in fixing their compensation." With few competitors the railroads freely charged high rates for their services, discriminated against local producers through long- and short-haul provisions, and lobbied vigorously against any legislative control over rates. They also combined to set regional rates and to provide rebates to larger, more-favored customers.[54]

Texans, like many rural Americans, felt defenseless in the face of railroad power, especially the railroads' control over the rate charged to haul goods. High rates reduced the profits of local producers and retarded growth. Individual producers and shippers could do nothing to stop the abuses and turned to the state government for help. The government quickly responded. In 1876 the state's amended constitution declared railroads public highways and railroad companies common carriers and authorized the legislature to "pass laws to correct abuses and prevent unjust discrimination and extortion in the rates of freight and passenger travel; to establish maximum legal rates; and to enforce such laws by adequate penalties." Three years later the legislature passed a regulation setting "50 cents per hundred pounds for every hundred miles" as the legal rate allowed and prohibiting discrimination toward persons or places. Four years after that it prohibited long- and short-haul differentials.[55]

These regulations, however, lacked enforcement machinery and as a result were ineffective in limiting railroad abuses. By 1891 political pressure against the railroads resulted in the creation of the Railroad Commission of Texas. The commission had both the authority to set rates and the power (through fines and court proceedings) to enforce these rates and other state laws regulating railroads.[56]

Faced with what they considered debilitating regulations, the Texas railroads challenged state rate making in the federal courts. Viewing railroads as a necessity for the economic well-being of Texas, the federal courts in Texas supported the railroads' position. In the 1881 case of the *Texas Express Co. v. Houston and Texas Central RR Co.*, the Northern District Court faced the question of whether the Texas *Revised Statutes* applied to rates charged to express companies that used their own cars to carry freight and passengers along the railroads' tracks. Express companies were known to be in existence when the statute was written; however, Judge A. P. McCormick ruled that, since the laws did not explicitly include express companies in its prohibitions, the statute did not apply to them. Until the state made such an explicit regulation, "the parties hereto and all others similarly circumstanced must be remitted to their right and power to contract . . . subject [only] to the limitations placed upon them as common carriers."[57]

When the state legislature instituted specific regulations, the Texas federal courts refused to uphold them. The best example of this failure occurred soon after the creation of the Railroad Commission. Afraid of the power placed in the commission, Texas railroads and their financiers turned to the federal courts to have the commission declared unconstitutional, or at least to have its rulings on the rates railroads could charge voided. In April, 1892, the Farmer's Loan and Trust Company of New York filed a petition in the Circuit Court of the Western District naming the Texas attorney general, the Railroad Commission, and the International and Great Northern Railroad defendants in a suit alleging that the rates established by the commission were unreasonable and unjust. It requested an injunction to prevent the commission from enforcing the rates and the attorney general from instituting additional suits to recover penalties for failure to conform to the law. Bondholders of other Texas railroads filed similar claims.

In May the circuit court granted the injunction. Finding the rates required by the commission unreasonable, the court perpetually enjoined the Texas Railroad Commission from enforcing any existing railroad rates or setting any new ones. The court further enjoined the attorney general from instituting additional suits against the railroads under any act or provision of the commission. Costs of the suit were charged to the state.[58]

The commission and the attorney general appealed to the Supreme Court, arguing that the original action was in essence a suit against Texas and thus prohibited by the Eleventh Amendment; that the penalties imposed by the commission were not excessive or unreasonable; and finally, that the commission did not deny railroads due process or equal protection of the law. The railroads repeated their arguments about the unconstitutionality of the commission and the unreasonableness of its rate limits.[59]

Commenting on the "great importance of the questions in this case," Justice Brewer, sitting as a circuit judge, ruled that the Texas Railroad Commission was constitutional. "There can be no doubt of the general power of a state to regulate the freights and fares that may be charged and received by railroads or other common carriers, and that this regulation may be carried on by means of a commission." This did not mean, however, that such a commission could set rates with impunity. If citizens of another state felt "aggrieved and injured" by the commission's rulings, they had the right to petition for relief in the federal courts. While the federal courts could not establish rates themselves, they could rule on the reasonableness of commission rates. Where rates were unjustly low, thus depriving the railroad of its constitutional right fully to enjoy its property, such rates could be struck down.[60]

Rates were only the first of the railroads' problems. High fixed expenses for both construction and operation made railroads an inherently risky investment. This risk was worsened by bad management, inept operations, and unfriendly regulations. Though enormous profits were possible, most railroads lost money. Between 1870 and 1900 over 700 of the nation's railroads at some point sought federal protection. Of that number, one-quarter were southern lines. These numbers totaled almost half of the railroads in existence in 1900–and over half of the South's lines.[61]

State courts offered little recourse for insolvent railroads. It proved politically difficult for state institutions to provide the help the railroads needed. Popular anger over the high rates that fostered the regulation movement did not stop when it came to insolvent railroads. Many of the railroads' opponents saw railroad failures as examples of the mismanagement to which they were opposed. To help the same railroads that were charging high rates meant political suicide.[62]

This void in support was quickly filled by equity receiverships in the federal courts. An equity receivership is a court-protected dismantling or reorganization of a failed business. Under the court's jurisdiction, control of the company is given to an appointed receiver whose job is to conserve and to reorganize the assets of the bankrupted company.

In its earliest forms, equity receivership was a means of maintaining a property before liquidating it to pay off creditors. The receiver was a conservator for the creditors' interests. With railroads the situation was a little different. Railroads exist to provide a service. If they fail to provide that service, their assets are practically worthless. By necessity, a railroad receiver had to operate and to reorganize the railroad to provide service and thus protect future profits. Merely holding the insolvent property prior to sale would destroy the railroad's practical value.

The federal courts quickly realized this difference. In the last third of the nineteenth century they restructured the equity receivership concept by emphasizing reorganization and long-term productivity over immediate disposal of the property to pay off creditors. This new type of receivership protected the railroad from its creditors, raised new capital through the selling of receiver's bonds, and generally trimmed the debt that had caused the railroad to fail in the first place. As Justice Bradley noted in 1872: "Rival creditors . . . may control the priority of their respective liens, and . . . stockholders may contest the validity of the claims of others, but all in subordination to the general object and purpose of suit–to obtain an administration of the company's assets and property."[63]

In the 1880 and 1890s, when growing competition, high fixed operating costs, and a general economic depression forced over one-third of the nation's lines into bankruptcy, receiverships played an even greater supportive role. One response by managers to the problem of high fixed costs and competition was to merge into large regional rail systems. State laws often prohibited such systems, however. Receiverships offered a means of getting around this prohibtion. Northern financiers would force troubled lines into bankruptcy by foreclosing on bonds that had been purchased for this specific purpose. The financiers would then request that a federal receiver be appointed. After the receiver had reorganized the railroad, the financiers would purchase the property "on behalf of former shareholders, who, as a condition to their participation in the new company, were assessed pro rata to raise the needed cash resources," for which they received "stock in the new corporation as a solace." Once in control, the financiers would then either lease or sell the line outright to one of the large rail systems. As long as the lines were kept officially separate (though they operated as one), state laws did not come into play.[64]

In this manner, much of the nation's independent railroads became regional rail systems, especially in the South, where northern capital dominated the business. By 1900 the Southern Railway, the Illinois Central, the Seaboard Air Line, the Atlantic Coast Line, and the Louisville and Nashville had acquired much of the region's independent lines and controlled over eighteen thousand miles of track.[65] In Texas, the Southern Pacific; the Atchison, Topeka and the Santa Fe; the Gulf Coast Lines; and the Missouri Pacific acquired most of the independent roads through lease agreements or by purchasing lines in receivership.

In the early 1880s, for example, Tom Scott's Texas and Pacific Railroad, an ambitious attempt to build a southern transcontinental line, was first forced into receivership and then acquired from the receiver by Jay Gould for $1.5 million. He immediately added the T and P to his growing Missouri Pacific system.[66] Gould's rival, the Southern Pacific, also used receiverships to acquire control of needed spur lines. In 1885, for example, it acquired the Houston and Texas Central, the Texas Central, and the Waco and Northwestern after they entered receivership.[67]

The Texas federal courts freely provided receivership protection to the railroads. They appointed "familiar faces" as receivers, masters, and trustees, people who would help the large lines acquire the failed road.[68] As the judges of the federal courts in Texas saw the problem, a failed railroad was useless to the state. Better to make its assets available to other, more competent, corporations. Where there was not the "slighest security or hope of meeting the company's just obligations," the Texas federal courts allowed the lines to be sold for the "greater good."[69]

Having set this policy, the federal courts in Texas separated themselves from the administration of the receivership as much as possible. The courts ruled that "all outlays of the receiver . . . made in good faith in the ordinary course of business . . . and with a view to advance and promote the road . . . are fairly within the line of discretion necessarily allowed him." Only in cases of "extraordinary" expenses would the court examine the receiver's actions. Similarly, the setting of the receiver's compensation was left in the hands of others. All the courts required was that the amount of compensation be adequate for the effort put out by the receiver.[70] While all this was done primarily to forestall even the appearance of impropriety, the result was to give the receiver a free hand in the operation and ultimate disposition of the line. Given the close ties between the receivers and the northern financiers who initiated the receivership process, the outcome in such a situation would inevitably be to the benefit of the large rail systems.

The effect of this policy was to decrease the number of lines operating in Texas and, thus, competition among the lines. Decreased competition, in turn, resulted in the general rise in rates that generated the regulatory movement; however, it also resulted in the creation of stronger and more financially secure railroads. As long as the existing railroads provided the transportation services needed by the state, the federal courts protected their investments and operations. Where the railroads failed, the courts worked to transfer ownership of the lines to someone who could provide this service.

Civil suits filed against the railroads in state courts also threatened them. As corporations covering extensive territory and employing large numbers of employees, the railroads found themselves defendants in tort and contract suits in state courts. Also numerous were suits contesting the imposition of a federal receivership. In all three cases, state statute and state judicial interpretation sought to limit federal jurisdiction. Yet, despite such opposition, the Texas federal courts continued to promote railroad development, accepting as many cases as possible and elaborating precise guidelines for future applications of removal jurisdiction.

The 1882 case of *Missouri, Kansas and Texas RR Co. v. Scott* typifies the Texas federal courts' views on the subject. The railroad sought removal to federal court after condemnation proceedings against it were initiated in state court, a motion that the federal court refused. Section 720 of the *Revised Statutes*, Judge Pardee of the Fifth Circuit ruled, prohibited a federal court from interrupting state court proceedings except in bankruptcy matters. There were, the judge noted before concluding, limits to how far this rule extended, however. The federal "statute prevent[ed] this court from granting the injunction asked for [but] it [was] *not* intended to decide that in proper cases where the U.S. court [was] first seized of jurisdiction" and later state proceedings were instituted, "the United States court [would] not lay its hands on the parties and control their proceedings, although thereby . . . indirectly stay[ing] or end[ing]" state proceedings.[71]

This point was made stronger in *Snow et al. v. Texas Trunk RR*, a dispute between various creditors over the priority of their liens on the railroad's property. In December, 1882, suit was filed in state court seeking to foreclose on the railroad and initiate a receivership. Soon after the proceedings began, other investors from outside of Texas requested the right to intervene in the proceedings.[72] The state court refused permission. The next day, without permission from the state court, these creditors filed suit in the Northern District Court.

The out-of-state creditors claimed the right to file in federal court under diversity jurisdiction. The original plaintiffs objected both to this argument in particular and to federal proceedings in general. Citing Section 720 of the *Revised Statutes*, they argued that, since state court proceedings had been initiated already, the petitioners needed the permission of the state court before filing in federal court. This permission had not been requested or granted. They moved that the case be remanded back to state court. Judge Pardee refused. Leave of a state court was not necessary for parties to intervene, the judge ruled. Having done all that they could to become parties in the state case, and having been denied this right, they had every right "sufficient for the purpose of removal." If the leave of state judges were necessary for removal to occur, then state courts could use that power to limit federal power indirectly. This was not the way justice should be structured.

> We take this occasion to remark that the proceedings disclosed by the record in this case eminently justify the wisdom of the removal acts of the United States. The intervenors are conceded to be large lienholders against the defendant company; they reside in distant states. Without notice to them, on comparatively small liens, the property on which their liens rest is seized by the consent of the defendants and put in the hands of a receiver to be managed indefinitely. They have no remedy other than to assert their rights in the court having custody of the property. That court, in defiance of specific statutory rights, refuses to hear their claims or adjust their rights. They may have had a remedy by appeal to the supreme court of the state, but it was wise policy, . . . to give them a choice of tribunals. "In the national Courts, [parties] may hope to escape the local influence which sometimes disturbs the even flow of justice."[73]

In these and other cases, the federal courts in Texas initiated and maintained a consistent policy toward removals. Striving for uniformity and predictability, the courts vigorously met challenges to their jurisdiction, reserving for themselves broad discretion over such matters. In general, the courts accepted removal cases whenever requested, failing to do so only where specifically prohibited by law. They justified this removal with the excuse that an alternate forum was a good thing for Texas; that out-of-state capital would be better protected by them than by the state courts. Combined with equity receivership and rate injunction actions, the removal efforts of the Texas federal courts resulted in a shield for the railroads, thus fostering growth and development for the region.

IV

As the Civil War and Reconstruction period came to an end, Texas remained a developing economy in a neocolonial relationship with major external markets and financial centers. This did not change over the next thirty years. In 1900, as in 1870, Texas remained dependent on outside capital to finance growth. Dependency allowed the Texas economy to grow, however. Protected by the federal district courts and promoted by other institutions, the state's railroads quickly expanded to serve most of its inhabited sections. With adequate transportation available, new extractive, agricultural, and commercial industries developed. These new industries expanded the scope of the state's economic structures, escalating the forces pushing for growth. Although they started out small, by 1900 these domestic industries had created a vibrant regional economy within the state.[74]

This growth had a significant effect on the state's federal courts. At first wary of federal law, operators of these new economic concerns soon saw the advantages offered by the national courts. Though much smaller than railroads, these companies also could benefit from the protections provided by the federal courts. Like the railroads, they too were threatened by the chronic instability of state politics and constantly faced financial disaster as fixed operating costs often outran revenues.

Starting in the mid-1890s, these new business leaders began to seek federal help. By 1900 the state's three federal courts had their dockets filled by new civil suits.[75] Judges complained that the new business coming before the courts added to the still-numerous suits from out-of-state companies and investors exceeded their capacity. One 1902 estimate of the case backlog was over six hundred, a number likely to grow with the discovery of oil at Spindletop in 1901.[76] Economic growth had led to a situation that made the creation of an additional court "necessary for the proper conduct of the Federal court business of Texas," Congressman Thomas Ball noted in 1902. While the "three district judges" already sitting in Texas were "young, active and vigorous men, devot[ing] their entire time to the business in their courts," he continued, the situation was growing beyond them.[77]

The result was the creation of the Southern District of Texas. On February 21, 1902, the House Judiciary Committee reported that "the great increase in population, the accumulation of judicial business, the vast area and the great distances from different points in the State of Texas, as well as the convenience of the people having business in the courts, and the relief of the judges" currently serving required an expansion of the Texas federal courts.[78] In a voice vote Congress agreed with this assessment. On March 4, 1902, President Theodore Roosevelt signed "a bill to divide the State of Texas into four judicial districts," creating the Southern District of Texas. It encompassed the southeastern counties of the state, from Polk, Trinity, and Madison to Starr, Hildalgo, and Cameron; it included the entire Texas Gulf Coast except for Jefferson County, and its western side ran from the Hill Country east of Austin to west of Laredo on the Rio Grande River. The new district court was to sit in Galveston, Laredo, Brownsville, and Houston at various times throughout the year. It was to have full authority over all "causes and proceedings of every name and nature, civil and criminal" capable of being brought before a distrcit court under the Constitution and laws of the United States. The act empowered the president to nominate a new judge, attorney, clerk, and marshal for the district. It concluded by setting the wages of the new court's personnel.[79]

The new Southern District Court would face the challenges the future held for Southeast Texas and would translate the changing needs of a growing region into action and policy. What follows is the history of that court.

2. "Awhir with a Buoyant Business Progressiveness"

THE PROGRESSIVE ERA, 1902–17

I

Texas entered the twentieth century "all alive and awhir with a buoyant business progressiveness." Fueled by the development of new markets, improved transportation networks, and an infusion of foreign capital, the state's economy, which had been rapidly expanding for the past twenty years, was finally ready to explode. The discovery of oil at Spindletop in 1901 provided the final impetus.[1]

Across the nation individuals rushed to exploit the region's resources. Almost overnight, the steady growth of the previous twenty years exploded into a frenzy of speculation and expansion. Farms and lumber mills doubled in size and profitability; so too did the cotton-pressing, cotton seed–processing, and lumber-milling industries. Oil generated over $240 million in investments in 1901 alone. Commercial concerns also grew rapidly. It was in these years that Texas banking, insurance, and construction became major concerns.[2]

Serious flaws existed in this expansion, however. Economic booms are notoriously short-lived, and the Texas boom was likely to be no exception. If growth were to continue unabated, Texas needed steady expansion of existing infrastructure matched with a slow and careful development of new commercial concerns. Unfortunately, neither occurred. A large part of the region's economic gains after 1900 resulted from wild speculation, questionable or even dangerous business practices, and potential rather than real gains. The foundation for sound economic growth existed, but, as much after the discovery of oil as before, Texas had a backward, developing economy tied in a neocolonial relationship with markets and financial centers elsewhere. Most railroads and banks were owned by non-Texans, as were many new manufacturing concerns. Without "foreign" investment the state's economy remained incapable of maintaining such high levels of growth. Even a minor downturn outside the state was capable of bursting the Texas bubble.[3]

Texas, moreover, was unprepared to cope with explosive rates of growth. True, the state had been growing steadily prior to the turn of the century, but its economic, social, and political structures had not kept pace. The aggressive conservatism of the "Bourbon Redeemers," who controlled the state through the late 1880s, viewed active government as anathema. Concerned primarily with issues of race and with their power centered largely in the agricultural economy of the region, Texas Bourbons had little interest in controlling the rising industrial and commercial sectors of the state. As long as industrial and commercial affairs did not upset the state's racial system, the Redeemers largely ignored it. The railroads alone were excepted from this lack of concern.[4]

Some efforts to control the state's growing commercial sectors were attempted in the 1890s under the leadership of Governor James Hogg. The state legislature created the Railroad Commission and passed strict laws regulating out-of-state corporations; however, these reforms were still in their infancy in 1900. When the boom came, the state's regulatory infrastructure neither controlled nor enhanced growth. The economy remained constantly in danger of failure. Optimism alone could not keep the boom running. More systematic efforts were necessary if it were to continue.[5]

Many of Texas' progressive business, professional, political, and civic leaders understood this dilemma. They welcomed economic growth. Most were intimately involved in the expanding economy. Yet, much as they approved of economic development, they perceived the associated dangers. They realized that uncontrolled development often produced questionable patterns of growth and that structural flaws in the Texas economy were fostering this insecurity.[6]

Their answer to these problems was greater regulation of the state's social and economic life through a mix of economic regulation, social control, and political reform. In the political realm, these reforms included the use of direct primaries, the creation of commission-type city governments, and the limiting of corporate influence in the electoral process. Socially, Texas progressives supported prohibition, improved education, and the limiting of the franchise to those who were "fit" to vote. One major economic reform predominated: the regulation of corporate power.

Texas progressives legislated in all three realms, but implementation, especially in the economy, was less than successful. Texas' problems went deeper than simple misbehavior by "foreign" corporations. Regulating corporations did little to halt the speculative boom. Worse, a conservative backlash beginning in 1906 hindered the progressive reform process.[7] Though great gains had been made in developing the state's economy, these gains rested on shaky foundations. Texas' economy was still immature, lacking an adequate foundation to maintain wild patterns of growth indefinitely.

What the Texas economy needed, if growth were to continue, was for some institution (or institutions) to watch and adjust its workings almost on a day-to-day basis, helping those members of the business community whose enthusiasm was not matched by their prudence pick up the pieces of their failed concerns, thereby assuring that key sectors of the economy remained viable and protecting the flow of external capital into the state. Many Texas progressives attempted to provide this service, to mitigate, if not completely forestall, the

Judge Waller T. Burns. From oil portrait, courtesy U.S. District Court, Southern District of Texas

dangers facing the region's economy. Focusing on key economic sectors, the region's banks, local governments, and chambers of commerce worked to foster growth and yet provide for stable working arrangements.[8]

II

It was in striving toward this end that the new Southern District Court placed its emphasis. The new court's judge, Waller T. Burns, typified Texas progressive business elites. He was born in a small town and became a lawyer in the late 1880s. In the twenty years prior to his becoming a judge, Burns built up one of the larger practices in the region. Working in Galveston and later in Houston, two of the major urban centers of Southeast Texas, Burns became intimately involved with the economic development of the region. His practice brought him into contact with almost every aspect of the region's economy. He served as counsel to a railroad, the Houston and Texas Central, "engaged in the trial of cases and questions arising in the United States Courts in Texas," and belonged to the committee that petitioned Congress successfully for funds to build the Houston ship channel. In the opinion of fellow Houston attorney James A. Baker, "few lawyers [were] better posted in the procedure and decisions" affecting the region than Burns.[9]

A lifelong Republican (most Texas progressives were Democrats), only in his political affiliation did Burns deviate from the average Texas progressive. The effect of this difference, however, was minimal. Though he was a Republican, Burns's attitudes differed little from those of his neighbors. In letter after letter sent to the president supporting Burns's nomination for the district judgeship in 1902, Texas Democrats echoed the words of Thomas Dodd, who noted that, "as a life long Democrat," it gave him "great pleasure to bear evidence favorable to this Republican." A "gentleman of the highest probity and exalted character," Burns "enjoy[ed] the confidence and respect of the people of Texas of all political affiliations." In fact, though a Democrat was also in contention for the judgeship, Burns received the support of most of the state's Democratic legislators, who noted that Burns, who had served in the state senate from 1896 to 1900, was a man Democrats could work with. Even the Democratic governor of Texas, Joseph Sayers, supported Burns over his democratic opponent for the bench.[10]

Such support was not surprising. Burns was a member of the progressive wing of his party. A leader of the "lily white" faction of the Texas Republican party, Burns's social and economic views differed little from those of progressive Texas Democrats. Like them, Burns sought a more orderly and cohesive community. He too believed that economic development required the founding of a society that carefully merged new ideas with old traditions. Individual responsibility, whether self-generated or imposed by society, was the key to this progressive vision, and Burns shared with other Texans a commitment to this goal.[11]

This commitment shaped Burns's personal and professional life. In letters to family and friends, he often gave advice on the proper way to live. In a letter to Lucy, a relative, the judge wrote that "life is too short to borrow either money or trouble, particularly the latter." To avoid this situation, the judge suggested in a letter to another relative that a man should work hard and avoid "the 'fire water' which brings us to grief." Burns's personal preference was for productive labor. Hard work brought its own rewards, the judge felt. For "light exercise" he favored the "digging of post holes upon a rocky section and us[ing] a crowbar with which to make an impression upon mother Earth." He did not feel "offended," though, when his friends "decline[d] this character of recreation," at least, as long as they made some attempt at productive work. The method was not important, it was the effort that counted.[12]

Professionally, Burns's commitment to productive behavior can be seen best in a letter he wrote outlining the District's bankruptcy policies. "The rule obtaining in the Southern District of Texas, . . . is to appoint a business man to take charge of the estates in bankruptcy" and to administer the estates with "rigid economy." Trustees were always people who "enjoyed excellent reputation[s]."

Where fees were allowed to counselors and trustees, they were always kept "moderate." The primary goal was always the efficient and conservative management of the estate. "Referees and Attorneys in this district understand that the Court uniformly insists that the expenses of administration are to be so restricted that the Creditors will receive the benefit of the estates, and that the same is not consumed by costs incident to the administration."[13]

The judge, in other words, was not antibusiness. As a Republican he believed that Texas needed a growing economy to develop. Once he became a judge, Burns had a mechanism to achieve this goal. The result was the use of such media as receiverships and diversity cases to uphold and expand growth. Such growth, the judge realized, could not be achieved by the court alone. Those whom the judge sought to help would have to help themselves as well. Moderation, dependability, and honest business practices, so the judge's progressive values informed him, were required if Southeast Texas' road to good times were to continue. If those entering his court were proved unwilling to live by these simple rules, Burns willingly demanded and forced such behavior. Combined with his commitment to the region, these two aspects of his values led him to push and pull on all facets of the region's infrastructure to foster development.

The motivations directing the district's U.S. attorneys mirrored those of Burns. Prior to the First World War two men served as U.S. attorney for the Southern District. Both, like Burns, were progressives. The first, Lock McDaniel, was a Roosevelt progressive; the second, John Green, was appointed by Woodrow Wilson. Both shared Burns's commitment to fostering a stronger, more balanced economy for Southeast Texas. This was especially the case for McDaniel. A close confidant and friend of Burns, McDaniel's background was very much like the judge's. Born and reared in Grimes County, McDaniel entered politics in 1877, when he was elected county treasurer. Three years later, after reading law with a local attorney, he became county attorney and then county judge. In the decade before being named U.S. attorney, McDaniel practiced law and helped lead the lily white faction of Texas Republican party. As U.S. attorney for twelve years, McDaniel's efforts matched those of Burns.[14]

Though a member of the Democratic party, Green's efforts followed McDaniel's lead. The son of a Methodist clergyman known as a supporter of civic reforms, Green was tied from an early age to the elite of Houston society. After graduating from college, he spent several years as city editor of the *Houston Post*. Leaving the paper to study law, he subsequently became an assistant district attorney in Houston. Allied with the progressive wing of Texas Democrats, Green viewed his function as U.S. attorney to be one of service to the region and its economic development. In the early 1920s this position would drive him to resign to protest orders from the attorney general to support higher telephone rates in Houston.[15]

Institutionally bound to serve the public agenda as set by Congress and the executive branch, both McDaniel and Green were nonetheless willing to follow the court's lead in placing the needs of regional development before those of federal policy. Like the judge, they saw private gain as producing the public good of regional development. Moreover, they agreed with Burns's vision of this development. They therefore raised few objections to the court's easy attitude toward many public law issues.

Finally, the many juries serving in the court fleshed out the bench and bar's active efforts to bring about development. In the first years of the present century, the jury played a greater role in the operation of a federal district court than is the case today. Trials were common, and most trials utilized the jury. This held for civil as well as criminal cases. The composition of the jury was also different. Federal jurors in the 1900s were selected from the same lists as state jurors. In Texas these lists included only registered voters. With the imposition of the poll tax in 1904, registered voters made up a minority of the state's total population. Jurors were almost always Anglo and tended to be wealthier than the state average. In fact, the typical federal juror came from the same business and agricultural sectors as did many of the state's progressives.[16]

Both these facts resulted in juries that held similar developmental goals to Burns's. The judge, in fact, worked hard to obtain juries that would hold such opinions. In letters to prospective jurors, he continually repeated his concern that "the Jurors . . . be drawn from the body of the District, rather than from [the] immediate locality" of the court. The judge held this concern because he felt that "local Jurors [were] more or less subject to local influences." Such influences meant that juries made their decisions based solely on preexisting relations with the parties involved and not with regard to the case's wider meanings. This "embarrasse[d] the Court" for it made it difficult to "administer Justice." By empaneling juries with members from throughout the district, the court assured that the needs of the entire district would be served by the decisions of the district's juries.[17]

The judge went to great lengths to guarantee that enough proper jurors were found. On one occasion, a juror wrote that he could not attend court as he needed to stay home and take care of his young son. Burns wrote back suggesting that the son "attend with his father" and stay at Burns's home, where the judge's "little fellows [could] take care of him." On another occasion, the judge excused a juror to consummate an important business deal, on the understanding that "as soon as [the] transaction [was] closed" the juror would "report for Jury service." When all else failed, the judge would explain the needs of the court and leave the decision whether to attend to the "good judgement" of the juror, hoping that logic would bring the juror into court.[18]

Shaped by the efforts of the judge, and to a lesser extent by those of the U.S. attorney, juries served as the final defender of private interests. In all criminal and most civil cases the jury had the job of interpreting the facts of a case. This power allowed it to make decisions based on local needs, interests, and beliefs. This predilection was reinforced by Burns's habit of leaving a wide latitude in his instructions to the jury.

Sharing a similar ethnic background and holding a common conception of the region's needs, this alliance of bench, bar, and jury worked for a common end: fostering the growth and development of Southeast Texas. Whether it was through expanding the equity process to include a wide range of economic sectors or through deciding on the guilt and punishment of a local criminal, an unspoken agreement on what was the "right" result of a case underlay every action and decision the court made.

III

Fostering growth was therefore a role for which the new federal court was well suited. It was also a role that was in great demand. "The litigation in this court," Judge Burns wrote to a prospective juror in 1915, "involves large property interests, together with many alleged violations of the Penal Code." Hearing on average two hundred to three hundred cases a year, the court was well placed to affect local business practices. It had at its disposal significant jurisdictions that dealt directly with the economic structures of Southeast Texas, jurisdictions that allowed the court to help shape the direction of the Southeast Texas economy toward stable patterns of growth.[19]

The court's equity and bankruptcy cases are a good example of how this shaping worked. Both equity and bankruptcy were intimately involved with the region's economic health. They provided safety nets for those who failed in the drive to strike it rich and supplied a means of maintaining key economic institutions before they failed. Through a judicious use of bankruptcy trustee- and equity receiverships, the court could keep necessary transportation, service, and manufacturing industries operating, despite economic difficulties. Thus the protected companies and numerous other businesses dependent on the services provided by these institutions survived.[20]

There was a profound need for this service. The railroad crisis of the 1890s, when over a quarter of the nation's lines failed and were placed in receivership, continued into the new era. Cutthroat competition, dwindling rates, increasing regulation, and rising costs continued to drive the nation's railroads to the brink of failure. The number of railroad bankruptcies became increasingly common after 1906. By 1915 over one-sixth of the nation's railroads, controlling some 41,988 miles of track, were under the protection of a federal receiver. Only the takeover of the railroads by the federal government in World War I halted this progression. Even so, the railroads continued having financial difficulties in the decades that followed.[21]

A real threat to Texas' booming economy existed. Railroads remained the primary form of transportation in the state throughout the prewar years. Without rail transportation, rapid development was impossible. Faced with the same problems threatening the nation's rail system as a whole, most Texas railroads were on the brink of failure. By 1915 many were unable to meet their financial and operational obligations and were forced to seek protection in a federal receivership.

In Southeast Texas, a number of lines sought federal protection. One of the larger ones was the International and Great Northern Railroad (I&GN). Serving North and East Texas, the I&GN was an integral part of the Missouri Pacific lines (MP). Though one of the largest rail systems in Texas, the MP was badly managed and on a number of occasions had to sell off local lines to keep solvent. The I&GN, one of the worst-run and least-profitable lines in the MP, was in the hands of a receiver more often and longer than any other Texas road.

The I&GN twice sought protection from the court in the prewar years, the first time from 1908 to 1911, when T. J. Freeman was named receiver. The second began in 1914 and lasted until 1922; the receivers in this case were James A. Baker of Houston and Cecil Lyon of Sherman.[22]

Another line requiring receivership protection was the St. Louis, Brownsville and Mexico Railroad (St L, B&M). It connected the Rio Grande Valley to the north, running from Brownsville to Houston and on to Texarkana. It was a part of B. F. Yaokum's Gulf Coast Lines (GCL), which controlled four additional roads in Southeast Texas. The GCL, in turn, linked through Yoakum to the Rock Island and Frisco line, which, in 1910 incorporated the GCL into its system. When, as a result of mismanagement and unprofitable conditions, the Frisco was forced into receivership in July of 1913, the fate of the St L, B&M came before Judge Burns. He named Frank Andrews, a local railroader, as receiver.[23]

The pattern leading to receivership was followed by most of the district's other railroads. In each case, the insolvency of the railroad forced the court to take operational control of the lines. The collapse of these lines would have limited, if not halted, almost every economic enterprise in the district. This the court chose not to allow.

The primary goal of the court in organizing a receivership was the continuation of transportation services, not the protection of the railroad's creditors. Often, when "the property was in bad shape," as Judge Burns noted in a 1915 letter, "creditors ha[d] no reasonable grounds to expect an early adjustment of their accounts," until every effort had been "made by the Receiver, under the direction of the Court, to put the property in such shape as to permit its operation." Only after the public's interest had been served and continued rail transport was assured did the court concern itself with creditors' rights. At that time, however, the court did work to minimize the creditors' losses.[24]

The court took a number of steps to assure that the lines were operated to provide maximum service. Multiple lines were placed under the control of a single receiver to provide for economies of scale and to limit costs. Where physical improvements were necessary for the efficient operation of the line, the court willingly authorized the issuance of receiver's certificates to pay for such improvements.[25] In order to assure that receivers viewed their jobs as a public service, the court sought out people who "enjoyed excellent reputation[s]" and who had the "ability to do things under adverse conditions." A foremost requirement for a receiver was to have a "feel" for the needs of the region and to have worked "for the development of this country." In many cases, the receiver was personally known to Burns. In all instances, receivers had to have a sterling personal and professional reputation.[26]

The court kept a close watch on every aspect of a railroad in receivership. Receivers were required to make monthly reports detailing every expense. Every special expenditure or capital improvement needed court approval. Before any major action was taken by the receiver, a master in chancery was appointed to hold hearings to examine the requests. After approval was given, the judge would periodically travel along the route to check on the road's condition.[27]

The Southern District's efforts to save the region's railroads were largely successful. The court appointed experienced railroad executives and business leaders to be receivers. With federal protection, the receivers were able to operate the lines productively, returning them to private control better run and more efficient railroads. For example, the I&GN was retired from its second receivership in 1922. At this time the line was in peak physical condition and operating at a profit. It had grown into the state's third-largest railroad and was still growing. The St L, B&M receivership, which ended in 1916, had a similar result. At that time the line, along with the rest of the GCL, was acquired by northern financial interests who reorganized the road as the New Orleans, Texas and Mexico Railroad. Frank Andrews, the road's receiver, was made head of the new line. Through efficient management the road, which had been losing money prior to 1913 and breaking even in 1916, became very profitable. By 1925 the line's stock had increased tenfold in value.[28]

Perhaps more important, the revival of the lines meant that the transportation service they provided to the region continued unabated. As the foregoing examples show, the region's railroads expanded their service while under court control. In its first year of receivership, the St. L, B&M raised $1,198,715 in new capital, $689,000 of which was spent to reballast roadbeds. In July of 1914 the line was authorized to raise an additional $300,000 for new equipment. Other lines focused as much concern on their infrastructure. The result was that efficient transportation was available throughout the period.[29]

Other businesses were also indispensable to the region's growth. Many of these were owned and operated locally. The trinity of oil, lumber, and agriculture played key roles in shaping the region's economy. Each either provided or utilized certain services the lack of which would have caused a ripple effect in the region's economy. Unstable economic times affected these businesses as much as they did the railroads. Realizing this fact, the court expanded the receivership concept beyond its traditional concerns with railroads to protect other local economic institutions.[30]

Consider agriculture. Following the completion of the St. Louis, Brownsville and Mexico road to Brownsville in 1903, South Texas was on the verge of an agricultural boom. With direct rail transportation between South Texas and the North now available, the year-round growing cycle, cheap land, and lush citrus crops of South Texas invited agricultural exploitation. Adequate irrigation was all that was needed to grow crops in South Texas' dry climate.

Private land and water companies quickly organized to meet this need. Headed by local people, these speculative companies bought unimproved land at low prices, constructed irrigation systems, and then sold the improved property to immigrants from the North. Hundreds of farmers from the East and the North settled in South Texas on lands irrigated by the private water companies. Towns, emerging to serve the growing agricultural sector, also drew on the companies for water and sewage treatment.

Soon after 1910, however, the boom ended. Poor crops and the beginnings of border troubles halted the flow of new immigrants. Already-settled farmers stopped paying water bills as bad harvest followed bad harvest. Without revenue, the private water companies soon went bankrupt. By 1915 only one private water company in South Texas had not sought court protection.[31]

The court administered these irrigation companies in much the same manner, and with the same goals, as it had the district's railroads. The San Benito Land and Water Company, a combined irrigation and land speculation concern centered in San Benito, a small community just north of Brownsville in Cameron County, is a good example.[32] At first business was good, but by 1910 the situation began turning ugly. In 1913, with over seventy thousand dollars in unpaid water rents and no new sales of improved lands, the company was unable to pay off its creditors. In addition, it owed twenty-nine thousand dollars in back state, county, and local taxes. A similar amount was due for 1913.

In July, 1913, the St. Louis Union Trust Company filed suit in the Southern District Court for the appointment of a receiver for the company, which request the court granted on July 31. S. A. Robertson and Fred Emert of Cameron County were named receivers. On appointment, the receivers immediately requested and were granted the right to issue sixty-five thousand dollars in receiver certificates. The court also ordered the receivers to "proceed with the collection of . . . past due water rents . . . with diligence and promptness" and authorized them to sue in state courts for the delinquent rents.

The issue of unpaid water rents lay at the bottom of the problem faced in operating the San Benito receivership. As Burns noted in February of 1914, "unless the water rent [was] promptly paid for the water used, the plant [could] not be operated by the Receivers." Most of the money raised by the receiver's certificates went for paying the company's large tax obligations and for buying improved machinery. Funds for operating the plant had to come from water rents. Without such revenue the company was "without money, and without credit, . . . [un]able to make purchases, large or small, without paying cash therefore."

Burns was serious in blaming the company's failure on the nonpayment of water bills by local farmers. If "the rent for water supplied by the" company were "promptly paid, that is paid from the proceeds of the sale of the crops grown upon lands contiguous to the plant, the Receivers would be able to operate" with little difficulty. To this end, in 1914 Burns threatened to refuse the issuance of any additional receiver's certificates to bail the company out. Failing a rise in revenue from water rents, the judge vowed to close the plant "and put a Keeper in charge."

Burns did not want to have to close the plant. He was "anxious to protect the farmers" and was willing to go "as far as possible" to keep the plant operating. He appreciated the important part that irrigation played in South Texas's agricultural economy. All he wanted was for "every water consumer . . . [to] do his part, by promptly paying his indebtedness."

The plant remained open. Despite the threats, the court took every action possible to keep it operating. To save money the judge "of [his] own volition" reduced the compensation paid the receivers to $1,800 a year. At one point he allowed them to withhold wages for the company's employees so as to continue operations. In 1914 Burns authorized the borrowing of money to meet expenses; in 1916 he allowed the issuance of an additional $79,000 in receiver's certificates. At all times, Burns pressed for the collection of past-due debt. On one occasion he even wrote to a farmer who had a complaint against the company for damages to his crop that the farmer should pay the rents "without regard to the question of damage." Ultimately, the rents were paid and the company recovered. On January 16, 1917, it was sold back to its original creditors at open auction for $125,000.[33]

The judge went to even greater lengths when necessary to protect the region's economic health. In 1915 a hurricane, comparable in strength to the storm that wrecked Galveston in 1900, crashed into the upper Texas Gulf Coast. Though few lives were lost, the storm resulted in millions of dollars in damage. A large part of this damage centered on the region's cotton crop, which had been stored at various locations along the coast. Following the storm, most of this cotton was strewn about, unidentified by any markings of ownership. In order to stave off a crisis, Burns, of his own volition and in the face of strong opposition from the owners of the cotton, appointed a receiver to take charge of all the unidentified cotton and to administer the property, collecing and selling it off at the best price the receiver could find. Within sixteen months of the date of the storm, this process was completed and the proceeds of the sale, exceeding seven hundred thousand dollars, were distributed to the more than four hundred owners of the cotton. Despite the early opposition to the appointment of a receiver, no appeals of Burns's decisions regarding the distribution of the money were made.[34]

Through its equity jurisdiction, then, the court worked to preserve key sectors of the economy needed for continued growth. From simple defenses of bankrupt business to complex restructuring of whole sectors of the economy, the court provided a shield to local business from both creditors and bad economic times. In return for this protection, it demanded, and sought to impose, a more stable and service-oriented infrastructure for the region.

More than this was required, however, if the region's development were to continue unabated. Protecting normal business operations was just as important to maintaining growth as supporting key sectors of the region's economy.

While most speculators stayed within the bounds of acceptable business behavior in their drive for success, many pushed those boundaries to the limit. Creditors frequently lost out as financially strapped business people failed to pay off their debts.[35]

The state still relied heavily on out-of-state capital to fund growth. Creditors, however, were not going to invest in Texas without a means of protecting their money. Somehow, a balance had to be struck between the need to defend economic enterprises and the need to sooth the legitimate fears of investors over unpaid debts. Involuntary bankruptcy was one option. Most receiverships and about one-third of all bankruptcies were instituted on the peition of creditors.[36] Bankruptcy, however, was an extreme response limited to specific situations. In addition, the protections offered the debtor by bankruptcy as often hindered as facilitated the payoff of debts.[37]

The court's private law docket provided an easier means to protect investor rights. Consisting almost entirely of diversity cases, the private law docket provided a neutral forum in which collecting debts and protecting other key business enterprises could be carried out. Suits were brought to recover debt, to prove title (a means of foreclosing on the property of a debtor), and to obtain damages (either personal injury or business-related). Also prevalent were suits brought by railroads to recover unpaid freight charges.[38]

These actions had a significant effect on the economy. Since most private law suits were diversity actions, these cases created an important bridge between local and national markets. Drawing on the court's ability to utilize a national common law independent of state court decisions, investors sought and found in the federal courts a uniform set of business standards, especially as related to the rights of creditors. Their goal was the creation of a stable marketplace in which investments would be safe, or at least in which the risks of investment would be known ahead of time. The existence of this standard gave creditors confidence about their investment's safety.[39]

The court took seriously the need to maintain proper protections for creditors, for both in-state and out-of-state investors. In one instance, a Colorado business came before the court seeking to recover from I. H. Kempner of Galveston, an investor in the construction company, a debt owed to it by the Taylor-Moore Construction Company, a Texas corporation. The plaintiff, the Leyner Engineering Works, sought to apply a Colorado statute that made investors liable for the total debts of any corporation doing business in Colorado if no local representative of the company had been named. The engineering company had sold to Taylor-Moore seventeen thousand dollars' worth of equipment, which was paid for by five promissory notes. Soon after, Taylor-Moore went bankrupt. As no local representative was named in Colorado, the plaintiffs turned to Kempner for their money.

The defendant argued that the Colorado act was a penal statute, in force only in the jurisdiction of its enactment. Since Kempner had invested in a company incorporated by the state of Texas, Texas' laws regarding investor liability should apply. In Texas an investor in a bankrupt corporation was liable only for the amount of original investment.

Judge Burns agreed with the defense's contention. Ignoring Colorado state court interpretations of the legitimacy of the Colorado statute, since how one defined a penal statute was a matter of "general jurisprudence," the court ruled that the Colorado law did not apply in this instance. To uphold this point, the judge restated the issues of the case as a question: "what law fixes the liability of stockholders, . . . the statute law of the state of incorporation . . . or . . . the enactments of every state in the Union in which the corporation may transact business?" To the judge the only logical answer was the former. For, "if the latter were true, it would invite immediate dissolution [of the corporation], for no sane person would become a purchaser of stock with the legal assurance that, in the event the corporation did business in a sister state–Colorado, for instance–and loss and disaster attended the venture, . . . a stockholder of Vermont, having subscribed and paid for a single share of the value of $100, would be called upon to make good the loss of every creditor, who elected to extend a line of credit to the insolvent corporation." "The subscriber," the judge continued, "looking for modest dividends as the result of his investment, would be called upon to separate himself from his earnings and stand forth a commercial pauper, having wronged no creditor, yet powerless to prevent his own destruction." Such a turn of events was a "monstrous" doctrine "hostile to the declared and recognized policy" of the law.

Before concluding, Burns cautioned on the limits of his decision. If someone invested in an out-of-state corporation, then the laws of the state that chartered the company would apply. An investor in a corporation was assumed to have "voluntarily agreed to the terms of the company's constitution," including the limits placed on it by state statute. If this had been the facts in the case, then Colorado's law would have applied.[40]

Despite this note of caution, Burns's decision in this case made clear his intentions to protect the normal business patterns of the economy. In most cases, that meant upholding the rights of creditors to a fair and safe return on their investment. Throughout Burns's judgeship, plaintiffs were two or three times more likely to win their suit than were defendants. In other cases, as in the foregoing example, stabilizing business relations required the defense of the debtor from excessive or illogical debts. This too the court allowed, as the still-significant number of defendants who won their cases shows (see table 1). In either case, the goal was to assure both creditor and debtor that when they made an agreement with a business partner, that partner would be held accountable for his or her end of the agreement. In this way members of the business community were able to operate with the assurance that their investments of time and money would be protected and adequate levels of credit would continue to flow into Southeast Texas.

Used in conjunction with the protections available in bankruptcy and equity proceedings, private law cases provided a means to counterbalance local and

Table 1
PRIVATE LAW CASES, 1903–17

Year	*Total for the Term*	*Judgment for the Plaintiff*	*Judgment for the Defendant*	*No. Dismissed*
1903	149	96	18	35
1904	51	10	16	25
1905	42	12	18	18
1906	43	7	11	20
1907	–	–	–	–
1908	12	3	1	8
1909	46	10	4	32
1910	62	14	8	40
1911	71	14	8	40
1912	50	14	9	55
1913	60	22	0	38
1914	67	20	5	42
1915	73	24	7	42
1916	66	12	1	53
1917	139	57	11	71

Source: Atty. Gen. Report (1903–17). No private law cases were listed for 1907. The numbers for 1908 are incomplete because of a fire at Houston, which destroyed records. Inconsistencies for total number of cases filed for the terms in 1905, 1906, 1911, and 1912 are the result of a filing error in the *Atty. Gen. Report.*

national needs. Where bankruptcy provided a haven for the debtor displaced by an unstable economy, diversity protected the interests of the creditor from the effects of the same forces. Both worked to the common goal of maintaining the components necessary for growth.[41]

Legal actions involving the federal government also played a role in fostering growth. One of the court's functions was acting as an enforcement and collection arm of the federal government. From internal revenue to customs to regulation cases, the federal government used civil actions brought in district courts as a means of penalizing those who evaded federal laws. These cases again brought the fate of Southeast Texas' development before the court. Many of the violations prosecuted were not the result of criminal behavior; rather, they grew out of normal economic activities. Other violations were the result of illegal actions. Most of these activities had a long history of practice in the region, however, and were once again closely related to legal business practices.

Public law cases fell into four general categories. The first consisted of suits against the railroads for violations of federal law regulating their operations. In 1893 Congress passed the Safety Appliance Act, which set standards for the conditions of railroad facilities, including both the rails and the trains themselves as well as switches used to shift trains between lines. Fourteen years later Congress passed the Hours of Service Act, which limited railroad employees to twenty-eight hours of continuous service. After such time, rail workers had to spend at least forty-eight hours off the job before returning to work.[42]

The second category of suits arose from the enforcement of the Safe Food and Drug Act of 1906. Passed by Congress in the wake of the uproar caused by the allegations of unsafe food processing in the meat industry in Upton Sinclair's *The Jungle*, the act regulated the preparation and labeling of processed food. Food found to be mislabeled was confiscated. A hearing was then held for the forfeiture and condemnation of the goods. If the processing company was found to be in violation of the act, the food, correctly labeled, would be sold at public auction.[43]

Immigration cases made up the third category of the public law docket. These cases arose from violations of the 1907 Alien Immigration Act, which denied entry to various classes of individuals, including anarchists, imbeciles, people with physical or mental defects, and potential paupers. Also added to this act were sanctions against those illegally employing these immigrants. It was these sanctions, sections four and five, that resulted in the bulk of civil prosecutions. The illegal immigrants themselves were taken care of through criminal deportation proceedings.[44]

The most common public law cases were *in rem* customs cases. Smuggling was endemic along the border with Mexico. For many in South Texas it was a normal part of life. With an overwhelmingly Hispanic population, South Texas viewed the border as a connective rather than as a divisive line. Trade flowed freely, ignoring international boundaries. In this situation, little distinction was made between commerce and smuggling; both arose out of essentially the same activities. When smugglers were caught by customs agents, they were tried criminally, while the smuggled goods were impounded and confiscated by a civil *in rem* suit. If condemned by the court, the goods were sold at auction.

In deciding cases arising in all four of these categories, the court found itself balancing conflicting local developmental needs and national priorities. Though the laws enforced were federal, the impact of enforcement was local. Texas' booming growth produced an economy that superficially resembled that of the nation as a whole. Important differences existed, however. Most notable was the fragility of the expansion of Texas' manufacturing and commercial sectors. While northeastern and midwestern industries, mature after years of growth, could survive the loss of revenue and service brought about by strict enforcement of federal laws, Southeast Texas could not. The region's business operated on a small margin of profit. All available capital was needed to finance growth. Strict enforcement of national laws did not make sense in this situation. Yet the court, as part of the national government, was duty-bound to uphold these laws. The problem facing it was to find a way to fit the enforcement of these laws into the Texas context.

This the court did. When clear cases of violations were brought before it, it prosecuted such behavior. The railroads were fined for using unsafe equipment and for working their employees too long. Food and smuggled goods seized by health and customs officials were condemned and sold at auction. Those employing or importing illegal immigrants were fined. In deciding guilt and in setting damages, however, the court took into account the context of such cases. For example, few railroads were ever fined the full amount requested by the government. In 1910 the U.S. attorney requested a fine of forty-five hundred dollars for the Missouri, Kansas and Texas Railroad for violations of the Hours of Service Act. Two years later, at the completion of the case, the railroad's fine was only five hundred dollars. That same year the Gulf, Colorado and Santa Fe Railroad was charged with a violation of the Safety Appliance Act. The request was for four hundred dollars; the fine was for only one hundred dollars. The same result occurred when the Gulf, Colorado and Santa Fe was brought before the court seven years later.[45]

The penalties placed on the other violations of federal law were usually just as light as those for the railroads. Most fines for immigration violations were under one thousand dollars, many well under. Smuggled goods and mislabeled food were confiscated; however, since they were ultimately sold at auction, the goods could be reacquired by the defendant. Also, given the high incidence of smuggling along the border, the number of condemnation cases was quite small.[46]

In reaching these decisions, the court achieved two results. First, its actions limited the effect of federal laws on the region by tempering legal dictates with understanding and limited punishments. The result was to protect the region's fragile economic structure from national laws that had little relation to local business realities. Second, these decisions placed a governor on excessive speculation, punishing those whose drive for wealth led them to cross the line into unethical behavior. In doing so the court once again sought to protect the region's continued growth, making it clear to those living in the district that limits on how one could join in the region's development had to exist if growth were to continue unabated.

This pattern of selective enforcement of federal statutes to protect regional development was reinforced in the district's criminal docket. Criminal cases constituted over half of the suits filed in these years, and the majority of these arose from economic issues. Most criminal indictments were for actions that could have been prosecuted as civil cases. The main difference between most U.S. civil and criminal actions was the focus of prosecution: civil cases went after property while criminal cases punished the individual. The wider impact of these decisions was the same. Like public law cases, the criminal docket operated as a check against excessive zeal in the pursuit of economic gain while not inhibiting legitimate economic initiative.

The economic focus of the court's criminal docket was pervasive throughout the district. In the two southern divisions, Brownsville and Laredo, the main concern was smuggling, which made up over 75 percent of the criminal docket. Internal Revenue and importation of cattle without proper inspection made up most of the remaining 25 percent. In the northern three divisions–Houston, Galveston, and Corpus Christi–the majority of criminal cases involved prosecutions for the operation of a retail liquor dealership without a license (a tax crime). In addition, such economically related crimes as counterfeiting, mail fraud, embezzlement, and theft from interstate commerce were also present.

As with civil prosecutions, the origin of many of these crimes rested in the normal course of business in the district. Smuggling is a good example. As noted earlier, for most of its history trade across the border between Mexico and the United States was common and a key part of the South Texas economy. Little distinction existed between commerce and smuggling. The goods being smuggled were in themselves legitimate; often only the failure to pay the proper customs fees was illegal. In fact, the most common goods seized by customs agents were cattle, sheep, goats, mules, and horses. Also commonly smuggled were small amounts of mescal, a Mexican liquor. All of these goods could be imported legally from Mexico. Those doing the smuggling, in turn, were usually poor Hispanic laborers. Often they smuggled to avoid paying import fees they could not afford. Only rarely did the amount of goods smuggled imply more professional smuggling. The same could be said for the importing of uninspected cattle. Ranching was carried out on both sides of the border, often by the same people, and with the same types of cattle. The number of cattle smuggled across the border was usually fewer than one hundred at a time. The only difference between a Texas cow and a Mexican one was a matter of inspection and import fees.[47]

The judge took these facts into account in deciding cases of this sort. Almost all smuggling cases in Laredo and many such cases in Brownsville ended with guilty pleas, as there was little doubt of the guilt. In pronouncing punishment for the crime, however, the court proved lenient. On average, a smuggler received between ten days and six months in the county jail. No smuggler received anything close to the maximum statutory sentence of two years imprisonment and a five thousand–dollar fine. Often, the jail sentence was waived for time served. Fines were rare and few cases of civil attachment of the goods smuggled were filed.[48]

A similar example of this attitude shaped prosecutions for the illegal operation of a retail liquor dealership (or RLD cases, as they were more commonly known). Many Texans after the turn of the century started small business enterprises as a way to tap into the state's economic growth. With Prohibition a priority of many in the state, and local options limiting the number of drinking establishments in the larger Texas cities, serving alcohol to a few customers in one's home was an easy way for a poorer Texan to join in this process. Little capital was needed to start up this sort of business, and demand was usually high.

Many in the district operated such businesses. Next to smuggling, RLD cases were the most numerous on the criminal docket. In the divisions of Corpus Christi, Galveston, and Houston, they made up almost half the criminal case load. To a lesser extent, they also filled the docket in Brownsville. Despite the large number of indictments, a significant number of these cases were dismissed on the motion of the U.S. attorney. Where defendants were found guilty, the punishments were again limited. On average, the minimum sentence of thirty days in the county jail and a one hundred dollar fine was imposed.[49]

Even before the trial, the judge sought to ease the burden on defendants in the foregoing categories. Affordable bail was set if at all possible. "In matters of this character," Burns wrote to the U.S. commissioner in Brownsville in 1913, "you [should] endeavor to ascertain the ability of these defendants charged with violations to give bond, and exercise your good discretion in endeavoring to fix the bond at such a sum as to make it possible, if not probable, that the defendant may be able to find sureties, thereby avoid[ing] the expense to the government of maintaining the defendant in jail and the better concerning the rights of men charged with violation of the law." The judge did caution on the need to "exact the personal assurance of the party charged with the crime, in the event he is a Mexican, that he will report to the next ensuing term of Court." If such assurance was given, however, the defendant was to be freed. The judge would even lower bail after it was set if he felt the defendant was incarcerated because of an inability to make bond. On one occasion Burns asked to know the amount of bail a prisoner could afford to pay, as "nothing [could] be gained by reducing . . . bail unless" the defendant "would be able to make bond in a reasonable sum."[50]

Even after a defendant was incarcerated, the court made every effort to see to the well-being of the prisoner. On hearing that the Harris County jail was "unsanitary and badly crowded," Burns authorized the transfer of two federal prisoners to another county jail. In 1913 the judge sent word to the sheriff of Webb County that, "unless federal prisoners committed to custody receive[d] proper care and treatment," they would be transferred to another jail. On a third occasion, he refused to send a female witness being held by the Immigration Department to the Webb County jail for holding prior to testifying in another case, noting that the jail was "not a proper place to confine a young woman." The judge continued, advising that "in no like instance [would] any female be committed to the Jail of Webb County or any other Jail on the Rio Grande" as it would be "an act of inhumanity . . . which the Court will uniformly decline to perpetrate."[51]

The key to the judge's actions rested in his belief that such crimes as smuggling and serving alcohol without a license were not serious offenses. This was a common view throughout the district. Even the local customs agents conceived of their jobs more in terms of local politics than of federal service.[52] Yet, as a part of the federal government, the court had the duty of enforcing federal statutes. The tension between public duties and private priorities resulted in both the high incidences of guilty decisions and the court's lenient sentences and concern for indicted and convicted criminals.

Not all criminal cases fell into these patterns. Crimes against property, such as embezzlement, counterfeiting, mail fraud, and theft from interstate commerce, were viewed by the court in a much darker light than were other types of crimes. Though taking up only a quarter of the criminal docket, these crimes loomed large in terms of the time the court spent on them. Such cases were more likely to go to trial, to take more time to complete, and to receive harsher punishments than crimes such as smuggling and RLD. Though almost all of these crimes had their origins in the unsettled economic times, they were destructive, not conducive, of growth. They were examples of speculation and unethical behavior run riot, tearing down the future many in the region sought to build. As Burns noted about the case of A. Brown, former postmaster of Madisonville, Texas, who used his office to embezzle funds: "Everyone . . . residing in Madison County is thoroughly satisfied with the fact that Mr Brown is now making his residence at Leavenworth . . . [and] would be pleased in the event his residence there could be made permanent."[53]

In such cases the judge did not lower bail, even when asked to by the prisoner. Where juries found the defendants guilty, the court's punishments were very strict. For example, in cases resulting from theft from interstate commerce, the minimum sentence granted was one year and one day in the federal penitentiary. Maximum sentences went up from there. Forgery and embezzlement also brought sentences in the penitentiary. As Burns noted in a letter to a forger he had sentenced to Leavenworth: "the act [of forgery] is regarded as a very serious offense." Even when the prisoner recanted his position and promised to live a law-abiding life, the judge refused to work for his early release, as he did for prisoners convicted of many other crimes.[54]

Combined, then, the district's equity, law, and criminal dockets worked effectively to foster Southeast Texas' social and economic development and struck a careful balance between the extreme options facing the region—unlimited growth versus stability, the needs of the creditor against those of the debtor, and limiting speculation while fostering initiative. In an ad hoc manner, the court provided necessary economic regulations and protections where no other institution could or would and filled the gap between what local and federal regulations existed and what was needed if growth were to continue. Where needed, the court provided a shelter through its equity and bankruptcy jurisdiction in which local business could weather economic downturns. At the same time it spurred growth by protecting creditors' investments through its private law docket. Again, the court simultaneously limited the extremes of speculation by sanctioning those who overstepped the bounds of acceptable actions while allowing for economic initiative through its civil and criminal cases. In return for this protection, the court demanded, and sought to impose, a more stable and service-oriented infrastructure. The rapid private development of Southeast Texas' economic resources was the result.

IV

Though most of the Southern District's business arose in response to Southeast Texas' economic development, not all of the court's cases involved economic issues. As a court of general jurisdiction, the Southern District heard a wide variety of cases.[55] A small but significant part of its time was therefore spent on issues only remotely related to Southeast Texas' development. While these cases were parenthetical to the court's primary concern, ironically, they provide a useful example of how different forces interacted to achieve the court's private economic goals. The *Reyes* case involving the trade with Mexico during that country's revolution is exemplary in this regard.

The Mexican Revolution posed a major problem for the United States and a crisis for Texas. Mexico in the decade between 1910 and 1920 staggered under a series of revolts and counterrevolts. The Mexican government changed five times during this period as the result of armed insurrection. This did not count the numerous unsuccessful attempts that were made. Most of these revolts originated along, and often over, the U.S. border. The United States was a main supplier of arms and ammunition for the different rebel armies. It was also often the safest ground available for the planning of a rebellion. Control of the railheads along the border at Brownsville, Laredo, and El Paso became the key to victory, and the border was second only to Mexico City in importance as a military target.

The United States could not ignore the fighting along its border, Texas could afford to even less. All agreed on the need to respond to this crisis. The problem was how to respond. The federal government's primary goal in this situation was to maintain peaceful relations with Mexico. Viewing the Revolution as a question of foreign policy, both Presidents Taft and Wilson acted cautiously in their dealings with Mexico; they did not want events along the border to set off an international incident. To keep the peace, the federal government sought through the customs process and the courts to strictly enforce neutrality laws prohibiting the export of arms, ammunition, and other military supplies to the various combatants.

For Texas the problem was somewhat different. It experienced the Mexican Revolution primarily as a border problem. With a population predominantly of Mexican descent, South Texas proved a fertile ground for involvement in Mexico's problems. Trade flowed almost unhindered across the border. So too did people, arms, and ammunition. Texas, whether it wanted to be involved or not, was a part of the Revolution.

The state's response to this situation was ambivalent. On the one hand, fear of disorder led Texans to argue for active defense of the border. The state's two governors during these years, Oscar Colquitt and William P. Hobby, repeatedly called on the federal government to send more troops to the border to enforce the nation's laws and protect Texas. When Washington failed to respond to the governors' satisfaction, they used the Texas Rangers and called out the state militia to maintain order. On the other hand, the close ties between Texas and Mexico that caused such fears also directly involved the state in the revolutionary crisis. State leaders could not ignore the links between Texas and events in revolutionary Mexico. Many Texans—including many of the state's political elite—became entangled in the Revolution as a result of friendship, kinship, politics, or business connections. Texans found it difficult to take a strict stance in all matters pertaining to protecting the border. In many cases, influential Texans, often with the support of the local power structure, ignored federal neutrality statutes. Even when such involvement ran afoul of federal enforcement of the neutrality laws, political expediency and popular attitudes stressed the need to compromise on the issues. Conflict between state and federal officials over border policy was often the result.[56]

The Southern District, as federal court in a local setting, was pulled in both of these directions, experiencing in full measure all of the confusions attendant to this conflict. Holding jurisdiction over customs, immigration, and neutrality laws for a two hundred-mile stretch of border, the court was intimately involved with the execution of neutrality policy. It had the duty of enforcing punishment for the breaking of these laws. Though a part of the federal government, however, the court was staffed from judge to juries by local inhabitants. Everyone was strongly in tune with the needs and attitudes of the region. As Texans they felt the same fears, and held the same connections to events in Mexico, as their fellow residents. This made enforcing federal policy a difficult proposition.

All this ambivalence came to the surface almost immediately following Francisco I. Madero's successful revolt in 1910. In the summer of 1910, seven-term Mexican president Porfirio Díaz ran for an eighth term as president. Díaz's opponent in the election was Madero. In an election filled with fraud and the misuse of official power Díaz was reelected. Madero contested the results. He fled to Texas and began to plot the overthrow of the Díaz regime. A few months later Madero's revolution successfully drove Díaz from office. Soon after, Madero was elected president of Mexico.[57]

In that election Madero's main opponent was a former general of Díaz's, Bernardo Reyes. A popular leader during Díaz's regime, Reyes felt that he could defeat Madero in the presidential election. It soon became apparent, however, that he could not. Reyes, in turn, fled across the border and began planning a new revolt to overthrow Madero.

Reyes centered his revolt in San Antonio and received warm support from the largely Hispanic population of South Texas. Almost immediately he began collecting money, supplies, and support for his revolt. Throughout the region, but especially along the border, Reyes supporters soon collected large amounts of guns and ammunition, horses, and field supplies.

The key to the success of the Reyes plan was open access across the border. To get this, Reyes needed government officials in Laredo, Brownsville, and El Paso willing to look the other way. As his plans took shape, he sought out such men, bringing them into his conspiracy. Included in this group were Francisco

Chapa, leader of San Antonio's Mexican American population and a lieutenant-colonel on Governor Colquitt's staff, and Amador Sánchez, sheriff of Webb County and political boss of Laredo. Both men were friends of Reyes before the Revolution and willingly offered to help him out with his planned invasion of Mexico. With their help Reyes was ready to act by November, 1911.

The federal government was also ready to act by November. The United States could not allow Reyes's plans to succeed. It wanted peace to the south so did not want to anger Mexican president Madero by allowing the planning and organization of a counterrevolution from Texas. Almost from the day Reyes entered Texas, federal agents worked their way into his conspiracy. By November they had acquired enough evidence to seek charges. On November 13 Burns ordered a federal grand jury at Laredo to investigate the rumors of a conspiracy to formulate a revolt against Mexico. Five days later, the grand jury passed an indictment against Reyes, Chapa, Sánchez, and nine other men. Utilizing blanket search warrants, federal and state authorities raided sites throughout South Texas, confiscating hundreds of rifles and horses and thousands of cartridges. In addition, wagonloads of saddles, blankets, and other supplies were found. Later that month, a second federal grand jury, this time sitting in Brownsville, returned updated indictments against the conspirators and named an additional twenty-four defendants. The Reyes conspiracy was dead.[58]

In the aftermath of this disaster, Reyes was captured, set free on a ten thousand–dollar bond, and fled over the border into Mexico. His followers, however, remained to be tried. On January 1, 1912, the trial of twenty-three of the thirty-six conspirators began in Brownsville. They were charged with multiple violations of the Neutrality Act and sections of the criminal code dealing with conspiracy.[59]

The trial drew wide attention. Many of the defendants, including Chapa and Sánchez, were politically influential. The defendants were represented by the state's top legal talent, Chapa by Jake Wolters, a confidant of the governor, the rest by Marshall Hicks of Houston. Lock McDaniel and Noah Allen represented the government.

In five days of hearings, the government put on a strong case to prove its contentions of a conspiracy to violate the Neutrality Act. Along with the physical evidence collected in the November raids, the government brought forth telephone and telegraph records detailing the extensive correspondence between the conspirators. Hotel bellhops and chauffeurs were put on the stand to testify. Even members of the conspiracy, granted immunity, testified to the scope and intentions of the plot. Almost seventy witnesses were called.[60]

Before the government could rest its case, the trial took a strange turn. Following a closed-door conference and on the assurance of the judge that none of the defendants would be sentenced to the penitentiary, thirteen of the defendants, including Amador Sánchez, changed their plea from innocent to guilty. Following immediately, the prosecution dropped its charges against nine of the lesser defendants. This left only Chapa to try.[61]

The case against Chapa was the strongest. Prior to the conference, the government had produced copies of three manifestoes written by Reyes calling for support for his revolution in Mexico. They had been prepared on the presses of *El Imparcial,* a San Antonio paper owned by Chapa. Other testimony had shown that Reyes had stayed in Chapa's home while in San Antonio, and that Chapa had procured a loan of some sixty thousand dollars for Reyes. Especially embarrassing had been the statements of John Bowman, Governor Colquitt's private secretary, who described a visit Chapa had set up between Reyes and the governor in October, 1910. Though Bowman described a short, formal meeting, the implication was clear that Chapa had attempted to use his influence to help Reyes in his plans. The testimony of Captain Juan Mirigo of Mexico City, one of the conspirators not on trial, added to this impression. Mirigo testified that General Reyes had told him that he (Mirigo) could operate in Texas "without fear," as "Colonel Chapa" was a friend and "would use his influence" to see that there would be "no interference from the government of Texas."

Chapa strongly protested his innocence. His attorney, Wolters, argued that all the evidence was the result of a political "frame-up." On the stand, Chapa readily admitted to helping his friend Reyes. But, Chapa continued, he helped many "prominent Mexican citizens" when they came to San Antonio. This included "endorsing drafts for them during their stay." As to all the evidence of his implication in a conspiracy–the letters, proclamations, and records–Chapa argued that he had never seen them and had no knowledge of their existence before the trial. In fact, Chapa testified that he had never seen Captain Mirigo before the trial.

The case went before the jury on January 10. It stayed out for the next twenty-four hours. Twenty-three hours into its deliberations it returned to the court, announcing that it was unable to reach a verdict. The judge refused, however, to let it adjourn undecided. Declaring that the case had been too long and expensive to retry, Burns ordered the jury to attempt to reach a majority decision if a unanimous one was impossible. In addition, he informed the jury that he would not inflict a penitentiary sentence on Chapa if a guilty verdict were returned. One hour later, the jury returned with an 11 to 1 vote of guilty.[62]

In setting punishment for the defendants, Burns continued to show great concern for the well-being of the conspirators. In sentencing Chapa, he stood by his agreement not to send him to the penitentiary. Noting that "I am well disposed towards you . . . and . . . that [the penitentiary] is not a place for men of your kind," the judge fined Chapa fifteen hundred dollars. Burns was just as lenient with the thirteen defendants who had pleaded guilty. "Distressed" at having to impose any penalty on these men at all, the judge fined Sánchez twelve hundred dollars and the rest six hundred dollars or six months in the Cameron County jail. When eight of the defendants who could not pay their fines requested that their jail sentence be moved to the Webb County jail, which was under the control of codefendant Sánchez, the judge agreed.[63]

In the months that followed, Burns continued his efforts in behalf of the defendants. In February, 1912, José Sandoval, one of the defendants serving six months in the Webb County jail, wrote to Burns explaining that his wife had died and that his children needed him. Moved by this plea, the judge paid Sandoval's fine himself and invited him up to Houston. After thanking the judge personally in Houston, Sandoval returned to Laredo, where he paid off the fines for the remaining defendants with a draft he had received from General Reyes's son.[64] The judge also worked for the pardon of Chapa and Sánchez, writing numerous letters in their behalf. So too did Lock McDaniel and numerous other Texas politicians. On May 29, 1912, Chapa's pardon was approved by the president. On February 9, 1913, Sánchez's pardon was approved.[65]

It would be a mistake to view Burns's actions, and those of the court as a whole, as motivated simply by political favoritism. While the political clout of the defendants may have played a part, the situation was more complex than this explanation allows for. It is unlikely that Burns was bought off or politically influenced. For one thing, the judge belonged to a different party from Chapa and Sánchez. Nor was he attempting to win over these men to the Republican party. In the next election, both worked to elect Woodrow Wilson, not President Taft. Further, Burns had been instrumental in federal efforts to stop the Reyes conspiracy. In 1911, when he charged the grand jury that indicted Reyes and his followers, the judge ordered the jurors to be vigilant in seeking out violators of the neutrality laws. Burns even promised to impose stringent sentences on offenders, a threat he did not keep.

Rather, this inconsistency was the result of the conflicting priorities faced by the court. As a federal court the Southern District had a duty to punish violations of the law. This it did. As a local court made up of individuals with personal contact with the defendants, however, it proved difficult to sanction these men for their activities. To Burns's mind, and to the jury, while these men were guilty of breaking the law, they were not criminals. They were good men, friends, and neighbors, the sanctioning of whom "distresse[d] the court." As Burns noted in sentencing the prisoners: "It was not the purpose of the court to sentence any of the defendants who had admitted their guilt to the penitentiary. To do so would be to give them a status which they neither had earned nor deserved. Personally . . . [the judge] regarded the prisoners with pronounced favor, but the law exacts a strict demand that the neutrality regulations be not violated and hence regards the offense as serious." The inability of the jury to decide on a verdict prior to being given assurances that none of the men would go to the penitentiary is also instructive of this feeling.

Pulled in two directions, the court responded to the Reyes conspiracy with strong indictments followed by "moderate" sentences. Despite the expectation of "criticism and censure" for its actions, the court and its judge felt this was the right thing to do.[66]

It was in this drive to do the "right thing," even in the face of public censure or conflicting national priorities, that the court's noneconomic, public cases merged with its private ones. No plot or plan existed to subvert national law;

far from it. The attempt was to apply national law, but interpreted to suit private needs and the requirements of Southeast Texas' development.

The unintended, but welcome, result was that the court became a tool for the creation of a "better" Texas—better as defined by the state's progressive business and political elite. The court's role was simple: it had to maintain growth and foster development in good times and bad. Lacking an adequate institutional infrastructure to stabilize the region's gains, Southeast Texas needed an institution to substitute for this missing infrastructure, to provide on an almost daily basis a counterforce to the wild fluctuations of the Texas economy.

In this endeavor the court was largely successful. The 1920s would observe the maturing of the Southeast Texas economy. Though still based on extractive industries like oil, cotton, and timber, Texas in the 1920s would have in place all the parts of a steady economy capable of surviving the tough times ahead. But before this could occur, the court had to deal with the effects of the First World War and excessive economic growth in the 1920s.

3. Trade Not Treason

PUBLIC LAW IN WAR AND PEACE, 1918–33

I

In its first fifteen years, the Southern District Court's top priority was promoting Southeast Texas' economic development through private, mostly corporate, means. Almost 90 percent of the court's time between 1902 and 1917 was spent on cases relating to some aspect of the region's economic condition. No other function, public or private, was allowed to stand in the way of this objective. As a result the court was extremely successful in fostering private economic growth. By 1917 the Southeast Texas economy had doubled in size. It had also become more diverse, with energy, mineral, and lumber enterprises joining agriculture as its foundation. Structural problems still existed, but the Southeast Texas economy was maturing and promised continued growth.

An important ingredient in the court's success in fostering this growth was the lack of competing public pressures to implement national or state economic or social policies. Few of the nation's laws at this time aimed at controlling individual or corporate action. Aside from one or two statutes regulating the operation of railroads, controlling taxes, limiting foreign trade, or making such actions as prostitution, interstate lotteries, or forgery federal crimes, most federal laws did not result in significant legal action in the federal courts. More to the point, except for the progressive-inspired railroad, prostitution, and tax statutes, none of these laws were backed by strong national enforcement policies. Rather, it was left to local officials, principally U.S. attorneys and federal judges, to set enforcement priorities. Even where national laws and policies were involved, federal courts could interpret the enforcement provisions of these laws as they wished.[1] Similarly, though state regulatory laws were much more common, the *Swift* doctrine gave federal judges the freedom to interpret those laws in light of "general common law doctrines." As a result, state statutes placed few limits on federal judges' freedom to act.[2] In such an environment it was easy for the Southern District Court to spend almost all of its time on private developmental issues.

With America's entry into the First World War, the federal courts' freedom to set their own priorities began to be challenged. War brought public issues to the fore. Federal statutes were passed instituting a draft, regulating foreign trade, and curtailing many actions that formerly had been private. Each of these laws was part of a coherent plan of wartime enforcement. From all levels of the government and from the public as well, pressures were placed on the federal courts to uphold wartime statutes and to serve specific public ends – pressures that the federal courts could not ignore. The return of peace, in turn, did not lessen public demands on their time, but increased it. Drawing on the wartime experience, new federal laws aimed at reforming the morals of the nation, such as Prohibition, were passed. Like wartime statutes, these laws were supported by a wide range of public and private agencies that pressed the federal courts to make enforcement their top priority.

These changes posed a dilemma for the court, one that was to continue to be troubling throughout the remainder of the century. How was it to balance growing public demands for action on specific social, political, or economic reforms with the already-significant private pressures to support regional economic development? Which of its two functions – private or public – should the court give priority?

During the war the answer to this dilemma proved easy, as few private cases came before the court. This meant that it, under its new judge, Joseph C. Hutcheson (Judge Burns died just as WW I was beginning), could place public cases foremost on its docket. Since many of these statutes affected private interests and the economic soundness of the region, however, the court administered these cases in light of its experience and interest in private matters. This was especially the case where federal statutes involved issues of trade and not treason, but also affected such noneconomic issues as the draft. The result was that, while the court served the public needs of wartime, it protected the long-term private developmental interests of the region.

Balancing private and public functions proved more difficult following the war. Armed conflict intensified Southeast Texas' growth, and so too did the peace that followed. Suddenly, maintaining growth was no longer the problem facing the region; rather, it was surviving the effects of too much growth coming too fast. The region's economy was in dire need of the stabilizing influence of the federal court. Yet, for the court to find the time to meet this need required it to limit its efforts in upholding Prohibition and other federal regulatory statutes. The opposite was true if Prohibition were to be enforced adequately. A choice between these two functions had to be made if either need were to be met.

The court chose the private function. Though faced with hundreds of Prohibition and other public regulatory cases, it settled these cases quickly, using guilty pleas and out-of-court settlements to move the public docket along quickly. Further, as a result of Judge Hutcheson's emphasis on private matters, and as a means of producing guilty pleas to speed up the process, the court limited its punishments in such cases. Only where defendants violated laws or trusts that affected the private side of the law did the court act strictly. The result was that while it functioned under public pressure as a definer, defender, and regulator of public morality and behavior, its emphasis lay elsewhere, in serving the needs of its private economic agenda. In making this choice, it set a pattern of ignoring or limiting enforcements of public matters in favor of private matters that was to remain for the next forty years.

II

In 1919 Justice Oliver Wendell Holmes, commenting on the large number of internal security prosecutions in the federal courts, described the national judiciary as "hysterical." Historians have concurred, pointing to a number of district courts, including the Southern District, as examples. Their evidence and Holmes' was the large number of convictions under the Espionage and Draft acts. Drawing on a small number of well-publicized prosecutions of domestic dissenters, these authors have assumed that all other prosecutions aimed at similar crimes. They argue that a lack of control among federal courts as well as a basic conservatism among the bench, the bar, and the jury led to "thousands" of prosecutions and judgments "based on standards of neither fair play nor common sense."[3]

This was not the experience in Southeast Texas. True, the same wild fears about loyalty affected Texas as the rest of the nation, but a close view of the district's case load makes clear that most of the court's efforts during the war focused on actions far removed from local dissent. Most of its cases aimed at assisting the war effort and at coping with unexpected wartime social tensions. The most common cases under the Espionage Act dealt with trade, not treason.[4] Far from being hysterical, the Southern District took a deliberate and conservative approach to the war and its role in the war effort. It treated the war much as it had the wild growth of the previous decade: as a problem that needed solving through a reasoned application of national and state laws to the local situation.

Whether the court's experience was typical or not, the war transformed its functions, expanding its role as a national tribunal in a local setting. Wartime legislation and executive policies greatly increased the range of federal laws applicable to citizens who never before had been much affected by national policies. Not since Reconstruction had the federal government become so involved in the everyday affairs of the nation. From conscription to price controls, from loyalty legislation to morals enforcement, the government used its nascent police powers to support and control the war effort. As during the Reconstruction years, the federal courts were primary enforcement mechanisms.

America's entry into the First World War rapidly expanded the court's case load. In 1918 alone 602 new cases were filed. Over 80 percent of these were on the criminal docket as a direct result of the war. Of 483 criminal cases filed in 1918, 368 dealt with the war effort. The war's secondary effects generated another hundred cases related to its wider social effects. This pattern continued into 1920.[5]

Nationwide, most war cases involved draft evasion. Draft resistance was a national problem. On June 5, 1917, almost 9.6 million men between the ages of twenty-one and thirty registered with Selective Service. Subsequent registration days added 14 million men. It soon became clear, however, that an unknown number had failed to register. Major General Enoch Crowder, judge advocate general and head of the Selective Service, calculated that over 15 percent of eligible males evaded registration; other estimates put the number at below 10 percent. Either way, somewhere between 2 and 3 million men had failed to register for military service by war's end.[6]

The Justice Department attempted to halt this trend, but results were mixed. Within the first six months of 1917, it arrested over six thousand men for failing to register. By mid-1918, over ten thousand accused draft evaders had been prosecuted in federal courts; by December, 1918, approximately half of those known to have evaded the draft were under arrest and under indictment, or had their cases settled in some other manner.[7]

The "average" evader was a young, poor laborer, isolated and alienated from American society by geography or social, racial, and economic status, a man at odds with the middle-class authorities who ran the local war effort. One observer described the resister as "always loafering [*sic*] around town, never seeming to have any thing to do." Most resisters were centered in the ethnic communities of large northern cities or the backcountry of the Appalachian, southern, and western states, including Texas.[8]

With its large Hispanic population, Southeast Texas had many displaced and alienated people. Discriminated against for generations, many of the district's Mexican Americans felt little reason to support the war.[9] Even before the draft was initiated, fear of conscription and rumors of a possible conflict with Mexico led thousands of Hispanic workers to return to their homeland. With the implementation of conscription the flow increased. The loss of workers quickly became acute. Governor James Ferguson requested from the president "a proclamation at once exempting all Mexicans from registration and selection during the year 1917." Wilson declined, but in order to procure enough labor for southwestern farms and ranches, the government implemented a temporary immigrant labor program, permitting the importation of large numbers of "temporary" (and hence not subject to the draft) Mexican laborers.[10]

Many Hispanics who remained in South Texas demonstrated their opposition to Texas Anglo society and the war by refusing to register for the draft or to report for induction. Despite the pressures local political leaders placed on the mostly poor Hispanic worker, thousands "of the ignorant laboring class" failed to register or fled to Mexico.[11] In Starr County, only four of the twenty-eight men called for duty in September, 1917, answered the summons. The county sheriff, himself a Hispanic, supported their inaction, arguing that "no foreigners of whatever nationality should have any fear of being forced into the military service." In late 1918 the sheriff's nephew, newly elected to replace his uncle, sought to escape the draft by filing a false affidavit with Selective Service. As late as May, 1919, the U.S. attorney still complained of the many "delinquents" remaining unprosecuted in the district's southern divisions.[12]

Over 98 percent of the district's draft cases arose in its southern half. Almost every case involved a Hispanic. In fact, despite a large German American population feared by civic and political leaders to be disloyal, only four men with Germanic surnames were indicted for failing to register. The number of non-Hispanics indicted totaled less than twenty, and this number included resisters from the district's sizable African American population.[13]

The death of Judge Burns impeded the court's response to the many draft cases. No judge was named to replace him until April, 1918. Until then, the district's dockets were covered by visiting judges. By the time the replacement, Joseph C. Hutcheson, Jr., took his seat, a backlog of cases existed. Hutcheson worked diligently and by war's end had disposed of the majority of draft cases.

Individually, draft actions posed few difficulties. The U.S. attorney only filed draft cases where "the facts were strong and the defendant was willing to plead guilty," because "it [was] impossible to prove their [the defendants'] age and almost impossible to prove that their failure [to register] in any respect was wilfull." Only where defendants fled to Mexico after registering did the U.S. attorney file indictments without a prior guilty plea. As a result of this pretrial selection process, 90 to 95 percent of indictments for draft resistance went to trial. Of these, nearly 100 percent ended with guilty pleas.[14]

Sentences varied as the war progressed. Early in the war, the court sentenced defendants to jail, usually for one to three months, followed by induction into the army. In the spring of 1918, as the American Expeditionary Force was heading for Europe, the court waived jail time and sent defendants immediately into the army. Finally, beginning in late 1918 and through 1920, remaining defendants received jail sentences of one to five months, often plus a $100 fine, after which the court released them without requiring military service.[15]

The court also served the war effort by enforcing domestic security measures. The Espionage Act of June 15, 1917, included thirteen sections, most of which dealt with defending against foreign espionage, defining the right of neutrals and interned belligerents, and protecting military installations. Other parts focused on domestic dissent and unlawful actions. One section provided for a ten thousand-dollar fine or imprisonment of up to twenty years or both for anyone who had "willfully [made] or convey[ed] false reports or false statements with intent to interfere with the operation . . . of the military . . . forces of the United States or to promote the success of its enemies . . . [or] cause[d] . . . insubordination, disloyalty, mutiny, or refusal of duty, in the military, . . . or . . . obstruct[ed] the recruiting or enlistment service of the United States." Adding strength to this section, Title XII gave the postmaster general authority to open and refuse to deliver "every letter, writing, circular, postal card,

. . . newspaper, pamphlet, book or other publication, . . . in violation of any of the provisions of this act." Other sections targeted the misuse of passports and the export of certain goods required for the war effort.[16]

These latter categories generated most of the court's domestic security cases. The Southern District heard 82 criminal cases relating to the Espionage Act: 64 in 1918 and 18 in 1919.[17] Of this number, 76 cases were prosecutions against Brownsville and Laredo merchants and laborers who had exported such merchandise as grain, flour, sugar, and lard to Mexico without licenses from the War Trade Board. In August, 1917, the president had declared these goods necessary for the war effort. Under the Espionage Act, it was a crime punishable by a fine of no more than ten thousand dollars and two years in jail to export prohibited goods without authorization.[18] Though proclaimed a felony in the statute, the court viewed these violations as minor infractions, for the amounts of goods traded south were usually quite small.[19] Minor too were the sentences imposed, as illustrated by the prosecution of José and Andrés Cisneros and Isidoro Cornea for illegally exporting seven sacks of flour, twenty-two sacks of sugar, and three sacks of corn. When José Cisneros evaded arrest the case against him was dropped. Andrés Cisneros and Cornea were captured and brought to trial. Cornea pleaded guilty and the court sentenced him to sixty days in the Cameron County jail. Andrés Cisneros pleaded innocent but the jury found him guilty. The court sentenced him to four months in the Cameron County jail and a fine of four hundred dollars. Few punishments under this category lasted longer or cost more than Cisneros's. Most jail sentences ran between one and three months; average fines were between one hundred dollars and four hundred dollars.[20]

In addition to criminal sanctions, the court heard thirty-two civil cases under Title VII of the Espionage Act for the condemnation and forfeiture of illegally exported goods. These cases all involved large amounts of goods. They were, however, only a small part of the total number of civil cases that could have been filed. Making a separate libel for each condemnation was both time-consuming and expensive. In cases where the amount of goods seized was small, it cost more to prosecute than was gained by the sale of the goods. U.S. Attorney Green repeatedly requested from the Justice Department the authority to condemn small amounts of seized goods under the customs and not the espionage law. Customs condemnations allowed for administrative disposal of goods worth less than five hundred dollars. The Justice Department refused to allow this every time, however. As a result, a larger number of cases "of apparent illegality" were never prosecuted.[21]

The remaining espionage cases involved more serious charges. Four cases of illegal use of a passport and five of causing insubordination and obstructing recruitment into the army came before the court. Unlike the illegal export actions, these seemingly involved legitimate security issues. In common with most other suits during this period, however, in reality these cases were minor and were quickly settled. Three of them were dismissed on the motion of the U.S. attorney; the rest entered guilty pleas. In the obstruction cases, sentences were longer than in other actions, each of the defendants receiving one year or more. Given the minor nature of the violations, however, these sentences were significantly lower than similar sentences made in other district courts. Those charged with passport violations, on the other hand, received fines of fifty dollars and served short terms in the Webb County jail.[22]

The war's indirect effects also swelled the court's docket. Texas was a favored training center for the military. More than thirty bases, airfields, and training camps housed several hundred thousand troops in the state. Housing so many soldiers caused problems, however. Prostitution and drunkenness, gambling and violence created endemic problems throughout the district. As one observer noted, suddenly "Houston [was] full of new women, . . . hundreds . . . from no one knows where." Other cities were similarly affected.[23]

To deal with these problems, state and local officials limited or prohibited the sale of intoxicating liquor to soldiers. Laws calling for stricter enforcement of prostitution ordinances were also passed. Houston even passed a law closing the city's saloons. But problems with disorderly soldiers and social turmoil continued throughout the war.[24]

The court aided in these efforts to defend the district's moral condition. Federal statutes prohibited serving alcohol to soldiers in uniform or the operation of a "house of ill repute" within five miles of a military base. By war's end, the court had heard 169 prosecutions under these two categories.

The more common suit was for serving drinks to soldiers in uniform. Most indictments for violating this law were made in Houston, though cases were filed in every division. The amount of alcohol involved in these cases was usually small. Most defendants were poor laborers who sold one or two bottles of beer or whiskey to a soldier. There was little doubt in most cases of the defendant's guilt. As in draft cases, most suits evoked guilty pleas. Sentences were usually short, entailing a few months in the county jail and, where the violation was more serious, fines of one hundred dollars to four hundred dollars.[25]

Prostitution cases also followed this pattern. A districtwide problem, prostitution loomed largest in Houston and Galveston. Most cases involved single prostitutes who entertained soldiers in their homes. Again, almost every case that reached trial ended with a guilty plea. As with alcohol cases, punishments were light, usually a few months in county jail, and fines were rare. In the few cases involving larger, more professional brothels, punishments included longer jail sentences, often in the federal penitentiary, and fines of up to one thousand dollars.[26]

By war's end, the court was intimately involved in regulating the social and economic affairs of the district. From implementing loyalty legislation to enforcing morals legislation, from prosecuting draft resisters to regulating foreign trade, the range of the court's regulatory functions was greatly expanded.

III

Peace did not halt these trends, but rather intensified the shift toward increased federal involvement in local affairs within both the Southern District and the nation as a whole. Established religious and social organizations, worried by a "rising flood" of radical, non-Protestant immigrant laborers, quickly grasped the potential uses of expanded national police powers to control the social transformations reshaping the nation. Even before the war began, statutes such as the Mann "White Slavery" Act, the Harrison Anti-Narcotic Act, and the Lottery Act pointed out the potential peacetime uses of federal police powers. With war on the horizon, movements such as the Anti-Saloon League and the American Purity Association quickly moved to harness the powers of the federal government to additional reforms. Drawing on the growing hysteria with wartime preparedness, these groups successfully convinced Congress and the nation that reforms like Prohibition and limited immigration were patriotic sacrifices necessary for waging war and creating a better America. Laws were passed prohibiting the sale of liquor to soldiers in uniform, banning prostitution within five miles of a military installation, and sharply limiting immigration from Mexico. Once in the war, additional restrictive legislation was passed: in August, 1917, Congress forbade the use of grains and foodstuffs necessary for the war effort for distilling liquor; in December it passed the Eighteenth Amendment (Prohibition), which was quickly ratified by the necessary two-thirds of the states. The Russian Revolution in 1917 intensified fears of alien radicals and the trend toward federal controls of individual behavior. These fears culminated in the October, 1919, passage of the Volstead Act enforcing Prohibition, the 1920 Palmer "Red Scare" raids, and the 1921 amendment to the Immigration Act, which strictly limited non–Western European immigration.[27]

For these and similar laws the lower federal courts were once again made the primary forum for enforcement. The impact on the federal courts' dockets was immediate and profound. By 1930 the total work load of the federal district courts had increased 270 percent. Most of this increase came on the criminal side of the docket, the total number of criminal filings increasing from 19,628 in 1917 to 87,305 in 1930—a rise of over 300 percent. During this same period the civil case load expanded at half this rate.[28] Most of this increase in criminal actions was the result of recent criminal statutes regulating personal behavior and, to a lesser extent, immigration matters. Social regulation and immigration prosecutions made up over three-fourths of all criminal cases filed during the 1920s; Prohibition cases alone numbered well over half. By mid-decade, even traditionally numerous crimes such as smuggling had paled into insignificance next to the onrush of Prohibition and, to a lesser extent, immigration cases (see table 2).

The Southern District experienced in full measure this increase of criminal case load during the 1920s. Numbering between seven hundred and eleven hun-

Table 2

CRIMINAL CASE LOAD OF FEDERAL DISTRICT COURTS, 1920–30

Year	Total Criminal Cases	Immigration and Morals Cases	Prohibition Cases
1920	55,587	7,768	7,291
1921	54,498	29,680	29,114
1922	60,722	40,778	34,984
1923	71,077	55,050	49,021
1924	70,168	52,421	45,878
1925	76,136	59,660	50,743
1926	68,582	51,440	44,743
1927	64,614	46,576	40,704
1928	83,372	62,471	55,729
1929	86,348	64,902	56,786
1930	87,305	69,986	56,992

Source: Atty. Gen. Report (1920–30).

Note: Moral regulation and social control cases included Prohibition, narcotics, prostitution, and peonage statutes. Immigration cases also included a small number of naturalization, war trade, and admiralty violations.

dred cases a year on charges varying from misdemeanors under the Volstead Act and the Immigration acts to felonies such as counterfeiting, smuggling, and postal fraud, criminal cases made up between half and two-thirds of the court's business (table 3). As was the case nationally, Prohibition cases made up the majority of the district's criminal docket. Evenly distributed throughout the district, violations of the Volstead Act composed between 60 and 75 percent of each division's criminal filings. By the end of the decade, the total fraction of Prohibition violations in the southern half of the district decreased to about 50 percent as immigration violations became more common. To the north, however, liquor prosecutions continued at this level until the repeal of the Eighteenth Amendment.[29]

Despite these impressive numbers, these actions received only routine effort. This was especially true for Prohibition cases. Throughout the federal court system such cases took on average three months to be processed as overworked district judges sought to clear clogged criminal dockets.[30] Yet in the Southern District, the time spent on Prohibition cases averaged but one or two days as defendants pleaded guilty on the first day and were sentenced on the second. Guilty pleas, in fact, made up around 90 percent of all Prohibition convictions throughout the decade; in some years they reached as high as 99 percent. With hundreds of cases entered on the docket every year, such speed was a necessity if any other work were to get done.[31]

Despite the speed with which the court tried defendants, punishment for these crimes was not given out thoughtlessly. Visits to jails and the awful burden of having to sentence defendants to them revealed to Judge Hutcheson the

Table 3

CRIMINAL CASE LOAD OF SOUTHERN DISTRICT COURT, 1920–30

Year	*Total Cases Filed*	*Criminal Cases Filed*	*Morals Cases Filed*	*Immigration Cases Filed*
1920	724	579	159	123
1921	1,190	810	664	N/A
1922	1,045	615	550	14
1923	1,198	954	854	14
1924	764	511	382	20
1925	973	676	489	24
1926	1,007	690	472	36
1927	1,318	928	564	44
1928	1,320	956	592	67
1929	1,688	1,298	713	275
1930	3,582	3,123	715	2,081

Source: Atty. Gen. Report (1920–30). Totals include other kinds of cases not reported separately here.

N/A means not available.

fact that "most of these persons coming before me for judgment and for jailing were not people set apart, public enemies, but average, ordinary, underprivileged common men." Such individuals did not deserve to be thoughtlessly sent to jail or fined excessive amounts of money. This was especially the case with those charged with misdemeanor Prohibition violations. These individuals, the judge believed, had "become offenders to make a living because their betters, at least their betters in having money and opportunity, would have and pay for what they took the chance to sell." Punishing the seller while ignoring the buyer was not, as the judge saw it, equitable. While the selling of alcohol exhibited a disregard for the law that Hutcheson abhorred, the concurrent lack of punishment for the buyer angered him even more. He viewed the crime of illegal entry to the United States in a similar light. Those charged with immigration violations were not criminals, but common people seeking a better life for themselves and their families. Long prison terms for such offenders were not right.[32]

As a result of these feelings, the judge's sentences in Prohibition and immigration cases were on the whole quite lenient for first- and even second-time offenders.[33] Take, for example, the February court term of 1921, held in Houston. Of thirty cases filed, twenty-three were Liquor Act cases. The remainder were for the illegal importation of cattle, theft from interstate commerce, mailing an obscene letter, counterfeiting, and violations of the Food and Drug Act of 1906. There was also one fugitive case that was remanded back to the proper district court. Of the twenty-three Prohibition defendants, the court sentenced only one to jail, a six-month term. The remaining twenty-two were given fines ranging

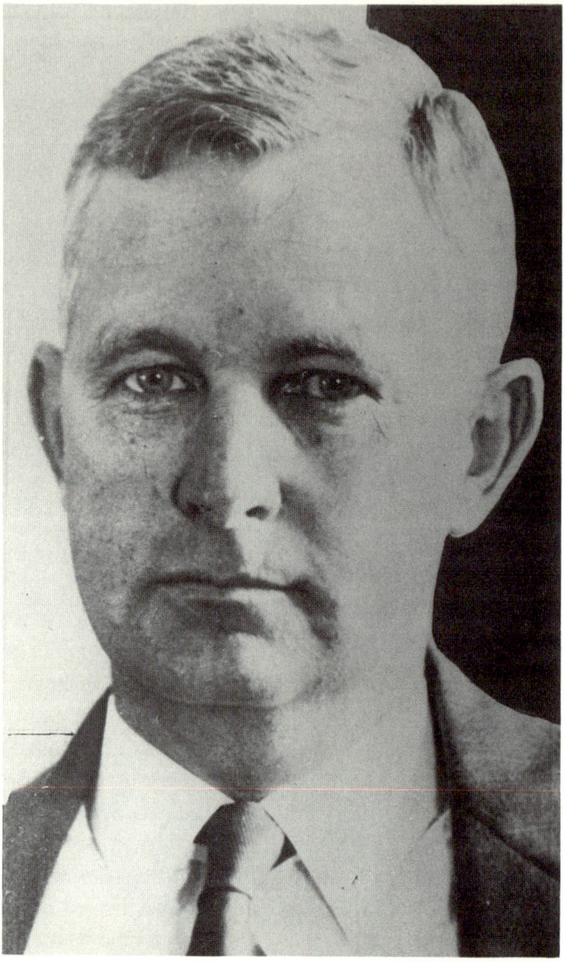

Judge Joseph C. Hutcheson, Jr. Courtesy Houston Metropolitan Research Center, Houston Public Library

from $25 to $1,000. Just over half (thirteen) received a $50 fine. Nine received fines of $100 and $250. Of the non-Prohibition cases, only the counterfeiter received a jail sentence (eighteen months); the rest were given fines of between $50 and $100.

Following 1925 and the creation of a federal probation, sentences of one to five years, "suspended upon good behavior," became common. Hutcheson, working through the Prison Conference and the National Probation Association was a pioneer in the creation of a federal probation law. Prior to its enactment in 1925, Hutcheson had adopted a system of dismissing, waiving, or delaying the sentences of "deserving" defendants, setting low bail, or using the pauper's oath in place of fines. With formal probation now allowed he used it liberally. In the July, 1928, term of the Houston Division, the court gave thirty-one suspended sentences out of a total of one hundred Prohibition cases. At the same time, thirty-seven defendants received fines of between twenty-five dollars and one thousand dollars and twenty-one defendants were given jail terms running from thirty days to one and one-half years. Two months earlier in Brownsville, Hutcheson had given eleven defendants suspended sentences out of a total of sixty-one Prohibition violators. The rest received short jail sentences (twenty-five received less than three months, and many of those were time served) or fines of under fifty dollars.[34]

A number of the district's residents complained about the court's "loose way" of "enforc[ing]" the Prohibition laws. As one Harris County district attorney wrote to the attorney general: "I have been in actual touch with the Liquor situation in Houston for three years now, and I know that the enforcement here has been only indifferent." Even the Justice Department felt frustrated at times with Judge Hutcheson's lenient view of Prohibition matters. Throughout the early 1920s, immigration officers had helped enforce Prohibition. Utilizing their powers to search automobiles for illegal aliens, these officers had also searched for smuggled alcohol, thereby expanding the number of officers available for Prohibition work. This service, in the view of a Justice Department memorandum, was "very helpful" in enforcing the Volstead Act. Yet in a 1927 case, Judge Hutcheson ruled that immigration officials could not make arrests for the transportation of liquor. Their job was the capture of illegal aliens, not bootleggers. Immigration officers, the judge related to the assistant superintendent to the Border Patrol, had "no more authority to apprehend a person transporting liquor than a private citizen." Since, by the facts of the case, it was obvious that the officers had in reality been searching for liquor and not aliens, the arresting officers had clearly overstepped the bounds of their authority. The judge thus threw out the case, noting at that time to the U.S. attorney, Henry Holden, that he would rule similarly in other cases of this kind. Holden and his office took the judge's warning seriously, for soon afterward Assistant U.S. Attorney Hardy warned William Whalen, district director of the Immigration Service, that if any of his men sought to enforce the Volstead Act, they would be "sent to the penitentiary for contempt of court." The result of Judge Hutcheson's position was that, "in order to avoid trouble with" the judge, "Patrol Inspectors working along the highways [were] compelled to let liquor laden cars drive past them."[35]

This is not to say that the court never gave long prison sentences. Despite his predilection for lenient sentences, if Hutcheson felt that a defendant was deserving of punishment, his verdicts could be strict, even severe. Justice, as Hutcheson understood it, required not only the protection of individual rights but the defense of society. Where individuals "willfully" and repeatedly denied the duty to act in a lawful manner, the judge always provided for the necessary penalties. As one contemporary commentator put it: "The Hutch is an old-time Southern hot-head, and a real overstepping of his ideas of right and wrong, and particularly his ideas of fairness and justice, was like monkeying with a naked bolt of lightning. He could and did 'dress down' offenders—criminals who had swindled poor people, officers who had taken bribes or had taken undue advantage of their authority, lawyers who didn't play by the rules—with a cold fury that made your skin crawl."[36]

Given a chance, Hutcheson sentenced repeat offenders severely. However, the judge's hand was often stayed by one of two considerations. First, the Volstead Act provided for only limited punishments. Throughout the nation, major smugglers were given trivial sentences under the act for lack of authority to provide longer jail terms. When a defendant could be charged under some additional law such as the Tariff Act of 1922, Hutcheson would give longer sentences. This occurred in 1924 when the members of the Galveston bootlegging gang of George Musey and John L. Nounes, reputed to be the "largest liquor smugglers in Galveston," were brought before the court. They were charged with conspiracy to violate both the Tariff Act and the Volstead Act, and Hutcheson chose to sentence them under the harsher Tariff Act. Nounes received two years in the penitentiary and a fine of five thousand dollars, the statutory maximum. Musey skipped out on his bond of ten thousand dollars to go to Canada before he could be sentenced. Other members of the gang received from six months to two years in jail and fines of five thousand dollars. In a similar case growing out of the British Schooner *Island Home* and the American tramp steamer *Lena*'s attempt to smuggle alcohol into Galveston, the court gave sentences of twelve to fifteen months and fines of five thousand dollars.[37]

Second, and more to the point, Hutcheson did not see Prohibition actions as deserving of more court time and effort. As previously noted, he saw the defendants in these cases as mere pawns in a national debate over morality. They were not hardened criminals, but average citizens forced by circumstances to break a law they had no part in passing. While the court was duty-bound to uphold the law, it had better things to do with its time than strictly punish such individuals.

For other serious crimes, where longer sentences were provided for by law and where the crime exhibited a greater disregard for social norms, such as counterfeiting and the possession and sale of illegal narcotics, the judge gave longer sentences. For example, in February, 1921, a counterfeiting case was heard in Houston. The defendant was found guilty and sentenced to eighteen months in the federal penitentiary. In May, 1925, four narcotics cases were decided at Brownsville. Three of the defendants were found guilty and one had his case transferred to another court. Of the three found guilty, each was sentenced to the federal penitentiary, one for a single year, the second for one year and four months, and the third for two years.

A listing of the court's attitudes toward crime and the proper extent of federal police power could continue indefinitely. But, perhaps the full flavor and extent of the court's handling of criminal matters can be best seen in Hutcheson's actions toward a "packed" grand jury in 1923. Though not dealing with a criminal case per se, this incident shows the extents (and limits) to which Hutcheson would go to see that justice was done in his court.

In February of that year, Edward Clarke, former acting imperial wizard of the Ku Klux Klan, was to be brought before a Houston grand jury on charges that he had violated the Mann "White Slavery" Act. Successfully indicting Clarke, however, was not expected to be achieved easily. During the early 1920s the Klan was a strong force in Houston (it had over eight thousand members in 1923). Given the size of the Klan, it was feared that the grand jury might contain Klan members who would refuse to indict Clarke. This especially worried Hutcheson. Several klansmen in the past had informed the judge that Klan membership imposed "an obligation when sitting on a jury, to give to klansmen different and other protections than those which the law gives other defendants." Though he had no great affection for African Americans, Hutcheson would not support or allow such a "reversing [of] the rule of law" to occur in his court.[38]

As a result of this fear of Klan involvement, prior to the impaneling of the grand jury, Hutcheson "took the precaution of having the department of justice investigate" the members of the panel and report to the court who on the jury were "members of the Klan." Then, in open court the judge asked each jury member under oath if he belonged to the Klan. Before letting them answer the judge warned them that he had had each of them investigated and that he now had the "facts." Hutcheson continued his warning, noting that to lie in answering a question from the court while under oath was basis for "prosecution for perjury." If, however, the members of the jury "voluntarily" disclosed their membership in the Klan and swore to uphold the duty of a grand juror, the judge would allow each to sit on the jury.

The judge then asked if there was a volunteer from the jury who wished to relate any affiliations he had with the Klan. When no juror immediately stepped forward, Hutcheson called the roll, "giving each man an opportunity to state the truth of the matter." From the questioning it soon became apparent that six members of the jury were Klan members and one was a former member. Hutcheson then asked each if he could, if necessary, do his duty as a juror even if it required ruling against a Klan member. The only response from the now-cowed jurors was silence. Taking this silence as an affirmation, the judge noted with sarcasm how pleased he was that "we are all going to do what is right, because we are members of the United States court, and [that] what we belong to on the outside don't mean anything when we get into the federal court." He then impaneled the jury, which, in March, 1923, indicted Clarke. No further action was taken against the jurors. Having forced them to fulfil their duty, the judge was willing to leave matters as they stood.[39]

Hence, even when a party was deserving of strict punishment, Hutcheson always sought the most appropriate sentence. His goal in criminal cases was reform, not punishment.[40] If a jail term was the appropriate sentence, such a sentence was given. Where, on the other hand, sarcasm and ridicule were the most appropriate response, it was used, and often with devastating effect. In cases where the defendant was "redeemable," probation "upon good behavior" would be used. The aim was to fit the sentence to the person behind the crime. As a result, when Hutcheson left the district bench for the Fifth Circuit Court of Appeals in 1931, he still used fines and probation more often than many judges, including his replacement on the District bench, Thomas Kennerly.[41]

Combining with these criminal cases in enforcing federal social legislation were civil actions. Suits were brought by the government both in equity and law to combat bootlegging. Most common were equity suits that sought to have property used for the manufacture or sale of alcohol declared a public nuisance. The federal courts had the power to order a property closed to all use for one year and one day if it was declared a public nuisance. Abating property in this manner served as a means of enforcing the Volstead Act and of civil punishment. Nationally, this became an increasingly popular option for combatting violations of the Volstead Act. Mabel Willebrandt, the assistant attorney general in charge of Prohibition matters, felt that "a determined injunction drive, padlocking and closing up soft-drink and other liquor dispensing establishments, will do for prohibition enforcement more good than scores of so-called hip-pocket cases." By 1923 the use of injunctive proceedings to combat liquor violations became a matter of policy for the Justice Department. From a start of 611 equity cases filed in 1920, nuisance-abatement actions quickly increased to a high of 15,455 in 1932. In most cases the government emerged victorious and the property was declared a public nuisance and closed for a year.[42]

Though less common in the Southern District than nationally, equity-abatement suits still averaged over 50 suits a year during the 1920s. In the 1930s, they became more common, reaching a high of 209 cases in 1932. Also in opposition to national trends, the court took great care in disposing of these cases. While it almost always granted a preliminary injunction when requested, the court was in many cases unwilling to make these injunctions permanent. If the owner of the property was involved with the violation of the law, the injunction was almost always made permanent. Often the owner was not the individual who had violated the law, however. Rather, it was a tenant or tenants who had been caught selling or manufacturing alcohol. Where this was the case, the court usually allowed the owner to rerent the property to new tenants on payment of a bond assuring that it would not be used to manufacture or sell liquor. In other cases, where the owner had acted quickly to evict the tenants, the court ordered the dismissal of the case.

This trend toward alternate sentences to closure became prominent as the decade progressed. From 1921 through 1924 most cases were terminated in favor of the government and the property was ordered closed. Following 1925, not only did judgments in favor of the government become less common, but in those cases the government won, a bond against the future use of the property for the manufacture or sale of alcohol was the common result. Also, as cases involving multiparty dwellings became more common, the court might have already dismissed the cases against most of the defendants when the government technically won its suit. As a result, only part of the property was closed off, which limited the preventive impact of the injunction.[43]

Adding to the impact of equity-nuisance injunctions were condemnations and forfeitures of vehicles and boats used in the transportation of alcohol. Prior to 1930 these condemnations were largely made under the National Prohibition Act, but as the decade progressed, more were filed under customs and internal revenue statutes. In 1927 this practice came under attack in a number of districts, including the Southern. Ruling in a case simply titled *US v One Fargo Truck*, Hutcheson concluded that, "where a car is found with smuggled liquor in it the Government had the option, in the present state of the law, to proceed under the customs or the prohibition statutes in the forfeiture of the cars as it is advised." Appealed to the Fifth Circuit along with three other cases, Hutcheson's decision was overturned. On appeal to the Supreme Court, however, the judge's interpretation of the law was upheld. As a result, after 1931 most condemnations were made under the Internal Revenue Code.[44]

Despite constitutional litigation challenging these condemnations, forfeiture suits were not very numerous before the 1930s. They averaged at most a few hundred per year nationally. Even after 1930, they never added up to more than a thousand cases per year. In the Southern District they were even less common. In most years before 1931, they numbered less than a dozen each for autos and boats. The origin of this small number may have rested with Judges Hutcheson and Kennerly. Both strictly required that all procedural safeguards be followed in forfeiture cases. As a result, the U.S. attorney could prosecute only the strongest cases of this sort. Though condemnations were few in number, their impact was to reinforce the general tenor of social control by the federal court. In most cases the vehicle was condemned.[45]

IV

Combined with criminal enforcement of nationally set social norms, civil condemnation and nuisance cases demanded much of the court's time and effort. As previously noted, such actions made up between half and two-thirds of the court's docket throughout the decade. Yet, in every way possible short of harming the interests of the individual defendant, the court strove to minimize this commitment. The result was that, while the court functioned in the 1920s as a definer, defender, and regulator of public morality and behavior, this function came second to serving the needs of Southeast Texas' private economic development.

4. Balancing Rights with Duties

PRIVATE LAW DURING THE TWENTIES

I

Despite the imposing number of cases it heard and its ties to national trends, protecting public morality was not the only, or even the primary, function served by the Southern District Court in the 1920s. Rather, as had been the case under Burns, the court's major efforts following World War I were aimed at serving the needs of private economic development.

This service was greatly needed. The social and economic transformations that had dominated the early years of the twentieth century did not end with the First World War but intensified. Rapid, even explosive, growth occurred at all levels of the economy. Cotton production, for example, increased by one-third, from 2,971,757 bales in 1920 to 3,793,392 in 1930. Crude oil production tripled in this decade, rising from 96,868 barrels to 290,457. The rate of growth in the new petrochemical refining and distribution industry was even more extreme. All of this economic development, in turn, facilitated a doubling of the region's population, with Houston alone growing by more than 111 percent—a rate of growth it has yet to exceed.[1]

Governor William P. Hobby described these economic changes as signifying a "new age" for Texas, and he was largely correct. By the end of the decade the region's social, political, and economic structures had matured into stable forms capable of generating sustained growth for the region. Yet, this growing maturity did not come any easier than earlier periods of development had. Local and state government remained ill-prepared to deal with growth. While the governor's office was often filled by a progressive, the legislature remained controlled by fiscal conservatives who felt little need to regulate local businesses, which, it should be noted, often did not want to be regulated. Local governments were too small effectively to control the rapid pace of development. As late as 1924 the City of Houston, with a population of close to 200,000, had only 1,350 employees and a budget of five million dollars. Other cities and counties in the state had even fewer resources at hand.[2]

All this made maintaining steady patterns of growth difficult. Worse, the boom mentality still shaped much of the Texas economy throughout the 1920s. Risky and speculative ventures remained the norm for many of Texas' industries. An unexpected economic downturn or the loss of a market could shatter the region's recent gains. Thus, as it had under Burns, the court sought in the 1920s to fill the gap, to protect the region's development from external forces that might have derailed its progress.

In this light, Judge Hutcheson's lenient sentences in Prohibition and immigration matters served the same protective and adaptive purpose as Burns's sentences in smuggling and RLD cases. In both situations, federal penal statutes threatened to disrupt the social or economic balance of the region. In the booming Texas economy of the 1920s, labor was at a premium. Much of the labor pool in Southeast Texas, in turn, was made up of immigrants and internal migrants whose opposition to Prohibition was long-standing.[3] As one Galveston mechanic who had been arrested for possessing whiskey and home brew beer noted in a letter to the attorney general: "I and my son are working hard in our business . . . and getting very thirsty[.] [B]eing used to having our beer and plain water not quenching our thirst as the beer did[,] I made a home brew of Malt Hops and Corn Syrup. It was not regular beer but it answered our thirst better than water did." Why, the man asked, had he been arrested and fined?[4]

To have strictly punished this sort of violation of the law not only would have deprived local businesses of the labor of convicted defendants, but would have disrupted the labor peace that was a necessary part of the Texas economy. A fine, after all, was a mild sentence for the manufacture, as opposed to simple possession, of alcohol. Jail terms were more common for manufacture. But, as noted Chapter 3, Judge Hutcheson realized that most of the Prohibition defendants were not criminals, but ordinary people taking actions that they did not consider illegal. To send most of them to jail for their actions would have done no good and, in fact, would have been counterproductive. On various occasions Hutcheson visited the local jails. What he found there "amazed" him. As he noted in an article in the *American Bar Association Journal:* "Leaving every other consideration aside, I was impressed with the economic and spiritual loss to society, through the effect on keeper and kept, of the practice of locking a man up in a cage and then after a time turning him out again on society, anti-social now after the treatment, training and associations he had there, when perhaps he was only unsocial and this in a limited way when he went in. This was not common sense. It was not democratic. It was not humane. It certainly was not social justice."[5]

With the professional bootlegger or the repeat defendant, the judge took a different view. These people, however, were not the average citizen. Hutcheson's goal in sentencing was reformation, not punishment. While supporting the economy was not necessarily his main goal in sentencing Prohibition defendants, by giving defendatns a second chance—by fining them or granting them probation—Hutcheson was able to help out in maintaining a peaceful work force for local industries and businesses.

The judge did this in other ways as well. As will be seen, Hutcheson proved open to organized labor's arguments that they should be allowed to organize themselves free from the influence of management. He believed that such organization provided stability to the workplace in that it gave the worker a stake in the region's development. The result, Hutcheson believed, was stability, and stability was what the region's economy badly needed.

Providing social and economic stability was, in fact, the court's primary aim under Hutcheson. Over two decades of wild growth had created a pressing need for economic stability. Southeast Texas needed to integrate gains already made without halting its forward progress. With government not providing needed regulations and leadership, and business unable to agree about the ways the economy should change, few constraints limited growth.[6]

The court was potentially a powerful player in this drive for stability. It could not only make, but enforce, decisions about standards of business behavior that were necessary if stability were to be achieved. More to the point, it could do so over a wide range of economic and social activities.

Area business leaders recognized this potential in the court, turning to it in increasing numbers as a source of ad hoc regulations and standards necessary for economic stability. This resulted in a change in the type of civil case brought before the court in the 1920s. Before the war, the average private civil case was an equity suit that sought either the creation of a receivership or an action somehow associated with a business in receivership. Even where suits did not involve the receivership function, the most common request was still for the court to order the transfer of property or property rights. In the 1920s, on the other hand, well over 80 percent of equity cases requested that an injunction be placed prohibiting or requiring the specific performance of some act. Injunctions were sought by cities and against cities, by corporations and against corporations; even labor unions sought injunctions to protect their organization.[7]

The effect of this change on the court's economic impact was significant. In an injunction hearing, its powers focused directly on the behavior of litigants. The request was for it to set and enforce standards of proper social, economic, and political behavior, to declare what was acceptable and what was not. By requiring that certain actions be taken or not, the court not only set standards for the region, but forced the region's inhabitants to live up to these standards.

The court did not shrink from imposing such standards; rather, it willingly set out to provide standards. The source of this willingness to act was Judge Hutcheson. A native of Houston, Hutcheson was a member of the region's social elite. His father, a former captain in the Confederate Army, had moved to Houston from Virginia following the war. Once in Texas, Hutcheson, Sr., quickly built up a strong law practice and political following and served two terms as a representative in the United States Congress. In 1900 Hutcheson, Jr., graduated from the University of Texas Law School as valedictorian of his class and began practicing corporate law with his father in Houston. In 1913 he became chief legal adviser to the City of Houston. Four years later he was elected mayor. Hutcheson, however, did not like being mayor of wartime Houston. As he once told his son, "nobody would be mayor of a growing city unless he was a knave or a fool. While I'm not a knave, I surely was a fool for being mayor." In 1917, following Judge Burns's death, Hutcheson put his name in for the judgeship. Selected as a compromise candidate from among twenty-seven applicants, Hutcheson was appointed to the district bench in April, 1918.[8]

A man of strong personality, remembered with awe, respect, and fear over twenty years after his death by those who practiced before him, Hutcheson's personality and judicial philosophy dominated the court during his tenure. More to the point, his judicial philosophy not only emphasized the need for economic, social, and political stability, but also stressed his duty to provide standards of ethical behavior to create such a stable environment.[9]

As a judge, Hutcheson placed his faith in "the natural law principles upon which our freedom depends." He had "faith in the rights of man, faith in the Constitution . . . , faith in law as liberator." Mostly, he had faith "in the principles and practices which, in Madison's immortal phrase, 'enable the government to control the governed, yet also oblige it to control itself.'"[10]

The idea of a government that controlled the governed but at the same time controlled itself, in broad terms, formed the foundation of Hutcheson's judicial philosophy. He was in many ways a man of the nineteenth century, believing implicitly in the importance of the individual and individual rights. He tempered this view, however, with an equally strong concern with the needs of what he called the "General Will." Law, to Hutcheson, had a purpose and a power to act to defend both the rights *and* the duties of all citizens. Where a right was enjoined, it was the job of a court of law to enforce the practice of that right; where a duty owed to society was not performed, the court's responsibility lay in enforcing the performance of that duty. Reaching a balance between individual rights and public duties was what law and justice were all about.

Achieving such a balance was not an easy process. Yet notwithstanding the difficulty involved, Hutcheson believed that the ultimate obligation of a judge was in "the pursuit of justice," defined as a balancing of rights and duties, of "social considerations . . . and strong common sense." "A sense of justice," the judge quoted in a speech, "must and should have an important influence upon every well organized mind in the adjudication of causes. Its proper province is to superinduce an anxious desire to search out and apply, in their true spirit, the appropriate rules of law. . . . In this it is like the polar star that guides the voyager."[11]

Hutcheson saw law as the bulwark of all freedom and prosperity. "Where there was no law, . . . there was no freedom." Without obedience to the law, the judge argued, there was no liberty. Yet once again, the foundation of this belief was the dictates of moderation and responsibility. Obedience to law was a duty of everyone, but only when law was viewed in its correct spirit. So viewed, "law . . . [was] not so much the limitation as the direction of a free and intelligent agent to his proper interest." If properly administered, law "prescribe[d] no farther than [what was] for the general good of those under that law." Where a law overstepped these bounds, it was invalid and needed correcting.[12]

In short, Hutcheson saw moderation and responsibility as underlying the court's function of defending law and justice. He linked his version of Madison's model of proper government to everyday behavior, for if a person acted responsibly and with moderation, that is to say, with due regard for the limits on individual wants, that person was acting in a "just" or "correct" manner. The result was "social order" and "social peace." Where individuals refused to live by this standard, it was up to the courts to enforce responsible behavior. In achieving this, Hutcheson stressed what he called the "Judicial Hunch," an internal, often illogical, and always personal search for the proper response in deciding a case. While "facts, facts and more facts are the stuff from which verdicts [were] made," judges had to do more than just rule on the facts; they also had to balance those facts in a search for the truth of the case; they had to decide what would be the "just" result based on these facts.[13]

In practical terms this view of law and its duties motivated Hutcheson to stress equitable results in his decisions. If the facts showed that one litigant had overstepped the bounds of proper behavior, had failed, in other words, to control personal actions, then Hutcheson would respond to this action by deciding in favor of the other litigant. Where both sides in a case seemingly acted in a responsible manner, justice required a more balanced, compromise decision. The goal was always to temper the demands of justice with the needs of the individual and the community, to read the dictates of law within the necessity of change.

The idea behind Hutcheson's judicial philosophy, then, was that if everyone acted with moderation and a concern for the needs of others–if private rights were balanced with public duties–stability would result. Where this did not occur naturally, it was Hutcheson's duty as judge to make this vision a reality.

II

This setting of standards occurred most often, and naturally, in the court's equity docket. In equity, litigants turn to the court to seek specific ends that can be achieved only by an affirmative use of judicial power. This was exactly what was demanded of the court in the injunction suits of the 1920s. In addition, equity cases required the court to make the sort of decisions that gave freest play to Judge Hutcheson's personality and judicial philosophy. In an equity proceeding, someone asked for justice, for a wrong to be be righted. Providing justice where no other forum could provide a remedy was, in fact, the origin of equity jurisdiction.[14] As a result of both of these facts, the court was able to provide the standards and regulations necessary for a stable economy most directly through its equity powers.

An early equity case before the court, *Galveston Electric Co. v. City of Galveston,* though determined on primarily technical grounds, laid the foundations of the court's efforts.[15] In 1920 the Galveston Electric Company, the owner and operator of Galveston's streetcars, wished to increase its fare from five cents to seven. The city, however, had an ordinance fixing "irrevocably" the fares of the city's streetcars at five cents. To get around this law, the streetcar company turned to the court for an injunction to restrain the city from enforcing this ordinance.

In an initial hearing the judge granted the injunction, temporarily overruling the ordinance as a potential confiscation of private property without due process of law. He then appointed Henry J. Dannenbaum master in chancery to look into the case and see if the five-cent rate actually was confiscatory and thus grounds for making the injunction permanent. In late 1920 Dannenbaum made his report, arguing that with fares set at five cents the company was not getting a fair return on the value of its property, which he set at two million dollars. He recommended that the injunction be continued indefinitely.[16]

The judge, however, disagreed. In a final hearing on the case, held in early 1921, Hutcheson reversed the decision of the master of chancery, concluding that "the ordinance was not confiscatory." Hutcheson reached this decision by a step-by-step reevaluation of the report of the master. Looking at such issues as the cost of reproduction, developmental costs, and depreciation, the judge ruled that the true worth the company's property was $1,500,000. Given an average yearly operating income of $618,000 and expenses of $475,395 the judge found that the company received a net return on its income of $142,405, or approximately a 9.5 percent return on its total value. This return, the judge ruled was "not . . . so plainly inadequate as to justify this court in interfering with the action of the municipality in the exercise of its rate-making function."[17]

Before he reached this position, however, Hutcheson spoke at length on the judicial function and powers in such a case, laying out what he felt were the proper limits to government rate making and the court's role in regulating this process. Ignoring the issue of an "irrevocable" rate limit (since the U.S. Supreme Court was at that time deciding on this issue), Hutcheson instead noted that the foundations of the rate-making power rested in tension between two principles of law: first, the police power of the state, which gave a state the power to regulate private property if such property were put to a public use; and second, the provisions of the Fourteenth Amendment, which guaranteed equal protection of law and prohibited the taking of property without due process. Both doctrines, Hutcheson argued, needed to be respected by the courts; both defended basic rights and duties. What resolved the tension between these two principles, he continued, was the "reasonableness" of a regulation. If reasonable (as defined by the courts) a regulation, though it by effect took a property in the public use, was acceptable. Only if the Galveston regulation was "unreasonable" should the rate be declared void.

Hutcheson was following the doctrine of the day in deciding the case in this manner. By the early 1920s the Supreme Court had handed down a long line of precedents on the judiciary's role in judging the "reasonableness" of a rate regulation.[18] Hutcheson, however, gave his own twist to this precedent. Quoting from the Supreme Court case of *San Diego Land Co. v. National City,* Hutcheson noted that "*judicial interference should never occur unless the case presents, clearly and beyond all doubt, such a flagrant attack upon the rights of property under the guise of regulations as to compel the court to say that the rates prescribed will necessarily have the effect to deny just compensation for private property taken for public use.*"[19] Hutcheson further noted (quoting this time from *Knoxville v. Knoxville Water Co.*) that "no injunction ought to be granted [enjoining a regulation] unless in a case reasonably free from doubt. We think such rule is, and will be, followed by all the judges of the federal courts." Although the High Court itself failed to follow this procedure with any great consistency, Hutcheson presented it in this case as an iron-clad rule, a specific guide for judicial decision making.[20]

Hutcheson deeply felt that "municipal bodies . . . should not force public utilities to apply to the courts for protection"; "it cannot but be a deplorable situation for any community to find itself in, if its legislative tribunal is so wanting in courage and fairness [that] the rates and practice which its public utilities are allowed to use are 'only those which fall just short of confiscation.'" However, he still felt bound by the facts of the case to rule that, while unfair and just short of confiscation, the rates were not unconstitutional.[21]

Hutcheson was unwilling to let the case remain at this stage, however. He concluded his essay on rate regulation by lecturing both sides on what constituted proper behavior in such a situation. Quoting from a brief he had written as Houston city solicitor in 1914, the judge noted that

> the courts ought not to bear the whole burden of saving property from confiscation, though they will not be found wanting where the proof is clear. The Legislature, and subordinate bodies to whom the legislative power is delegated, ought to do their part. On the other hand, the companies to be regulated will find it to their lasting interest to furnish freely the information upon which a just regulation can be based . . . [for] it is not amiss for me to say that the [city] council occupies a somewhat different position from that of a court, . . . and it should be its aim and purpose not merely to pronounce a legal judgement as to what rate would be short of confiscatory, but to arrive at and agree upon a fair rate though said rate should be considerably in excess of the lowest rates which the courts would sustain and allow.

"In other words," Hutcheson continued, "if the company exhibits a spirit of fairness and concession, with the view of agreeing upon a fair and reasonable rate, it is clear that the council is not only authorized, but should endeavor, to meet them in that spirit." Hutcheson concluded his lecture with a warning: "If at any time it should appear to me that any order made by me in this or any similar case now or hereafter pending before me is being used by the parties to it for any other purpose and to any other extent than its terms express, . . . this court will, of its own motion, or upon application of the other party, amend or vacate the order so as to deprive the offending party of its benefits, and to that end the decrees in this and similar cases will be drawn."[22]

Hutcheson was very serious in making this warning. In numerous cases throughout the decade, the court freely used its equity powers to demand that businesses and governments "exhibit a spirit of fairness and concession" in their dealings not only with each other, but with other segments of the economy as well. Where they failed to do so, the court acted quickly and with force to reverse the situation.

A particularly vivid example of this active demand for ethical behavior and the results if action was not forthcoming occurred in the 1928 case of the *Brotherhood of Railway and Steamship Clerks, etc. v. Texas and New Orleans RR Co.* The case began in July, 1927, when the Brotherhood of Railway and Steamship Clerks of the Southern Pacific Lines, a local union representing clerical workers of the Texas and New Orleans Railroad, requested a temporary injunction against the Texas and New Orleans to enjoin the railroad and its officials from forming, supporting, and recognizing as the sole representative of the employees a company union known as the Association of Clerical Employees, Southern Pacific Lines. At issue was an allegation by the brotherhood that the Texas and New Orleans, a subsidiary of the Southern Pacific, was attempting to break the brotherhood and replace it with the company-controlled association. If this occurred, argued the brotherhood, it would mean the end of effective representation for the workers. More important, the brotherhood argued, the association had been formed by fraudulent means and for the sole purpose of denying the brotherhood the chance at arbitration for a ten-cent-an-hour pay raise.[23]

Deciding this case raised three problems for the court. First, the brotherhood's call for an injunction was a case of first impression. The union was asking for the injunction under the Railway Labor Act of 1926.[24] No case on this issue had arisen under this act. The only case relating to the problems raised in this controversy, the *Pennsylvania Railway* case, was of questionable applicability. As a result, the judge had no precedents to help him decide what the law required. In fact, he had no guide to help him decide if he should even hear the case at all.[25]

The second, and related, problem lay in the use of an injunction to assist a labor union in combating an attempt to create a company union. Most instances of injunctions being used in labor disputes prior to 1927 had been by companies attempting to enjoin a union from striking. As a result, little experience existed as to how to use an injunction to help a union.[26] Further, because of past abuses of the injunctive process in labor disputes, section 52 of the Judicial Code prescribed that "no restraining order or injunction shall be granted by any court of the United States or a judge thereof in any case between an employer and employee . . . growing out of a dispute concerning terms or conditions of employment, unless necessary to prevent irreparable injury to property or to a property right."[27] Was a limit on the right to organize a union freely a "property right" within the meaning of this act? Was the act even applicable to such a situation? Again this question raised an issue of first impression for the judge to decide.

Finally, though with less concrete impact, was the social pressure this case placed on Hutcheson. The judge was a native Texan, born and reared in Houston. He was a respected and established member of the Houston bar and community and as a result had close social contact with the elites of the city. Included in this social group were the officials and attorneys of the Southern Pacific. The judge's half-brother, Palmer Hutcheson, was even a member of the Southern Pacific's main Texas counsel, Baker and Botts.[28] Thus for Hutcheson to help the union was at the same time to attack his social peers. While none of these social forces placed any overt or unique pressure on him, it did give the conflict a confusing extra dimension.

Though the case raised problems, Hutcheson's judicial philosophy provided a blueprint for the court's actions. He started his decision with the assumption that Congress and the courts had both the power and the duty to "insure that in the settlements of [labor] disputes each side shall be represented by those of its own selection, uninfluenced by the action of the other," and that the right to "work and to continue to work under arrangements which will insure fair wages and working conditions is a proper right . . . [that] the court has the power . . . to protect." Given this duty, Hutcheson ordered that the temporary injunction requested by the brotherhood be placed on the Southern Pacific Railroad to enjoin the railroad and its officials from "in any way or manner interfering with, influencing, intimidating, or coercing . . . any of said clerical employees" of the railroad from "their free and untrammeled right of self-organization." Specifically, the railroad was prohibited from supporting in any manner the Association of Clerical Employees, Southern Pacific Lines. The order did not, however, prohibit the association from attempting to organize without company help. If the association could organize and gain the support of a majority of the clerks without company help, the judge would not hinder this process. The key issue was the guarantee that "employees should have the right to organize in the manner that they please, so long as they are not influenced and coerced by their employer." The form this organization took was beyond the concern of the court.[29]

All in all the decision was a mild one. Little but a hands-off attitude was required of the railroad. Hutcheson's goal was to balance the gains and the losses of both litigants. Both sides claimed to be happy with the decision. John Crocker, attorney for the brotherhood, noted how the decision was "all we wanted." Edward Tallichet, counsel for the railroad, argued that "they got about 12.5 percent and we got the balance. While it means that our officers can not advise the men to enter the new union, it guarantees the men the right to organize themselves as far and as freely as they like."[30] It seemed as if the dispute between the union and the railroad had been amicably solved.

Events were to prove such optimism wrong. As Hutcheson was soon to note, "before the ink was hardly dry upon the order of injunction" the railroad had "proceeded to nullify it [the injunction] by recognizing as truly representative the association, all of whose authorizations had been filed with the defendant . . . before this suit was filed, and the most of which had been obtained, as found by the court, by the use of means in violation" of the law.[31]

As a result of such activities, the brotherhood brought before the court information alleging that the railroad had violated the temporary injunction. In October, 1927, Hutcheson issued an order to the Texas and New Orleans Railroad to show cause why it should not be held in contempt for its actions. Four months later he handed down his decision on the contempt charges. In words strikingly more strident than those used in the original injunction decision, the judge noted that, "[w]hile it is hard to believe that a Railroad and its officials would deliberately seek to set at naught both the legislative and the judicial power of the United States, it is difficult to avoid the conclusion that the violation of the statute and of the injunction which followed its violation, was the result of a strong and settled purpose to defy both, and that the spirit of heady violence to obtain its ends, which has so often exhibited itself in these labor disputes, in the conduct of employees when the injunction was the other way, is not absent here."[32]

The railroad had clearly arranged it so that it "would be in a position of surely having a vote on both sides of the table, its own side and that of its employees." This sort of action the court could not allow; it simply was not right. Hutcheson felt it incumbent on himself, in line with his stated philosophy, to take stronger action. He therefore ordered that a remedial order be entered that completely disbanded the association as currently constituted as the representative of the workers and that reestablished the brotherhood as the sole representative of the clerks until such time as the workers chose to change their representation in a vote without "dictation or interference." Further, the officers of the Texas and New Orleans were limited in all ways from affecting the freedom of activity of the brotherhood, even where they were acting on their own authority and initiative. The judge then ordered the rehiring of all members of the brotherhood who had been fired for their organizational activities. Finally, Hutcheson, in a private meeting in his chambers three days later, threatened the officers of the Texas and New Orleans with jail sentences if they did not accept the dictates of the order within ten days.[33]

Hutcheson's ever-stronger actions in the *Brotherhood* case emphasize the court's ultimate aims in deciding equity cases during the 1920s. His goal was the establishment of a stable and equitable working environment for the railroad's employees. Hence, at first, he sought to have as little direct effect as possible on the labor dispute as a whole, simply demanding that all sides play by the rules. By 1928, with the growing evidence of management's failure to live by the injunction's dictates, he actively denounced one side of the conflict and chose by judicial fiat the brotherhood as the workers' sole representative. Thus, while in the first injunction hearing Hutcheson was only willing to see "proof . . . sufficient to show that there has been enough activity of company officers, whether upon real or apparent authority is immaterial, to bring about a condition of company influence on self organization" of a workers' union, by the later contempt hearing he saw "the evidence of activity in violation of the statute, and of the injunction occurring since," that presents "an appearance of purpose and of resolution . . . which is wholly inconsistent with the claim of the defendant of neutrality between these rival associations."[34] The actions of the railroad had not changed between the first hearing and the second (though perhaps they had intensified somewhat); what had changed was Hutcheson's anger at the railroad's continued failure to follow the court's orders. No matter what other factors came into the case, this ignoring of the dictates of the law as set out by the court could not be allowed to continue.

The judge's increasing anger at the intransigence of the railroad only intensified when, in April, 1928, the railroad asked for a rehearing on the injunction and the contempt charges. In this hearing the railroad once again argued that it had done no wrong and that its actions were completely legal. It requested that both the contempt charge and the injunction be vacated.

Rather than vacating the decisions as requested, however, Hutcheson proceeded to defend and expand on his decisions in language as strident as that used in the contempt hearing. To the judge the continued failure of the railroad to change its actions constituted a conspiracy, a conspiracy from which "every proceeding taken thereafter sprang . . . and . . . which explains the vigorous and determined effort to seat the company union as the sole representative of the employees and gives full color to the persistent efforts thereafter to destroy the influence and activity of the Brotherhood." A wrong clearly existed, and by Hutcheson's view of the law, a wrong required a remedy. It was the duty of the court to create a remedy for a wrong wherever possible. Given the blatant actions of the railroad, the judge made the injunction permanent and continued the contempt order in full force. Thus, despite the social and legal pressure, Hutcheson held to his 1921 warning that he would hold litigants to a standard of moderation and responsibility in their actions.[35]

Just how far the court would go to uphold this conception of equitable justice may be seen in the 1932 case of *Constintin v. Smith*. Though this was an Eastern District of Texas case, and Hutcheson was by this time on the circuit court bench, it exemplifies the strong commitment he had to the goal of stability and to the setting of proper standards of behavior while on the Southern District bench. At issue in this case was a Texas oil conservation act that limited the output of Texas oil pumps in an effort to raise the price of oil in a depressed market (oil had by this date fallen to ten cents a barrel). In the face of district court opposition and organized resistance to the act, the governor of Texas, Ross Sterling, had declared earlier that year that "an organized and entrenched group" of oil producers was "in a state of insurrection against the conservation laws." The governor therefore declared a state of martial law over the East Texas oil fields and sent the state militia under the command of General Jacob Wolters to restore order. In response, oil producers turned to the Eastern District Court and obtained a temporary injunction to the martial law order. The governor, however, ignored this order, arguing that martial law superseded any injunction. The case then was appealed to a three-judge court with Hutcheson presiding.[36]

Though this case raised many issues, of interest here is the view that the governor had misused his power in calling out the militia. The governor claimed that he had called out the militia only to prevent violence, not oil production. Questioning his counsel, Hutcheson asked: "Do you mean, that the Governor . . . is stopping oil production, not for the benefit of the industry, but because he is afraid people will begin shooting at each other?" The counsel answered yes. Hutcheson could not believe what he heard. As he saw it, the only riot apparent in East Texas was "a riot of producers trying to get oil out of the ground." The problem with the governor's argument was twofold. First was the partisan nature of the proclamation of martial law. In the hearings Hutcheson wondered aloud if the state militia was taking orders from the big oil companies, so perfect did their actions fit the needs of these companies. Governor Sterling, in fact, was a former president of the Humble Oil Company. Second was the fact that civil courts still existed in the region. This made the calling of martial law a violation of the first article of the Texas Constitution's Bill of Rights. Given both these facts, Hutcheson saw the proclamation of martial law as invalid.[37]

Hutcheson went on to note that "when the governor calls out the troops in Texas, he calls them out, not as a military, but as a civil officer." As such, he (and the militia) were at all times under the dictates and duties of civil law. "There [is a] difference between the unquestioned right of the Governor to call out the militia, which all authorities concede, and his right to erect himself and them above the law, giving [the militia] superpowers." Military control was simply unacceptable. "Under constitutions like ours, military dictatorships may not be established by executive fiat." Property rights were to be adjudicated by the courts and not by executive decree. Only the single instance of an attack on the nation could change this doctrine. Having established all these points, Hutcheson therefore ruled that the defendants "have been without warrant of law interfering with and illegally depriving the plaintiffs of their undoubted right to operate their own properties in a prudent and reasonable way . . . and, that, from further interference, . . . they must be enjoined."[38]

It should be emphasized that Hutcheson was not against conservation or the regulation of the oil industry per se. Though he had overturned proration laws in *MacMillan v. Commission* and *Henderson v. Commission*, Hutcheson did accept the right of the state to conserve its oil resources; he questioned only the methods used. Where the issue was protection of resources, Hutcheson allowed a wide scope to the state's conservation program. Even in *Constintin* the judge permitted the state militia to stay in the oil fields to "help" the Railroad Commission in its legitimate regulation of the oil fields and conditioned his decision so that the plaintiffs could not drill indiscriminately. In 1933 Hutcheson endorsed a revamped proration law. The issue requiring strong action in this case was not the regulation of the industry, but the governor's overstepping of the bounds of legitimate executive power. And this overstepping the judge could not allow.[39]

Had the governor acted with greater discretion in enforcing the proration laws Hutcheson's response would have been different. It was not only the ends that one had to be concerned about, the judge was saying, but the means as well, for if means used to achieve even a proper end were immoderate or aimed at harming another individual, the result would be flawed though the goal itself was acceptable.

This insight formed the basis of the court's equity decisions throughout the 1920s. Faced with a series of discrete problems in which not only the results but the methods used to achieve a certain end were challenged, the court responded by demanding that all litigants follow the path of moderation and show a concern for the needs of others. The means had to justify the ends, the court repeatedly held, and where individuals did not act in such a manner, the court forced compliance.

III

The attitudes exhibited in equity also shaped the court's actions in other civil suits it decided. In such diverse categories as admiralty, patents, and commercial law, a common thread – the need to provide stability to a shaky economic infrastructure unable to mediate the effects of growth – shaped both the process and the outcome of litigation.

Even in the relatively technical arena of admiralty law, the court sought to set standards for everyday behavior. Admiralty cases almost always raised complex issues of fact and law; the primary focus was determining the cause and legality of a series of events. Yet despite these difficulties, the court worked to provide general standards of responsible behavior that could be used in similar circumstances.

Since the district encompassed a coast over six hundred miles long and contained three major and growing ports, admiralty was a significant part of the Southern District Court's case load.[40] The court heard numerous admiralty cases that raised issues of great complexity. In deciding these cases, Hutcheson simplified this complexity and as a result created general rules of behavior by applying the dictates of his judicial philosophy.

Specifically, utilizing the judicial hunch, Judge Hutcheson sought to impose an equitable and balanced result in admiralty cases, one on which future behavior could be based. In a 1929 article he described how this process worked. Noting how "collision cases in admiralty furnish excellent illustrations of the difficulty of arriving at a sound fact conclusion by mere reasoning upon objective data," he argued that, "in these cases, as every trier knows, the adherents of the respective ships swear most lustily in true seagoing fashion for their side. . . . If a judge were compelled to decide the case by observing the demeanor of the witnesses alone, he would be in sad plight, for . . . the shrewdest, smartest liars often make the most plausible and satisfactory witnesses, while the humblest and most honest follows often, upon the witness stand, acquit themselves most badly." "Fortunately," the judge continued, "in these cases the judge may, reconciling all the testimony reconcilable, and coming to the crux of the conflict, . . . re-enact the drama and as the scene unfolds with the actors each in the place assigned by his own testimony, play the piece out, watching for the joints in the armor of proof, the crevices in the structure of the case or its defense." Having done this, the judge then replayed "over and over" in his mind the facts of the case "until finally, when it seems impossible to work any consistent truth out of it, the hunch comes, the scenes and the players are rearranged in accordance with it, and lo, it works successful and in order."[41]

Utilizing this procedure, Hutcheson was able, even in a technical case requiring the objective weighing of complex facts, to evaluate those facts by a subjective standard. In this manner, his personal conclusions as to the equity of the case—that is to say, his conclusions based on a uniform standard of behavior of who was at fault and deserving of censure—affected the decision.

This process worked in any number of admiralty cases; however, one example is sufficient to show the pattern. In early 1928 the *Hornby Castle* was steaming up the Houston ship channel. Ahead of the *Castle* were two vessels: the first, a barge traveling slowly in the same direction as the *Castle;* and the second, the steamer *Cody,* traveling down the channel toward the *Castle*. Following customary practice the *Castle* signaled that it would pass the barge on its left and then cross the channel to pass the *Cody* on its right. The *Castle* then proceeded to pass the barge successfully. The ship swung too wide in passing the barge, however, and, in danger of grounding on the bank, collided with the *Cody.*

Though neither party disputed these facts, the case still raised complex questions. First, there was a dispute as to why the *Castle* was unable to avoid missing the *Cody.* The *Castle*'s counsel argued that the *Cody* was traveling too fast and as a result made it impossible for the *Castle* to avoid hitting it. The *Cody*'s attorney replied that the cause of the accident was negligence by the *Castle*'s pilot.

Second, the case raised a problem of law. Established doctrine denoted that, once signals had been made establishing a pattern for passing in a narrow channel, it was the duty of each vessel to follow that pattern. If a ship broke this agreement, it was at fault for the collision. At the same time, an equally valid doctrine existed that argued that, once a ship was in danger, all preexisting contracts as to passing in a channel were voided. Avoiding a collision, and fault for a subsequent accident, thus became the duty of the ship not in danger.[42]

Since both doctrines were equally valid if applied to the case of the *Castle* and the *Cody,* what the law required and, as a result, who was at fault, depended on Hutcheson's interpretation. He noted that "under the circumstances the burden rests heavily on the *Castle* to relieve herself from fault," for it was the *Castle* that took the active part in the collision. Barring proof of wrongdoing by the other ship, or of a sequence of events beyond the control of the crew of the *Castle,* the fault for the accident rested with them. While the judge listened with considerable interest to the *Castle*'s argument of innocence, "upon further reflection and considerations," he felt that its crew's position was "without evidence to sustain it." As the judge interpreted and evaluated the testimony of the litigants, the facts did not justify the *Castle*'s position. This being the case, the crew of the *Castle* had acted irresponsibly and was at fault for its negligence.

The effect of such decisions was to set an outer limit on individual and group action. Stressing individual responsibility, Hutcheson used the law to rein in what he considered irresponsible action. Where corrective action was necessary, the court freely used its powers to achieve such ends. Yet for actions within these limits, actions considered responsible and proper, the judge stressed compromise as an equitable solution.

The emphasis on compromise and moderation in most actions at equity and law was implicit in these cases. While the American judicial system requires that there be a winner and a loser in a case, where both sides in a litigation acted in what the judge considered a responsible manner, Hutcheson attempted to balance the punishment to match the extent of fault. Where no fault existed on either side, Hutcheson worked to balance the interests and needs of both parties. This is clearly seen in his criminal decisions. It is also visible in the early stages of the *Brotherhood* case, where, prior to the railroad's offending the judge's sense of propriety, the injunction required only minimal action by both parties. Even in admiralty, once fault had been distributed in a collision case, the decision was for only the amount of damages caused by fault.

The impact and extent of such an emphasis on balance also affected the district's commercial cases. Along with injunction, criminal, and admiralty law, commercial cases filled out the bulk of the court's business. Consisting of such diverse actions as bankruptcy, title, patents, customs, taxes, and debt collection, commercial law matters affected the individual member of the public to a greater extent than any other type of action facing the court except perhaps criminal and injunction actions. More so than in other types of suit, it was on commercial matters that individuals relied on the court to serve their private economic interests. Further, the commercial jurisdiction of the court was potentially a powerful tool to shape the law. It was in commercial cases that the federal common law powers granted to federal court by the 1842 Supreme Court decision of *Swift v. Tyson* most often came into play. Utilizing diversity jurisdiction the courts were given the power to decide how the economy of the nation would operate.

As with other forms of actions, in commercial matters a concern with setting business standards shaped the court's decisions. Where the actions of one litigant bespoke irresponsibility, the court ruled against them; however, the issues facing the court in commercial actions were often ones in which fault was either nonexistent or equally shared. Given the often uncertain nature of business, cases came before the court in which all parties had acted responsibly, or at least were at equal fault. Lacking issues of responsible behavior to weigh, in such situations the court focused on achieving balanced results in its decision.[43]

Take, for example, a 1926 case arising between the St. Louis and San Francisco Railroad and the Republic Box Company. The Republic Box Company had contracted with W. S. Clark, the shipping agent of the Gulf, Colorado and Santa Fe Railway, to ship materials to the East Side Packing Company of East Saint Louis. In the contract, the Republic Box Company clearly stated that the boxcars would be shipped over the Santa Fe Railroad at a rate of 32.5 cents per hundred pounds of goods. The exact route to be used, however, was left to be decided by the railroad. The goods were subsequently delivered by the St. Louis and San Francisco Railroad, acting for the Santa Fe Lines, which received the payment of 32.5 cents per hundredweight of goods delivered.

At issue in this case was the adequacy of this rate. While 32.5 cents was the legal rate for railroads shipping directly between Houston and Saint Louis, where there was a need for transshipment of the goods to a second carrier to complete shipment, this was legally an undercharge. Because of the particular routing of the Santa Fe lines, which owned no direct tracks to Saint Louis, the railroad had to contract with a second railroad, the St. Louis and San Francisco, to haul the goods to East Saint Louis. The St. Louis and San Francisco, in turn, was legally entitled to charge more than 32.5 cents per hundredweight for its efforts. Having received only 32.5 cents, the railroad was suing the Republic Box Company to recover the balance it felt it was legally owed.

The case therefore raised an issue in which fault was either nonexistent or, interpreted another way, evenly distributed. The railroad claimed that it was simply seeking a just return for its efforts. The box company had specified shipping on the Santa Fe lines, which required the use of the St. Louis and San Francisco line. Congress through the Interstate Commerce Commission had ruled that the St. Louis and San Francisco Railroad was entitled to a larger return than 32.5 cents. The court therefore had no recourse but to uphold the law and have the box company pay the railroad the balance. In response to this, Republic Box argued that it had contracted with the Santa Fe lines to ship the goods at 32.5 cents and was not liable for any undercharge caused by the Santa Fe's decision to ship along a line with a higher legal rate than that specified. If fault existed, it rested either with the shipper, the Santa Fe, for choosing the wrong carrier, or with the St. Louis and San Francisco for agreeing to ship at such a low rate. In either case, liability did not rest with Republic Box.

In deciding this case, Hutcheson was being asked to weigh the dictates of law—the requirement that the railroad could charge a legally determined rate for its services—with the needs and responsibilities of an individual shipper—the box company's right to set by contract the parameters of its responsibilities. Both litigants had acted in a responsible manner: the railroad had delivered the goods as promised; the box company had not attempted in any way to shortchange the shipper of the contracted return. At issue was an unavoidable dispute growing out of the complexities of commerce. Rather than two wrongs conflicting, this case raised the necessity of weighing and balancing two rights.

A winner in the case still had to be named. Hutcheson chose to support the contentions of the defendant, the Republic Box Company. In doing so, he acknowledged the justness in the railroad's contention that "instances of individual hardship cannot change the policy which Congress has embodied in [a] statute." He quickly went on to note, however, that "it is also true that courts will not literally enforce rates where the individual circumstances of the particular case make it certain that the invocation of the principle is an absurdity."

While the railroad's position was largely valid in and of itself, the effects of the use of such a position, the judge felt, would be unacceptable. To require, as would occur if the railroad's position was accepted, that a shipper so know the "tariff [rates] better than railroad agent[s]" as to refrain from shipping on a line that could charge a higher rate than was contracted for, was "unreasonable." Rather, the judge continued, such cases of under charging should be disposed "with an eye as much to the practical injustice of the particular case as to the sanctity of the general rule." Such an action would "[compel] railroad companies and their agents to exercise ordinary care and good faith in quoting and applying rates, or to abide by the consequences of their failure to so act." This would make "the business of shipping freight . . . not . . . as perilous to the shipper as it has been"; this was an action Hutcheson found in the best interests of both the nation and the local economy.[44]

IV

The ultimate effect of all this standard setting was the creation of a system of ad hoc regulation for local businesses. Where requested, the court set, and then enforced, standards for the smooth operation of the region's economy. These regulations ran the gamut from the proper extents of government regulation to issues of negligence in admiralty. All resulted in creating necessary stability for that sector of the economy.

The key to this system, in terms of both its success and its limits, was that the court only acted if requested to do so. Local business wanted only promotional help from local, state, and federal government; actual regulations were actively fought. However, with the region's rapid economic growth, some regulation was necessary. Unable to initiate litigation, the court provided a "safe" forum for regulation. Local business felt confident that the court, as a limited forum, would serve its interests without the danger of providing too much regulation, too much control. Tied socially, politically, and ideologically to local business concerns, the court provided just this service. If Houston, Galveston, and Corpus Christi were "free enterprise cities" the court was the safety valve that allowed that free enterprise to work; it provided the necessary rudder to stabilize the wild pace of growth.[45]

By 1929 this informal system of promotion and informal regulation had reached peak effectiveness. Business was booming and few limits to continued growth were apparent; however, troubles lay just ahead. The stock market crash of 1929 cut the Southeast Texas boom as it did the rest of the nation's. Though it took longer for Texas to feel the full weight of the depression, by the early 1930s, the state was in need of help if chaos was to be avoided. This need posed new challenges for the Southern District Court's goal of promoting growth and helping those in need. It also exacerbated the tensions between the court's local concerns and its role as a part of the federal government.

5. Keeping the Law within Reasonable Limits

PUBLIC LAW DURING THE DEPRESSION

I

The full impact of the depression did not strike Southeast Texas until late 1932, but its effects were becoming apparent by early 1930. Markets began to dry up and businesses to fail. Voluntary and involuntary bankruptcies grew yearly, reaching 158 in 1930, 213 in 1931, and 302 in 1932. This did not count the numerous businesses verging on insolvency. Unemployment also became a growing problem. In Houston the number of unemployed seeking the city's help in finding jobs grew from 607 in 1929 to 789 in 1930. One year later it had risen to 2,231. Galveston had 1,011 seeking work that year. These were only the worst off. Many other destitute Texans relied on the help of family and friends, or simply went without.[1]

The problems were even more extensive in rural areas. Few Texas farmers had shared in the prosperity of the 1920s as farm parity, the difference between what farmers got for crops and what they paid for services and manufactured goods, dropped yearly throughout the decade. Most farmers were already on the edge of poverty by 1929. The depression provided a final blow. As declining crop prices reduced the parity value to half of what it had been before World War I, many Texas farmers could not recoup the costs of planting. By 1930 almost half of the state's farms were in danger of foreclosure.[2]

Despite these trends, Texans refused to admit that something basic had gone wrong with the economy, that good times were gone forever. "The country is safe," declared the Texas-based *Cotton and Cotton Oil News* in late 1929. "Its resources have not been lessened by a single ton of coal, or by a single bushel of grain, or a bale of cotton, or by a single industrial building. These things are still here, and the country will go forward on a sounder, saner and safer basis than since the wild gambling boom started a few years ago." Few in the state disagreed with this prognosis, and many went further in their optimism.[3]

Texans had faith that their economic problems could be solved privately. The *Dallas Morning News* (January 15, 1931) "steadfastly set its face against tin-cup-and-blue-goggles trips to Washington for 'relief' for Texans." "Are we going to let our own flesh and blood beg on the steps of the National Capital" it asked. Its answer was a resounding no. Other Texas papers also advocated private relief, stressing that the state's greatness had been achieved through self-reliance and not dependence on outside help. Dependence on Washington "encourages paternalism and vitiates state morale," the *Galveston News* (September 5, 1930) declared. Business journals joined in this chorus, stressing Texas' ability to raise local relief funds. Business leaders such as Houston's Jesse Jones also echoed this line, arguing that for Texas, at least, the depression was a minor, and solvable, problem.[4]

The depression was not, however, a minor problem. By 1932 Texas' economic difficulties became impossible to ignore. Not only were businesses, farms, and banks failing, so too were local governments. Cities and counties were unable to pay for rising relief costs. Local charitable relief efforts also proved inadequate to meet the region's escalating needs. As the *Houston Chronicle* reported on May 8, 1933, available funds had simply run out.[5]

Texans could no longer deny the depression. In November, 1932, they joined the rest of the nation in voting Franklin D. Roosevelt and his New Deal into office. For the next year, support for FDR was widespread; even the state's conservative business community welcomed the New Deal's economic reforms. Yet despite having turned to the federal government for help, Texans refused to give up their belief in their own ability to solve their economic woes; they were too proud to go completely on the dole. What they wanted from the federal government was financial and organizational assistance to complement local reconstruction efforts, not federal regulations.

Welcoming federal help at first, Texas business leaders soon questioned the need and efficacy of federal legislation. What they had first seen as temporary relief measures had quickly become unwanted regulation of "private" matters. In Houston, for example, most of the city's bankers welcomed the help provided by the Reconstruction Finance Corporation (RFC) when a crisis shook the banking community in early 1933. When the New Deal passed stronger regulations for the nation's banks, however, Houston bankers were less pleased. The state's experience with the National Recovery Administration (NRA) and the Agricultural Adjustment Administration (AAA) were similar: welcomed at first, by 1934, they were attacked as socialistic and un-American.[6]

The court's experience during the depression grew out of these mixed feelings and motivations. Texans turned to the court during bad times as they had during good as a source of authority and standards applicable to private use. Through the court they sought to meet, and solve, the difficulties posed by the depression. The answers they sought, however, often conflicted with the concurrent efforts of the federal government to implement structural changes in the national economy. This forced the court into a conflict of interests. On one hand, it was a part of the federal government, bound to enforce federal statutes. On the other, as a court of private law concerned with the needs and wants of the district's inhabitants, it was ambivalent about the federal government's

Judge Thomas M. Kennerly. Courtesy Houston Metropolitan Research Center, Houston Public Library

role in combating the depression. During the depression, both state and federal government took a more active stance toward regulating private property. This troubled the state's many conservative business leaders; it also bothered the court's new judge, Thomas Kennerly, appointed in 1931 by President Hoover.

Described by many who knew him as a warm-hearted, Christian man, Kennerly felt strongly for those harmed by the depression. He understood the need for reform and regulation if the depression were to be defeated and the distressed helped; however, he was also a man of strict legal beliefs and values.

He was born in 1874 in Lee County, Texas, and admitted to the bar in 1893 after reading law with a local lawyer. He moved to Houston in 1897, and was appointed six years later as a referee in bankruptcy by his close friend and fellow Republican Judge Burns. In 1907 Kennerly resigned his position and became chief counsel to the Houston Oil Company, a position he kept until his appointment as district judge in 1931. With his legal roots in the nineteenth century and his social roots in the business elite of Southeast Texas, Kennerly was a perfect example of the conservative "black-letter judge." Unable to "be persuaded to do anything which he does not sincerely believe to be RIGHT," the judge often felt constrained by the dictates of the law "as he understood it." That understanding, however, like that of his good friends Burns and Hutcheson, was based on respect for individual rights and property. Any regulation that took the property of A and gave it to B was invalid, the judge felt.[7]

Worried by the steady growth of national law and power, and questioning the validity of an economy of scarcity, Judge Kennerly ultimately proved unwilling to accept the costs of expanded public regulation; he saw these laws as unfairly helping one segment of the nation at the expense of another and, holding them up to a "reasonableness standard," found them costly, dangerous, and invalid.[8] Thus, as in the past, the court's response to the conflicting forces pushing on it was to stress private needs and concerns over national policies. This preference took both a negative form, as the court invalidated national laws that denied basic private property rights, and a positive form, as the court worked to help Texans rebuild their shattered economy.

II

The depression transformed the federal courts' regulatory function as the nation's views of its causes and solutions shifted. The decade started with Prohibition and other federal social regulations forming most of the court's criminal case load. Within a few years, social regulations of this sort had disappeared from the docket. They were replaced first by immigration and state regulatory cases, that is, actions combining social and economic issues. These cases, in turn, were replaced by suits arising from New Deal economic reforms. By decade's end, except for foreclosures under the National Housing Act (NHA) of 1937, public regulation litigation had almost disappeared from the court's dockets.

These changes broke down into three stages. The first came during the early 1930s, when the Hoover and Roosevelt administrations used traditional, limited means to combat the depression. The second stage occurred during the early days of the New Deal, arising in response to the Roosevelt administration's economic reforms. The last stage came after 1937, as New Deal economic reforms either died or were slowly accepted as part of the nation's economy and thus no longer needed special judicial enforcement.

In the last years of the Hoover administration, the federal court's criminal and public law dockets grew rapidly in response to efforts to combat the depression through traditional, limited means. "Traditional" in this case meant the use of the federal courts to strictly enforce existing laws and regulations and to support local relief efforts.[9] As a result, in the early 1930s Prohibition filings rose to new heights, reaching an all-time high of 65,992 in 1932. Safety regulations, such as the Food and Drug Act, Hours of Service Act, and the Safety Appliance Act, also remained active on the docket. In addition, revenue regulations within the customs and tax laws, long subsumed under the category of Prohibition, began to reappear in significant numbers.[10]

One of the more intensive efforts to fight the depression through traditional means of enforcement involved the immigration laws. In 1929, under pressure from nativist groups, President Hoover, in order to free jobs for out-of-work Americans, ordered the removal of all illegal aliens in the United States and set into motion a policy of encouraging the "voluntary" emigration of all aliens, legal or illegal. Though enforced nationally, the impact of this policy was felt most by Hispanics in the southwestern states. Hundreds of thousands of undocumented Mexicans and Mexican Americans were induced to return to Mexico "voluntarily" (though often under intense pressure from welfare officials). This process was called "repatriation." It is estimated that 286,099 people of Mexican heritage departed between 1930 and 1932; Texas Mexicans accounted for 132,639 of this number. By 1937 some 458,057 Mexicans and Mexican Americans had been repatriated.[11]

Illegal aliens who refused to leave voluntarily, or who were caught illegally entering the country, faced criminal proceedings in the federal courts. In 1929, 1,351 persons were convicted of illegal entry, or reentry after deportation, into the United States. Almost all were deported, either immediately or following a short jail sentence. The next year the number of those convicted jumped to 6,717. Thereafter the number convicted for illegal entry dropped slowly to pre-depression levels.[12]

As with repatriation, the majority of judicial deportations occurred in Texas. From 1929 to 1932 the Southern District alone processed between 20 and 30 percent of all immigration cases. In 1929, 275 cases were filed in the Southern District; in 1930 this number jumped to 2,081. Thereafter the numbers declined slightly, to 1,831 in 1931, and 1,375 in 1932. Immigration matters alone totaled almost 75 percent of the court's criminal docket through 1933; added to the still-numerous Prohibition cases, they made up over 90 percent of the criminal docket.

Most immigration cases arose along the border in the Rio Grande Valley, but a significant number came from the cities to the north. Starting in 1931 federal agents staged immigration raids in cities across the country, the largest occurring in Los Angeles, El Paso, Phoenix, and Houston. In Houston the 1931 raids netted 152 illegal aliens. This was "more than quadruple" the number processed by the Houston immigration service in 1927. More raids followed, and the number processed steadily grew. By late 1931 the immigration service needed an additional 3,060 square feet of office space because of "increased deportation activities." This need lessened slightly after 1933, as the number deported decreased.[13]

As had been the case with smuggling and Prohibition cases, the court's handling of these immigration matters was largely routine. Ninety-nine percent of defendants pleaded guilty and were in court no more than one or two days. In most actions, those convicted of simple illegal entry received time served and were immediately deported; those charged with illegal reentry received jail sentences of thirty days to one year before deportation. The only break in this pattern occurred when a defendant was concurrently charged with Prohibition and smuggling violations. In those cases, jail time, usually from six months to over a year, was almost always given, even if the immigration violation was a first offense.

Despite the perfunctory nature of immigration proceedings, their impact on the court's operations was significant. The number of cases filed was staggering. By 1930 immigration cases outnumbered Prohibition cases by more than two to one, alone doubling the court's work load. Never before had the court had so many similar cases on its docket. Quick action had to be taken if only to clear out local jails filled to overflowing with illegal aliens. The court did this, but only through great effort by all personnel and occasional delays in other sections of the docket.

The impact on the region's Hispanic population was also significant. Most immigration cases followed a common pattern. Defendants were caught either attempting to enter the United States, often for the second or third time, or already in the United States without adequate documentation. This lack of documentation was not surprising. Prior to 1917 the border had been fully open, so no documentation was needed to enter. Since 1917 the border, while technically closed to unlimited movement, had in reality remained open. As long as a need existed for Mexican labor, few barriers were placed in their path to the North. The depression, however, caused a decline in the need for Mexican labor. With strict enforcement of the immigration laws, many long-time residents in this country were technically illegal aliens and were deported. The result was a disruption in the lives of the state's Hispanic community that took decades to ease.

The impact on efforts to combat the depression was less significant, however. The defendants were not, on the whole, criminals. Most were common laborers caught by bureaucratic red tape. The court realized this fact. Torn between the dictates of statute law and the realities of the border problem, it tried to clear these defendants out of jail as fast as possible and ignored the effects letting them loose would have in efforts to close the border.[14] As the large number of reentry cases suggests (reentry cases averaged approximately one-third of all immigration cases in the 1930s), deportation proceedings had little deterrent effect on Mexicans wishing to live in this country. Nor did they result in increased jobs for Anglos. When the farm economy slumped, no jobs were available. As the farm economy turned around in 1934 and 1935, farmers in the Rio Grande Valley turned again to undocumented Mexican workers, preferring them to Anglos. By the end of the decade, the border was as open as it had been in the 1920s.

The court was more successful in combating the depression when it merely supplemented or enforced federal relief efforts initiated by other federal agencies. Though federal efforts of this sort were not numerous, their economic impact was greater than their numbers would suggest. The most prominent federal effort to stabilize the economy was initiated by the comptroller of the currency to prop up the nation's banking system following the stock market crash of 1929.

In 1931 hundreds of banks were insolvent and many more neared collapse. Realizing the need for quick, drastic action, President Hoover created institutions, such as the Reconstruction Finance Corporation, to pump capital into the system. For many banks this help came too late. Though the comptroller tried to save as many banks as possible, thousands of banks were forced to close their doors. In these cases the comptroller had no option but to initiate liquidation proceedings. Following the banking crisis of 1933 and the passage of the Emergency Banking Act designed to deal with this crisis, the comptroller's ability to save faltering banks expanded. The new banking act gave the comptroller the power to appoint special receivers, known as "conservators," to operate insolvent banks, in conjunction with the federal district courts. The conservator's main function was to reorganize failed banks, resorting to liquidation only in extreme circumstances.[15]

Texas' banks had already endured two years of tough economic times by 1929. Following the stock market crash, this decline became a plummet. Faced with what historians have described as an "overexpanded banking system, . . . the decline of real estate values, problems in the oil and gas industries, and a gigantic surplus of cotton," local banks experienced huge losses of revenue. Even the strongest verged on insolvency and some crossed the line. By the end of 1933, fourteen Houston banks, more than half the city's banks, had closed their doors. To the south, the number of failed banks was even greater.

In Houston and Galveston federal reorganization was not needed to save the banking system. Local bankers successfully united to shore up and merge failing institutions before their loss undermined the system. Sounder banks banded together and bailed out, or bought out, such insolvent banks as the Marine Banking and Trust Company and the Public National Bank and Trust of Houston. In Galveston the large Hutchings, Sealy and Company Bank merged with the South Texas National Bank to protect assets. Despite the rapid decline in the number of banks active in the region, no Houston bank folded with its deposits unprotected; no Galveston bank failed at all. Only one Houston bank, the Public National, was forced into receivership by the comptroller.[16]

Elsewhere in the district collective effort proved less successful. By early

1933 seven additional Texas banks, all found to the south of Houston, were insolvent and were placed by the comptroller into the hands of a receiver. These included the City National Bank and Trust of Corpus Christi, the Trinity National Bank, the First National Bank of Bishop, the First National Bank of Mathis, the First National Bank of George West, the First National Bank of Corpus Christi, and the Corpus Christi Bank and Trust.[17]

In order to facilitate the recovery, the comptroller named a local banker, Malcolm Meek, receiver for each of the banks. Meek's priority as receiver was to regain solvency while providing necessary banking services to the region's inhabitants. To succeed he needed first to raise capital by recovering unpaid loans, by selling assets, and by collecting unpaid capital stock assessments from bank stockholders. Only then could he reorganize the daily operations and lending policies of the banks. To do both, he needed the help of the court.[18]

It willingly provided help. In its familiar role of protecting business from failure, the court moved confidently toward reorganizing the banks. Understanding the complex nature of reorganization, it allowed Meek a free rein in his efforts. It quickly approved every sale of assets requested by Meek. In capital assessment cases and suits to recover loans, Meek almost always won his suit. The court did not even require the usual monthly progress report; it merely accepted a final report on completion of the sale.[19]

In each of these endeavors, Meek was largely successful. With the help of the court, delinquent loans and capital assessments were repaid. This capital allowed the banks to make new loans to the region's businesses and farms. As the loans were repaid, the banks' finances were brought into order. By the end of the decade the receiverships were ended and the banks returned to their stockholders.

In addition to enforcing federal relief efforts, the court served a second public role in the Hoover era by evaluating the legitimacy of state economic regulations. In 1930 and 1931 Texas also sought to combat the depression through traditional, limited methods of relief and reform. Neither the governor nor the legislature saw a need for radical responses to the depression. In his first message to the legislature Governor Ross Sterling made no recommendations for special measures, stressing, rather, the need to keep state expenditures to a minimum and to wait for good times to return. The Forty-Second Legislature willingly followed the governor's suggestions. It passed few relief measures, refused to grant local governments the right to raise additional money to pay for local relief efforts, and actually raised taxes on sulfur, natural gas, cement, and cigarettes to help balance the budget.[20]

What relief measures the legislature did pass were aimed at regulating traditional sectors. Two reforms in particular were challenged in the federal courts. The first sought to regulate the oil and gas industries while the second regulated the use of the state's highways by trucks. In both cases, the laws were challenged because of the selective nature of their enforcement provisions. Though both implemented needed reforms in important sectors of the economy, they also acted to aid one segment of the economy at the expense of another.

The new law served the large major oil producer at the expense of the small independent. As noted in chapter 4, Texas' response to the low price of oil was proration, a limit placed on the amount of oil that could be pumped from any well in a particular field. Originally a conservation measure, proration also acted as an economic regulation, limiting supply and raising prices. Such limits better served the interests of big producers. They could afford to sell less oil now to obtain a higher price later; with limited capital most independents could not afford to wait. The regulations, however, did not take this difference into account. As Judge Hutcheson noted in the *Constintin* case, so perfectly did the state government's actions fit the needs of the big oil companies that it was hard to believe that state regulations were not written to serve the interests of those companies.[21]

Production limits of some kind, everyone agreed, were a necessary response to the chaos of the East Texas oil fields. Oil was already at ten cents a barrel in 1931 and seemed likely to drop even more. The question for the federal courts was whether the choices made in setting needed limits were constitutional. Most of the cases dealing with this issue arose from the Eastern District, where the large oil fields lay. In these cases, the Eastern District Court, arguing that the costs of regulation were unevenly distributed, that the limits set were so low as to transcend public necessity, and that state laws were not followed, first declared proration unconstitutional under the Fifth Amendment of the United States Constitution and the conservation provisions of the Texas Constitution.[22] In the *Constintin* case, the governor was held in contempt for declaring martial law to enforce proration. By 1933, however, changes in the administration of proration were contemplated that would more evenly distribute the costs and gains of regulation. In April of that year, the Texas attorney general advised the state Railroad Commission that the only way to obtain the federal court's support for a proration order would be to raise the allowable production level and to get rid of a flat-rate method of allocation.[23] He recommended that it be replaced with a flexible rate based on estimated potential output. This formula would satisfy the district court's complaint of inequitable distribution of the costs of regulation. Swayed by the argument, the commission implemented new rules governing proration. In a series of subsequent cases, the federal courts accepted this new proration plan.[24]

One of these cases arose in the Southern District. In May and June, 1933, suits challenging the new proration laws were filed. Only one, *Boxrollium Oil Co. v. Smith*, was decided. The rest the court settled by referring to this decision and other Eastern District cases.[25]

The facts in *Boxrollium* were typical of many proration cases. The Boxrollium Oil Company held a mineral lease on five acres of land in the Conroe oil field near Houston. In July, 1933, the Railroad Commission issued an order limiting production in the field to 16 percent of potential flow and production. For this field, 16 percent averaged 83 barrels per well per day. In addition, each well was allowed to pump an extra 16.5 barrels for every acre it was set on. The plaintiff with its five-acre lease could draw roughly an extra 80 barrels of oil each day.[26]

The plaintiff had no complaints with the concept of limiting production. What the company objected to was the actual production to which its well was limited. In its original complaint, the company argued that its well was capable of producing thousands of barrels of oil a day. Further, this oil could be withdrawn without damaging the ability of the field to produce oil in the future. For the orders of the Railroad Commission to limit the well to merely 163 barrels when it could produce thousands, the plaintiff concluded, was a "void and illegal . . . taking . . . [of] the property of [the] complainant without due process of law, in violation of the fourteenth amendment."[27]

In a supplemental complaint, the oil company also objected to the different amount of production allowed wells of similar potential. Other wells on five acres of land were allowed to pump 180 barrels a day. Such a difference was not equitable, and was even discriminatory, it argued. Further, and worst of all, the oil company complained that other producers were illegally pumping from 7,000 to 9,000 barrels a day from a "wild well," in effect stealing the plaintiff's oil. In both cases, the plaintiff felt that its property, in terms of potential earnings, was being taken as a result of the Railroad Commission's order. Its request was for an injunction prohibiting the commission from enforcing the proration rule.[28]

In deciding the case, a three-judge court, consisting of circuit judge Hutcheson and district Judge Kennerly and Grubb of the Northern District of Alabama, dealt only with the latter two complaints. They felt that the plaintiff's acceptance of the idea of proration denied the early constitutional challenge under the Fourteenth Amendment. If the Railroad Commission had the right to order a production limit, then the existence of an order limiting production was not unconstitutional. Only if the order limiting production was unreasonable or took the property of A and gave it to B would the limit be liable to challenge. Yet this was not the case. "While it is true that by various comparisons, and methods of figuring, some minor inequalities may be shown" under the system of percentage output production, "plaintiff's allowable production is materially increased by the use of the method complained of." For an injunction to issue "plaintiff must [first] make out a case of irreparable injury to itself." This it had not done. As to the fact that others were allowed to produce more oil then the plaintiff, this the court denied as unsubstantiated. The court found that the distance between the plaintiff's well and the illegal wells was great enough that the plaintiff experienced no loss "as would entitle it to equitable relief." An illegal act was occurring, but the plaintiff had suffered no monetary loss. Since the regulation evenly distributed the costs of conservation, and the presence of the illegal well did not materially harm the plaintiff, the injunction was denied.[29]

The result of this decision, along with other decisions reached in the Eastern

District, was to stress that the state could limit oil production if the regulation set limits that allowed all wells within the field to make a profit. This did not mean that all wells had to have equal limits, but rather that no well could be slighted on purpose to the benefit of others. Even the existence of wells pumping illegal "hot oil" did not necessarily change the evenness of the regulation. As long as no one individual was harmed to the material benefit of another, the federal courts would allow proration for economic purposes to continue.[30]

The court came to a similar conclusion in cases challenging the state's new highway regulations. The need for regulation of Texas trucking was clear. The state's highways were heavily used by trucks of all types. The result was a growing cost for the state in terms of both road deterioration and accidents. In 1930 over 450,537 tons of goods were carried by class A trucks; an unknown amount was added by class B and private trucks. As with proration, the legislature's response to this problem solved the issue of trucks on Texas highways in a highly selective manner.[31]

Supporters of strict highway regulations benefited from the laws passed even more than did oil producers. In May and June of 1931, three bills came out of the Forty-second Legislature regulating the use of the state's highways by trucks. Bill 335 set standards limiting the use of the highways by contract or private carriers. Bill 336, regulating common carriers, added strict weight and size limits. Bill 628 regulated the transportation of cotton by trucks on the highways. All three bills were primarily aimed at the transportation of cotton from the interior to the Gulf ports by truck, though only Bill 628 did so explicitly. Cotton was the state's largest crop and, next to oil, its most important industry. In 1930 Texas harvested 3,793,392 bales of cotton, 26 percent of the nation's total harvest. Even with depressed conditions, this harvest was worth an estimated $388,767, over 50 percent of all farm revenues.[32] Most of this cotton was ultimately exported through the ports of Houston, Galveston, Texas City, and Corpus Christi and prior to 1930 had been moved mostly by rail.

The problem revolved around the condition of the cotton when moved. In order to save space, freighters and exporters required that cotton bales be compressed. Two types of compression were common. Standard compression, averaging 22 pounds to the square foot, was used for domestic transport while high-density compression, 33 pounds to the square foot, was used for international export.[33] During the 1920s most Texas cotton had been compressed twice. First, inland presses compressed it at standard compression to facilitate rail transport to the ports; once in the port, a high-density compression was done before shipping abroad.

By mid-decade, some inland presses were converting to high-density compression. Inland high compression eliminated the need for a second compression in the ports. With 54 high-compression presses inland by 1929, port compresses were losing a significant and growing percentage of their business. The port presses responded to this threat by encouraging the movement of uncompressed cotton directly to the ports by truck. Since such cotton had to be compressed only once, merchants were able to make higher profits from uncompressed, trucked cotton. Initially drawing only from areas adjacent to the ports, with improved road conditions and low costs due to not having to pay for a first compression, cotton moved by truck began to arrive in Gulf ports from as far away as the Red River, over four hundred miles from the coast. In the 1928–29 season 451,885 bales of cotton were moved by trucks to the Gulf Coast ports. Just two years later the figure had jumped to 2,000,712 bales out of a total production of 5,320,000 bales. The movement of cotton by trucks challenged the inland presses and the railroads.[34]

They responded quickly to this challenge. Prior to 1931 the motor freight industry was practically unregulated in Texas. Although the Railroad Commission held jurisdiction over trucking within the state, the only regulation limiting truck owners' freedom concerned what could be placed on the truck; no limits existed on weight, size, or shape, or the condition of the vehicle. Even the limits placed on all common carriers by the common law were of little use in Texas, as most trucking was done by private carriers who contracted directly with shippers. This was especially the condition with cotton trucking. Increased use of the highways by unregulated trucks resulted in many accidents and a noticeable deterioration of the roads. Demands for some regulation was already present by the late 1920s. Weight and size limits, however, were potentially devastating to the cotton trucking industry.

The railroads and their allies quickly marshaled support for new regulations to control the trucking industry. With the legislature dominated by rural representatives, little pressure was necessary to get action. Within days of opening of the Forty-second Legislature, bills regulating the trucking industry in general and the cotton trucking industry in particular were before the legislature. All were strongly backed by the railroads and the inland compressors. Of the three finally passed, the one most destructive of moving cotton by truck, Bill 628, was actually written by Carl Callaway, general counsel for the Texas-Oklahoma Compress Association, an association of inland compressors.[35]

Combined, all three bills made it impossible for cotton to be shipped uncompressed by truck, and difficult for compressed cotton to be so shipped. Bill 628, passed in May, 1931, prohibited the movement of more than ten bales of uncompressed cotton or twenty bales of compressed cotton beyond a fifteen-mile limit. A larger load could be carried if the truck bed was fully enclosed in a box of wood or metal one and one-half inches thick. However, in June, Bill 336 limited all "commercial motor vehicle[s], truck-tractor[s], trailer[s] or semi-trailer[s]" outside of incorporated city limits to a weight not to exceed seven thousand pounds. Since ten bales of uncompressed cotton weigh almost seven thousand pounds, this concession was meaningless in light of Bill 336. This limit of seven thousand pounds was well under the average carrying capacity of most trucks. Declaring all trucking to be a business affected with a public interest, Bill 335 required all private carriers to be licensed by the state before operating on the state's highways. It then granted the Railroad Commission the power to refuse these licenses in any area where "adequate service" was already provided by other carriers, including, presumably, railroads.[36]

Within a month of their passage, challenges seeking injunctions prohibiting law officers from enforcing these new regulations were filed by the trucking industry in both state and federal courts. Numerous intervenors, individuals, and companies similarly affected by the law seconded the plaintiffs' objections. Each plaintiff was also an intervenor or codefendant in the other suits. In the three cases actually heard, each of the plaintiffs was represented by the same counsel, the Houston firm of Fulbright, Crooker and Freeman.[37]

The first case to be heard was *McLeaish v. Binford.* McLeaish and his partner, George Herder, Jr., were cotton merchants in Weimar, Colorado County, about 120 miles west of Houston. They owned eight trucks, capable of carrying from 10,000 to 12,500 pounds of cotton each. Each season they bought uncompressed cotton from farmers around Weimar and shipped it to Houston on their trucks. In 1930 they transported over fifteen thousand bales of cotton. They had plans for shipping more than this amount in 1931.[38]

McLeaish sought to enjoin enforcement of Bill 628. He and his partner alleged that "it [would] be economically unsound and inadvisable for them to transport their . . . cotton from Weimar . . . to Houston over . . . the public highways by motor vehicles . . . carrying loads of only ten bales of uncompressed cotton . . . , instead of loads of 20 or 25 bales as heretofore [were] transported." To do so would force them into bankruptcy. Nor, they argued, was it feasible first to compress their cotton and then to ship it by truck. Such a procedure would cost an additional one dollar for every bale shipped. This destroyed all the financial benefits of shipping by truck. In fact, when the extra expense of hauling the cotton to and from the compress was added, it cost more to ship compressed cotton by truck than by rail. Since McLeaish and Herder had invested "many thousands of dollars on the purchase of [their] trucks, and in equipping them for the purpose of hauling their . . . cotton" to market, and since the "Act has so limited and restricted the hauling of said cotton . . . as to make [it] undesirable, impracticable and virtually prohibitive from an economic standpoint" to remain in business, without the help of the court, the partners complained that they "[would] be forced to abandon the business of hauling cotton by truck" and lose their investment.

The inequity of this result was that "the carriage of uncompressed bales of cotton is no more hazardous to the public safety and no more injurious to the public highways than cotton compressed to [standard] density." The distinction the act attempted to draw between compressed and uncompressed cotton as related to highway safety was "[an] arbitrary discrimination without reason or any justified distinction, . . . [a] mere . . . pretense and device to force all cotton to be carried by the railroads and to foster the business of interior compresses by discriminatory and arbitrary legislation." Rather, the act was a discriminatory regulation with "no reasonable relation to the safety . . . nor . . . preservation of the public highways." It was therefore unconstitutional as it took the plaintiff's property without due process of law in violation of the Fourteenth Amendment.[39]

Texas responded to these allegations by stressing the pressing needs that existed for highway reform. It strenuously denied that limiting the number of bales to be moved by truck was "not of advantage in the protection of the public highway." Pointing out the "tremendous increase in the transportation of cotton over the highways . . . by truck" in the last years, and using pictures of crashed cotton trucks to prove its point, the state alleged that "a serious traffic menace [existed] on the highways," which had resulted in "an unwarranted destruction of" the state's roads. By limiting the transport of cotton over the highways, the state concluded, this very real problem was solved. The act was therefore not unconstitutional, but rather was a proper police regulation of a public convenience.[40]

The central issue in the case, as the three-judge court of Hutcheson, Kennerly, and Bryant noted, was whether the regulations in Bill 628 were a legitimate response to a real problem or a legislative action in support of the interests of one section of the economy at the expense of another. As Hutcheson remarked in his opinion: though "every presumption sprints in [the state's] favor to support the bill against attack, . . . [if] on its very face the classification, . . . or the means adopted to effect the desired end, appears arbitrary, unreasonable, or oppressive" the court has the duty to enjoin that regulation.[41]

Hutcheson noted that the intent of the state was clearly to drive cotton off the highways. "The point was not contested, but was urged by defendants' counsel as one of the prime accomplishments of the act." The "crux" of the problem, therefore, was whether this particular end was reasonable. While the plaintiffs clearly showed that "the legislative genesis of the act" rested with those who benefited most by its passage, the defense showed just as well that a real problem in relation to cotton trucking also existed. Was the law's supporting of the inland compressors and the railroads the primary purpose of its passage, the court asked, or merely an unintended effect? The court felt that it *was* the purpose of the act. "If the Legislature," Hutcheson wrote, "could have passed an act forbidding the use of the highways to uncompressed cotton, and compelling it to be compressed in the interior and hauled to market by rail, it could have passed the act in question, for that is what the act does, and judging its purpose by its effect, what it was designed to do."[42]

Concluding, the court went to great pains to note that it was not opposed to state regulation of the highways. All three judges, "believe[d] that the Legislature had the power to classify carriers of cotton compressed and uncompressed and impose regulations and restrictions upon their use of the roads reasonably related to and calculated to remove the dangers and abuses which the Legislature finds to be attendant upon that movement." The difficulty in the present case, and the reason they enjoined the enforcement of the law, was that the legislature's restrictions went unreasonably beyond what was needed to remove the problem defined.

This proved to be an important concession when *Sproles v. Binford* and *Stephenson v. Binford* came before the court one month later. Though aimed at the cotton industry, the regulations in both Bill 335 and Bill 336 were written to include all trucks using the state's highways. This difference resulted in a different outcome from *McLeaish*, one supporting expansive state powers over the highways.

Plaintiff's arguments in both cases were similar to those of *McLeaish:* the laws as written would unconstitutionally force truckers out of business to the benefit of others (the railroads). Sproles, owner of the Sproles Motor Freight Lines, a common carrier in the Houston area, had one hundred trucks most of which were over thirty-five feet long and could easily carry in excess of seven thousand pounds. While Sproles did not move cotton, he was joined in his suit by W. T. Stevens, a contract carrier of uncompressed cotton. Both complained against the act's weight and length limit, arguing that to follow it would force them to operate "unprofitably." In addition, Stevens complained of section 3(f) of the act, which limited the size and weight of packages moved by truck to under thirty cubic feet with a weight of five hundred pounds and totaling only fourteen per truck.

Complaining about Bill 335, Stephenson, a contract carrier with an exclusive contract with the Southwest Freight Company, argued that the power granted to the Railroad Commission to "refuse permits to contract carriers" on consideration not only of highway conditions and the fitness of the applicant, but of the adequacy of existing transportation "prevailing along the route proposed," was unconstitutional. The "Legislature may not by its fiat convert a contract carrier into a common carrier," even though its powers of regulating the safety of the highways, "regulate private business done upon them" Stephenson argued.[43]

The state's response in both cases was the same as in *McLeaish*. Filing only one brief for both suits, the state attorney argued that each act was a legitimate response to a pressing problem. Since the highways were public conveniences for the use of all Texas residents, the state was within its rights to regulate not only the goods carried over these roads but the means used to transport these goods. Limiting the size and weight of trucks using the public highways was but an application of the state's police powers. Similarly, the licensing requirement under Bill 335 was a proper police regulation necessary for ending congestion on the state's roads.[44]

In *Sproles*, the three-judge panel of Hutcheson, Kennerly, and West of the Western District of Texas accepted most of the state's explanations, acknowledging the limits placed on trucks by Bill 336 as within the state's police powers. "This Act, in so far as it regulates . . . the size of vehicles and loads, the speed thereof, and makes provisions for the safety of the public and the protection of the highways . . . is well within the power of the Legislature" to enact, wrote Kennerly. Nor did they view the limits set as arbitrary. "[W]e are asked to substitute our judgement as to the manner of limiting such gross weight of vehicle and load, . . . for that of the Legislature. That we may not do." The only problem the judges had with Bill 336 related to the limits placed on the size, the weight, and the number of containers that a truck could carry. This limit, placed in addition to the weight limits made by other sections of the act, they felt excessive. The court therefore granted a partial injunction prohibiting enforcement of this section of the act. On rehearing one year later, however, they withdrew the injunction as unneeded in light of the actual practice of enforcing the law.[45]

Unanimity broke in *Stephenson,* but the decision of the court remained the same. Judges Hutcheson and West agreed with the state that contract carriers were businesses affected with a public interest. They also agreed that the right to use the highway to carry on one's business was a "privilege" and not a "right." As a result: "We think it perfectly plain that, as he never had a right on the roads, but merely a privilege as to them, it is too much to say that, when the state undertakes to impose upon him conditions different from those characterizing him at common law, his privilege flowers under the Fourteenth Amendment into a right which the state may not impair." If the state wished to, it could completely deny the use of the highways to contract carriers. The plaintiffs, Hutcheson concluded, had no cause to complain about rules merely limiting commercial use of the highways. With no right threatened, they had no cause for the court to hear.[46]

Judge Kennerly, on the other hand, saw a sharp distinction between a private and a common carrier. As private concerns, they were not subject to special public duties. The act in question, Kennerly felt, "in no real sense concerned traffic safety and highway protection," but merely regulated private business concerns. He concluded, as a result, that the injunction should have been granted.[47]

Despite Kennerly's dissent, the court once again supported "reasonable" state regulation of the public highways. As it had with oil proration, the majority felt that the reforms effected by the law outweighed the actual costs to individual truckers. The state had not only a right but a duty to pass laws regulating industries necessary to the well-being of the state. The only limit on this duty was that the costs of this regulation be evenly distributed.

Both *Sproles* and *Stephenson* were appealed. In both cases the Supreme Court upheld the court's decision, basing its opinion on the lower court's findings of fact and law. "[W]e perceive no constitutional ground for denying to the state the right to foster a fair distribution of traffic to the end that all necessary facilities should be maintained and that the public should not be inconvenienced by inordinate uses of its highways for purposes of gain," wrote Chief Justice Charles E. Hughes in upholding the district court's ruling in *Sproles.* "This is not a case of a denial of the use of highways to one class of citizens as opposed to another, or of limitations having no appropriate relation to highway protection . . . [it is rather a discrimination] apply[ing] to all persons and to all products . . . as the District Court found." Like the district court, the Supreme Court was willing to allow the state legislature to shape commercial development as long as the means were not blatant.[48]

III

The New Deal changed both the number and the type of public cases brought before the federal courts. Committed to attacking the depression through "new" means, and distrustful of the mostly conservative, Republican federal bench, the Roosevelt administration sought to deemphasize the regulatory role of the federal judiciary.[49] In its first year, the New Deal repealed Prohibition and toned down enforcement of the immigration laws. With its own reforms, the New Deal avoided litigation as an enforcement mechanism whenever possible. Many New Deal acts replaced the district courts with bureaucratic boards and commissions, such as the National Labor Relations Board (NLRB), as the forum for hearing complaints under a particular act. Appeals from these boards, in turn, went directly to the circuit courts of appeals, cutting the district courts out of the regulatory process.[50]

The New Deal also avoided litigation by not filing, or selectively filing, enforcement actions. Roosevelt's attorney general, Homer Cummings, advocated "caution and avoidance" in litigating under the National Industrial Recovery Act (NIRA) and the Agricultural Adjustment Act. The directors of the agencies created to implement these acts agreed. Distrusting litigation as a means of enforcing the law, they preferred using personal and political pressure to halt violations. "We have tried not to take any action that could be brought into court," boasted Hugh Johnson, head of the National Recovery Administration in mid-1933. Jerome Frank, general counsel of the Agricultural Adjustment Administration, shared this feeling. "There will be little in the way of litigation" for his office to deal with he declared in August, 1933. Negotiating and drafting marketing agreements was to be its primary job. Both agencies largely achieved their goal. Neither organized a litigation department until early 1934, and, until 1935, kept them understaffed.[51]

The New Deal could not, however, avoid litigation in the federal courts entirely. Within six months of implementing the first NRA codes, violations had become common.[52] By the end of 1933, over ten thousand complaints alleging code violations had been filed with the NRA. To halt this flood, the NRA began selectively prosecuting "locally well known chisellers."[53] Deterrence was the aim of litigation and results were demanded. As Blackwell Smith, head of the NRA Legal Division, outlined the goal in an April, 1934, memorandum: "Objective: Results; Methods in General: Machiavellian – the end justifies the means (almost)." The result of this policy was that, while NRA filed fewer than six hundred cases by the end of 1935, more were in the offing.[54]

Enforcement under the AAA followed a similar pattern. At first cautious over litigating in the federal courts, difficulties in one major farm industry, the dairy industry, forced the AAA's hand. The dairy industry involved millions of farmers and thousands of distributors and operated nationwide. Operating both inter- and intrastate, the industry was plagued with instability. Almost as soon as a marketing agreement was reached, producers and distributors violated it. Two distributors in the Chicago area soon challenged the constitutionality of the marketing agreement. Arguing that the agreement was "confiscatory of their business," they sought an injunction from the Circuit Court of the District of Columbia to stop enforcement of the Dairy Code. The court refused to grant these injunctions. Drawing on a state case, *Nebbia v. New York*, the D.C. Circuit Court accepted the existence of a national emergency and fully backed the AAA's authority to regulate the dairy industry and, by implication, other farm industries. Emboldened by its success, and facing continued violations of the law, the AAA reevaluated its position on litigation and in mid-1934 began an aggressive enforcement campaign in the courts. One year later hundreds of enforcement cases had been filed.[55]

Also bringing the New Deal into court were equity suits filed against the NRA and the AAA. As occurred in the dairy industry, challenges were filed by producers and distributors seeking to enjoin the individual NRA codes and AAA marketing agreements. Angered by uneven or nonexistent enforcement of the codes, most plaintiffs argued that the acts or codes violated the Fifth and Fourteenth amendments of the Constitution. Each sought to halt enforcement by national and local officials. Less numerous than federal prosecutions, these suits added another one hundred cases to the federal courts' public law dockets.[56]

The Southern District heard eighteen cases relating to NRA and AAA enforcement.[57] Most of these actions were dismissed uncompleted following the invalidation of the NRA and the AAA by the Supreme Court in *Schechter v. the United States* and *U.S. v. Butler* in the spring and summer of 1935. Before this occurred the court completed three of these cases, two challenging the NRA and a third, the AAA.

In line with the Supreme Court's ultimate decisions against the NRA and the AAA, the Southern District's opinions in these cases show a discomfort with extensive government regulation of private business. Following the line it had taken on state regulation of oil and the highways, the court appreciated the need for action but questioned the methods chosen to implement these reforms. Faced with having to make a decision, it again turned to a "reasonableness" standard as its guidepost in judging these regulations.

The issue first came before the court in the *Boggus Motor Co. v. Onderdonk et al.*, filed in September, 1934. The Boggus Motor Company was a retail car dealership in Harlingen, Texas, "one of 50 or 60 Motor Retail Dealers" operating in the Rio Grande Valley. On October 3, 1933, the president approved a code of fair practices for the retail motor trade to regulate costs, hours, and wages. Soon after, meetings were held among car dealers throughout the Valley over whether to accept the code. J. L. Boggus, president of the Boggus Motor Company, led the movement to accept federal regulations. On May 7, 1934, his company along with most, but not all, car dealerships in the Valley assented to the code.

The company "vigorously" supported the code initially. J. L. Boggus was a member of the Local Advisory Committee to the NRA. He often wrote to L. H. Onderdonk and Z. E. Avery, the local NRA field adjusters, demanding stricter efforts to enforce the code, especially the price-control sections. His efforts, however, soon proved unsuccessful. As the court later noted in its decision, "the whole situation remained in a state of more or less confusion insofar as the Motor Retail Dealers in the Valley were concerned." Some retailers "did not assent to the Code" while others, "who [had] assented to the Code wholly or in part" failed to comply with its price-fixing sections.[58]

In late 1934, under orders from Washington, all efforts to enforce price controls were stopped, much to the anger of Boggus and his supporters among the Valley's car dealers. Feeling frustrated at the high number of infractions, they threatened to "appeal to some source to let us out of the code" unless the entire code was enforced. A petition, including the names of thirty-nine of the Valley's fifty dealers, was drawn up complaining of the lack of enforcement. It was sent to various enforcement bodies of the NRA with little result, or so Boggus thought.[59]

At this time, the field adjusters, Onderdonk and Avery, charged the Boggus Motor Company with violations of the wages and hours sections of the code. Boggus strenuously denied these charges, claiming they were filed in response to his leadership of the petition drive. Boggus was later proved innocent of all charges; however, prior to this vindication, these charges resulted in a heated dispute between Boggus and the field adjusters. The agents threatened Boggus with criminal prosecution, civil penalties, and an injunction closing his business. In repeated visits to the dealership, they demanded that they be allowed to inspect Boggus's books and to interview his employees, which disrupted business. The dispute quickly become quite personal. Angered by the continued harassment, Boggus filed for an injunction enjoining both Onderdonk and Avery from interfering with his place of business. In a supplemental complaint, Boggus added the name of Douglas McGregor, the U.S. attorney for the Southern District, to the request.[60]

By the time the case came to trial on November 19, 1934, the actual dispute had worked itself out. Both Onderdonk and Avery had been transferred to East Texas, charges were never filed against Boggus, and the NRA sought to ignore the whole episode. This raised the question of whether Boggus had a valid claim that the court had jurisdiction to hear. "It is pressed upon me that the National Industrial Recovery Act and such Code are constitutionally invalid, and that for that reason, relief by Injunction should be given [to the] Plaintiff," Judge Kennerly wrote. "Assuming, but not deciding, that they are invalid, Plaintiff is not entitled to relief in Equity . . . except upon showing of some clear ground of equitable jurisdiction." This, the court ruled, Boggus had not provided. "The function of an injunction is to afford preventive relief, and not to redress wrongs (grievous though they may be) already committed." The facts of the case clearly showed that, "insofar as the Defendants Onderdonk and Avery are concerned, and insofar as the prosecution of Plaintiff in the Courts by them is concerned," no future wrongs were apt to occur. Not only were charges never filed against Boggus, but the "root of the controversy," the actions of Onderdonk and Avery, were clearly "abandoned" by the NRA when the field adjusters were transferred.

The judge refused to rule on the constitutionality of the NIRA for this same reason. Though Kennerly had doubts about the constitutionality of the act, he was troubled by the late date of Boggus's challenge to the NIRA. "Up to the time Plaintiff was accused of violating the Code, neither Plaintiff nor its President, . . . questioned the validity of either the NIRA or the Code. Indeed, Plaintiff had assented to the Code, and Plaintiff's President had aided in its enforcement, and was pressing for the prosecution of others thereunder. It was when Plaintiff was accused of a violation of the Code that it began to claim invalidity." With this in mind the judge ruled that the constitutional challenge presented no "'actual controversy,' but only a hypothetical controversy or question." Hypothetical cases were not, Kennerly declared, within the court's jurisdiction.

Despite all this, the judge's decision did not go completely against Boggus. Though he dismissed the case with all costs to be paid by the plaintiff, Kennerly included a provision allowing "for future amendments by the Plaintiff, should a contingency" arise in which he was threatened with a real and future loss as a result of illegal efforts to enforce the code. Were this to occur, Kennerly concluded, the court would have jurisdiction to decide the issues of the case and could act in an appropriate manner to protect Boggus's interests.

In a case filed one month after *Boggus* and argued on the same day before Judge Bryant of the Eastern District, the court had the opportunity to rule on the merits of the NIRA. This case involved the Carter Kelly Lumber Company, which sought an injunction enjoining Douglas McGregor, U.S. attorney for the Southern District, from enforcing the price-fixing sections of the Lumber and Timber Code, approved August 19, 1933.[61]

The lumber industry had been hard hit by the depression. Already fragmented as a result of "widely scattered producing areas, a large number of firms running from very large to very small . . . and severe competition within . . . the industry," the lumber industry was racked by "cut-throat competition." The industry giants were especially hard hit by the price wars. When the NRA began to draft a code for the lumber industry, the giants demanded and received specific price and production control. Section IX of the Lumber Code contained elaborate provisions for setting the price of lumber. Later, this section was amended to allow individual code authorities to determine when "an emergency existed in the lumber industry" and to respond by setting new limits on prices and production.[62]

On July 16, 1934, the Southern Pine Association, the administrative authority for the southern lumber industry, certified the existence of an emergency and issued new price limits for "practically all grades, sizes and species of lumber and timber products." These prices, W. T. Carter, president of the Carter Kelly company, argued were set so high that they could not sell their lumber.

Worse yet, the price limits caused this loss to the benefit of other sections of the industry. "Numerous discriminatory and inequitable differentials, in the classification of mills according to their size and production capacities, . . . allow competing members of the industry . . . taking different classifications, to absorb the entire demand of certain types of lumber manufactured by these plaintiffs, at prices substantially less than these plaintiffs are authorized to sell lumber under the prices fixed" by the association. None of these prices, Carter further noted, were related in any manner to the actual costs of business. Carter not only had customers wanting his lumber at a lower price, but he was willing to sell the lumber at that price. Section IX of the Lumber Code of the NIRA, and by implication all price setting under the NIRA, was therefore an unconstitutional taking of the property without due process of law, Carter concluded.

Before turning to the court, Carter had sought administrative relief from the Southern Pine Association, but had been refused. This had left the company in a difficult position. On the one hand, it could sell its lumber at prices below the fixed cost and run the risk of fines up to five hundred dollars a day for violating the law. On the other, it could withdraw from the market, "permitting their stocks of lumber to be destroyed by bugs and worms . . . shutting down their mills, . . . putting between 750 and 1,000" out of work, and generally causing "certain ruin" for the company. Either choice resulted in an "intolerable" situation and made it "impossible" for the company "to continue the manufacture of lumber upon a reduced scale or any other scale." Faced with the unpleasant choice between paying large fines or bankruptcy, the plaintiff turned to the court as its only source of relief.[63]

The Justice Department responded to these claims by stressing the need and fairness of both the NIRA and the Lumber Code. Lawyers reminded the court that "the depression and partial paralysis of the lumber industry brought about by ruthless price cutting" had "produced a disastrous effect upon interstate commerce." Both the sources and the "free-flow" of commerce were destroyed by the "crippling and eliminat[ion] of producers," as well as "greatly diminishing, paralyzing and stagnating . . . sales" for those who survived. Drawing on "cost data gathered from a large number of representative operators, the Lumber Code limited the dangers of price wars by setting minimum prices providing for "reasonable production costs." The U.S. attorney did acknowledge the possibility that the plaintiff had suffered losses while the price code was in effect. He denied, however, that the code was at fault. The past year "had been [one] of extremely subnormal demand, and relatively few operators have been able to dispose of their entire production." The fact that the plaintiff had customers for his lumber at prices lower than the controlled level was, in turn, a direct result of the existence of price controls. "Under a program of cost protection price control, it is natural that opportunities have been presented [for] selling below the set price." However, "such opportunities would not have existed if the Industry had been permitted to engage in cut throat competition." Ultimately, the outcome Carter Kelly strove to achieve was no different from that which it claimed for the present Lumber Code: helping one lumber company at the expense of all others. This, as the plaintiff himself had pointed out, was unconstitutional. No cause for an injunction, the U.S. attorney concluded, therefore existed.[64]

With no troubling jurisdictional issues to complicate the case, the court's decision and order dealt directly with the constitutionality of the NIRA and the Lumber Code as it related to price fixing. The decision went completely against the government. Declaring the NIRA provisions as to price fixing an unconstitutional taking of private property without due process of law, the court on November 30 ordered both the NRA and the Justice Department to refrain from enforcing the price-fixing provisions of the Lumber Code against the plaintiff. Five days later, after three days of hearings, it made the injunction permanent. The injunction remained in force until February, 1935. At that time, pursuant to an agreement between all parties involved in the case, the court dissolved the injunction on a joint motion to the effect that the NRA was no longer fixing prices in the lumber industry. The court, however, made clear that the plaintiff retained the "right to institute further action . . . in the event that [the] suspension [of price fixing] was again attempted."[65]

Though focused exclusively on the price-setting sections of the Lumber Code, this decision placed the entire NIRA in jeopardy, much as the Supreme Court's *Panama Refinery v. Ryan* ruling on the Oil Code had placed the petroleum industry in jeopardy.[66] Both declared sections of the NIRA unconstitutional and further hinted that the NIRA would be viewed unfavorably within their jurisdictions in future cases. Nationally, the Justice Department tried once again in the *Schecter* case and lost; in May of 1935 the NIRA was declared unconstitutional by the Supreme Court. In the Southern District, the U.S. attorney took the court's hint and refrained from enforcing the NIRA. As a result, the NRA was a dead letter in Southeast Texas over five months before the Supreme Court acted.[67]

The same pattern occurred with the AAA. Buoyed by the favorable decision in *Nebbia v. New York*, the AAA had energetically litigated in early 1935. In March of that year five cases were filed against distributors of citrus products in the Rio Grande Valley. One month earlier, an injunction suit had been filed by the Rio Valley Fruit and Vegetable Company, one of the defendants in the enforcement cases, that sought to enjoin enforcement of the AAA. Of these six cases, only one, involving the Rio Valley Fruit and Vegetable Company, actually went to trial. The remaining five cases were held pending the disposition of this case.[68]

The facts in this case were straightforward. The Rio Valley Fruit and Vegetable Company was a wholesale cooperative distributing South Texas citrus fruit throughout Texas. On October 20, 1934, the Texas Citrus Control Committee, the regulating body under the AAA for the Texas citrus industry, defined eight categories of grapefruit, encompassing some 25 percent of the total grapefruit crop, and limited distribution exclusively to these eight categories. The committee further prorated the amount of classified grapefruit that any company could sell. Soon after the order went into effect, the Rio Valley Fruit and Vegetable Company, which had never voluntarily assented to the AAA citrus program, violated the committee's rules not only by selling classified grapefruit beyond its prorated limit but also by selling an unspecified amount of unclassified grapefruit. In addition, the fruit company never paid the one cent per box assessment the committee charged to all Texas citrus wholesalers. The committee requested an injunction enjoining the company from selling any unclassified fruit, from selling classified fruit over its set limit, and asked it to pay the one cent fee.[69]

The fruit company responded with charges of its own. Pointing to the Supreme Court's partial negation of the NRA in *Panama Refining Co. v. Ryan,* the fruit company argued that the AAA unconstitutionally delegated legislative powers to the president and the secretary of agriculture. More to the point, the fruit company charged that the act set unreasonable regulations on private property, "unlawful[ly] discriminat[ing] against [the] defendants and other similarly situated" in violation of the Fifth Amendment. It was impossible, the company contended, for an independent wholesaler to sell only classified grapefruit. "In order for an independent shipper . . . to procure grapefruit for shipment, it is necessary . . . to purchase from the grower what is commonly referred to as 'orchard run' fruit; in other words such shipper must buy all class and grades of fruit as are found in the orchard." This lot in turn included all types of unclassified fruit, which were "equally as wholesome . . . as classified fruit"; they differed only in their appearance, "being . . . not as attractive as . . . classified fruit." Further, a market for unclassified fruit existed. If independent wholesalers were prohibited from selling the unclassified fruit that they were forced by the market to purchase from the producer, they would be forced out of business. This, the fruit company argued, was inequitable and should not be enforced by an equity injunction.[70]

In the preliminary hearing on the injunction in March, 1935, Kennerly agreed with the defense's contentions. Ruling only on the issue of the preliminary injunction's potential effect on the citrus industry and not on the constitutionality of the case, the judge denied the injunction. He felt that, given the short time remaining in the citrus season, allowing the defendant the freedom to ship as it pleased would "not materially affect the grapefruit market, nor materially injure Plaintiff, . . . or their prgram." Implementing an injunction, on the other hand, would produce "great and irreparable loss and damage" to the defendant.[71]

Two months later, the judge ruled on the constitutionality of the Citrus Committee's rule and the AAA. After reviewing the workings of the statute, Kennerly declared the "provisions of the Act . . . Constitutionally invalid" and ordered the government not to enforce the act against the defendant. This decision drew on the Supreme Court's May decision in *U.S. v. Schecter* that the NRA was an unconstitutional transfer of legislative power to the president. Kennerly, relying fully on the precedent value of *Schecter,* did not elaborate further on his reasons for declaring the act unconstitutional. In his earlier decision on the preliminary injunction, however, the judge had hinted at an alternate reason for his decision. In that ruling he noted how the facts clearly showed the committee's rule to be "unreasonable and an unlawful discrimination in favor of shippers of grapefruit included in the eight grades of fruit fixed . . . by the Committee, and against . . . shippers of grapefruit not coming within such eight grades." Such an unreasonable law was clearly unconstitutional.[72]

The court's position toward the AAA was the same as its position toward the NRA. In both cases the court refused to accept unquestioningly the nation's powers to regulate industry and agriculture. As it had with similar regulations, the court subjected the regulations to a "reasonableness" standard. Unlike with the state laws, however, the court found the federal statutes unreasonable and hence unconstitutional. Worried by the steady growth of national, as opposed to local, laws and questioning the validity of an economy of scarcity, Judge Kennerly proved less willing to accept the costs of federal regulation; he saw these laws as unfairly helping one segment of the nation at the expense of another, and this he felt was wrong.[73]

While these were not easy decisions for Kennerly to make, he felt constrained to do so. As his dissent in *Stephenson v. Binford* and his decisions in the NRA and AAA cases showed, any regulation that took the property of A and gave it to B went beyond this line; however, respecting individual rights and property as the basis of society, the judge felt he had no other option but to declare these laws unconstitutional.[74]

IV

The invalidation of the NRA and the AAA by the Supreme Court by 1937 pushed the New Deal's litigation strategy back to its earliest forms. Frustrated by the largely conservative federal bench, the New Deal stopped trying to enforce its reform and regulatory legislation in the federal courts. Wherever possible, bureaucratic boards were employed to replace the lower federal courts' enforcement duties. Hence the new AAA, passed in 1937, set up stronger bureaucratic enforcement mechanisms than its predecessor had. Where enforcement in the federal courts proved unavoidable, the New Deal simply did not file. Even the successes of the New Deal in the Supreme Court after 1937, when it upheld the NLRB and Social Security, did not change this trend.

Regulatory enforcement of economic reforms was replaced by a renewed emphasis on traditional civil law cases. These included increased filings under the food and drug laws, the tax laws, and the public safety laws. While none of these had been dropped from the docket during the early years of the New Deal, their relative importance had declined as the court dealt with the effects of new economic regulations. Most impressive in the revival of civil law cases were food and drug condemnations. Beginning in 1936 national filings under this law more than doubled in number, from 722 to 1,845. Dropping slightly in 1937, the number of filings quickly returned to this mark in 1938 and grew even greater in 1939. The others followed a similar pattern.[75]

Joining this revival of traditional regulatory litigation was a new type of case that had its origins in the earliest days of the New Deal. In the first hundred days of the Roosevelt administration, Congress passed a series of acts aimed at helping farmers and homeowners retain their debt-ridden property. These acts included the Emergency Farm Mortgage Act, providing for the refinancing of farm mortgages; the Home Owners' Loan Act, providing for the refinancing of home mortgages; and the Farm Credit Act, providing for the reorganization of agricultural credit. One year later, Congress passed the National Housing Act of 1934, which expanded efforts under the Home Owners' Loan Act by insuring funds earmarked for renovating dilipidated housing. Combined, these acts provided millions of dollars in loans to needy Americans.[76]

The recession of 1937 threatened the survival of these programs, however. Hurt by the economic downturn, many farm- and homeowners defaulted on their loans, especially those who had borrowed federally insured money under the National Housing Act. Prodded by the holders of these notes, the government instituted foreclosure proceedings in the federal courts to recover the money paid to the note holders. By late 1937 these procedures accounted for almost one-quarter of all public, nonequity civil filings; in 1938, almost 30 percent. These high numbers continued well into the 1940s.[77]

In the Southern District, foreclosure cases followed the national norm. Almost nonexistent before 1937, government foreclosure cases entered the docket suddenly and significantly. Prior to 1937 only a few farm credit cases were filed. By 1938 foreclosure cases made up 25 percent of the public law case load. In the Houston Division, as elsewhere, housing foreclosure cases were the most numerous category in the law docket.

Most of these cases involved small sums. The defendants were usually small home- or farm owners who had taken out either direct or federally insured mortgages or home improvement loans. Representative of most defendants were H. L. Martin and his wife, Fay Mae, who had purchased on credit goods from Lack's Auto Supply Company to improve their car. So too were Louis and Maggie Bruchart, who purchased goods on credit to improve their home. Both had paid back a portion of their debt before stopping payment. They had every intention of continuing to pay back their loans; tough times made this impossible, however. Owing less than two hundred dollars apiece, both families still found it impossible to pay off their loans and had to default.[78]

In these and similar cases the court's decisions were foreordained. Once the validity of the claim was settled, the court had little discretion in its actions. As the government's primary collection agency, it was duty-bound to enforce the law. Though Judge Kennerly was troubled by the harm this caused local citizens, as a "black-letter law judge," he had no other recourse. Contracts had to be upheld. As a result, most of the court's housing and farm loan cases were decided in favor of the plaintiff. Fines equaling the amount of the loan outstanding plus interest of 6 percent were levied.

Along with the always-heavy criminal docket and the occasional equity condemnation, this was the extent of the public law docket in the last years of the 1930s. More concerned with finishing the construction of the welfare state, and later on with foreign affairs, the New Deal withdrew from the federal courts wherever and whenever possible.

V

Recalling the political situation in mid-1934, former governor William P. Hobby noted the "gradual disintegration of the feeling of Texas business toward the New Deal." Having survived the immediate shock of the depression, Texas business viewed with growing concern the growing trend toward what it saw as socialism. "More pronounced today than ever before," the *Texas Weekly* wrote in a July, 1934, editorial "is that sharp divergence in social philosophy which aligns believers in government control of private life and business against believers of individual initiative, self-reliance, and enterprise." This, the *Weekly* concluded, boded ill for Texas and the nation. Francis Law, president of the First National Bank in Houston, agreed. "We are living in a world of change," Law wrote, and "in many respects the old order has passed. Under it, many grievous mistakes were made and abuses suffered, and these must never be allowed again." But, Law concluded, it was not necessary "to destroy the foundations of this government or of its business structure" to solve these problems. "We need only to repair and rebuild the superstructure." Destruction, however, seemed to be the New Deal's goal.[79]

Forced to turn to the federal government for help in the darkest days of the depression, Texans, especially the state's conservative political and business elite, refused to give up a belief in their ability to solve their own economic woes. What they wanted from the federal government was financial and organizational assistance to complement local reconstruction efforts, not federal regulations. Welcoming federal help at first, Texas business leaders soon questioned the need and efficacy of federal legislation as the bite of the depression lessened. What initially were temporary relief measures quickly became unwanted regulation of "private" matters. This shift Texans opposed, both politically and in the courts. As Sherwood Avery, former chief of the NRA enforcement division in Texas, noted years after the NRA died: "I don't think the NRA was properly administered. We did not keep attuned to public opinion. We used harsh methods, we 'cracked down' as Old Iron Pants Hugh Johnson (first head of the NRA) admonished the organizations to do. At first, (1933–4) the people were scared but, as soon as they felt they were to live, they rebelled against regimentation and harsh administration."[80]

In the short term, this opposition was largely successful. Both the NRA and the AAA were successfully challenged in the courts. In the long term success was less forthcoming. The federal regulatory state was in place to stay as World War II and the postwar economic boom completed the transformation the New Deal had started. Before this occurred, however, Texans showed a positive side to their aversion to federal regulation. Seeking private answers to the problem of the depression, local business turned to the Southern District for help in restructuring the region's economy.

6. Regulation without Restriction

PRIVATE LAW DURING THE DEPRESSION

I

The Texas society that opposed the New Deal was shaped by what scholars have called the traditionalistic-individualistic impulse. Combining rule by a small, paternalistic elite with the idea that government's sole job was to protect and promote the use of private property, this impulse sharply limited the accepted scope of governmental action. The business and legal elite that ruled Texas wanted government to build roads, to provide police protection, and to construct and protect harbors, roads, and bridges. Beyond such basic services it had few needs or wishes for government action. It especially did not want government restriction of business, an endeavor that it regarded as essentially private in nature.[1]

The New Deal's reform programs overstepped the line Texans drew between proper regulation and restriction. Welcoming government action at first, Texans balked when the New Deal's relief efforts shifted to restrictive regulations. The result was the short-term invalidation of many of the New Deal's most ambitious reform programs. Yet something had to be done to combat the depression's effects. Left to itself, the Texas economy was slowly tearing itself apart. Merely opposing federal programs was not going to save the state's economy from collapse. With thousands of businesses failing or failed, this was a fact Texas business painfully understood. But how to combat the depression without turning to restrictive government regulation and destroying the existing private economic system?

Once again the Southern District Court provided answers for many Texas business leaders. Thirty years of working to foster and stabilize Southeast Texas' growth had made the court's regulatory powers an accepted part of the local business environment. Business saw the court's adaptive, fluid regulation as a useful resource for supplementing private efforts to stabilize the economy. The court sheltered and reorganized insolvent business, recovered unpaid debts, ruled on the rights and duties of litigants, and enforced the completion of contracts. These were indispensable services in bad economic times and business saw the court as a safe forum in which to obtain these services. As a court of law, the Southern District had limited regulatory powers; it could neither initiate litigation nor rule on issues beyond the immediate scope of a case. By focusing their arguments on specific concerns, litigants were able to limit the court's power while at the same time procuring indispensable services.

Judge Kennerly's presence on the Southern District's bench added to the perceived effectiveness and safety of the court. Like his predecessors Kennerly was a member of the social and economic elite of Southeast Texas. Trained in a nineteenth-century style of jurisprudence and having served as a referee in bankruptcy and as the chief counsel of Houston Oil Company before becoming judge, Kennerly's judicial and economic philosophy differed little from that of the litigants appearing before him. He viewed the court's job in largely economic terms: its primary function was to protect private property and foster the commerce and industry that made this property socially useful. Any action that threatened private property was a danger that had to be stopped. Other issues came second (though often a close second), hence the judge's opposition to the NRA and the AAA.

The very points of his judicial philosophy that led Kennerly to oppose federal regulatory efforts made him support private actions to reform the economy. The depression threatened the system that fostered private property. If business was unable put its own house in order, government would be forced to step in and restructure the economy. The NRA and the AAA were a hint of things to come. Kennerly thus welcomed suits aimed at reorganizing insolvent or inefficient businesses; he provided definitions of legal rights and promoted rules of proper conduct for new economic situations. He saw such suits as the most efficient method of solving economic problems; it was also, he felt, the proper method.

Where property rights were not threatened, but merely in confusion, the judge was just as receptive to business needs. With his strong Christian values, Kennerly stressed balance and compromise in his decisions. Known among admiralty lawyers as "mutual fault" Kennerly, the judge always sought a settlement that balanced competing wants and needs. A supporter of the pretrial conference, Kennerly was happiest when the opposing sides worked out a settlement before the case came to trial. If a trial was unavoidable, he still sought to satisfy all participants with his decision. This preference was strictly limited by a harder edge to the judge's personality, however. Where the the law was explicitly on the side of one litigant, or where one litigant was clearly at fault and not deserving of help, the judge took a strong partisan position. Kennerly's benevolence was always limited by his opinion of the law's dictates.[2]

Starting in early 1930 large numbers of local and national businesses began to seek help from the court. By 1934 private civil filings (which for most of the court's history had numbered fewer than 150 per year) topped 384. They remained near this level for the remainder of the decade. Combined with bankruptcy suits, which added an additional 100 to 200 cases a year, private civil suits outnumbered public civil actions by more than three to one (table 4).[3]

Table 4
PUBLIC CIVIL, PRIVATE CIVIL, AND BANKRUPTCY FILINGS, 1930–39

Year	Public Civil Filings	Private Civil Filings	Bankruptcy Filings
1930	286	173	158
1931	229	184	213
1932	407	288	302
1933	349	293	211
1934	72	384	134
1935	93	334	187
1936	129	296	140
1937	119	248	118
1938	253	329	135
1939	229	269	118

Source: Atty. Gen. Reports (1930–39).

These cases arose directly from the economic disruptions of the period. Though they involved many different issues, litigants generally sought two related services. The first was help in protecting and, where necessary, fairly dividing the assets of businesses and individuals harmed by the depression's economic disruptions. The second was the creation and enforcement of new standards of business practice, ones applicable to a new economic reality of depressed prices and insecure investments.

In the unsettled days of the depression, the court moved quickly and confidently into its familiar role of protecting business resources from difficult economic times. Drawing on procedures worked out over the last thirty years, and creating new ones where needed, the court supplemented private efforts at reform—creating receiverships, organizing industries, and mediating between different sectors of the economy—serving in a new economic setting its traditional function of protecting and fostering the private economic development of Southeast Texas.

II

The number of equity and bankruptcy receiverships grew rapidly after the stock market crash of 1929. At first, most cases involved out-of-state businesses already placed in receivership by other district courts. As the Texas economy fragmented and local businesses began to fail, however, companies centered in the Southern District were soon forced to seek federal protection.[4]

Encompassing a wide range of business concerns, equity reorganizations in the 1930s were larger and more complicated than had been the case thirty years earlier. Along with public utilities such as railroads and irrigation companies, private concerns such as sugar and lumber mills, department stores, and investment companies sought help in restructuring. In addition, the request for receiverships came from more varied sources. Petitions came not only from majority bondholders and stockholders, the traditional source of receivership suits,[5] but also from management and minority creditors. Often more than one creditor filed suit. Complicating matters even more, these multiple suits often took differing forms, with petitions for an accounting of the company's books and foreclosure on liens joining standard receivership requests.[6]

The scope of the problems facing the court was immense. No sector of the Texas economy escaped the effects of the depression. Small businesses and large corporations failed; casual laborers and multimillionaires sought protection from their creditors. Often one failure led to another, as suits for receivership, accounting, or foreclosure forced many of those involved into personal bankruptcy or other forms of extended litigation. The opposite also was true. Even where only one suit was filed, it often involved multiple creditors holding conflicting claims to the assets of the failed company. It was up to the court to balance these conflicting claims by slicing a suddenly small economic pie.

Though cases of this sort were of a unique nature, how the court treated competing claims to scarce resources can be seen in the admittedly extreme case of Houston millionaire John Henry Kirby. Kirby's economic fall in the 1930s, and the subsequent efforts of the court to lessen the impact of that fall, clearly shows the various demands placed on the court for help and how different cases quickly became interconnected. It also demonstrates how the court's response to those cases was manifested through both formal and informal actions. Finally, it uncovers the competing pressures shaping these actions, including Judge Kennerly's personal wish that no one get hurt by the court's performance of its duty, his goal of protecting and maintaining economic growth for Southeast Texas, and his commitment to private control of economic structures as the means of achieving this development.

By the early 1930s Kirby was one of the richest men in Texas. He had grown up poor near Peachtree Village in Tyler County. Admitted to the bar of Tyler County in 1885, Kirby began to acquire wealth by serving as local counsel to northern speculators in East Texas timberlands. He quit the law in 1890 and began to speculate in East Texas land, lumber, and railroads. By 1900 he owned two railroads, a lumber company, and over half a million acres of timberland.[7]

Kirby had even grander dreams. Following the discovery of oil at Spindletop in 1901, Kirby saw an opportunity to combine lumber and oil into a successful and profitable investment. Joining forces with New York City corporate attorney Patrick Calhoun, grandson of John C. Calhoun and one of the nation's foremost corporate lawyers, Kirby sought to organize two new concerns, one for oil and one for timber. The idea was that the lumber company would purchase 1.1 million acres of timberland, which it would sell to the oil company; that company, in turn, would lease back to the lumber company the right to cut timber on these lands. The expectation was that the revenues from lumbering would support both companies until oil was found.[8]

By October, 1901, the plan was ready to set into motion. Two companies, the Kirby Lumber Company and the Houston Oil Company, were chartered. Kirby then transferred his personal timber holdings to the Houston Oil Company and began buying additional land. Profits, however, came slowly. The lumber company produced less revenue than expected and failed to replace funds spent on acquiring new timber rights. As early as 1902 Kirby Lumber had trouble paying the fees owed the oil company. Kirby needed additional capital. A $500,000 loan from the Santa Fe Railroad helped keep the two companies afloat, but only for a time. In 1904 Kirby's luck ran out. Worried over the lack of revenue, Maryland Trust, holder of most of the two companies' bonds, forced both into receivership.[9] If both companies were to be reorganized successfully more capital was needed.

Desperate to save his dream, Kirby solved his problems by acquiring a $3 million loan from the Santa Fe Railroad. The railroad needed a steady supply of railroad ties and lent the money in return for a long-term contract for ties. In addition, Kirby was prohibited from shipping the rest of his lumber on other carriers, thereby guaranteeing steady use of the railroad's lines. To protect its investment, the railroad was given a lien on 29,667 shares of common stock in the Kirby Lumber Company, 66 percent of the lumber company's common stock, and a majority of Kirby's holdings in the company.[10]

Recapitalized, both the oil and the lumber companies rebounded from receivership and went on to profitable futures. Kirby's ties to the Santa Fe did not end, however. As the loans came up for repayment in 1914, 1919, 1922, 1928, and 1931, they were renewed, extended unpaid, or closed out with money acquired from new loans made by the railroad. The result was that much of Kirby's wealth rested on the continued willingness of the Santa Fe Railroad to maintain a permanent loan of over four million dollars in return for a first mortgage on Kirby's holdings of common stock in the lumber company.[11]

This arrangement proved profitable to both Kirby and the railroad for more than twenty years. On May 9, 1933, however, it began to fall apart. On that day, John Henry Kirby filed for personal bankruptcy. Hard hit by the stock market crash and the depression that followed, Kirby's personal finances crumbled after 1929. Though Kirby listed assets of $12,995,360.74 and liabilities of only $12,276,171.00, many of his assets were unsalable. As the "depression not only continued, but grew worse," Kirby related in a press release, his "property . . . [became] unmarketable."

> Four years ago my properties were reasonably and fairly worth $30,000,000. I then owed about $8,000,000, the great bulk of which was for security debts, accommodation paper, and endorsements for others. [However,] the earnings on my properties declined to a point where my income was exhausted, interest accumulated, taxes increased, and property values went down to an unheard of low level, with property hardly saleable at any price. After two years of effort to stem the

tide, I was reluctantly forced to the conclusion that the expected favorable upturn in values was too long deferred to be of practical help to me.[12]

In normal times, Kirby's personal difficulties would have had little effect on his lumber company, but in normal times Kirby would not have been bankrupt. At the end of his press release, Kirby assured the public that "this proceeding does not in any manner affect the Kirby Lumber Company or the Kirby Petroleum Company, financially or otherwise, nor does it affect any other corporation in which I am a director or an officer. Only my personal affairs and fortune are involved." However, Kirby's business associates were not as confident of this fact.[13]

Afraid of losing its $4 million investment, the Santa Fe Railroad threatened in October to call in its loan. Kirby had not paid interest on the loan since May, and the railroad was worried that if it waited with Kirby's other creditors for the estate to be liquidated, it would not regain its full investment. Writing to A. E. Kerr, trustee of the Kirby estate, the railroad stated that failure to pay the interest due would force it to foreclose on its lien on Kirby's 29,667 shares of common stock in the Kirby Lumber Company.[14]

Kerr objected to any proposed sale of the stock. As trustee of the Kirby estate, it was his job to protect Kirby's assets for the good of all his creditors. The contested stock formed more than 50 percent of Kirby's net worth. At fair market value, the stock was worth well in excess of the $4 million due. For Kerr to allow the Santa Fe to sell this stock would deprive Kirby's other creditors of the benefits of its sale.[15]

In addition, Kerr questioned the validity of the loan agreement. In his opinion, the agreement between Kirby and the Santa Fe Railroad was in violation of the Elkins Act of 1906, the Sherman Antitrust Act, and other antitrust laws. In arguing this point, Kerr noted that the agreement limited Kirby Lumber to the exclusive Santa Fe Railroad for moving its timber, provided for the purchase of rail ties by the railroad at below-market cost, and prohibited Kirby Lumber from acquiring any additional bonded debt without the prior approval of the Santa Fe. All of this, Kerr held, resulted in an illegal rebate in the form of restraint of trade. Kerr argued further that the loan was in reality part of a joint venture in timber cutting between the lumber company and the railroad. As such, the loan was never meant to be paid back. It was for these reasons that Kerr had failed to pay the interest due on the loan in the first place.[16]

Kerr threatened to bring suit to halt any attempted sale of the stock, but never did so. On January 20, 1934, the Santa Fe took the initiative. Through its subsidiary, the Southwestern Lumber Company of New Jersey, the railroad brought suit in the Southern District Court seeking a temporary restraining order requiring Kerr to prove his claims to the stock and, failing to do so, to be enjoined from disturbing the sale of the stock as set out by the loan agreement.[17]

At the same time that the Santa Fe initiated its suit against Kirby's stock, other creditors sought legal protection for their investments in the Kirby Lumber Company. Though also hard hit by the depression, Kirby Lumber was not insolvent in January, 1934. The company's total assets were well in excess of its liabilities, but poor sales had created a chronic cash shortage, making it impossible for the company to pay off its short-term obligations. Unless business conditions improved, this looked like a long-term problem.[18]

Filing its petition on the same day as the Santa Fe, K. H. Mastin and Company, an insurance firm, brought suit against the Kirby Lumber Comany for unpaid debts. Mastin and Company held $11,371.68 in unpaid notes for premiums protecting portions of Kirby Lumber's mills and timberlands. Afraid that Kirby's personal financial difficulties would harm the already-shaky finances of the lumber company and "certain" that if other creditors were individually to press their claims for payment on the lumber company the resulting litigation would "create an irreparable injury and loss to the [company] and to its creditors," Mastin and Company sought the appointment of a receiver.

Mastin and Company proposed that the receiver take over and operate the lumber company "as a trust fund for the payment of [its] creditors." Immediate liquidation of the lumber company's assets was unlikely to realize even a percentage of the company's true worth. Worse, such action would scatter the "administrative, technical and sales forces" on which much of the intangible value of the company rested. "Unless a Receiver be at once appointed to take charge and possession of the property and assets of [the] defendant," Mastin and Company claimed in its petition, "the defendant will be subjected to a multiplicity of suits and conflicting litigation in this and other courts, . . . its assets will be dissipated and sacrificed [as] some creditors . . . secure preferences over other creditors . . . [and the] defendant's business will be interrupted and destroyed." If Mastin and other creditors were to regain the full value of their debt, it was necessary for the court to "preserv[e] the value of [the] defendant's property and assets as a going concern" until the present economic difficulties had ended.[19]

Mastin and Company was joined in its suit by the Western Improvement Company, an investment concern, which held a $150,000 note from the lumber company. This debt had been acquired in December, 1931, when Kirby Lumber was unable to pay off a loan from the Houston Oil Company. Rather than have the note become past due and force the oil company to initiate foreclosure proceedings against the lumber company's property, Kirby had asked the investment company to purchase the loan in return for a second mortgage on sections of the company's property. This was agreed to. In January, 1934, however, Kirby Lumber failed to pay the interest due. Worried about the loan's security, the Western filed a foreclosure suit on January 20. Five days later it joined its suit with that of Mastin and Company and seconded the demand for the appointment of a receiver.[20]

On January 24, Kirby Lumber consented to the appointment of a receiver. With dozens of creditors seeking immediate payment of their debts, and two who had already filed for a receivership, a friendly receivership was the only available means of saving the company from total liquidation. As Kirby saw it, he had little choice in the matter.

With no opposition from the lumber company, Judge Kennerly ordered Kirby Lumber into receivership the next day. He named former state senator McDonald Meachum receiver. A corporate lawyer and associate counsel for the Houston Oil Company, Meachum had a clear understanding of the issues involved in the lumber company's receivership. He was also an experienced receiver, having successfully reorganized the Signal Oil Company in the late 1920s.[21]

As receiver, Meachum's job was to turn the company around and pay off its debts in full. To do this he was given full authority to "preserve, manage and maintain" the company's property "as a going concern." This included the right to contract and sue, to hire and fire, and to work the property as needed. As was traditional in the district, the court reserved "the right to pass upon and approve any and all contracts" and "legal proceedings" entered into by the receiver and also demanded periodic reports on the status of the receivership.[22]

Court protection did not end Kirby Lumber's problems. As part of his order, Judge Kennerly required Meachum to pay "all expenses incident to the creation . . . or administration of . . . the business; all monies due . . . to employees . . . [and other] claims for labor and services . . . [and all] taxes . . . [due] on any of the properties belonging to the . . . company." Last, he was to hold the "balance of the funds" subject to "further orders from the Court." Yet, to pay off each of these debts in full, Meachum was forced to use money earmarked for long-term obligations to cover more immediate ones. On two occasions in particular, he sought authority to use funds deposited in a sinking fund created for the repayment of the company's $30 million first mortgage to pay back taxes and purchase needed insurance. In both cases, the court approved the request and the withdrawal was made.[23]

It was these actions that caused renewed difficulties. The Whitney National Bank of New Orleans, trustee for the company's bondholders, disapproved of Meachum's use of money earmarked for redeeming the company's bonds to pay off more immediate expenses. The bank had held off pressing any claims on the lumber company throughout January and February in hopes that the receiver would protect bondholder investments as he successfully reorganized the company. Meachum's use of the bond funds to pay off short-term debts and unpaid taxes threatened these investments, however. To protect the value of the bonds, the bank filed a foreclosure suit on March 6, seeking either the liquidation of the company (which would mean immediate repayment of the bonds) or the appointment of a receiver to protect bondholder rights. After a short hearing, the court combined this suit with those filed in January and once again named Meachum receiver.[24]

Combined, these cases posed practical and personal difficulties for the court. Kirby was a personal friend of the judge. One of the first cases Kennerly had faced as a referee in bankruptcy was the 1904 Houston Oil receivership. For two years Kennerly worked alongside Kirby to save the oil company. In 1906, when Kennerly reentered private practice, his first client was the same Houston Oil Company, for which he became chief counsel. Kennerly retained this position until he entered the bench in 1931. Professional contacts had led to social ones. Despite belonging to different political parties, both Kirby and Kennerly held similar political views, especially in their dislike of Franklin Roosevelt and his New Deal. Each respected and liked the other.[25]

Kirby's economic difficulties troubled Kennerly. As a friend, Kennerly wished to protect Kirby. But, as a judge, it was his job to safeguard the interests of all litigants. As Kennerly saw it, Kirby had taken on his debts in good faith, planning to pay them off on time and at full value. His creditors had lent money or provided services to him with the same expectations. That Kirby was unable to pay off these debts was "no fault of Kirby, and no fault of the plaintiff. It [was] a condition of many of humankind."[26] None of the litigants deserved to be hurt. The problem was how to help Kirby without harming the interests of his creditors.

Adding to Kennerly's problems were the wider economic effects of these suits. Kirby Lumber was one of the largest lumber companies in Texas. Employing seventeen hundred persons and contracting with hundreds more for goods and services, the company provided a livelihood for between fifteen thousand and twenty thousand individuals. Liquidation meant unemployment for the company's employees and hardship for their families. It also meant more difficulties for an East Texas economy already hurt by the depression.

Balancing the needs of defendant, the plaintiffs, and the region was a difficult goal. What was best for one group was not necessarily good for another. Whose rights should the court protect first? Which would better serve the needs of the region, and should this have any effect on the judge's decision?[27]

Kennerly's answer to this dilemma was to seek to balance the costs and benefits of settlement among the claimants as equally as possible, limited only by the law's specific dictates. As had been the case when he ruled on the proper extent of public economic regulations, the judge felt that it was unjust for one claimant to receive a benefit or pay a cost that was greater than that of similar parties. While the dictates of American law required that a winner and a loser be declared, the judge sought to balance the costs paid by the loser with the gains acquired by the winner so that neither gained an "unearned" benefit or paid an "unjust" cost.

With this goal in mind, Kennerly willingly provided bankruptcy protections to Kirby in 1933. He realized that it was unlikely that Kirby would ever be able to pay off his creditors in full; the value of the Kirby estate had fallen too much. By appointing a trustee to conserve and divide the estate up systematically, Kennerly assured that each creditor received a fair share. While all would lose some part of the value of their investment, none would go away empty-handed. At the same time, bankruptcy allowed Kirby to retain at least some of his personal property and to live his life free from the worry of paying his obligations.[28]

The same reasoning shaped the decision to appoint a receiver for Kirby

Lumber. Receivership protected the company from immediate and chaotic dismemberment by its creditors. This solved three problems. First, it assured that the rights of all the lumber company's creditors were protected. In any settlement of the company's status the court could assure that the settlement would be an equitable one in which all creditors received their fair share of the company's worth.[29] Second, it kept the company operating. This saved the jobs of thousands of workers and protected the Texas economy from potential disaster. In addition, by keeping the company operating, it raised the possibility that the company's fortunes could be turned around and its creditors paid off in full. Finally, receivership sheltered John Kirby's interest in the company. The receiver, Meachum, was a friend of both the judge and Kirby. In appointing Meachum as receiver, Kennerly assured that Meachum would allow Kirby to retain significant influence in the company's operations. In 1935 a friend of Kirby's noted how "[Kirby] continues as the head of the Kirby Lumber Company today, working side by side with the receiver, . . . a compatriot who knows and understands the Kirby mind and soul."[30]

Balancing the costs was more difficult in the Santa Fe case. The railroad had a legitimate claim on Kirby's common stock. The loan agreement specifically gave the Santa Fe the right to sell the stock if payment were withheld for over thirty days. By the time of the trial, Kirby owed the railroad over six hundred thousand dollars in interest and capital payments. No plans to pay this or any future interest existed. To allow the stock to be sold, however, would deprive Kirby's other creditors of its worth. It would also cost Kirby control of the company.

Kennerly had to make a choice between litigants, specifically between the railroad and Kirby's other creditors. As the law then stood, only one claimant could receive the value of the stock; the question was, which one? In making his choice Kennerly fell back on the dictates of contract law. And the law favored the railroad. "That [Santa Fe] is entitled, under the law, to sell the stock, to pay the principal and interest . . . of its debt, . . . I entertain no doubt," the judge wrote. Though Kirby's other creditors would be "deprived of the . . . value" of the debt, the facts of the case and the law's meaning were "clear." The Santa Fe Railroad had a superior claim on the stock through its first mortgage, and thus had the right "to sell the stock under such safeguards as equity would impose." Only if the proceeds of the sale exceeded the amount of the debt would Kirby's other creditors have a right to claim a portion of the stock's value.[31]

All this depended on the invalidity of Kerr's claims as to the illegal nature of the loan agreement and the railroad's connections with Kirby Lumber. If the "defendant [was] right on the questions he raise[d] as to the validity of the plaintiff's" lien on the stock, then the sale should not be allowed, the judge noted in his decision. These contentions were not supported by the facts of the case, however. "My conclusion," Kennerly ruled, "is that [the business relations between the railroad and Kirby Lumber] do not constitute a violation of [federal] statute." Basing his conclusions largely on Kirby's own testimony, the judge felt that these ties were a normal part of doing business. "I do not think the simple purchase by a railway company of ties from a shipper, and/or the loaning by a railway company of money to a shipper at the usual, customary, fair and reasonable rate of interest, where there is no evidence that under and by such transactions the shipper's property is transported at less than tariff rates, and no other advantage is given the shipper, . . . violates the law."[32]

This decided, Kennerly ordered that an agreement be written between the railroad and the lumber company for the immediate sale of the stock. This agreement was to fix a minimum sale price for the stock, one that was large enough to cover "the expenses of the sale, plus the amount of the principal, interest and attorney's fees." Any returns beyond this amount were to be given to Kerr for distribution to Kirby's other creditors.[33]

This left the problem of protecting Kirby's interest in the company. Officially, there was nothing the judge could do for Kirby. With the sale of the stock his ownership of the lumber company was at an end. Unofficially, however, the judge still watched out for his interests. Soon after Kennerly's order to produce an agreement, the lawyers for both the lumber company and the Santa Fe came to the judge's office and told him they had a decree. They asked Kennerly to read it and tell them what he thought of it. Before he even read the order, the judge asked what the lawyers had done for "the old gentleman [Kirby]?" "Well," the lawyers replied, "we didn't do anything for him." "You mean," asked the judge, "you took his company, his stock, his office and everything that he had, and left him nothing at all? . . . I don't want to read that decree," Kennerly declared, "go over it again and work with it a bit to give the old man something." A few days later, the lawyers returned and told the judge that they had a decree that he would approve of. The lawyers had put in the decree that Kirby would have an office and a secretary plus all necessary expenses for the rest of his life. "Now that sounds more like a decree that I would want to read," the judge replied.[34]

The Kirby case was unique as to size, the power of those involved, and the close ties of the litigants to the judge. Kennerly's mix of official and unofficial action, however, his emphasis on protecting and balancing the interests of all the litigants involved in the case, and his insistence on retaining economic resources in as productive a form as possible were typical of the way he operated receivership cases during the depression. Even if he did not personally know the litigants and even if the economy of entire counties rested on the outcome of the case, Kennerly strove to balance the needs of both the litigants and the region within the requirements of the law.

For example, in November, 1930, D. H. Burnham of Illinois, a minority stockholder in the otherwise family-owned Arcola Sugar Mills Company of Fort Bend County, brought suit for the appointment of a receiver, an accounting of the company's books and the liquidation of the corporation. Burnham held four hundred of the company's seventy-five hundred shares of stock, acquired in 1921 from Kate Scanlan, president and majority stockholder, as security for a nineteen thousand dollar debt. Burnham held this stock for nine years in place of repayment. As the economy became more depressed, however, he required a more liquid form for his capital. Sale of the stock on the open market, though, was unlikely to recover even a portion of the original debt, nor was selling the stock back to the company an option. On a number of occasions prior to 1930, Scanlan had made it clear that she was not interested in paying off the debt.[35] If Burnham was to recover the full value of his investment, he needed the help of the court.

The problem with satisfying Burnham's request was that the sugar company was not insolvent. Normally, insolvency (or at least the inability to pay off short-term debts) was a prerequisite before a federal court would impose a receivership.[36] The company was in a state of disorganization, however. As originally set up in 1903, its assets consisted of an eighty-six hundred–acre sugar plantation and a sugar mill. By 1914, however, all sugar manufacturing operations were discontinued. The mill equipment was sold off the following year. Thereafter the company operated its eighty-six hundred acres as a general farm and generated a small profit growing cotton and corn. In addition, Scanlan, who owned 90 percent of the company's stock, treated the company as if it were her personal property, mingling her personal finances with those of the company to the point that it was impossible to separate the company's assets and liabilities from her own. In essence, as the court was later to note, Scanlan gave herself an interest-free loan of over one hundred thousand dollars of the company's money. This misappropriation of funds was hidden, in turn, by financial records so "inadequate" that the court found it impossible to discover the company's exact financial state.[37]

It was this disorganization that Burnham relied on to support his request for judicial action. Prior to turning to the court, he had complained of Scanlan's misappropriation of company funds to the company's officers (all of whom were her relatives or close friends). Nothing was done, however. Burnham argued that, despite the company's solvency, the change in business function, the keeping of inadequate books, and, most of all, the subsequent inaction of the company's officers placed his investment in jeopardy. Only through the appointment of a receiver empowered first to reconstruct the company's books and then to liquidate the assets so discovered could the protection of his investment be assured.[38]

The company denied all of Burnham's contentions, including his ownership of the stock. Judge Kennerly, however, was convinced both of Burnham's ownership of the stock and of the need for the court to act. Given the "abandonment of the corporation of the purposes of its incorporation," and the obstructive action of its officers when Burnham sought satisfaction, Burnham was due "some character of relief" from the court, the judge ruled. The question was, what sort of relief was appropriate? Kennerly had no wish to harm Scanlan any more than was necessary to protect Burnham's interests. Nor did he wish to disrupt a going economic concern unless it was absolutely necessary. To this end, after he had decided to grant Burnham's request for relief but before he reached formal judgment, Kennerly asked the opposing counsel to "suggest in their briefs the character of relief which would best conserve the Estate and be least expensive."

Arcola Sugar, however, refused to compromise. In its brief the sugar company continued to deny Burnham's right to demand liquidation of the company. Article 1387 of the Texas Revised Civil Statutes of 1925, the brief read, limited minority stockholders to seven methods for obtaining the dissolution of a chartered corporation. Running from waiting until the charter expired to the insolvency of the company, none of these methods involved instituting a federal receivership and obtaining liquidation of the company for changes in business functions or criminal actions on the part of the company's officers. Burnham would simply have to wait for the company's charter to expire, find a way to gain a majority of the company's stock, or sell out, the brief concluded.[39]

Angered by the company's unwillingness to compromise, the judge saw no option but to grant Burnham's request for liquidation. As he noted when summarizing the dissolution methods proposed by the company, if Article 1387 were held to control in this situation, Burnham would be denied "adequate relief" for his legitimate concerns. This was wrong. As the judge saw it, Burnham was due some form of relief. Kennerly had hoped to save the farm from liquidation, but since the sugar company would make no suggestions as to how to achieve this relief short of dissolution, liquidation was his only choice.[40]

Hence, even where the issues were small and the parties involved politically unimportant, producing a compromise decision protecting the interests of both the litigants and the wider economy was foremost in Kennerly's mind. Equity or the law's dictates often forced the judge to rule against one litigant, as in the Kirby bankruptcy case or the Burnham case. But, even in such cases, the judge still strove to limit the disruptions caused by the court's actions, for in protecting these business leaders from harm, Kennerly also protected the region's private economy.

The effect of such actions was that, during the depression, the court took the traditional supportive function of bankruptcy and equity to new extremes. In the past, bankruptcy petitions such as Kirby's would have brought only a minimal response from the court. Traditionally, in bankruptcy matters, the court appointed a bankruptcy referee who handled, largely unsupervised, all of the details in liquidating the bankrupt's property. The referee, in turn, operated through the trustee, elected by the bankrupt's creditors, who saw to the actual liquidating of the property. Yet, with hundreds of individuals seeking protection, many of them powerful men like Kirby and all involved in some way in the region's economy, the court felt a duty to take a greater interest in such proceedings. Hence, though federal bankruptcy statutes strictly limited the right of a participant in bankruptcy proceedings to seek review from a district court judge, Judge Kennerly expanded the right to review in bankruptcy matters. In

December, 1933, for example, the Walker-Craig Company, creditor to J. W. Ainsworth, a bankrupt Brownsville grocer, sought review of a decision of the referee in bankruptcy to disallow its claim. Though the proper filing procedure had not been followed in appealing the referee's decision, the judge agreed to hear the case and overturned the referee's decision.[41]

The same willingness to provide protection to those needing help shaped the court's decisions in foreclosure suits. Often, at the end of its decision in a foreclosure case, the court reserved "all questions, issues, matters, and things not . . . disposed of . . . for further adjudication, . . . [so that] any party to [a] cause may at any time apply to the Court for further relief . . . in any matters not herein specifically provided for." When new issues were raised or new litigants appeared, the court issued supplemental decrees.[42]

The judge's efforts to help those in need occasionally went beyond the litigants in a case; they also included the receivers he appointed. Most receivers were personally known to Kennerly and many were in need of work. The judge's son, Everton Kennerly, tells a story from around 1937, when he was returning from Huntsville, where he had attended court and saw Sam Davis, a fellow lawyer, "with his thumb out" hitching a ride. Everton picked Davis up and drove him home to Houston. On the way he asked Davis why he was hitching a ride. Davis replied that things were bad for him. "I don't know where my next meal was going to come from" Davis admitted. "I am a desperate man." Returning home, Everton told this story to his father, asking him to help Davis, whom the judge also knew. A few weeks later, Everton received a call from Davis, thanking him for his and his father's help. "I'm calling from a phone in my own office. It's been years since I've had both at the same time." After hearing of Davis's problems, the judge had appointed him receiver of a small oil company.

Of course, Kennerly could not help everyone entering his court, nor did he attempt to do so. Most bankruptcy or receivership cases were handled by a referee and never really came before the judge. Kennerly only stepped in if the issues of the case posed special or troubling problems. Also, where legal doctrine or statute went against a litigant, as in the Santa Fe case, the judge followed the law's direction, even if it cost a litigant a fair return. Finally, the focus of the court's actions was toward helping those who already had property. Unemployed laborers or sharecroppers did not turn to the Southern District for help. As always, the Southern District was first and foremost a court for the business community.

Yet, despite these limits, Kennerly on the whole successfully balanced competing claims on scarce resources. In 1936 the Kirby Lumber Company was released from receivership, its creditors paid off in full, and its operations put in working order. Other receiverships had similarly successful ends.[43] Even when a company had to be liquidated, the costs of this process were equally borne by all its creditors and investors. While not every claimant could be helped, enough were helped to keep the economic system—battered but seaworthy—afloat.

III

The court's services in preserving scarce economic resources ameliorated only part of Southeast Texas' economic problems. Renewed growth was also needed if the depression's effects were to be negated. This, in turn, required a shift in business's economic practices.

Before 1930 the Southeast Texas economy, built on the existence of abundant resources and abundant finances, grew at a rapid pace. Welcomed at first, this growth soon began to strain the region's infrastructure and threatened to limit future growth. Stability became a priority among the region's economic elite, and business practices, standards, and rules were adopted by local business to provide cohesion and stability in an economy founded on consistent growth. The system did not always work efficiently, but major crises were avoided.

The depression changed everything. For the first time since the turn of the century, the region suffered a sustained contraction of the economy. Suddenly, structures and practices created to provide stability faced unforeseen problems. Government intervention supplied some, but not all, of the standards and rules that business needed to survive in the new economic reality of depressed prices and insecure investments. In those areas where federal regulations did not help, the court offered an alternate and familiar source of standards and rules, one to which business leaders seeking answers to financial and operational business crises for which past practices were no guide quickly turned.

These requests for help came in the form of lawsuits involving conflicts between two or more litigants. The issues, however, went far beyond the immediate action requested. Business needed general rules of practice, and it was through the court's decisions that it sought those rules. Often the court simply provided a forum for a negotiated settlement, which it would back by its authority. Where the court did make a decision its emphasis was to help business and the region, but always within the limits set by the law.

One of the first sectors of the economy to seek help from the court was the oil industry. State and federal regulations provided some standards aimed at solving the industry's overproduction problem, but left other difficult issues unresolved. One of the most troubling was the validity of oil and gas leases.[44]

When the East Texas oil field was discovered in 1930, the major oil producers moved cautiously. Before initiating large-scale leasing campaigns, they awaited the results from other test sites. Their hesitation allowed small independent producers to lease the best sites by 1931, thereby locking the majors out. The effect on the industry was devastating. Along with costing the majors a share of the East Texas field's vast oil reserves, their failure to act quickly also fostered opposition to proration in East Texas.

Where the majors dominated a field, proration was generally supported; they could afford to pump less oil in the short term for a larger return in the long. The independents who dominated the East Texas field could not afford to wait for a return on their investment. With limited capital and large debts to pay, they had to pump as much oil as they could immediately or go out of business. The result in East Texas was a free-for-all that harmed the entire industry by lowering prices and wasted large amounts of oil by overproducing.[45]

The majors learned their lesson in East Texas. Thereafter, whenever new fields opened, they secured adequate leases to control the field and dominate its development. In the race between the majors and the independents to acquire new leases, corners were sometimes cut and less-than-honest methods used.[46] Subsequently, suits claiming fraud were brought in state court. The oil companies, using diversity jurisdiction, preferred that these cases be removed to federal court.

In this manner a series of oil and gas lease suits were brought before the Southern District Court beginning in 1933. The first were brought by residents of Polk County against the Sun Oil Company of New Jersey. In April and May, 1932, Sun Oil had initiated efforts to acquire mineral rights to small tracts scattered throughout Polk and nearby counties. J. F. Darnell, a leasing agent of the company, had the job of securing these rights. He, in turn, subcontracted with O. C. Garvey, a "highly trained and skillful Mineral Lease man," to cover a ten-by-twenty-mile section of Polk County. Garvey purchased the mineral rights on his own behalf, using his own money, and later transferred those rights to the company at an agreed-on price of $1.25 per acre for a mineral lease and $2.50 for a mineral deed. Garvey's profit came from the difference between what he paid the landowner and what he received from Darnell.[47]

By June Garvey had fulfilled his contract, obtaining mineral leases and deeds that were subsequently transferred at the agreed price to the oil company. Not everyone was happy with this result. Some of the farmers who had sold mineral deeds, as opposed to leases, complained that Garvey had acquired those deeds fraudulently. They thought they had sold Garvey "an ordinary commercial ten year Mineral Lease, with 1/8 royalty to Lessors, and the usual drilling obligation on the part of [the] Lessee." But, in fact, as a result of "fraudulent representations" by Garvey, they had actually executed a mineral deed. Instead of a lease in which ownership remained with the lessor and which had a yearly fee of fifty cents per acre due if drilling was not started by a set date, the landowners transferred to Garvey ownership of all the minerals on the land, "except a 1/8 royalty" should Garvey or his assigns "elect to develop the land for minerals and should obtain production in paying quantities." Garvey was under no obligation to develop the land.

It was undisputed that Garvey had acquired the mineral deeds by fraud; however, since he had already transferred his rights in the property to Sun Oil, the question arose whether Garvey's fraud invalidated the oil company's interest in the minerals. Sun Oil professed no knowledge of Garvey's fraud until after purchase. Unless Garvey had acted as an agent of the company at the time the deeds were signed, legal doctrine, the company's lawyers claimed, held that his fraud did not bind the company and thus invalidate its ownership of the minerals.[48]

In the first of these suits, *J. H. Bush and Wife v. Sun Oil Co.* (April, 1934), Garvey's status was the only issue in contention. Bush, through his lawyer, argued that Darnell's contract with Garvey to purchase mineral rights in effect made Garvey an agent of the company. As agent, his fraud was the company's fraud and the contract was invalid. Sun Oil responded that Garvey was an independent contractor and thus only personally liable for his fraudulent actions.

Judge Kennerly concentrated on the provisions of the contract. If Garvey was Sun Oil's agent, the minerals in Bush's land would have passed immediately to the defendant with the signing of the deed. Yet the contract specifically noted that Garvey was to purchase the land with his own money and then sell the mineral rights to Sun Oil. This was "a fact inconsistent with the view that Garvey was [the oil company's] Agent." If Garvey was the company's agent, Sun Oil would have been bound to purchase the leases he acquired whether they were the ones the company wanted or not and at the price Garvey had paid. Garvey, however, received more from the oil company than he paid for the deed, and in one case, had a proffered lease rejected by Darnell. Viewed in this light, the judge argued, it was clear that "Garvey was not Defendant's agent, and that [Sun Oil] . . . was not bound by the fraudulent conduct of Garvey in connection with the Deed from [Bush and his wife]." Kennerly therefore upheld Sun Oil's rights to the minerals and enjoined Bush and his wife from thereafter asserting any rights to the oil.[49]

With this decision, the remaining six cases against Sun Oil were quickly settled, five out of court four months later, with Sun Oil retaining ownership of the minerals in return for an additional cash payment of between one hundred dollars and three hundred dollars per plaintiff. The sixth case, *D. R. Bush and Wife v. Sun Oil Co.*, was remanded to state court.[50]

Subsequently, the court allowed exceptions to the foregoing rule. On October 31, 1935, it held that when a fraud was perpetrated and its instigator retained a right in that property, judgment against that person or company could be had. The court later held that, where an oil company contracted for an oil lease, it was bound to fulfill all the lease's requirements. Fictitious drilling or payments would not satisfy the court. In this case, ownership of the minerals was returned to the landowner.[51]

Similarly, Austin County residents sued G. T. Blankenship and the Farmers Mutual Royalty Syndicate, Inc., an investment cooperative from Oklahoma, claiming that the syndicate was bankrupt in December, 1931, when its agent, T. P. McLain, purchased a one-half right in their mineral holdings in return for syndicate stock. The company's bankruptcy was not made known to the farmers until after the transaction was completed. In addition, plaintiffs claimed that McLain lied to them when he completed the deed. They were told that the deed was for a "non-participating royalty conveyance," which would entitle the defendant to no rights beyond sharing any royalties acquired by the landowner if and when the mineral rights were leased. In reality, the deed transferred total ownership of one-half the minerals to the syndicate and Blankenship and the right to veto any contract for mineral development made by the landowner.

Before trial, a compromise settlement returned complete title in the subsurface minerals to the landowners except for a one-eighth share of any royalty the owners might gain in leasing the land for development. This right to a one-eighth share was to be held by the Farmers Mutual Royalty Syndicate for "twelve years or as long thereafter as oil or gas is produced therefrom in paying quantities." The royalty interest did not give the syndicate any right to "participate in lease bonus money or in delay rentals, but only in production from said property," or to hinder any leasing plan agreed to by the plaintiffs.[53]

The decisions on these fraud cases favored and strengthened the ability of oil companies to obtain mineral leases and deeds. The use of independent leasing agents was common in the industry.[54] If the court had ruled that they were direct agents of the company, their use might have been curtailed, and the oil companies would have had to conduct expensive title searches and other verifications to assure themselves that no fraud had been practiced.

Not all conflicts over mineral rights involved fraud. In many litigations litigants held conflicting claims to the same mineral rights or disputed lease provisions. Most of these cases involved oil companies holding mineral leases to the disputed land. Their opponents were landowners who claimed that the oil companies had in some manner subordinated the owner's rights to the minerals, usually by paying inadequate royalties. Afraid that these claims would threaten the validity of their leases, oil companies brought suit to validate their title to the minerals. In line with its equity decision, the court usually upheld the companies' titles, occasionally requiring them to pay additional fees to the landowner.[55]

In some cases the order of who sued whom was reversed. Landowners who felt that the oil company was shortchanging their royalties would sue the oil company for return of title plus damages. In one prominent case, dozens of landowners sued a number of oil companies, including the Humble Oil and Refining Company, for title and damages of over $2.5 million. After five years of litigation (1936–41) the court again confirmed the defendants' claims to the land, but required them to pay damages to plaintiffs for failing to supply full royalties.[56]

By 1936 the court had set the basic ground rules. Where an oil company used fraud to gain a lease, or failed to live up to the full dictates of the contract, the court held it accountable. Beyond this limit companies were free to acquire mineral leases by practices resulting in losses for landowners.

Insurance was another industry searching for answers to problems it could not solve alone. By the 1920s it was among the nation's most profitable businesses, but chronic uncertainties, including unfriendly state regulations, insecure investments, and excessive claims litigation, threatened ruin. The arrival of the depression only made these problems worse.[57]

Contested claims were the most common source of uncertainty in the 1930s. Arising when more than one individual claimed the benefits of a policy, this opened the insurer to "the hazard of double liability and to a liability in excess of the amount which it actually owes, . . . [and] in addition, . . . to enormous vexation, harassment and expense in answering and trying to keep up with and otherwise protect itself [from] . . . various claims."[58] In accident cases, problems existed with the extent of insurer liability. Although liability insurance policies listed the conditions under which they operated, accident victims still attempted to bring insurance companies into court whenever possible, even when the company, in its opinion, was contractually free from liability. The result was extended litigation in state courts and potential liability beyond the express provisions of the policy.[59]

Afraid that depressed economic conditions encouraged expensive and time-consuming litigation, insurance companies headed off multiple and unreasonable suits in the state courts by exploiting, first through interpleader and then through declaratory judgments, the federal courts' equity powers. Interpleader is a motion made to an equity court by someone holding a thing of value claimed by a group of people. The individual making the motion places no claim on the thing of value and wishes to turn it over to the proper owner; however, this person does not know which claimant has the best right to it. The holder, worried about possible harm from proceedings brought by various claimants, petitions the court to force the claimants to litigate their title between themselves. If no compromise is worked out by the defendants, the judge then decides who has the right to the thing of value.[60]

Interpleader suits could be filed in state court, but insurance companies preferred to file in federal court under diversity jurisdiction. As did other large businesses, the insurers felt the federal courts provided more uniform and sympathetic results in their decisions. More to the point, once suit was filed in federal court the insurance company was protected from multiple suits filed by different claimants.[61] It was with this end in mind that Congress in 1917 and again in 1926 expanded the federal courts' statutory equity jurisdiction to include interpleader for "any casualty company, surety company, insurance company or association or fraternal or beneficial society" in which the amount in dispute was larger than five hundred dollars and diversity of citizenship existed.[62]

In the Southern District, interpleader suits tended to follow a general pattern. For example, in December, 1930, the Chicago Fire and Marine Insurance Company came before the court under diversity jurisdiction and the Interpleader Act of 1926. In January, 1930, the company had insured G. H. Shepard's San Angelo home against fire. On March 24, this house burned, causing damages of one thousand dollars. Three weeks later, the company issued a check for one thousand dollars payable to G. H. Shepard, the National Bond and Mortgage Corporation, and Henry Laithe, trustee for the Maryland Casualty Company of Baltimore. The latter two recipients held mortgages to Shepard's home and were included on the policy so that their interest in the property "would not be invalidated by any act of neglect on the part of the insured."

The check was never cashed. As the insurance company noted in its petition, "the three recipients could not agree among themselves as to the division of the funds, and in fact each . . . claimed all of said funds for himself, . . . making claim against" the insurance company for the whole one thousand dollars. Adding to the difficulties, a fourth defendant, William Cameron and Company, also claimed the money, arguing that Shepard had assigned it the proceeds of the policy.

Faced with four claimants, each demanding one thousand dollars and threatening to bring suit in state court to recover this money, the insurance company turned to the Southern District Court for a settlement. "Plaintiff," the insurance company argued, "is only interested in having the claims of said parties properly litigated and the money awarded to whoever may be entitled to same, and this plaintiff properly discharged and released and acquitted under its said policy, settlement and check and the various suits and claims filed and made against it."[63]

When the court accepted this case, the defendants reevaluated their position. Faced with a choice of taking the case to trial and accepting the judge's decision or reaching a settlement among themselves, they chose the latter option. When the case came up for trial on November 14, 1931, the court was informed that a settlement was reached, with William Cameron and Company receiving the one thousand dollars less court costs and attorney fees. Accepting this settlement, the court ordered that William Cameron and Company receive the one thousand dollars and perpetually enjoined the defendants from "instituting or prosecuting any suit or suits in any court against [the] plaintiff arising out of this controversy."[64]

In cases where no settlements were reached, the results of the judge's decisions were largely the same. In August, 1938, Samuel Merkur, owner of the New York Fur Company, a retail and repair establishment, purchased ten thousand dollars in fire insurance for his property and the property of his customers from the National Liberty Insurance Company of America. Four months later, Merkur's store was destroyed by fire. A five thousand dollar settlement was agreed on and paid. Rather than using this money to pay off his creditors, however, Merkur fraudulently used it to purchase a house from H. Seltzer.[65] In February, 1939, Merkur's creditors claimed the proceeds of the policy, which had been paid to Seltzer. In order to avoid extended litigation, the insurance company removed the case to the Southern District.

Examining the facts in the case, Judge Kennerly agreed with the creditors' contention that Merkur was guilty of fraud in using the proceeds of his policy to purchase a house, but, the judge decided, this fraud did not invalidate Seltzer's claim. Articles 3996 and 3997 of the Texas *Revised Civil Statutes* of 1925, the Texas law with respect to fraud and fraudulent conveyances, held that a debtor was "entitled to a . . . homestead exception under the Constitution and other Laws of Texas, [and] may appropriate all or any part of his property to the purchase of a homestead, and that his creditors may not prevent his doing so." Since Selzer had no knowledge of Merkur's fraud and had presented a valuable consideration for the five thousand dollar policy, he was entitled to the proceeds. Kennerly ordered the money paid to Selzer and cleared the National Liberty Insurance Company of all future liability.[66]

For the insurance industry, then, the motion of interpleader in the federal courts provided a quick and secure means of policy settlement. No matter what the outcome of the case or how the decision was reached, insurance companies fulfilled their needs for a decision regarding distribution of the money and freedom from future suits. The same general result was reached, though by a different means, by the second equity power used by the insurance industry to create certainty–the declaratory judgment.

In June, 1934, Congress passed the Declaratory Judgment Act, which "in cases of actual controversy" allowed the "Courts of the United States . . . to declare rights, and other legal relations of any interested parties petitioning for such declaration, whether or not further relief is or could be prayed [for], . . . such declaration . . . hav[ing] the force and effect of a final judgement or decree."[67] For the first time, parties in dispute over a contract, deed, lease, will, or other written instrument could turn to the federal courts and receive a listing of each litigant's responsibilities and rights, costs and gains. This declaration, though "not followed by a decree for damages, injunction, specific performance, or other immediate coercive decree" was conclusive as to the legal rights accruing under the facts of the case. In any future litigation arising from this dispute, the declaration would stand unchanged as the foundation for any orders or decrees. As a result, in most cases the declaration "suffice[d] to settle [the] controversy."[68]

Declaratory judgments were like a life preserver to the insurance industry. Insurance companies faced hundreds, perhaps thousands, of cases a year about their contractual liability. Usually associated with auto collisions, but also including other forms of accident and life insurance, these litigations developed when policyholders were involved in incidents that the insurers felt were not covered by the policy. In such cases the insurance company withheld payment, arguing that it was not liable under the policy's provisions. If the injured party or parties disputed this claim, however, and threatened to include the insurance company in future litigation the company faced a dilemma. Should the company, at great expense and a possible "waiver of its defense of noncoverage" defend the policyholder in litigation? Or should it refuse to help, protecting its claim of noncoverage, and take the chance of a negative judgment in state court? A declaratory judgment solved this dilemma. Conclusively listing the insurance company's liability to the insured, it made clear the company's options. If the company was held liable under the policy, it defended the policyholder or paid the claim; if not, the company could safely refuse to act, protected by the federal court's declaration of its duties.[69]

Within a year of the Declaratory Judgment Act's passage, insurance companies were calling on the Southern District Court to provide this service. Two of the first cases, one decided in favor of the insurance company and one against, show the pattern of the court's response and how it served the insurance industry's need for stability.[70]

On June 9, 1935, a Ford coupe driven by Sidney Plummer, Jr., age eighteen, collided with a truck driven by Murry T. York, killing York and injuring the truck's other passengers. The Ford belonged to Carl Short, Inc., an oil drilling company and Sidney Plummer, Sr.'s, employer. It had been lent to Plummer, Sr., for use in carrying out company business; Plummer, Sr., was supposed to be the only driver of the car. On the night of the accident, in fact, Plummer, Sr., had informed his son that he was not to use the car.

Following the accident, Murry York's heirs and the other passengers in the truck initiated suit against the Plummers, Carl Short, Inc., and the Ohio Casualty Insurance Company. Ohio Casualty had insured the car for up to ten thousand dollars of accident liability, but it refused to pay any claims. The policy specifically limited the coverage to employees of Carl Short, Inc., and others provided with the "express or implied consent" of the insured for company business. Since the car was not on company business when the accident occurred—Plummer, Jr., was joy riding—and no consent was given for the car's use, Ohio Casualty felt it did not have to cover the accident. Worried that juries in state courts might disagree with this interpretation of the contract, the company brought suit under the Declaratory Judgment Act.[71]

Arguing in the alternative, the defendants in this case, including not only the Plummers and Carl Short, Inc., but the injured parties in the accident, held first that the court had no jurisdiction to hear the case but that it properly should be heard in state court, thereby implying that the federal Declaratory Judgment Act was an unconstitutional extension of the federal courts' powers. They went on to argue that, if the case could be heard in federal court, it should be heard on the law side of the docket, and not equity. This would open the facts to a jury, which commonly was believed to be biased toward the injured parties in insurance cases. Finally, if the judge did rule on the case, the defendants asserted that his ruling should go against Ohio Casualty. Plummer, Jr., they noted, had driven the car in the past with his father's permission. This past permission provided the implied consent needed for the insurance policy to cover. Ohio Casualty was therefore "bound and obligated to defend" the Plummers in all suits filed against them and, further, to pay any judgments.[72]

Ohio Casualty denied each of these points. Taking as a given the constitutionality of the court's jurisdiction, the company pointed to both the specific provisions of the policy limiting use of the car and the elder Plummer's prohibition on the night of the accident. Together, the company argued, these facts proved that the policy was invalid in this situation.[73]

Before ruling on the facts of the case, Judge Kennerly discussed the legitimacy and constitutionality of the statute. Questions existed about the right of insurance companies to seek a declaratory judgment for matters of "liability as distinguished from a right." The Eighth Circuit Court of Appeals held that the act was limited to rights only. Other circuits disagreed. So too did Judge Kennerly. The law's intent, as Kennerly understood it, was to provide certainty, and the judge saw little difference between certainty over rights and that over contractual liability. In both, the result of the court's actions was the same specific listing of each litigant's legal rights and duties. All this depended, of course, on the law's constitutionality. The judge, however, saw the addition of declaratory judgments to the federal courts' jurisdictional powers as well within Congress's constitutional discretion. He also felt that the suit was a proper equity action. "While I would be unwilling to hold that actions at law may not in certain cases be brought and prosecuted under the act, it is clear that the powers conferred by the act upon the District Courts . . . [are] of an equitable nature, and one generally exercised by courts of equity, rather than by courts of law."[74]

With the constitutionality and jurisdiction of the act upheld, the outcome of the suit depended on the facts of the case and how they related to the law's intent. The judge saw these as favoring the plaintiff. "It is clear that the car at the time of the collision was not being used with either the express or implied consent of either Carl Short, Inc., Carl Short, or Plummer Sr., . . . or of any person named in the provision[s]" of the policy. "It follows" Kennerly concluded, "that plaintiff should have judgement" in its favor and be protected from future litigation.[75]

Two weeks after the Ohio Company filed for a declaratory judgment, the Commercial Casualty Insurance Company of New Jersey did the same. This case involved a July 5, 1935, collision in Fort Bend County between a Plymouth coupe, owned and operated by T. E. Humphrey, Jr., and a car driven by A. P. Pierce, Jr., whose passenger was W. R. Tull. The Plymouth was insured by Commercial Casualty for twenty thousand dollars accident liability.

Unlike the Plummer case, no one disputed the fact that Humphrey was at fault for the accident and protected under the policy. Rather, the company sought a declaratory judgment because it felt that Humphrey had violated the policy after the accident, thereby invalidating the agreement. The policy said that "the assured [Humphrey] shall not voluntarily assume any liability or interfere in any negotiations for settlement, or in any legal proceedings, or incur any expense or settle any claim, except at the assured's own cost, without the written consent of the company." Immediately following the accident, however, the company argued, Humphrey had "without the plaintiff's knowledge or consent, voluntarily assumed liability to the defendants and voluntarily agreed to pay the other defendants their damages sustained as the result of the accident." Commercial Casualty felt "no duty to defend Humphrey or to pay any judgement which may be recovered against him by the other defendants." Yet unless the court sustained this belief, the company faced the possibility of multiple suits over this accident.[76]

The defendants denied that Humphrey had in any manner assumed liability or interfered with negotiations for settlement. The insurer was therefore still "bound and obligated under its policy . . . to defend . . . Humphrey in any action brought against him . . . for damages growing out of such collision and to pay off, within the limits of the . . . policy, any judgements . . . that may be rendered."[77]

With no challenges to the constitutionality of the act, the court went directly to the facts of the case in reaching its decision. As Judge Kennerly saw it, Commercial Casualty's liability depended wholly on whether Humphrey had violated the contract after the accident. If he had not done so, as the judge ultimately decided, then it followed that Commercial Casualty was "liable to Pierce in the amount of any judgment recovered by Pierce against Humphrey, in accordance with the terms and provisions of the policy."[78]

Commercial Casualty appealed this decision, asking Judge Kennerly to reverse his holding.[79] Yet despite its discomfort with the court's decision, the company had achieved its main goal in bringing suit: it knew that it had to defend Humphrey and cover the costs of his accident. Winning freedom from fiscal responsibility would have been nice, but knowing its exact liability was a necessity if the company were to plan for the future and thus survive. As with interpleader, in declaratory judgment cases the insurance companies won no matter which way the court ruled.

The court's declaratory rulings also provided stability in a second way. These decisions provided a kind of blueprint for the limits of proper business practice in the insurance industry. In so ruling, the court informed insurance companies of the limits to their rights to restrict their liability contractually. Where clear violations of the provisions of a policy occurred, the companies were protected. Otherwise, they had to live up to their agreements, even if so doing caused them significant expense.

The court took a similar position toward insecure investments. As the largest single long-term investor in the nation, insurance companies had more to lose than most as the investment market collapsed. The sudden decline in the value of stocks and bonds caused by the depression forced many insurance companies grave difficulties. Many were forced to foreclose on their investments, turning credit investment into ownership. For example, by 1937, the Metropolitan Life Insurance Company was the nation's largest owner of farmland, holding over seven thousand farms in twenty-five states.[80] Yet such investments were not the worst problem faced by the industry. Public securities that could not be foreclosed on, such as municipal bonds, caused insurance companies greater difficulties.

By the mid-1930s "defaults by municipalities had become a national problem." It was estimated that by January 1, 1934, some 1,729 counties, cities, and irrigation districts were in default of their bonded debt. This number included over thirty-seven cities with a population of thirty thousand or more and hundreds of county road and improvement districts. The total investments involved added up in the billions of dollars.[81]

Defaults in public securities left large investors such as insurance companies in a difficult situation. In most of cases, the only available option if their investments were to be saved was to restructure the municipality's debt load, replacing the old bonds with new longer-term, lower-interest issues. The idea was to accept an immediate loss of interest revenue and thereby protect the longer viability of the debt.

Restructuring of this sort was a difficult task, however. When a municipality or other local taxing district was in default of its bonded debt, the usual response was to organize a bondholders' committee, which negotiated a reorganization plan. This plan, known as a "refunding agreement," listed the existing bonds involved in the agreement, issued new replacement bonds at a lower interest rate, and set up a procedure for replacing the old bonds with the new. Involvement in this plan was completely voluntary, however. Under existing laws nothing prevented a bondholder from retaining old securities and demanding payment at the old, higher rate of interest. Further, any creditor of a defaulting community had the right to seek a writ of mandamus against the officers of that community and demand immediate payment of past-due interest. "Such mandamus proceedings were . . . decided without reference to the rights of the other bondholders or to the debt problem in its entirety." The only issue examined by the court was the relations between the debtor and the creditor. If the court found that a valid debt did exist and that payment had been defaulted, it could order payment and, if necessary, the levying of taxes for the satisfaction of this particular debt. With such tools at their disposal, dissenting bondholders had the potential to be a serious nuisance and delay reorganizations as the money necessary to fund the restructuring was diverted to pay them off. And, if enough bondholders dissented, they transformed from nuisances into significant barriers to successful reorganizations.[82]

In most cases of municipal default, it proved impossible to garner unanimous support for a reorganization plan. While most large investors were willing to take a long-term view of debt readjustment, many small investors were not. As Justice Cardozo noted in 1936: "experience makes it certain that generally there will be at least a small minority of creditors who will resist a composition [reorganization plan], however fair and reasonable." Thus large investors faced the dilemma of surrendering to dissenting creditors, ignoring their demands, or fighting them in court. In most cases, they chose the last option, seeking methods by which to minimize the disruptive effects of minority bondholders through the equity powers of the federal courts.[83]

This was the situation in the Southern District in December, 1933, when the Hidalgo County Water Control and Improvement District No. 1 defaulted on its bonded debt, forcing a majority of its creditors to initiate the first of many bond suits to be brought before the court. Throughout the district, but especially in the southern half, municipalities, counties, and local taxing districts faced enormous debts loads. These debts, totaling tens of millions of dollars, had been approved by local voters in the development craze of the 1920s. For instance, Hidalgo County Water Control and Improvement District No. 1, one of half a dozen water control districts in the county, had an outstanding debt of almost two million dollars in 1934—and this was after the county already had paid off almost half of the contracted debt.[84] These bonds were funded by local property taxes and used to build and maintain roads and irrigation projects. The depression, however, lowered property values in the Rio Grande Valley by as much as 70 percent. This decline in property values devastated the tax base of local communities. Even with lower property values, residents were unable to pay their taxes. Faced with a taxpayers' revolt, many county boards lowered property taxes. The result by 1933 was default by dozens of communities on their bonds; dozens more followed in the next years.[85]

At the request of large investors and the defaulting communities, creditor committees were organized to attempt to restructure the debt load to more manageable levels. In the case of Hidalgo County Water Control and Improvement District No. 1, the committee consisted of business leaders and bankers Frank Calvin, John Getz, R. W. Crummer, Lon Hill, Jr., John R. F. Rives, and John L. Hunt. On December 7, 1933, the committee and the board of the water control district reached an agreement. Their plan called for issuance of 1,675 new bonds, each worth $1,000 to be called Refunding Bonds series 1934. Unlike the bonds they replaced, which paid 6 percent interest from their issuance, the new bonds paid interest along a sliding scale, starting at 2 percent and increasing one percentage point every three to five years until 1960, at which date the bonds paid a steady 6 percent. The plan called for these new bonds to be traded at par value with the old and for the water district to create a sinking fund setting aside $2.10 for every $100 valuation of taxable property to pay the interest and principal.[86]

The committee, cognizant of bondholders who opposed this plan, sought to head off any attempts to disrupt the plan. Two days after the agreement was signed, Frank Calvin and the other members of the Creditors' Committee brought suit in the Southern District Court against the water district, its board of directors, and the bank in which the water district deposited its funds. Using the dissenter's tool of the equity mandamus suit, the committee claimed that the water district's default on its obligations to pay interest on its outstanding bonds had caused real and potential harm to the holders of these bonds, that, as these "wrongs . . . complained of [were] of an official nature," the complainants' "rights to damages, if existent [were] doubtful" if brought in a normal suit at law. "The duties sought to be enforced arise by virtue of a trust relationship, and the intervention of a court of equity is necessary to enforce the trust duties herein set out[:] . . . to marshal and distribute said District's assets, . . . to distribute and allocate it taxing and assessment powers among claimants who have trust interests . . . and contractual rights therein, and . . . to restrain the arbitrary and inequitable exercise of official power under color of right." In other words, if the bondholders were to receive justice, it was necessary for the court to apply its equity jurisdiction to this case, to "determine the measure of complainants' rights and respondents' wrongs" and to prevent the "impairment, . . .

sequestration, . . . and distribution of funds" to others before the plaintiffs were paid.[87]

Though worded as a complaint against the water district's board of directors, in reality this complaint was an attempt to acquire court protection of the refunding agreement. By having the court rule the existing bonds "valid and binding obligations of . . . Hidalgo County Water Control and Improvement District No. One" and the water district in violation of this obligation, the court had the power to order that the provisions of the agreement be carried out. This did two things. First, it made the agreement a "binding contract" to which all who agreed to it had to adhere. Second, it allowed the court to order the use of tax money already on deposit or to be collected for the payment of this specific obligation. This protected the sinking fund from being used to pay dissenting creditors.

Judge Kennerly willingly provided each of these services. After summarizing the refunding agreement, he ruled it a "just, proper and equitable" settlement and ordered its implementation. In addition, he went beyond the agreement's provisions, ordering the water district to withdraw half of its present funds, some $22,987.32, and to use this money to start the sinking fund called for in the agreement. He also ordered that any proceeds from delinquent taxes be added to this fund.[88]

The reorganization of Hidalgo Water Control District No. 1 set a pattern for subsequent bond cases throughout the district. As cities, counties, and taxing districts in the Rio Grande Valley defaulted on their bonds, refunding committees were created and negotiations between the committee and municipal officials on the exact method of refunding were entered into. Subsequently, an equity suit would be filed in the Southern District Court seeking enforcement of the agreed-on refunding plan. In all but a handful of these cases, the result was automatic, the court quickly approving the negotiated reorganization plan and ordering immediate enforcement of its specific provisions.[89] Thereafter, as was common with other equity suits, the court retained jurisdiction to assure the smooth operation of the ordered plan.

On a number of occasions, retention of jurisdiction proved a necessary precaution. Despite specific court orders requiring payment of interest to bondholders, some county and state officials refused to authorize the distribution of funds. Where this occurred, the court quickly created supplemental orders requiring immediate payment and threatening contempt hearings if the order was not immediately complied with. In one case, when the comptroller of the state of Texas refused to authorize the use of tax money already collected to pay interest on Hidalgo County road improvement bonds, the judge held the comptroller in contempt, releasing him only after he changed his position and distributed the money.[90]

Judge Kennerly did everything in his power to help private investors protect their capital through bond reorganizations. But there were limits to how far he would go in helping bankrupt municipalities reorganize their debts. He saw the court's role as supportive of the private efforts of the municipality and its creditors to restructure the municipality's debt; it merely acted to assure compliance with the final refunding contracts worked out by these parties. At no time did the court take independent action affecting anyone except those involved in the litigation. This was an important limit to the judge's thinking; to violate it would take his court beyond the proper limits of mandamus equity jurisdiction and the constitutional protections of private and public property.

Kennerly held this position as early as the Hidalgo Water Control District No. 1 case. Before concluding his decision in this action, the judge made it clear that his decree involved only the rights and obligations of those bondholders who had formally agreed to the restructuring plan. Listing those bonds involved in his ruling (approximately 60 to 70 percent of those extant) the judge held that "no findings herein contained . . . shall inure to the benefit of any holder of any other bond or obligation not adjudicated in this decree." While the remaining bond-holders might be deserving of the same protections as the plaintiffs in this case, it was their choice to make. For them to receive court protection, they would first have to join in a refunding agreement with the municipality.[91]

In 1934, with municipal bankruptcies at an all-time high and suits by minority creditors hindering the restructuring process in hundreds of localities, Congress attempted to ease the refunding logjam by passing the Municipal Bankruptcy Act. This act formalized the procedures of municipal debt reorganizations along contemporary lines, but added one significant difference. As with these earlier cases, the intent of the new act was to provide legitimization and enforcement for restructuring plans worked out beforehand by a municipality and its creditors—to provide, in other words, a sort of "'short receivership' to be employed at the end rather than the beginning of readjustment negotiations." Once the plan was accepted by the court, however, it became binding on all creditors, whether they had agreed to it or not. In this way the problem of the dissenting minority was simply circumvented.[92]

This last aspect of the law troubled Kennerly. Though few public debtors invoked the act in the two years following its passage, a number of these cases were filed in the Southern District.[93] The first of these to come to trial involved Cameron County Water Improvement District No. 1.

Organized in 1914 along with seven other water improvement districts, Cameron County Water Improvement District No. 1 embraced some forty-two thousand acres of land and had outstanding, in 1934, over eight hundred thousand dollars in long-term, 6 percent bonds. Like other irrigation districts in the Rio Grande Valley, Cameron County Improvement District No. 1 faced grave financial difficulties as a result of the depression. As the district noted in its petition: "about two and a half years ago the country entered into a general financial depression causing great reduction in the price which the farmers received for their fruits and vegetables; the price being placed at such a low basis that even it did not pay the cost of production, thereby making it impossible for the farmers of said District to pay their Flat Rates and bond tax." With the farmers unable to pay their taxes, the irrigation district was insolvent and unable to "meet its debts as they mature[d]." Having already garnered the support of 30 percent of the bondholders to a refunding plan, and confident that "upon hearing" an additional 30 to 40 percent "of bondholders" would agree to the plan, the irrigation district petitioned for a court-ordered reorganization under the national Municipal Bankruptcy Act.[94]

Soon after its filing with the court, the bankruptcy petition was contested by creditors holding just over 5 percent of the irrigation district's bonds. This opposition gave the judge the opportunity to rule on the act's legitimacy. Kennerly did not waste this opportunity. In a short decision, he declared the national Municipal Bankruptcy Act unconstitutional on December 1, 1936.

Kennerly did this for two reasons. The first involved the constitutional separation of powers between the federal government and the states. Noting that the bonds in question were "contracts, constitutionally and statutorily executed by the state of Texas, through petitioner, its local agency," the judge asked if "Congress [had] the power to confer upon [the] Court [the] jurisdiction to readjust" this debt. His answer was a resounding no. Congress had passed the Municipal Bankruptcy Act as a temporary relief measure under emergency powers first used to combat the depression in 1933. As the act noted in its prologue: "There is hereby found, determined and declared to exist a national emergency caused by increasing financial difficulties of many local governmental units, which renders imperative the further exercise of the bankruptcy powers of the Congress of the United States." Yet even granting the emergency to be real, the judge still felt that all this was of "no consequence if [the act was] contrary to the federal Constitution." "The leading case under the [Bankruptcy] act of 1898 . . . while holding section 8, article 1, of the Constitution to be broad in its scope, falls far short of being authority for the view that Congress may confer jurisdiction upon this court to readjust, in the manner provided in this act, bonds issued by a sovereign state and/or its agency, and payable out of funds provided by taxation, except by permission of such state." As Texas had not yet given this permission, "I conclude that Congress has no such power." To have held otherwise, Kennerly continued, "would be not only to go far beyond the real purpose and meaning of section 8, article 1, of the Federal Constitution, but to strike down the long-recognized rule that under our dual system of government (national and state), one government may not by its laws impair the sovereignty of the other."[95]

Kennerly also voided the Municipal Bankruptcy Act out of a concern for its coercive nature. At various points in his decision, he noted how the irrigation district never claimed or showed that any "effort [had] been made . . . to collect the tax levied to pay the bonds." Nor did the petitioners show any valid reason why this money could not be collected through tax delinquency proceedings in the state courts. All the irrigation district claimed was that "during one or more years of 'financial depression,' the price received by farmers for their fruits and vegetables has been below the cost of production, making them unable to pay their . . . tax[es]." Did this include all taxpayers and all the taxable property in the district? The petition did not say. The judge was also troubled by the irrigation district's apparent disregard for the interests of minority bondholders. Nowhere did the petitioners claim that the refunding plan was in the bondholders' best interests. Rather, the petition noted how the refunding plan was "*absolutely satisfactory to the Cameron County Water Improvement District Number One*."[96]

With both of these points in mind, the judge did not look kindly on the irrigation district's petition for help. "Clearly," the judge wrote, "petitioner by its petition does not present a case authorizing this court to strike down more than 50 percent of the face value of the bonds held by contestants, and require contestants to receive, . . . approximately 49.8 percent of their face value, when so far as appears from petitioner's petition, there may be funds available, or funds may become available, by the slightest diligence on the part of petitioner in collecting the tax levied to pay the bonds in full. . . . Clearly, the act of Congress, if valid, does not contemplate or authorize a proceeding so unfair and inequitable."[97]

The judge's point was clear. His court would help those seeking security in troubled economic times, but not if this help gave an unfair economic advantage to the litigants or threatened private property rights. Where other business leaders or investors were involved in a dispute but chose not to become involved in the case, the court limited the range of its decision so as not to harm the dissenters' interests. As always, the court wished to balance the costs and benefits of its actions when helping businesses. To this end, it continued throughout the 1930s to provide the more limited mandamus protections for municipal refunding plans. One case, filed in November, 1936, even involved Cameron County Water Improvement District No. 1.[98]

It is here that bond suits join with insurance and oil lease cases as examples of how the court required limits in the actions of private business and public officials at the same time it redistributed scarce financial resources. As long as both acted in good faith and made no attempt to force others to join their agreements, the court supported and protected their efforts; where the opposite was true, the court refused to help and even hindered such actions. While individual businesses might be harmed by the court's decisions, as a whole, business got what it needed from the court: general rules of practice suited to a new economic reality.

IV

Judge Kennerly's objections to the Municipal Bankruptcy Act stand as a symbol of the court's judicial philosophy throughout the depression. Split between various overriding goals—combating the depression's effects, helping business, and upholding the law—the court acted in both negative and positive ways. Always, the aim was to balance the costs and gains so that no one individual or group was unduly harmed and in this way to assure that the law's protection or property was maintained. Only by meeting both of these needs could the court's goal of fostering private regional development for Southeast Texas be maintained.

7. Public Policies and Private Concerns

THE SECOND WORLD WAR

I

America's entry as a combatant in the Second World War broadened the federal government's role in American life to unprecedented levels. Wartime expansion required centralized government setting of production and transportation priorities, directing of the use of raw materials, and control of labor allocations. It also required strict regulation of many actions once deemed private; rationing, price and wage controls, and increased taxes attended the transfer of private resources to public use.[1]

The Southern District Court, as a part of the federal government, supported these military and economic regulatory efforts by condemning land for military use and enforcing the draft, prosecuting violators of price controls and rationing, and seeking to stabilize an economy and society transformed by war. It provided these services unhesitatingly, devoting most of its time and effort between 1941 and 1945 to servicing this public agenda. This shift toward public issues was made possible as prewar obstructions to the court's execution of public services almost vanished during the war.[2]

The Second World War was generally popular with the business and political elites who shaped the federal court's private agenda—at least in the first years. Motivated by both patriotism and the opportunities for sharing in wartime profits, people from all levels of the business community—corporate executives who joined the federal bureaucracy as "dollar-a-year-men," members of the small business community who staffed local draft and rationing boards—placed themselves staunchly behind the war effort. This was especially the case in Texas and the other western states, where local business "saw the war mobilization program as an unusual opportunity to secure long-desired manufacturing facilities," thereby "accelerat[ing] industrial development" and creating an "increasingly diversified and self-sufficient" regional economy.[3]

Wartime government controls, therefore, did not evoke the same negative responses inspired by similar controls passed in the 1930s. Motivated by patriotism, profits, and satisfaction in sharing in government, Texas and national business accepted government regulations as necessary evils and raised few challenges in the courts. Where private, non-war-related cases were filed, they were either quickly completed or placed on the inactive docket until the war was over.[4]

Yet the concerns that motivated the court's private agenda were not forgotten. Where cases involved property rights or the proper extent of government controls over property and person, the court's actions were still motivated by anxiety over the need for continued regional development, a belief in the sanctity of private property, and a determination to limit government regulation to its "proper" sphere of influence. While business might have found government economic practices acceptable, Judge Kennerly was not so sure. He fully supported the war effort, but worried that the government might go too far in directing the economy and so threaten important protections of private property. It was not that he expected the government to overstep constitutional protections in its efforts to win the war, but an unintentional attack was always possible.

Two other judges assigned to the Southern District in the 1940s felt, on the whole, the same as Kennerly. In 1938 Congress had authorized a second judge for the Southern District of Texas to sit primarily in the southern three divisions, and FDR had appointed Texas governor and former state attorney general James V. Allred. Allred resigned in May, 1942, to run for the senate and was replaced by Allen B. Hannay, son of a former U.S. attorney and a state judge since 1930. Like Kennerly, both Allred and Hannay were members of the region's political/business elite: while in private practice, each had served as counsel to local and national businesses. Although Democrats and holding more liberal views than Judge Kennerly, both Allred and Hannay agreed with Kennerly that private property was the foundation of American society and that the role of the law was to protect the proper use of that property. Where they differed from Kennerly was in the amount of government regulation they saw as compatible with this conception of the law. Allred, a New Deal liberal, was especially willing to accept more government intervention in the economy than was Kennerly; however, even Allred saw the government's powers as limited when they moved beyond regulating for the public good to taking private property without adequate compensation. The rule of law, Allred maintained, had to be upheld at all costs. Hannay's views fell somewhere in between. The result was continuity in the court's decisions despite the addition of a second sitting judge.[5]

While the court's preoccupation with private interests did not hinder its enforcement of federal wartime statutes within the Southern District, it did shape the court's approach to executing those regulations. Sitting almost as a review board on the propriety of government statutes, the district's judges demanded that proper procedural limits be followed consistently. Whenever they felt that government actions threatened basic rights they warned the government of its errors and, when necessary, sought to constrain the government into maintain-

Judge Allen B. Hannay being sworn in as judge, August, 1942. Courtesy Houston Metropolitan Research Center, Houston Public Library

ing essential procedural safeguards. This was done even when the court's action in some way hindered the government's legitimate war efforts. Where safeguards were maintained and rights protected, however, the court enforced federal wartime statutes to the fullest.

The private agenda also came into play in the court's response to the economic and social transformations caused by the war. By 1945 a full 70 percent of its private civil cases were the result of economic changes caused by the war effort. Mobilization had brought industry to the region and the attendant economic and social costs of industrial work. The Texas legal system, however, was unprepared to deal with these costs, especially as they related to labor and industrial accidents. Created at a time when Texas had few industrial workers, and hence few industrial accidents, the Texas Industrial Accident Board proved unable to cope with the flood of new cases brought on by war. Ultimately it was left to the courts, including the Southern District Court, to settle these issues. Drawing on the values that underlay its private agenda and its tradition of creating new business rules in response to changing economic patterns, the court's handling of these cases worked to integrate the needs of Texas' new industrial reality into the region's preexisting social, economic, and political structures.

Judge James V. Allred. Courtesy *Fort Worth Star-Telegram* Photography Collection, Special Collections Division, University of Texas at Arlington Libraries

Though no longer the court's primary concern, the private agenda therefore still motivated its actions throughout the Second World War and shaped its perspective toward the public and private issues it ruled on while not significantly lessening its service to the public agenda.

II

As in World War I, in the Second World War Texas was a favored site for military bases. By war's end, the army had constructed or expanded fifteen major training posts and ten airfields in Texas. Along the coast, the navy added to the military's presence with an air training station and numerous watch and repair bases.[6]

In most cases, the proposed sites for military bases were held by private owners. It was necessary therefore, for the government to initiate condemnation proceedings in the federal courts to transfer the land to public ownership. Even before Pearl Harbor, two major and over a dozen minor military condemnation petitions were filed in the Southern District to acquire military bases, storage facilities, or training grounds. The largest, the Corpus Christi Naval Air Station, was filed in 1940. Encompassing over twenty thousand acres in three counties, the base ultimately represented government investment of over $100 million. By war's end it was the navy's largest training facility. The army acquired sections of Matagorda Island and Matagorda Peninsula as bombing test sites. Stretching along the Texas Gulf Coast for over one hundred miles, these properties comprised thirty-five thousand acres. The remaining less-massive takings ran down to the few acres necessary for gun emplacements along the Gulf Coast.[7]

America's entry into the war brought more condemnations. From January, 1942, to June, 1946, 256 condemnation actions were filed in the Southern District. At first, they were implemented solely for airfields and training depots; as the war continued, an increasing number were for munitions plants, shipyards, and other facilities for war production, particularly for petrochemical plants to produce synthetic rubber and phosphates. Condemnations were also used to improve port facilities on the Houston ship channel and to build oil pipelines from Texas to the East Coast.[8]

The court's role in condemnation suits varied as the proceedings progressed. The first steps, transferring possession and title of the land to the government, required little beyond administrative action from the court. Various acts of Congress gave the secretaries of the army and the navy authority to condemn all lands "necessary . . . to provide for the establishment of" a military base or depot. Takings for factories and transportation facilities were made under the authority of the Federal Works Agency and the Reconstruction Finance Corporation. Where especially large takings were proposed, Congress usually provided special authority. In all cases, it appropriated funds to purchase the land.[9]

Since the government's right to take the land was undisputed, the court merely was required to review the "Petition in Condemnation" to ensure that lands were taken for a public use, that the owners had been informed of the taking, and that enough funds had been deposited in the court's registry to assure "payment of [a] just and adequate compensation to the parties entitled . . . as a result of [the] condemnation suit." These requirements met, the court was bound by law to order possession transferred to the government. In cases where speed was necessary, as with military bases, the court granted the government possession the same day the petition was filed. In all cases, possession was granted within a short time of the petition's filing.[10]

The court then appointed three commissioners to judge the land's value at current market prices. Statute prescribed that these commissioners should be residents of the county of the taking and be "familiar" with property values in the region. The court varied the commissioners' occupations to increase the chances for familiarity. In Corpus Christi, for example, a lawyer, a realtor, and a lumber dealer were commissioners. These were also semipermanent positions, with the court appointing the same commissioners to hear proceedings in several similar cases.[11]

If both the landowner and the government were satisfied with the commissioners' award, the court continued in its administrative role and ordered final title transferred to the government and compensation paid to the landowner. The case then closed. If one or both parties were not satisfied with the commissioners' award, however, the court's role shifted from administration to adjudication, for statute gave any participant the right to demand a trial. This trial was not an appeal of the commissioners' decision but a full hearing, with the court investigating all the facts and reaching its decision independently of the commissioners' report. This allowed the court to shape the results of government action and set what the judges felt were necessary limits on the condemnation process.

Most proceedings in the Southern District ended with the commissioners' award. A number of takings were contested, however, as the U.S. attorney's office in Houston was under orders to object to all awards in excesss of the amount deposited in the court's registry. Landowners, in turn, objected when they felt the awards did not take into account the total value of their land or the future earnings in that land.[12]

The most common cause of dispute was the value of subsurface oil and gas on condemned property. Some proposed bases, test sites, and factories embraced potentially valuable oil reserves. If included in the final valuation of the land, these mineral rights expanded the cost to the government, often beyond what the War Department deemed proper; if omitted, the award undervalued the property.

In December, 1940, the Justice Department, concerned over potential costs in valuing oil reserves and before any commissioners' report on mineral values was in, ordered the U.S. attorney to "have no further negotiation with oil company representatives respecting possible agreement on value on lands" pending further instructions.[13] Those instructions, when they came, were to negotiate mineral rights apart from title with the landowners, especially for the large Corpus Christi and Matagorda Island/Peninsula condemnations.

Over the next year partially unsuccessful negotiations continued between the government and the landowners. Both sides desired the retention of the mineral rights by the owners, but they disagreed on the method of returning those rights.[14] The government wished to amend its original petition of condemnation "to exclude the oil, gas, and other minerals in and under the land, but denying the owners thereof the right to take such oil, gas, and other minerals for a period of ten years or such lesser period as the Secretary of War may determine to be consistent with the public interest."[15] The majority of the landowners felt that, "under the original declaration of taking, title to the land in fee simple passed to the government and that the court is without power to permit . . . the declaration of taking . . . to be amended." Rather, they "attack[ed] the original declaration of taking and ask[ed] that it be set aside in its entirety as void and ineffective," since it clearly took more property than was needed for public use. This achieved, the government could recondemn just the land needed.

After almost a year of deadlocked negotiations, the government moved to amend its declaration of taking, leaving it to the court to decide which method was proper. In January, 1942, the court, in a joint decision by Judges Kennerly and Allred and noting the importance of this motion in reference to the "thousands of acres of coastal land" involved in condemnation proceedings within the district, disagreed with "the landowners' contention that the declaration of taking does not contain a sufficient statement of 'the public use' for which the lands were taken." Instead, it accepted the landowners' contention that the government's motion for an amended taking was improper.

Examining the statute under which the condemnation was made, both judges felt that it was "clear . . . that fee-simple title to the land was vested in the government by and at the time of the original declaration of taking and the simultaneous order of the court . . . declaring such title had vested in the government." It was true, the judges noted, that the court had retained jurisdiction of the case for "such further orders, judgments and decrees as may be necessary." But this was "patently for the purpose of carrying out the remaining provisions of the statute dealing with the award and distribution of compensation for the lands." Thus, while it was clear that "the Secretary of War, . . . at the time of [the] original declaration, [was] not aware of the fact, well known in Texas, that our coastal lands have considerable potential mineral value; and that in the very understandable urge of preparing for national defense . . . failed to take into consideration the possible cost to the government of acquiring these mineral estates," this fact was immaterial to the case. "The only question for us to determine is whether or not the Secretary has the statutory authority to amend the declaration and thereby eliminate those mineral rights." The court did not find the authority. "We are of the opinion that the government's title may not be divested without the consent or approval of Congress. We do not find such consent expressed in any existing statute. There is no express authority for the filing of an amended declaration."

Holding that even in wartime property rights had to be protected from arbitrary government action and that proper legal procedures were mandatory, even if both sides desired a common result, the court ruled against both the government and the landowners. The original taking having been valid, the judges ruled, the land and minerals remained in the government's hands unless and until Congress directed otherwise.

The Justice Department went to Congress for this authority (which, on October 21, 1942, it received, the condemnation subsequently being modified on March 17, 1943).[16] Meanwhile, government lawyers continued to search for other methods by which to limit the cost of mineral rights on condemned lands. Two months after the court's decision in the Matagorda case, the U.S. attorney made another attempt to lower costs by filing a motion in some of the Corpus Christi air base condemnations that asked the court to give special instructions to the commissioners, particularly that they be instructed that "the United States of America in this case is condemning the fee simple title, . . . [and that] it is your duty to assess the value of the land taken as an undivided fee simple absolute, without regard to whatever separate ownerships existed in the property on the date of taking." The assumption behind this instruction was that where one individual owned the land and another the mineral rights and the values of those rights were adjudged separately, the value of the minerals would be more than if they were valued together. The hope was that adjudging the value of land and minerals together would keep down the cost to the government.[17]

Judge Kennerly refused to accept this logic. Protecting the landowners' right to a full return on condemned property seemed to him to deserve priority. "The assumption that the Commissioners [in ruling separately on the land and mineral values] would find a greater value for the whole tract than they would if they proceeded as indicated by the suggested rule is without merit" he wrote. "The Statutes of the United States and of Texas, indeed the Federal Constitution itself, contemplates that when private property is taken for public use, the owner or owners, . . . must be compensated, and such compensation cannot be made except by determining under the Statutes the value of the property taken from each owner. It is clear that in all cases, the Commissioners should hear and report not only the value of the entire title taken in a tract of land, but also the value of each separate interest, ownership, or claim therein." The judge denied the government's motion for instructions.

Hindered once again in achieving its cost-cutting goal, the government had no option but to seek a jury trial to attempt to lower the costs of condemned land in those cases in which it felt the award was too high. Five such motions were filed in early 1942, going to trial by court order on June 9.[18] After days of conflicting testimony on the mineral value and a heated debate over the court's instructions to the jury, the jury decided for the government and awarded the landowners less compensation than the commissioners had.[19]

The government was pleased by this decision. The cost of this land was lowered and a better precedent created for valuing potential mineral reserves. The defendants were not as pleased with the jury's decision. One, the Eagle Lake Improvement Company, appealed the decision, arguing that three mistakes had been made in the trial. First, the court had allowed a sick juror off the jury during its deliberations, so that compensation was decided by a smaller body than the statutory and constitutional dozen. Second, the court's charge to the jury had minimized the potential worth of the minerals under the land and was thus both wrong and misleading. And, finally, the jury's verdict was "insufficient" and "not supported by the evidence." The company sought a new trial before a new jury.[20]

Ruling in February, 1943, Judge Hannay denied the company's motion. The defendants had received a "full and fair trial and . . . no error was committed therein which necessitat[ed] a new trial." Texas law allowed a jury in a civil case to continue deliberations even when a sick juror withdrew, as long as nine jurors remained. Further, condemnations of land by the government were not common law but statutory suits, and the Seventh Amendment's requirement of a jury of twelve in common law suits did not apply. The court had acted properly in allowing the jury to reach a verdict as it had.

With regard to the defendants' argument concerning how best to compute the value of subsurface minerals, the defendants had proposed that the jury base its award on the potential value of the oil less cost of production; the government argued for valuation only on present value. The court had properly accepted the government's definition in its instructions.[21] As Judge Hannay noted in quoting Justice Holmes's dicta in such cases: "the question [the court had to answer] was, what has the owner lost? Not, what has the taker gained?"

Responding to the complaint that the jury had ignored defense evidence, the court simply upheld the jury's right to decide the facts as it saw fit. Quoting from a recent Southern District of Georgia decision, the judge noted that, "while a jury has no right arbitrarily to ignore or discredit the testimony of unimpeached witnesses, so far as they testify to facts, and that a willful disregard of such testimony will be grounds for a new trial, no such obligation attaches to witnesses who testify merely to their opinion; and the jury may deal with it as they please, giving it credence or not as their own experience or general knowledge of the subject may dictate." The allegedly ignored testimony complained of was, in fact, mere opinion. Therefore, the jury "had an exclusive right" to ignore it and "their findings [in] such questions should not be disturbed."

As long as procedural protections for the rights of property holders were maintained, the court hesitated to hinder the rapid transfer of title to the government. Where the jury ruled in favor of higher compensation, the court was equally adamant that title should transfer and payment of compensation be made. In late 1942, for example, the government objected to the commissioners' awards in four tracts taken in the Buffalo Bayou improvement condemnation. The commissioners had awarded compensation of between $34 and $89 per acre, depending on the tract. At trial, however, the jury awarded significantly higher compensation, from $70 to $125 per acre. Arguing that the jury's awards were excessive, that the court's charge to the jury had been wrong, and that certain evidence presented to the jury was invalid, the government sought a retrial. Like Judge Hannay at Corpus Christi six months earlier, Judge Kennerly rejected the motion, holding that any errors in either the instructions or the testimony that might exist did not affect "the substantial rights of the parties." The judge further held that "the government and landowners . . . had a fair trial" and that no further proceedings were called for.[22]

On the whole, the court's decisions in condemnation suits were not anti-government. Its unwillingness to allow modifications in original takings forced the government to use the potentially unsuccessful method of litigation to lower costs, yet the court never refused the government's condemnation petitions. In fact, Kennerly's and Hannay's belief that the jury's decision should stand unchanged in condemnation cases ultimately helped the government more than landowners; in most instances, with Holmesian reasoning (what has the landowner lost, not the taker gained) shaping jury decisions, the jury's verdicts were for lower values. The court's sole concern centered on the Constitution's provisions protecting property rights and assuring that local landowners received fair compensation for their losses. If the commissioners or a jury were satisfied that a compensation amount was adequate, the court upheld them. Thus, despite the court's limited effect on the government's immediate aim of acquiring lands cheaply, its decisions in these cases placed a cap on government action. Even a nation at war, the judges implied, had to follow the law and respect private property rights. Though emergency could motivate government action, it was no excuse for failing to maintain the Constitution's protections of private property.

Of course, the converse—that property owners had to respect the government's right to successfully fight the war—was also true. The judges had no wish to hinder the war effort. They merely sought to ensure that this endeavor was carried out in what they considered a proper and constitutional manner. The war demanded government limits on many personal freedoms. Foremost were regulations limiting the movement and sale of heretofore unregulated private property. Of equal impact were laws affecting personal status and mobility. These and other regulations the court allowed, always demanding, however, that traditional procedural protections be followed scrupulously. Even when government action resulted in confiscation of private property, the court supported government action if the authority to act was clear and the procedures used were sound.

The best example of the judges' willingness to allow limits on property and person was foreign trade. In July, 1940, Congress passed an act to "expedite the strengthening of the national defense." Section 6 of this act gave the president, if ever he "determine[d] that it [was] . . . in the interest of national defense," the right "to prohibit or curtail [by proclamation] the exportation of any military equipment or munitions, or . . . material or supplies necessary for the manufacture . . . or operation thereof." In mid-1941 FDR used this authority to create the Board of Economic Warfare. He empowered it to regulate foreign trade in goods "necessary for the nation's defense." Subsequently, such disparate items as steel pipes and gaskets, used automobiles and auto parts, and synthetic fiber materials were placed in this category. To export these and other goods required a license from the Board of Economic Warfare. Failure to obtain this license resulted in confiscation and forfeiture of the goods and possible criminal prosecution. On June 30, 1942, Congress approved FDR's actions and expanded the president's authority to prohibit or limit the exportation of "any articles, technical data, materials, or supplies, . . . as [the president] shall prescribe." This second act remained in force throughout the war.[23]

The Southern District heard just under half of all prosecutions brought under the 1940 and 1942 Export Control acts. Most were civil forfeiture cases involving small items of everyday commerce such as rayon dresses, pipes used in oil drilling, or used cars. None of these goods were prohibited from export. In each case the violation was in failing to obtain a license from the Board of

Economic Warfare. In well over 90 percent of the cases, the goods seized were found in violation of the law and were forfeited to the United States.[24]

As might be expected, objections were quickly raised to these forfeitures. In a series of suits heard in late 1942 and early 1943, the owners of confiscated property argued that the two acts under which their goods had been confiscated were unconstitutional and the seizures invalid. Neither act, the owners pointed out, defined what goods the president could declare as necessary for national defense. Rather, as Judge Kennerly himself noted in *U.S. v. 251 Ladies Dresses*, decided in the summer of 1943: "it was left for Executive decision as to what articles came within the bounds of" the two acts. This, the owners argued, placed too much discretion in the hands of the executive, allowing the president to regulate all aspects of foreign trade in contravention of Congress's constitutional duty to regulate such trade. Such transfer of legislative authority to the executive was clearly prohibited by the Constitution; its violation therefore voided the law's operation.

Yet even if the president had ample authority to prohibit or limit items from exportation, the owners went on to argue, he had not adequately used this authority. "[N]o law nor lawful regulation" was in force "at the time of [the] seizure under which [their property] could be lawfully seized and forfeited," the owners held. Both acts clearly named the president as the sole determiner of which goods were to be prohibited from being exported. Yet at no time had he made up a list of prescribed items. The regulation under which their goods had been seized was written not by the president, but by the Board of Economic Warfare. While the board had been created by presidential order, this was not an adequate substitute for the president making the list himself. The board was meant to enforce executive orders, not to create them. And, the owners concluded, as the board was an inadequate source for regulations, the seizures were again invalid.[26]

Despite the similarity of these arguments to positions that Judge Kennerly had accepted in the past, the judge upheld the government's right to seize and confiscate these goods. In explaining his reasoning Kennerly drew on the decision of Judge Campbell of the Northern District of Illinois in a similar case. Quoting from that decision, Kennerly held that "in our consideration of this question we must not forget that there is a wide difference between the grant of power to the President in matters that are of internal control, and those affecting our dealings as a nation with foreign nations, where the President is the representative of this nation[.] [W]ho could more properly decide, for our national defense, which of certain articles described by the Congress, should not be exported or their exportation curtailed, than the Commander in Chief of our Army and Navy? The defense of this country must not be required to await armed attack, but must be prepared for when we are threatened." When dealing with issues of foreign policy and defense, the judge continued to quote, Congress wisely "stated its policy, established the standards," and left the details of the plan's operation to the president. Congress "did not grant legislative powers to the President, but only the power to determine as a fact which of the articles described by the Congress should not be exported or their exportation curtailed." This was not only constitutional, Kennerly concluded, but proper.[27]

As to the validity of the posted regulations, the judge's opinion followed directly from his view on the acts' constitutionality. Since the president's sole action under the act was determining "in fact" what goods were necessary for national defense, he could legitimately transfer this duty to a subordinate better qualified to make this determination. The owners' contention that the Board of Economic Warfare's regulations were invalid was therefore "not meritorious."[28]

As long as the goods seized were on the government's list of prohibited items and were confiscated in the act of being illegally exported, the court supported the government unquestioningly and ordered the goods forfeited to the United States. Where questions as to the illegality of either the goods seized or the intent of the exporter arose, however, the court held back from immediate condemnation. Where it became apparent that government officials had violated the rights of the owner in seizing the property, the court refused to order forfeiture.

An event of this sort occurred in fall, 1942, when Rafael Nava Urrutia, a Mexican citizen, was arrested while attempting to illegally export two used cars to Mexico. Nava had purchased both cars – a 1940 Packard Coupe, which he proposed to resell once in Mexico, and a 1941 Chrysler convertible purchased for his personal use – in Dallas and had them driven to Laredo, where, on the morning of November 5, 1942, he was stopped by customs agents and informed that he was in violation of the law. Nava, who was unfamiliar with the laws respecting exportation of cars from the United States, inquired of the customs agent what actions he needed to take to legally export his cars, especially the Chrysler. Informed that he needed to declare his property and in this way obtain an export license, Nava drove back to Laredo proper and executed a Shipper's Export Declaration. Returning to the customs office with the document, Nava was questioned at length by customs agents about his intentions and, despite having recently filled out the necessary paperwork for obtaining a license, was subsequently advised that both cars were seized in the name of the United States and that he was to be detained in jail for violations of the Export Control Act. Nava employed counsel and under his advice refused to sign a written statement of the facts prepared by the customs agents unless the attorney was permitted to read the statement first. The customs officers denied this request. Nava was subsequently indicted by the grand jury and brought to trial on criminal charges, in large part because of his failure to sign the report. Civil action was also taken against the two cars.[29]

This situation first came before the court on April 21, 1943, at which time the criminal case against Nava came to trial. The proceedings of the jury trial were only half done when the judge brought the trial to a quick end. Following the close of the government's case, and on his own motion, Judge Kennerly directed the jury to retire and declare a verdict in favor of the defendant. Nava never "intended to unlawfully export [the] two cars," the judge told the jury. "[W]hen [Nava] went to the customs office with his sworn declaration . . . he was making an effort to find out in what manner he could lawfully export the cars and what the law and regulations were on the subject[.] He intended to comply with such laws and regulations, and would have done so had he not been arrested and jailed." It was never Nava's intention to "*unlawfully*" export his cars, the judge repeated, and he should not be punished for simply being unfamiliar with the laws. Following this instruction, the jury returned the verdict as directed and Nava went free. Three months later, the civil suit to condemn Nava's cars ended with a similar result. Noting how "the evidence [was] similar to that at the trial of the criminal case," Judge Kennerly maintained his position on Nava's innocence and ordered the cars returned to him.[30]

Cases of this sort were few. In most export suits the illegal nature of the goods seized was without question and the court's order of forfeiture automatic. It took an exceptional set of circumstances and evidence of official misconduct, such as in Nava's case, before the court would question the government's contention that seized goods were exported in violation of the law. Where evidence of this sort was found, the court acted quickly to rectify the situation and return the seized property.[31]

A similar pattern followed when the court heard price control and rationing suits. Concurrent with its grants to the president of power over foreign trade, Congress authorized FDR to prepare plans for regulating the domestic economy in the event of war. Following Pearl Harbor, these plans were brought forward and the recently created Office of Price Administration (OPA) given the job of rationing key commodities and fixing maximum prices for consumer goods and rents. By the spring of 1942, the OPA was ready to act. On April 28, it issued General Maximum Price Regulations for all major commodities and classifications of rental housing. Known as the general freeze, these regulations required all merchants to accept as a ceiling the highest price they had charged in March, 1942. Subsequent regulations adjusted the maximum rate allowable to meet the changing demands of wartime inflation. Prices remained controlled until November, 1946. At the same time, the OPA initiated ten major rationing programs requiring the use of ration coupons to purchase such basic merchandise as gasoline, food, clothing, and automobile tires. More rationing programs followed as the war progressed. By war's end, most consumer goods required coupons for purchase.[32]

Price controls and rationing proved difficult to enforce. "Most of the [nation's] population, businessmen included, agreed as a general principle that controls were at least a necessary evil during the war emergency." This support, however, often worked best at an "abstract" level. Price ceilings and rationing brought government control to sectors of the economy it had never before touched. This caused problems. As an OPA pamphlet published after the war described: "Most of the sellers subject to controls were businessmen unaccustomed to such outside interference in the operation of their businesses, and in many instances resentful of it on principle . . . Since the regulations being enforced often set new and unusual restrictions on customary practices, violation of these restrictions did not in themselves seem heinous offenses, either to the violators or to the general public generally." The result of such feelings was "countless unreported overceiling sales, overcharges for accommodations and sales without valid coupons"–violations that individually were of "minor consequence and usually the result of careless disregard, not malicious intent," but that collectively caused a major crisis in enforcement of the law.[33]

Recognizing the impossibility of "obtaining convictions" for so many minor infractions, the OPA's litigation strategies aimed rather toward assuring "compliance" with the law. The goal was to keep people from breaking the law in the first place, not to punish offenders. Ironically, the best way to do this, OPA officials knew, was to prosecute all violations and thus let merchants know that failure to follow the law would lead to civil and criminal sanctions. The problem was to find a way to spread this fear of prosecution without attempting the impossible task of prosecuting all violators. Experience with enforcing Prohibition and price agreements under the NRA and the AAA stressed the usefulness of civil injunctions over criminal sanctions in this regard. While civil sanctions allowed violators to escape punishment for their past acts, they prohibited under threat of contempt of court all future violations. In addition, civil injunctions were easier to win than criminal cases. Criminal proceedings required proof of violation beyond a reasonable doubt, civil injunctions, only a preponderance of evidence. Also, since civil suits did not cause defendants any monetary loss–they were only prohibited from further acts in violation of the law–compromise decisions were simpler to obtain and the success rate against violators could be near 100 percent. (The actual percentage of OPA court victories was 94.) All this made civil injunctions a cost-effective way of assuring future compliance with the law while at the same time publicizing the willingness of the OPA to prosecute violators.[34]

Most of the OPA suits heard by the court were for civil injunctions enjoining overcharges of the maximum price ceiling or sales without valid coupons by local merchants and manufacturers.[35] This simplified the court's job considerably. As was the case nationally, OPA officials in the Southern District brought civil injunction suits, in large part as an inducement in out-of-court settlements. Suits were filed only after evidence of violations had been discovered, and, confident of their case, OPA officials used this litigation as a foundation for quick compromise decisions. As a result, most OPA injunction cases ended with consent decrees, occasionally with the defendant denying the truth of the allegation of wrongdoing, but usually stipulating as to its correctness. The court merely validated the agreement, providing for enforcement if its provisions were later violated.[36]

In a small number of cases, the OPA requested that civil damages be assessed by the court, either in addition to an injunction or alone. As with injunction cases, many were settled by stipulated agreements. Some, however, were contested. Here the court did look closer at the facts of the case and the legitimacy of the OPA's authority. As with export control cases, however, the court upheld the government's right to act. All the judges demanded was that, in setting damages, the sanction fit the scope of the violation. Thus, in a case against Joseph Epstein, owner of the Capital Wholesale Drug and Liquor Company, the OPA demanded treble damages of $189,909.93 while the court levied fines of only $50,000.[37]

Price control suits followed the pattern set by condemnation and export forfeiture cases. Where the government's statutory authority was clear and officials followed proper procedures, the court allowed the government a free hand in war-related activities. If anything, price control and rationing suits proved easier for the court to approve, as few of the defendants in these cases experienced monetary losses as a result of court actions. With defendants warned of the need to follow the law, any future violations could be sanctioned with no doubt about the propriety of the government's actions.

A third and final area in which the court accepted government regulations was the draft. This proved the easiest for the court to support. Not only were no property rights threatened, but ample precedent existed for the government's right to implement this procedure. The only questions raised concerned the propriety of a peacetime draft (Selective Service was reinstituted in 1940 as part of the nation's prewar preparations). Yet even here, few questioned Congress's authority to act; the dispute was one of public policy, not law.[38]

In addition, few challenged the law's administration. Despite initial worries by the Justice and War departments, few cases of draft evasion or opposition occurred prior to the outbreak of war. Through 1942 the director of Selective Service "received and investigated some 67,194 report[ed] violations – 31,845 cases [which were] closed and 35,349 cases still pending" with the arrival of war. Of the closed cases, most did not involve intentional opposition to the draft. "Investigations of the reported delinquents disclosed that in the majority of cases, the violation was unintentional in character and that there was no effort on the part of the registrant to evade his obligations under the Act," Lewis B. Hershey, director of the Selective Service Administration, wrote in his annual report. With the outbreak of war and the induction of millions of men selective service cases become more common. Yet even then, the number of willful violations was small – the "proportionate increase in such cases" being "less than the proportionate increase in inductions." Most violators were again draft resisters in a technical sense only. In such cases, the Department of Justice's general policy was "to secure compliance with the act rather than to prosecute unintentional or technical violations." The vast majority of draft violators "were later permitted to register without the institution of criminal proceedings."[39]

Registration in the Southern District followed the national pattern. As registration ended on the night of October 17, the district's U.S. attorney, Douglas McGregor, informed the attorney general that there had been no complaints, arrests, or disorders in the Southern District over selective service. In the following weeks he reported the discovery of only a handful of violators. As of December, 1941, only sixty investigations into potential violations had been made and few of these led to indictments.[40] Following Pearl Harbor the number of violations remained small. Between July, 1941, and June, 1946, the court heard 423 selective service cases. Approximately half were filed in the Houston Division. The remainder were equally spread among the other divisions. Further, many of these cases did not involve the court in any litigation. Of the Houston Division's 122 draft cases in calendar 1942, for instance, 43 involved draft violators from other districts. All that was required of the court was that it transfer the case to the appropriate court.[41]

Still, administration of selective service did involve significant limits on deeply held beliefs in personal mobility and occupation and raised questions about the limits of government power, questions that the court did acknowledge. Yet, as with other government regulations, the court's response to these questions was limited to jurisdiction and procedure. Where both were adequate, the court refused to act against government wishes.

The court heard three types of draft violation cases during World War II. The first, failing to register, was not very common. Most men failing to register were not indicted, but, rather, allowed to register late. Those who were indicted stood an even chance of being acquitted, usually because they were able to prove that they were not required to register.[42] Those found guilty, however, received sentences of from one month to one year and one day, depending on the facts of the violation.[43]

Similarly, few prosecutions for those failing to report for induction into the armed forces were filed in the court. Of those that were filed, many were fugitive cases from other districts. All that was required of the court in these cases was to transfer the defendant back to the original district. Where the defendant was from the Southern District, the court took a severe stance. Most were found guilty and sentenced to the federal penitentiary for terms of two years or more.[44]

Most common were indictments for failure to answer questionnaires sent out by local draft boards or failure to notify these draft boards of changes in address. It was a felony to not return a draft board questionnaire because they were used in classifying the registrant's dependency and employment status. Often the reason the defendant had not returned the questionnaire was that he had failed to inform his draft board of his proper address. As a result, he had never received questionnaire. Well over half of the district's draft cases came under one or both of these categories. As with failure to register and report for induction, most men charged with this crime pleaded guilty. Punishments varied depending on the reason for the failure to inform. Where the failure was unintentional or of short duration, defendants received sentences as short as one hour in the custody of the U.S. marshal. More willful violations brought jail sentences. Many of these sentences, however, were commuted to probation on the understanding that the sentence did not prevent the defendant from entering the army or the navy.[45]

The only true challenge to the administration of the draft involved Jehovah's Witnesses, who claimed religious deferments from military service. Church doctrine taught that all members of the church were ministers. The Selective Service Act classified ministers and seminary students as class IV-D, exempted from military service and training. Local draft boards, however, refused to classify Jehovah's Witnesses as ministers unless they had attended a seminary and devoted their full time to activities of the sect. Most were classified as conscientious objectors and when called up for military service were ordered to noncombatant military service or other occupations of national importance. Holding to their conception of themselves as ministers, those Jehovah's Witnesses called up refused induction. They were then charged with failure to report for induction and brought to trial in the federal district courts.[46]

The court heard a number of cases involing Jehovah's Witnesses. Most defendants made similar arguments. First, they denied that the indictment against them showed any act "which constitute[d] an offense against the laws of the United States." Having been misclassified by their local draft boards, they were merely upholding their rights in refusing to report for military or other national service. Second, they argued that the Selective Service Act violated the First and Fifth amendments. The act allowed appeals directly to the president "on the grounds of dependence"; it did not allow for appeals by ministers wrongly classified. By ignoring the need of ministers to appeal, the act limited the defendants' free exercise of religion and denied them due process of law. This clearly invalidated the act as an unconstitutional violation of the defendants' rights.[47]

Both arguments were raised in one of the first of these cases to be decided by the court, that of the *U.S. v. Elton Julius Haberman*. In an oral opinion, Judge Kennerly noted the significance of the case, as "the case involves, in a way, one of the sacred rights of men, the right to worship God according to the dictates of their own consciences." For this reason, Kennerly had agreed to "hear the evidence in its entirety, . . . [listening to] all that the members of the Draft Board and the Government witnesses . . . and all that the Defendant and his associates had to say" on the issue. The judge was especially interested by the constitutional argument; however, this interest was not matched by acceptance of the argument's validity. "This is a new question to me," Kennerly exclaimed, "but it does not strike me as having merit." The judge, therefore, denied the constitutional demurrer.[48]

Moving on to the invalidity of Haberman's classification, the judge again disagreed with the defense's arguments. As to their contentions that the defendant was a minister, Kennerly agreed that "there [was] no question in the world but what these good people who are worshipping God as they want to worship Him, call [and regard] this Defendant a minister of religion. . . . [That] under their definition of a 'minister of religion' he [is] a minister." The question was, did this make Haberman a minister under the law? Drawing on a decision of seven days earlier by Judge Holmes of the Southern District of Mississippi that, "in the construction of the Act," the language to be used was to be given its "common and ordinary meaning[s]," Kennerly had to answer no. "I do not think that he is a minister . . . within the meaning of the Act," he concluded.

The same held true on whether Haberman had a fair hearing from his draft board. The judge had listened "with a great deal of interest" to all the testimony, both for and against Haberman. And, keeping in mind that it was "not contemplated under the draft law that [the] boards [would] sit with as much ceremony and conduct their hearings with as much exactness as a court of justice," Kennerly found that "a fair hearing" had been held. Not only had the board listened to everything that the defendant had to say, it had accepted a "number of letters and documents and other papers" introduced by Haberman. "I do not think that any right of the Defendant was struck down in the hearing before the Board or before the Appellate Board." After hearing all the relevant facts, both boards had reached what they felt was a proper decision. As long as the defendant's rights were protected in reaching this position, as they were, it was not proper for the court to replace it with its own view. Besides, the judge agreed with the boards' choice.

Because he was correctly classified, Haberman had violated the law when he refused induction. Though he clearly respected the defendant's religious motivations, Kennerly had no choice but to sentence Haberman to thirteen months in the federal penitentiary.[49]

The remaining Jehovah's Witnesses cases ended with similar results. Having found Congress's authority to institute a draft adequate, the only real question before the court was whether the classification procedure used by the War Department was constitutionally sound. Where local draft boards had clearly examined all relevant materials in making a classification, the court found the procedure sound, refusing, as it had with the jury in condemnation suits, to replace the boards' opinion with it own.[50]

Though no longer the court's primary consideration, the private agenda still affected its enforcement of the federal domestic war effort, shaping that effort while not significantly hindering it. As long as basic procedural protections were provided, the court supported federal regulations. Where they were not provided, however, it prohibited enforcement.

III

The private agenda also came into play in the court's response to the war's wider economic and social effects. The Second World War culminated the Texas economy's hundred-year transformation into economic maturity. Situated halfway between the Atlantic and the Pacific coasts, and with easy access to deep water on the Gulf, Texas became a favored site for war industries. A quarter of all the synthetic rubber plants, a fifth of all the styrene plants, and half of all the petroleum-based butadiene plants built by the Reconstruction Finance Corporation were in Texas. Around Dallas, Southern Aircraft, North American Aviation, and Consolidated Aircraft constructed two major and a number of minor airplane factories with federal help. Houston received new steel mills, munitions plants, and shipyards; Texas City inherited a new tin smelter, the world's largest; Corpus Christi was the site of one of the larger shipyards on the Gulf Coast. In all, only California and Illinois received more federal money for building war facilities than Texas.[51]

Merging with an already expanding private manufacturing sector, this wartime expansion resulted in an explosive rate of growth for Texas manufactures. Between 1939 and the end of 1944 the number of Texas manufacturing plants increased by more than a thousand, from 5,376 to 6,500. At the same time, their productive output, as measured by the value added to the state's economy, more than tripled, from $448,523,000 to $1,900,000,000; the number of workers employed more than doubled, from 125,115 to 380,000; and the wages paid out nearly tripled, from $196,747 to $520,000. By 1947 Texas ranked twelfth on the basis of value added to the economy by manufacturing. Eight years earlier it had ranked but fourteenth.[52]

Over the long term, this growth in manufacturing signaled the maturity of the Texas economy.[53] More immediately, however, it posed a challenge for the state's economic and legal institutions as industrial expansion resulted in a corresponding increase in worker accidents and fatalities. This, in turn, produced an unmanageable flood of workers' compensation cases before the Texas Industrial Accident Board (TIAB). It was thus left to the courts, including the Southern District Court, to provide a forum in which the problem of injured industrial workers could be settled. In line with its prodevelopmental values and its tradition of demanding the adoption of new business practices in response to changing economic patterns, the court's judges understood the importance of workers' compensation cases. They appreciated the need simultaneously to protect the new manufacturing sector from the potential financial ruin of large compensation awards while assuring that the industrial worker's legitimate needs for injury compensation were met. Both were necessary components of the economic well-being of the region.[54]

Created in 1913, the TIAB was intended as an alternative to the uncertain, costly, and time-consuming system of using damage suits in the courts to provide industrial workers with accident insurance. Progressive for its time, the Employers Liability and Workmen's Compensation Law, which the TIAB supervised, guaranteed workers compensation on the basis of 60 percent of their average weekly wages, up to a maximum of $15.00 per week. The act also provided for one week of medical aid. Amended at various times, by the 1940s, the act provided for a maximum weekly compensation of twenty dollars and expanded the amount of hospital coverage available. Compensation, however, was limited to 401 weeks of coverage.[55]

The TIAB, however, created at a time when Texas had few industrial workers and hence few industrial accidents, was a modest organization that lacked the resources to investigate the merits of more than a small number of claims. When the flood of new cases brought on by increased war manufactures arrived in the 1940s, the board suddenly faced more cases than it could suitably handle—one former employee recalled sitting up until midnight on many a night with a board member making scores of awards just to keep up with the large number of cases docketed, and then only at the cost of superficial and hasty judgments. This insufficiency of resources forced the TIAB to rely extensively on evidence supplied by the worker, the employer, and the insurance company. Since few workers knew their rights, however, nor had counsel when they came before the board, in most cases only the employer's and the insurance company's estimates of the situation were available. This allowed employers and insurance companies to shape the board's compensation awards so that they matched, and hence legitimated, settlement offers already made by the insurance company. (In most cases the insurance company had already made an offer and begun payments to the worker by the time the TIAB heard the case.) Threatened by dire financial difficulties if they refused settlement, lacking legal counsel, and faced with a board decision likely to set compensation at a level close to that already offered by the insurance company, most workers accepted settlement and did not contest the board's decision.[56]

In some cases, however, no agreement between the worker and the insurance company could be reached before the board met. This most often occurred when the insurance company was unwilling to assume the costs of compensation and hence either refused to make a settlement offer or made one so inadequate that the worker refused to accept. Occasionally the source of contention was the worker's demands for more compensation than the insurance company offered. In either case, where no prior agreement could be reached, employers and insurance companies used their influence on the board to deny the worker any award from the TIAB.[57] Left without any compensation for injuries, the worker usually turned to the state courts to appeal the board's decision.

In those cases in which the employer or the insurance company was from outside of Texas (in 1945, 102 out of the 121 casualty and surety insurance companies licensed to operate in Texas were chartered outside of the state), the case would often be removed to the federal courts under diversity.[58] Insurers did this for any number of reasons. First was convenience. Rather than having to litigate suits in a dozen or more county courthouses, cases could be heard in one place and before the same judge—a judge whose views on issues of workers' compensation the insurance company's lawyers were already familiar with. This allowed the lawyers to estimate the outcome of a case if it went to trial and so advise their clients on whether to settle out of court.

Speed was a second reason. Though federal dockets were crowded, state court case loads were worse. Delays between filing and settlement in state courts ran from six months to over a year and complaints by plaintiff lawyers that workers' compensation claims were allowed to languish on the docket were common.

This did not occur in the federal courts, where judges attempted to get cases of this sort off the docket as quickly as possible.[59]

Finally, there was the reason of safety. Though most workers' compensation cases, state and federal, ended with an out-of-court settlement, there was always the possibility that no agreement could be reached and the case would have to go to trial. Texas law allowed for trials *de novo* on appeals from the TIAB. Tradition held that these appeals would be jury trials. Past experience argued that federal juries would be less biased against the insurance company than state juries. This made the federal courts a safer forum in which to litigate.[60]

Almost unknown before 1940, workers' compensation cases soon made up 70 percent of the court's private civil docket.[61] Most arose in the Houston and Galveston divisions, where the majority of the new industries were centered. A smaller number of suits were filed in Corpus Christi. Almost none arose from the Valley's two divisions. The majority of these cases involved workers whose compensation claim had been denied by the TIAB. The board's stated reasons for denial varied. In the majority of cases the TIAB refused the claim because the plaintiff had failed to establish that the injury occurred "in the course of employment" or that it was a "compensable injury" under the Texas workers' compensation statute. In other cases, the board refused compensation because the worker had not filed his claim within the statutory period of six months or proved "good cause for [the] delay" in filing. A small number of suits arose in response to what the worker felt was an inadequate award by the TIAB. An even smaller number of cases were initiated by the employers or their insurance companies against what were felt to be excessive TIAB awards.[62]

Most suits were settled out of court. Faced with the high costs of litigation, not to mention the real possibility of large jury awards, defendant insurance companies sought the certainty of agreed-on settlements. Plaintiff workers, in turn, now represented by counsel and also cognizant of the costs of litigation, usually found these offers agreeable, or at least acceptable, as the highest return they were likely to get short of a costly jail trial. Settlements averaged between $300 and $2,500, with most falling between $1,000 and $1,500. This was not only significantly higher than the amount given by the TIAB, but also greater than awards given for similar injuries, most of which averaged less than $1,000. In no case, however, did the amounts agreed on come close to the statutory limit of $8,020.[63]

Though the court's role in these proceedings was largely an administrative legitimization of the independent decisions of the litigants, neither Judge Kennerly nor Judge Hannay conceded any of its authority over these matters. In every case in which a pretrial settlement had been reached, both judges first ensured that a written agreement laying out the terms of the settlement had been signed and filed with the court. Next, they reviewed the evidence in the case, satisfying themselves that the evidence supported the imposition of a settlement and that its outcome was "fair, just and equitable, and to the best interests of all parties." Only then would they agree to the settlement.[64]

In fact, though few descriptions of the judges' actions in such cases exist, the large number of pretrial agreements strongly implies that both judges actually encouraged such agreements. The recollections of those who practiced before the court reinforce this conclusion. The Texas federal courts were known for their rapid handling of compensation cases. The judges understood the importance of quickly settling such claims in a manner acceptable to both the worker and the employer. Wherever possible, they pushed lawyers to settle out of court. Where no agreement could be reached and the case went to trial, the court's decisions also were quickly made and aimed at balancing the costs of the accident between the litigants.[65]

Thus, though the court's role in most compensation suits was limited, the impact these cases had on the region's development was not. Placed in conjunction with similar suits in state court, these actions helped maintain a balance between the legitimate needs of the growing number of industrial workers in the region for adequate compensation for industrial injuries and the needs of their employers and the insurance industry for protection from excessive compensation awards. The court provided a final forum in which the individual costs of industrial growth could be divided peaceably.

IV

Though not the court's primary concern during the Second World War, the private agenda still motivated and constrained many of its actions. It shaped the court's response to such public issues as the draft, price controls and condemnation suits and opened its doors to such private issues as workers' compensation. While none of this significantly lessened the court's service to the needs of the public agenda, it showed its continuing adherence to private matters over public policies. With the end of the war and the return of private suits, the court was set to return to its old habits and priorities. As will be seen, however, the changes of the previous twenty years posed new challenges to the private agenda's dominance.

8. The More Things Change

PUBLIC AND PRIVATE LAW IN THE POST–WORLD WAR II ERA, 1946–60

I

The end of World War II marked an important turning point for southeast Texas and the Southern District Court. Following a brief readjustment period while local industries shifted to civilian production, the region's economy began a period of sustained growth that would last into the 1980s. This growth transformed the region's economic structures and, with them, the role the court played in shaping and sustaining economic growth. By 1960 the Southeast Texas economy no longer depended on the services of the court to maintain its rapid development and the court had begun to shift its priorities from serving primarily private economic needs to fulfilling publicly defined objectives.

The postwar economic boom underlay these changes. By 1955 Texas industrial products were valued at over $5 billion and the state was the leading producer of oil, petrochemicals, natural gas, carbon black, helium, sulfur, cotton, rice, beef cattle, wool, and mohair. It competed also in shipbuilding, iron and steel manufacturing and aircraft production. Texas petroleum alone was a $3 billion a year industry, generating $275,369 in salaries and paying $188 million in state taxes annually.[1]

More significant than the pace of growth, however, was the mature and stable manner in which development took place. Unlike earlier periods of expansion, Texas' post-war growth did not inordinately strain the region's economic or social fabric. When asked in 1958 what he thought was the greatest problem facing Texas, Governor Allan Shivers chose the West Texas drought threatening agriculture. The labor tensions, business instabilities, and price wars that attended this intense economic expansion did not concern the governor or other state and business leaders. Instabilities existed in the economy, and many long-term costs of growth were apparent, but, as they did not threaten the state's continued development, they were largely ignored.[2]

One reason for this relative economic stability was the blossoming maturity of the region's business sector. Much of the expansion was in large, established industries and businesses that, with exceptions, controlled the resources needed for rapid development. This control, in turn, permitted these businesses to dominate the pace and direction of expansion. In the oil and gas industry, for example, the large majors controlled the new pipelines to the North and the East, built the new refineries, and developed the new fields. In petrochemicals, major companies like du Pont and Monsanto built most of the new plants and controlled growth.[3]

Big business, in turn, was increasingly capable of coping with the developmental costs inherent in rapid growth. Business had learned from the depression and the war the need for industrywide cooperation to stabilize markets and the beneficent role the public sector played in achieving this end. Following the war, American business reorganized, adopted managerial innovations, expanded markets and intraindustry cooperation, and began a forty-year reconciliation with public regulators. The result was a "refurbished" business community capable for the first time of maintaining "a stable, relatively predictable environment for business activity."[4]

By channeling patterns of growth into established economic and social frameworks, cooperating to create stable market relations, and taking care not to grow faster than the economy could accommodate, business successfully tempered the disruptions attending Southeast Texas' rapid growth. Where these efforts proved inadequate, or where cooperation broke down, business turned to various government bureaus or administrative agencies to correct these problems. The willingness of these agencies to provide such services—and to do so in ways acceptable to business—constituted a second reason for the stability of the post-war boom.

Just as members of the business community accepted government regulation, most Americans accepted the corporation. Economic regulations during the depression taught the public that controls over corporate excesses were possible. During the Second World War, efficient industrial production helped to make Allied victory possible and placed business in a more positive light. In the prosperous postwar years, both lessons combined to make corporate styles of control "appear to be more of a boon than a social problem." When business turned to the public sector for assistance, government agencies from the local to the national level willingly lent a helping hand in ways once resented as intrusions into private prerogatives.[5]

All of this affected the Southern District Court. Up to this time, the court's priority had been to fill the needs of the regional business community for a stable and predictable business environment. With the business community in control of the pace and direction of growth, and with largely friendly government regulations blunting problems too large for business to handle, the Southern District's services were less essential. In effect, the court had worked itself out of a job. Cases directly affecting the region's economic structure were no longer a part of its docket.

As demands for the court's private functions was declining among area businesses, pressure for a more active public role grew. The rise in governmental activism partly underlying this change slowly expanded the court's public duties. At first a limited and controllable trend, this movement toward expanded public functions would only grow more intense in the future. By the last years of the period, it would be impossible to ignore.

Little of this trend was apparent in 1946 when the court opened its first postwar term, nor for much of the next fifteen years, as it faced a flood of familiar public and private cases. These cases broke down into four categories of legal action. The first involved public civil suits arising from problems raised by the Second World War and its aftermath. These suits included such diverse issues as overtime compensation, housing controls, and industrial reconversion costs. A second group, criminal immigration suits, originated in the war's reshaping of the American labor market. The third category was private actions, most of which took the form of appeals from the rulings of the Texas Industrial Accident Board or tort suits on insurance contracts and personal injury matters. Last, civil rights suits formed a novel class of burdens, and opportunities, for the court, as for the nation.

These cases were coming in larger numbers than ever before. By 1950 the court was hearing around one thousand private and three thousand criminal suits a year. By 1955 criminal cases had more than doubled while civil rose to a high of almost fifteen hundred. Thereafter, criminal actions dropped to roughly one thousand filings a year while civil cases continued to grow, reaching nearly two thousand filings in 1958 (table 5). When immigration suits are re-

Table 5

U.S. Civil, Private Civil, Total Civil, and Criminal Cases, 1946–59

Year	*U.S. Civil Cases*	*Private Civil Cases*	*Total Civil Cases*	*Criminal Cases*
1946	337	455	792	2,256
1947	536	500	1,036	1,959
1948	535	576	1,111	2,106
1949	482	728	1,210	2,251
1950	259	792	1,051	2,822
1951	185	719	904	8,339
1952	367	806	1,173	6,484
1953	291	949	1,240	3,720
1954	334	1,111	1,445	5,068
1955	268	950	1,218	2,947
1956	293	1,059	1,352	1,175
1957	648	1,142	1,790	743
1958	421	1,482	1,903	704
1959	362	655	1,017	824

Source: AO Report, table C1 (1946–59).

Judge Ben C. Connally. Courtesy Houston Metropolitan Research Center, Houston Public Library

moved from this list, the largest segment of the court's case load remained private diversity suits–long the foundation of its emphasis on private matters. Add in the fact that many technically public suits involved issues affecting private needs and rights, and it should not be surprising that the Southern District's judges remained committed to a private agenda. If the state's political and business leaders ignored costs that did not threaten future development, the judges ignored the economic, social, and political changes transforming their docket.[6] This "business as usual" predisposition existed both for sitting judges Kennerly and Hannay and for the three added in the 1950s.

The first two joined the court in 1950 (though they had been appointed in 1949), filling positions recently created by Congress, one a permanent addition to the district bench, and the other, initially a temporary position lasting the lifetime of the appointed judge, but later made permanent.[7] Ben C. Connally, son of Texas Senator Tom Connally, won the permanent seat, and James V. Allred, former Southern District judge, the temporary one. The third new judge, Houston lawyer Joe McDonald Ingraham, was named replacement for retiring Judge Kennerly in 1954.[8]

As before, the three came from Texas' social, political, and economic elite. Allred was a former governor of Texas and federal district judge. Connally was a senator's son and partner in the Houston law firm of Butler, Binion, Rice &

Judge Joe McDonald Ingraham. Courtesy Houston Metropolitan Research Center, Houston Public Library

Cook. The sole Republican, appointee Ingraham, had been an associate of another of Houston's largest law firms before entering solo practice and was head of the Harris County Republican party.[9]

All three new judges were experienced private civil lawyers. They shared similar backgrounds and attitudes with the court's older judges. Each actively supported the court's developmental goals and agreed with Judges Kennerly's and Hannay's approaches to achieving these goals.[10] Hence, despite the changes occurring both nationwide and in the court's crowded dockets, only in the late 1950s would the court begin to change its priorities. Until then, it stressed its private functions, as it had for the past fifty years, largely ignoring public issues in favor of private matters.

II

For the United States, the Second World War was a social, economic, and political event as much as it was a military one. Global conflict and its aftermath transformed the nation and the world, laying the foundations for the cold war, the civil rights movement, and the beginnings of the postwar economic boom, all of which generated persistent domestic problems that were to trouble the nation for over a decade. A number of these lodged in the Southern District Court's dockets.[11]

Though all were public suits brought under familiar federal civil and criminal statutes, each raised difficult questions about the border between public power and private needs and required the court to rule on the legitimacy of government polices that, in various ways, allegedly harmed the interests of private individuals and businesses.

In contrast to its wartime decisions, the court's answers to these postwar dilemmas exhibited an increased uneasiness about federal intervention in everyday life. Its negative rulings stressed that private needs could no longer be ignored now that the war was over, that the lines separating public from private matters still existed and should be honored.

This strident protection of traditional private rights contrasted with the views of the U.S. Supreme Court and the Fifth Circuit Court of Appeals, both of which increasingly accepted public policy priorities. As never before, both higher courts began to reverse the district court on public policy matters.[12] Reversals did not stop the judges, however. Throughout the postwar period, they continued to hold the federal government to strict standards of responsible and limited action.

The court could not, however, contain all the problems deriving from the war. One of the first dilemmas to come before it, though pregnant with possibilities for court action, was one such problem. In 1938 the Fair Labor Standards Act (FLSA) established a national minimum wage and mandated a forty-hour work week for "persons employed in interstate commerce." Work beyond forty hours was deemed overtime and ordered paid at time and a half. The act did not, however, define the exact meaning of such terms as "work," "hours worked," and "employment." Rather, it was left up to custom, past practices, and contractual agreements to define when work began and ended and when overtime came into effect.[13] This system worked only where concord prevailed between labor and management over hours worked.

During the Second World War such concord quickly broke down. Mobilization brought a significant rise in the hours laborers worked. Management, seeking to keep costs down and in accordance with past practices, limited overtime by narrowly defining hours worked as only those hours in which the laborer was actually producing. Workers objected and, unable successfully to work out their problems with management, sued for overtime pay. By early 1944 the issue was in the Supreme Court, which issued new, broad, definitions of "work."

In *Tennessee Coal Co. v. Muscoda Local* (1944) the Supreme Court held that the purpose of the FLSA was clearly "remedial and humanitarian" and should not be "interpreted or applied in a narrow, grudging manner." Therefore, "work" in a coal mine included the time spent getting from the mine opening to the active shift as well as the act of digging coal. In *Anderson v. Mt. Clemens Pottery Co.* (1946), this definition of compensable work was extended to all types of industrial labor. "Work" was defined as the time spent walking from entry gates to the work station, and such preliminary activities as donning aprons and preparing equipment.[14]

Encouraged by these decisions, and anxious that peace not erode wartime gains, hundreds of local labor unions filed overtime compensation suits under the FLSA as the war came to a close. The Southern District heard forty-eight of these cases. Most arose in the Houston Division and involved plants and factories along the Houston ship channel. All were brought by local unions "in and on behalf" of all the workers in the plant, whether union members or not. They argued that, under the Supreme Court's recent interpretations of the FLSA, workers at these plants had not received compensation for wartime labors, compensation now estimated in one suit alone, that against the Todd-Houston Shipbuilding Corporation, at over eight million dollars.[15]

The defendant companies, as might be expected, argued that in computing hours worked they had followed customary practices. Compensable work involved productive labor, not the time spent getting to and from the workplace.[16] Given the Supreme Court's decisions, however, these companies understood that such arguments were unlikely to win.[17] Therefore, defendant companies lobbied Congress to redefine "time on the job" in a manner immunizing employers from liability for past unpaid overtime. They were joined in this call by the Truman administration, which—with most war contracts let on a "cost-plus" basis—feared that the cost of any overtime awards would be borne ultimately by the federal government. Under significant pressure, and with many members of Congress agreeing with the president that to let these suits be decided in favor of the unions would mean economic upheaval, Congress passed the Portal-to-Portal Act of 1947, limiting the extent of overtime compensation claims under the FLSA.[18]

The Portal Act divided the work process into three phases—preliminary, postliminary, and principal—and required compensation only for the principal work activity. Preliminary and postliminary activities (getting to and from the job, changing into work clothes, punching in, and so on) were made noncompensable under the act, unless the right to receive payment for these actions was specifically placed in the worker's contract. In addition, the act placed a two-year statute of limitations on all overtime litigation, including claims already filed in federal courts, thus nullifying the definition of work under which these suits had been brought. This effectively denied federal jurisdiction and so aborted union claims for overtime.[19]

The Portal Act was clearly biased in favor of employers. But Congress's constitutional authority to limit federal courts' jurisdiction to shape a particular outcome in pending litigation was unassailable.[20] Judge Kennerly and the other district court judges hearing these cases were forced to rule that, since the act was constitutional, the plaintiff unions lacked a valid case to press and therefore dismissed all of the overtime suits for lack of jurisdiction.[21]

By contrast, the court's power to shape interactions between private rights and government polices was not impaired concerning the second postwar dilemma to come before it—rent controls. Congress did not bar the court from hearing rent control suits. Instead, it left the federal courts as primary enforcers of rent controls. This allowed the Southeast Texas court to rule on the propriety of peacetime regulations affecting individuals and businesses.

In 1945 the "American housing establishment was worth less than . . . it [had been] sixteen years before." Great shortages existed in low- and middle-income housing, the type of housing millions of veterans sought.[22] In October, 1945, Congress removed controls on building materials but little new housing resulted. Rather, as federal housing expediter Wilson Wyatt noted in 1946, private builders chose to construct "a rash of race tracks, mansions, summer resorts, bowling alleys, stores and cocktail bars," all of which produced a higher rate of return than residential housing.[23]

The Truman administration tried to assure adequate supplies of low-cost housing. It created the Office of Housing Expediter (OHE) to encourage the construction of new, low-cost residential housing and reinstituted price and allocation controls for building materials. It also continued wartime rent controls for most residential categories. The idea was that rent controls would guarantee that present housing remained affordable while the housing expediter saw to the construction of new low- and middle-income housing units adequate for future needs.[24]

The first part of this program soon failed. Truman's Veterans' Emergency Housing Program (VEHP), initiated in early 1946 by the housing expediter to construct 1.2 million housing units for veterans, depended excessively on public controls of construction materials. When under intense political pressure Truman ended price and allocation controls on all commodities except sugar, rice, and rents in November, 1946, the VEHP was effectively derailed. New housing became wholly a product of the private marketplace, the federal government only insuring home construction and improvement loans under the National Housing Act of 1934.[25]

Rent controls were retained through 1950. It was the enforcement of these controls that brought the housing problem into the federal courts. Postwar rent controls were unpopular. High demand for housing matched with rising commodity prices led many landlords to exceed legal rent limits; this posed serious challenges to the Truman administration's goal of maintaining adequate low-cost housing for veterans. The job of enforcing rent controls was originally given to the OPA, which regulated rents as part of its postwar anti-inflation program. Following its wartime practice of using the federal courts to enforce its regulations, the OPA filed some thirty thousand federal price control suits in 1946, a significant portion of which involved housing violations. The next year it added some thirty-two thousand cases to the federal docket, rents once again making up a large part of this number. Following Truman's termination of anti-inflation price controls in November, 1946—which led to the dissolution of the OPA—rent control enforcement became the duty of the OHE.[26] The OHE continued to follow the OPA's enforcement practices. In 1948, the first full year in which the OHE had control over rents, it filed some fifteen thousand rent control cases. Thereafter, the number of suits dropped rapidly as federal rent controls were phased out.[27]

Most of these rent control suits were civil actions.[28] Government lawyers realized the impossibility of obtaining criminal convictions for so many minor infractions. While criminal suits punished past misdeeds, civil injunctions barred future violations of the law. This made civil suits easier to win than criminal actions. In the latter the government had to prove its charge beyond a reasonable doubt; in civil suits, it had only to provide a preponderance of the evidence. Evidence of overcharges were often so easy to find—the testimony of renters was usually enough to prove that overcharges had occurred—the government was almost assured of either decisions or compromise settlements in its favor in a civil action. Quick settlements both discouraged future violations and taught the general public important lessons about the effectiveness of enforcement.[29]

The court heard approximately 757 rent control cases from the end of the war through 1950, of which 738 were civil in nature and 19 criminal.[30] Few of these cases went to trial or were settled by consent decrees. Rather, the vast majority were dismissed uncompleted, occasionally by agreement of the parties, but more often on the motion of the government or by order of the court.[31]

In those cases that did go to trial, the court—in contrast to its wartime habit of upholding all government price regulations as long as procedural protections were maintained—was antagonistic to rent control prosecutions, especially where restitution and damage awards were at issue. In *Tighe E. Woods, Housing Expediter v. Carrie Haydell et al.*, for instance, the OHE brought suit against Carrie Haydell, owner of a Houston boardinghouse, for rent overcharges totaling over $2,000. Charging that Haydell had willfully violated a May, 1945, OPA regulation that set the maximum weekly rent for a room in a boardinghouse at $3.25, (Haydell was charging $8), the OHE sought to enjoin future violations as well as collect restitution for the tenants and punitive damages based on the $2,000 excess rent.[32]

While admitting the overcharges, Haydell claimed that her violation was not "wilful." She had never received the order setting the $3.25 maximum rent. Had she known of this new regulation, Haydell implied, she would have obeyed it; therefore, recovery for her violation of the rent control laws should "be [only for] the amount of the actual overcharge." Punitive damages and restitution were unnecessary and uncalled for. So too was an injunction; Haydell was already abiding by the new legal maximum.[33]

The OHE argued that Haydell's actions had been willful. Nonreceipt—or a claim of nonreceipt—of the new regulation was an inadequate defense. As long as the regulation was mailed to the correct address the defendant was accountable. Second, one of Haydell's tenants, an R. H. Williams, had testified that in August, 1946, he had questioned Haydell as to the propriety of an $8 per week rent. Yet, at no time did she check with the OPA or later the OHE to confirm this rate. This failure, the OHE contended, proved willful violation of the law.

Full restitution, punitive damages, and an injunction prohibiting any future violations were the proper responses from the court.[34]

Judge Kennerly's "Findings of Fact and Conclusions of Law" acknowledged that the overcharge had occurred, but accepted Haydell's argument that the violation was not "wilful, nor the result of [a] failure to take practicable precautions against the occurrence of such violations," this despite the government's precedents that the act of mailing a regulation was prima facie evidence that the defendant knew of the order (hence making violations "wilful") and evidence that large overcharges had occurred. The government was entitled to recover only the computed overcharge for the one resident who questioned the rent ($147.25), "but no more, and [with] no other relief." As to the tenants' right to restitution, the judge again turned the government's argument around, holding that since the tenants had "willingly and knowingly" paid this overcharge they were not entitled to restitution.

Kennerly's decision was quickly overturned on appeal by the Fifth Circuit. "Although the lower Court found that overcharges in excess of $2,000 had been collected," the appeals panel wrote, "he allowed a recovery by the Expediter of only $147.25. We think this was in error. Whenever it is determined that there has been an overcharge, damages for the full amount of such overcharges should be awarded."[35]

Yet Kennerly's point was clear. The wartime crisis had ended. No longer was the mere existence of a federal statute prohibiting some act adequate justification for the government arbitrarily to affect private individuals. The government once again would have to show both the need for the statute and the willfulness of the defendant's violation of the law before the court would order punitive damages and enjoin future actions.

This message infused the court's rent control decisions. In *Woods v. Tate* Kennerly once again found that overcharges had occurred, but that fault for the violation lay with the government for failing adequately to inform the defendant of the new rate. The order establishing the new maximum rent, the judge noted, had been addressed to one Jack Ragusa, a former owner of the property, not Mary Tate, It was "questionable" if the defendant had ever been informed of the new rate prior to this suit. With this in mind, Kennerly was "compelled to find that Plaintiff ha[d] not established" that Tate's violation was "willful" and thus deserving of punitive damages. A judgment in favor of the defendant resulted. In *Woods v. Selber et al.*, Kennerly—though holding that the OPA's maximum rent for Selber's property "was plainly oppressive"—ruled that the order setting the maximum rate bound the defendant. However, the defendant's violation of this order was "unwillful," and the judge ordered payment of only a small fraction of the actual overcharge and refused plaintiff's motions for restitution and an injunction.[36]

Similar examples abound.[37] In almost every local rent control case decided by the Southern District, the government lost. The burden of proof had changed. Before, it was enough for the government to show that a law prohibiting some act existed and that basic procedural protections had been followed. Now the government not only had to show the existence of the law, but had to prove that the order setting maximum rates was known by the defendant and that an intentional violation had occurred. Failure to meet either of these latter criteria resulted in the court's refusal to order damages or issue injunctions.

Although most of these decisions were reversed if appealed, their effects on the court's case load and on the region were significant. The government's evident unwillingness to bring rent control suits to trial in the Southern District resulted from Kennerly's negative decisions. He was holding the government to a high standard of procedural and substantive proof, a standard that the OHE found it could not meet. After 1948 government lawyers stopped trying to enforce rent controls in the Southern District. Most such suits were dismissed uncontested, and federal attorneys refused to file new cases.

To the court, a strong line existed between private and public matters. Yet these cases were overturned on appeal, a fact illuminating a growing separation between the court's views and those of superior federal tribunals as to where this line should lie. Both of these trends were to continue in the third—and most dramatic—postwar dilemma faced by the court: the *Consolidated Texas City Disaster Cases.*

On April 16 and 17, 1947, Texas City, a municipality of some ten thousand people situated forty-five miles southeast of Houston, was rocked by two massive explosions coming from the direction of the port. Smoke rose up to block out the sky. Two aircraft circling overhead fell like "300-lb chunks of ship's steel." A fifteen-foot-high wave surged across the harbor. Barges and boats of all sizes came aground, some ending up over two hundred feet from the shoreline. Every house within a mile of the blast collapsed and every window within two miles broke. Oil and chemical plants worth an estimated $125 million burned uncontrolled. Gas and water mains broke like straws. Hundreds died in the blast and fires that followed while countless others were injured. The city, as one police warning put it, was plunged into "pluperfect hell."

Next morning the enormity of the catastrophe became evident. The dead numbered 512—399 identified and 133 missing—and nearly 2,000 were injured. Almost six hundred structures were destroyed or damaged, with losses totaling nearly $200 million. Personal injury and death claims added an additional $15.5 million in losses. In one day, Texas City was nearly wiped off the map.[38]

The disaster had its origins in two postwar dilemmas: the rush to convert war industries to peacetime applications, and the growing cold war tensions. As such, it raised questions similar to those posed by overtime legislation and rent controls, namely, how far should public policies go if they resulted in detriment to the interest and well-being of private citizens?

With the end of the Second World War, a frantic search for peacetime applications for war industries had begun. Fearful that the sudden halt of war production would lead to a postwar depression similar to the one that had followed World War I, the government sought peaceful uses for wartime industries, especially functions that required minimal retooling. One of the most troubling industries in this regard was munitions. Vitally important to the war effort, hundreds of munitions and ordinance plants had been built by the end of the war, becoming major industrial employers in a dozen states. Peacetime demand for munitions was expected to be low, however. If these jobs were to be saved, a new use for output of a munitions plant had to be found.[39]

Meanwhile, in Europe, famine in the fall and winter of 1947, along with rising superpower tensions, threatened the stability of Western Europe. The destruction of Europe's transportation systems, industries, banking facilities, and political institutions was proving too big a problem for the region to solve alone. With winter imminent, the Truman administration feared that Western Europe would collapse without U.S. economic support. One result was the Marshall Plan's massive effort to feed and rebuild non-Communist Europe with American aid.

But bad harvests and the end of food rationing in the United States had resulted, by late 1946, in rising domestic food prices and declining stockpiles of grain available for export. More grain production was needed, both at home and abroad, if domestic inflation and foreign starvation were to be avoided. The key to growing more food, in turn, was fertilizer. With enough fertilizer, both the United States' and Europe's food problems could be solved.[40]

Concerns of the munitions industry thus blended with cold war needs. One of the key ingredients in modern munitions, ammonium nitrate, was also an effective fertilizer. It could be produced from existing plants with little retooling and investment. The answer to both the economic reconversion and cold war problems seemed to have been found.

Ammonium nitrate was, however, very dangerous if improperly handled and stored. Another compound, ammonium sulfate, would have been preferable because it was safer, but facilities for its production were limited. Faced with two pressing needs that the use of ammonium nitrate as fertilizer would solve, and with no good alternatives available, the government chose to ignore the risks and order production and distribution of fertilizer-grade ammonium nitrate.[41] This decision to proceed with the production of ammonium nitrate fertilizer despite the known dangers led, ultimately, to the Texas City disaster.

The immediate cause of the April 16 and 17 explosions were two ships, the *Grandcamp* and the *High Flyer,* each loaded with ammonium nitrate fertilizer. A fire in the *Grandcamp,* likely started from a cigarette and worsened by improper handling of the fire, caused the first explosion. It led to a later blast in the *High Flyer* in which most of the deaths occurred. If neither ship had been loaded with ammonium nitrate, the fire on the *Grandcamp* would not have resulted in an explosion and the disaster that followed would not have occurred. If nothing else, the government had been negligent in unwittingly shipping a dangerous product without adequate safeguards and warnings to the public.[42]

Angry at the government for its apparent negligence and appreciative of the fact that only the federal government had pockets deep enough to pay for the costs of the explosions, suits against the United States multiplied quickly in the Southern District Court. In all, some 424 cases were filed by individuals and major corporations, local government agencies, and insurance companies, incorporating 8,485 plaintiffs–1,510 who sued for wrongful death, 988 for personal injury, and 5,987 for property damages (over $200 million worth). The amount of individual claims varied widely, from the few thousand dollars necessary to repair a damaged home to the multimillions needed to replace refining and manufacturing facilities. Most suits averaged between $50,000 and $200,000 and involved a mix of property damage, personal injury, and wrongful death claims.[43]

Earlier, cases of this sort would not have been possible. The doctrine of "sovereign immunity" prohibited citizens from suing the government, unless it first agreed to the proceedings. In most cases the government had refused permission. Barred from the courts, injured citizens had only private congressional bills as a remedy–a costly and uncertain method of redress. In the mid-years of the twentieth century, however, the expanding presence of the federal government matched with the effects of modern technology brought a flood of claims before Congress for settlement. Swamped by these petitions, Congress sought alternative forums in the federal district courts.[44]

In August, 1946, the Federal Tort Claims Act (FTCA) conferred jurisdiction on the federal district courts to hear claims "for injury or loss of property or . . . death caused by the negligent or wrongful act or omission of any employee of the Government while acting within the scope of his office or employment." This negligent act had to be done "under circumstances where the United States, if a private person, would [have been] liable to the claimant," and "in accordance with the law of the place where the act or omission occurred." Further, the jurisdiction granted to the district courts would not apply "to any claim based upon an act or omission of an employee of the Government, exercising due care, in the execution of a statute or regulation," or to "any claim . . . based upon the exercise or performance . . . [of] a discretionary function or duty." The Texas City disaster cases were brought under this act.[45]

It was physically impossible for Judges Kennerly and Hannay to hear 424 cases, even with the help of visiting judges. Kennerly therefore consolidated the Texas City disaster cases, ordering the creation of a "Working Committee of [seven plaintiff's] Attorneys . . . to prosecute [one] consolidated suit" as a test case for the others. The court's decisions as to matters of fact and conclusions of law in this test case, *Dalehite v. U.S.*, would apply to all the other cases.[46]

Over the next year, lawyers for the government and the plaintiffs combed the nation collecting evidence. In late 1949 the trial, expected to last ninety days and involving the testimony of hundreds of witnesses and examination of thousands of pieces of evidence, began. The burden placed on the court was enormous. By trial's end, the testimony and evidence spread over twenty thousand pages, plus attorneys' briefs.[47]

Litigants did not make the judge's job easy. Each made strong arguments stressing those issues most likely to support his or her position. The plaintiffs emphasized the government's negligence in "manufacturing . . . [and allowing to be] . . . handled, transported and shipped . . . without warning to anyone of the danger in the densely populated city . . . of Texas City, . . . a very dangerous commodity," ammonium nitrate. If the government had not decided to manufacture and ship the ammonium nitrate fertilizer, plaintiffs pointed out, the explosion would never have happened. Or, the decision to produce the fertilizer having been made, if the government had provided adequate safety regulations pertaining to the storage and shipment of ammonium nitrate fertilizer, the explosion might have been avoided. To have done neither, and to have left the city in ignorance of the dangers associated with ammonium nitrate, was clearly criminal negligence. The government, in other words, had acted negligently by both commission and omission, causing by its failures the death of hundreds and the destruction of much of Texas City. This, the plaintiffs argued, was the sort of offense the FTCA was designed to remedy.[48]

The government denied both the court's jurisdiction and the plaintiff's right to sue under the FTCA. Government lawyers explained that *Grandcamp* and *High Flyer* would not have made a private individual under like circumstances liable. Many causes led to the explosions. Sole blame was not the presence of fertilizer. Therefore, the FTCA could not come into play. The plaintiffs had failed to "charge any specific negligent or wrongful act or omission against any particular employee or agent of the United States," as required under the FTCA. Blaming "[e]verybody from the President to dishwashers in the cafeteria," as one plaintiff's lawyer had done, did not make an adequate case. Last, and most important, the decision to use ammonium nitrate as a fertilizer was a discretionary act, brought under a "statute or regulation of the United States," and hence explicitly protected from prosecution under the FTCA. Even if the government had been negligent–and the government denied it–the court lacked jurisdiction. Combined, all three arguments denied the plaintiffs' right to bring the case and the court's right to hear it under the provisions of the FTCA.[49]

In the end, it would be Kennerly's choice as to which of these arguments was valid. A negative answer regarding either the applicability of the FTCA or the government's negligence would bar recovery; a positive response meant recovery. The judge had to decide how far the government could go to advance a legitimate public policy before the negative effects of that policy on private citizens made the government accountable for its actions. His decision, in turn, depended on his views of the government's liability as a manufacturer of fertilizer. Should the government-as-manufacturer be viewed as a private actor whose negligence invoked the FTCA, interpreted broadly, thus holding the government to full liability? Or was the government's decision to manufacture fertilizer an act arising from its prerogative or duty, thus demanding strict interpretation of the FTCA? If private, the issue on which the case would turn was the government's negligence in allowing the fertilizer to be manufactured and shipped; if public, the limits of the FTCA defined the answer.

As a black-letter law judge, Kennerly's first impulse was to interpret the FTCA strictly. This would result in an expanded federal government free to affect citizens and unchecked by accountability, an end the judge clearly disliked. To limit the FTCA meant that the federal government would be held to different standards than were private individuals. If a private company had produced and shipped ammonium nitrate knowing the dangers involved and an explosion had occurred, that company would have been liable for its actions to the extent that it was negligent. Should the fact that those to blame in the Texas City explosion might have been acting under the authority of federal policy provide them with a greater level of legal protection than a private individual had? The judge was unsure. Tradition said yes; equity and justice, no. Last, innocent sufferers wanted remedies. The judge's heart bled for their losses. They were his neighbors and in need. To limit the FTCA would deny these people a remedy for their hurt and potentially harm the region's continued development. Surely there was something his court could do. After all, where there was a wrong, there was supposed to be a remedy; this was a legal maxim to which Kennerly had always held. Yet just what the judge could do under the law to help these people remained in question. The limits of the FTCA were specific and, if viewed as the primary issue in contention, controlled the case.

With few precedents to guide his decision, an inner voice arguing that a remedy had to be found for the wrong that had occurred, and a basic distrust of the increasingly active federal government shaping his views, Kennerly chose to view the government's role in the Texas City case in essentially private terms. This view allowed him quickly to bypass the jurisdictional issues raised by the defense and attend to the plaintiffs' claims of government negligence.[50] Here the judge found a "record filled [with examples of] . . . blunders, mistakes, and acts of negligence, both of omission and commission, on the part of the defendant, its agents, servants, and employees, in deciding to begin the manufacture of this inherently dangerous Fertilizer."

Ample evidence existed, the judge ruled, both before and after manufacture of this fertilizer began, as to the dangers of fire and explosion if it were improperly handled. "Such facts [as] learned by Defendant . . . showed that such Fertilizer should not be manufactured, in that it was, under certain conditions and circumstances, most dangerous . . . to the public." Yet despite the known risks, Kennerly continued, "Defendant's servants, agents and employees, negligently went forward in the manufacture, handling, distribution, shipping, etc. of such fertilizer." Worse yet, having reached its decision to prodice the fertilizer, the government then failed in its duty "to notify and advise all the carriers handling [the fertilizer], including the Steamships *Grandcamp* and *High Flyer,* [as well as] the city and State Officers at Texas City, of the dangerous nature . . . of such Fertilizer, [so that the public] could protect themselves . . . against the danger of fires . . . and explosions." "From beginning on down," the judge concluded, the entire fertilizer program was a mistake—a plan so dangerous in its very conception that it constituted a public nuisance whose mere undertaking was wrong and deserving of censure.[51]

With negligence established, equity dictated that the government be held fully liable under the FTCA and that a decision be entered in favor of the plaintiffs. On May 4, 1950, Kennerly provided this remedy. Ruling that the government was liable under the FTCA and had in fact been negligent in its actions leading up to the Texas City explosion, he entered judgment in the consolidated cases in favor of the plaintiffs and ordered the government to pay for all damages resulting from the April 16 and 17 explosions.[52]

The government immediately appealed this decision to the Fifth Circuit. It argued that Kennerly had erred in accepting jurisdiction under the FTCA as well as in overstating the government's negligence in producing ammonium nitrate fertilizer.[53] Sitting en banc, the Fifth Circuit, in a four to two split, reversed Kennerly's decision and entered judgment in favor of the government on the grounds that the plaintiffs' suits were barred by the FTCA. For the majority, Judge Richard Rives gave two reasons for limiting the scope of the FTCA. The goal of the FTCA, Rives explained, was not '"the creation of new causes of action but acceptance of liability under circumstances that would bring private liability into existence.'" The act was intended to "waive immunity from recognized causes of action . . . , not to visit the Government with novel and unprecedented liabilities." The legislative and judicial history of the FTCA, in turn, showed no evidence that liability for negligence as a manufacturer was an "accept[ed] liability" in this regard. Nowhere in the record of "the legislative hearings . . . [was] the liability of the United States as a manufacturer or shipper . . . discussed." Rather, Congress spent most of its time considering cases arising from the "negligent operation of motor vehicles" by government employees. In the absence of explicit mention by Congress of negligence in manufacturing, and with ample evidence that Congress intended the act to cover such minor liabilities as automobile accidents, Rives argued, it was illogical to assume that the FTCA was intended to cover the events surrounding the Texas City disaster. More to the point, the judge continued, the government's actions in this case were discretionary acts specifically protected from suit by the FTCA. The fertilizer program, Rives noted, "was designed to meet the immediate and pressing problem of increasing the food supply of the devastated areas of the world following . . . World War II." "Weighing the magnitude of the risk against the utility of [an] act," Judge Rives argued, was what a "discretionary act" was all about. It was not the place of the courts to judge by hindsight the correctness of that decision. "Much the same public policy forbids the courts to exercise jurisdiction over discretionary functions or duties of executive officers, as protects the government from being sued for the errors of the courts themselves in the exercise of their discretionary functions." Given the facts of this case, the judge concluded, "it can hardly be argued that the dangers of explosion from [ammonium nitrate fertilizer] were so well known prior to the disaster that judgement or discretion were not called into exercise as to whether it should be manufactured at all and under what safeguards and warnings it should be distributed."

Kennerly had erred in choosing to view the government's actions in the Texas City case as private in nature and hence in minimizing the importance of the jurisdictional issue. Though mistakes were made by the government, these mistakes were the result of the hard choices public officials faced in trying to fulfill national policy. To expect the government to be an "infallible judge" of all the possible outcomes of its actions in such a case was wrong. Such a decision "would impose on the Government . . . an unreasonably high degree of duty, almost to the point of being an insurer." It would create a hindrance on the actions of public officials and paralyze the government's ability to fulfill its governing function. This had been the reason for Congress's prohibition on suits against discretionary actions.[54]

Appealed to the Supreme Court, this view was subsequently affirmed in a 4–3 decision. Starting "from the accepted jurisprudential principle that no action lies against the United States unless the legislature has authorized it," Justice Reed argued that it was clear to the majority that Congress had "never contemplated that the Government should be subject to liability arising from acts of a governmental nature or function." One need only read the FTCA "in its entirety to conclude that Congress exercised care to protect the government from claims, however negligently caused, that affected the governmental functions." Nor was there "any doubt" in the majority's mind that "the cabinet-level decision to institute the fertilizer export program was a discretionary act." The "decisions held culpable [by the district court] were all responsibly made at a planning rather than operational level and involved considerations more or less important to the practicability of the Government's fertilizer program." Though some negligence might have occurred, "as a matter of law, the facts found [did not] give the District Court jurisdiction of the cause under the Tort Claims Act," thus making the negligence issue moot.[55]

Since the Supreme Court agreed with the Fifth Circuit that Kennerly had erred, and both viewed the government's decision to produce ammonium nitrate fertilizer as a discretionary act, the core issue became the scope of the FTCA. Given its provisions, the plaintiffs were without a case to press. If plaintiffs wished compensation, they would have to seek it directly from Congress.[56]

Kennerly was hardly alone in his views of the government's liability, however. Justice Jackson's dissent, Justices Frankfurter and Black concurring, also questioned the broad protections of government action allowed by this decision. Jackson's objections rested on the "fear that the Court's adoption of the Government's view in this case may inaugurate an unfortunate trend toward relaxation of private as well as official responsibility in making, vending or transporting inherently dangerous products." Our interdependent society, Jackson explained, "must exact greater care than in more simple days and must require from manufacturers or producers increased integrity and caution as the only protection of its safety and well-being." "We [who oppose the majority's opinion] believe it is the better view that whoever puts into circulation in commerce a product that is known or even suspected of being potentially inflammable or explosive is under an obligation to know his own product and to ascertain what forces he is turning loose. If, as will often be the case, a dangerous product is also a useful one, [the manufacturer should be] under a strict duty to follow each step of its distribution with warning of its dangers and with information and directions to keep those dangers to a minimum." Liability under the FTCA existed. Failure to apply the law meant that "the ancient and discredited doctrine that 'The King can do no wrong' . . . ha[d] merely been amended to read, 'The King can do only little wrongs.'"[57]

Soon the dissenters' view would gain priority within the Supreme Court.[58] More immediately, the minority opinion emphasized the gulf between the federal appellate courts' acceptance of expanding government authority and the Southern District Court's continued distrust of this authority. That the federal system's trial and appellate courts differed in their vision was unsurprising. Each level had different duties and institutional outlooks. The Fifth Circuit and the Supreme Court were appellate courts. They viewed such events as the Texas City disaster or rent control in terms of their legal and public impacts, hence their expansive focus on legislative intent. As a trial judge, Kennerly dealt with the immediate needs of litigants, hence his private approach to the problem. As time passed judicial values changed and became more accepting of government powers, but holding the users of those powers to strict standards of responsibility. Until that time, however, the judges of the Southern District would hold to their own stricter standards by denying government powers.[59]

III

A second category of actions in this period, criminal immigration suits, also caused difficulties for the court. Like public civil suits, immigration cases raised questions about the proper scope of government powers to curtail the rights of private individuals and businesses freely to contract for labor. In this case, however, there was little the court could do to settle the issue. Its role in immigration matters was largely administrative. Well over 90 percent of all immigration defendants pleaded guilty. In some years the number stood at 100 percent. The presiding judge merely passed sentence. First-time defendants received suspended jail terms of thirty to ninety days and were deported; repeat offenders were also required to serve all or part of their jail terms before deportation.[60]

It was the vast numbers of immigration cases filed with the court in these years that transformed this topic into a dilemma. The Second World War and the steady expansion of the U.S. economy that attended it had strained the state's large agricultural sector. Domestic migrant farmworkers had fled to new, higher paying industrial jobs created by the war. Suddenly without workers, Texas agriculturalists turned again to Mexico. By 1945 tens of thousands of Mexicans were legally in this country as temporary agricultural workers through a *bracero* contract labor program. Legal *braceros*, however, filled only a portion of farmers' labor needs.

Angry at the discrimination its nationals experienced in Texas, the Mexican government strictly limited the number of *braceros* in Texas. Many Texas farmers further considered the program's labor scales too high and clogged with red tape to be effective. Many Texas farmers preferred using illegal workers. Illegals came cheaper, could be hired and fired at will, and were easier to control. With farmers actively recruiting illegal workers a literal flood of illegal Mexican laborers was soon drawn into the country in search of work. This trend continued following the war, the postwar boom drawing still more illegal aliens across the border.[61]

By the early 1950s this flood of illegal Mexican workers became a political issue. Labor unions, social reformers, and nativist groups complained that illegal immigrant labor was simply a new form of peonage, one fostering vagrancy, child labor, and the displacement of native workers. Farmers who simply let their illegal workers go at the end of the picking season argued that without cheap illegal labor the cost of picking their crops would be prohibitive.[62]

Despite the farmers' objections, pressure against the illegals' presence grew so great that the federal government was forced to respond to the "wetback problem." In 1952 Congress passed a new immigration law making it a felony "to recruit, transport, conceal, or harbor illegal aliens." Concurrently, various federal agencies and departments joined in a series of enforcement programs, culminating in 1954's "Operation Wetback," aimed at stemming the flow of illegals from Mexico. Between 1950 and 1956 almost 3.25 million illegal aliens were sent back to Mexico. Operation Wetback alone accounted for the arrest and deportation of over one million undocumented workers.[63]

The majority of those arrested were administratively processed by immigration officials and allowed "voluntarily" to cross back into Mexico. At the program's high point in 1954, thousands of Mexicans were crossing the border into Mexico every day from El Paso, Laredo, and Brownsville. A small percentage of those arrested, however, were formally charged in the federal courts.[64] These latter cases produced the court's immigration dilemma.

Though only a fraction of a percent of the number of illegals administratively processed,[65] these cases nonetheless produced a sharp growth in the number of illegal immigration suits before the court. In 1950, 2,350 immigration cases were filed. The next year this number jumped to 7,813. Declining somewhat in 1952, to 5,901, and further still in 1953, to 3,100, immigration suits rebounded in 1954 to 4,681, only to decline once again in 1955, to 3,569. Thereafter the number of immigration cases filed began to decline rapidly, totaling 701 in 1956, 380 in 1957, and a decade low of 336 in 1958. Not until the 1970s would the number of immigration suits filed in the Southern District top the thousand-case mark.[66]

Individually of little consequence, save to the persons involved, taken as a whole these actions posed significant administrative and practical problems for the court. Though most defendants pleaded guilty, it still took time to hear the thousands of cases before the court. It seemed that every time one of the judges "cleared out" the jail in Brownsville, Corpus Christi, or Laredo, he was called back to do it again. As Judge Kennerly explained in a 1949 letter, "about every 6 weeks" or so, "it was necessary for [either me or Judge Hannay] to stop whatever he may be doing and visit [the court's three southern divisions] to dispose of [immigration] cases and try to prevent the expense of keeping prisoners in jail for a long period." Once there, as Hannay explained in a similar letter, it took the judge sometimes as much as two weeks to process these immigration cases, leaving only one week or less in which to hear any civil matters on the docket. Nor could the judges in good conscience put this duty off. Conditions in South Texas jails were so bad that regular court action to empty them was essential. "I have seen many of our small cells, say 10 by 12 feet, with as many as 10 or 12 men housed in them," South Texas Congressman Lloyd Bentsen reported. "We do not have a place for them. They have to stay in those jails . . . until we have a Federal judge sitting down there."[67]

This problem worsened as the numbers of immigration violators increased in the next five years. Already busy with an active civil docket, the court found itself unable to keep up with the flood of immigration suits without causing significant delays in other areas. The addition of two judgeships in 1950 allowed the court only to keep up with the increased flow of cases resulting from such efforts as Operation Wetback. To do even this, Judge Allred was forced to spend close to 100 percent of this time shuttling between the three southern divisions of the district simply hearing immigration cases, and it was often necessary for the other three judges to travel to one of the three southern divisions to help Allred out. Not until the government began limiting its enforcement of the immigration laws after 1955, primarily by making illegal immigrants into legal *braceros,* did the court's immigration problems ease.[68]

In effect, immigration matters posed as great a challenge to the court's private priorities as did public civil matters, but they took a completely different form. While public civil cases raised questions about the content of the court's priorities, immigration cases challenged its ability to provide any services at all. Only the addition of the two extra judges in 1949 kept the court from collapsing under the strain imposed by so many immigration suits. And more "floods" of public cases were soon to be filed with the court.

IV

Hundreds of private civil suits also burdened the court. While these numbers did not compare to the thousands of cases illegal immigration generated, they made private civil suits the second most numerous category of action before the court from 1945 through 1958. In contrast to earlier years, when equity and contract matters made up the majority of private civil suits, most postwar private actions were diversity tort cases. Comprising primarily insurance and personal injury actions, tort suits totaled over 80 percent of the court's private civil cases, in some years, 90 percent (see table 6). The remaining private civil cases consisted of diversity suits involving real property and contract matters and federal question actions under such statutes as the Jones (Seaman's Personal Injury) Act and the Federal Tort Claims Act.[69]

These tort actions seriously affected the court's traditional emphasis on private matters. Unlike earlier contract and equity cases, the tort suits of the 1940s and 1950s did not provide a good mechanism through which the court could, as appropriate, preserve or reshape the region's economic ways. Most tort actions involved integrating individual needs and concerns into existing economic structures and business practices, not creating new ones. Tort actions required different responses from the court than did equity or contract matters. In contract or equity cases, the court's main function was to discern litigants' legal relationships, obligations, and reciprocal advantages and then to provide a plan by which these relationships could best be implemented. In a tort suit, its duty was first to ascertain to what extent each litigant was responsible for some adverse act or event and then to compute the compensation due the more-injured party. In nontort cases the court's decisions directly affected the way business was carried out; in tort matters, the court could affect the future actions of the litigants only by setting high compensation awards. In the 1950s, however, few tort cases involved large enough amounts of money to affect the region's economy. In addition, since most tort suits were settled by agreement of the parties, the ability of the court to set compensation was curtailed.[70]

These trends largely neutralized the court's ability to achieve its private agenda in the years following World War II, at least in private actions. Having successfully attained its long-held goal of local development, the court ironically found itself out of a job as the large businesses on whose litigation it depended to implement its agenda no longer turned to it. At the same time that public issues were increasing, pressure on the court to implement its private agenda was quietly lessening. And, unlike what obtained with its public actions, the court could do little to redress the drift. This shift in emphasis can be perceived in the first category of tort suits to appear on its docket after World War II: appeals from the Texas Industrial Accident Board.

TIAB cases made up over two-thirds of all insurance cases faced by the court from 1946 through 1958; they were the largest single source of tort litigation in the postwar period. In terms of their content, these workers' compensation cases were almost identical to similar appeals filed during the war; the major difference was their greater number. As with wartime suits, most postwar TIAB cases originated in the state's industrial, transportation, and construction sectors. Growing rapidly in response to the postwar boom, these industries employed increasing numbers of workers. More workers, in turn, meant more

Table 6

PUBLIC, PRIVATE, DIVERSITY, AND INSURANCE SUITS IN SOUTHERN DISTRICT, 1946–59

Year	*Public Suits*	*Private Suits*	*Diversity Suits*	*Insurance Suits*
1946	305	427	392	313
1947	503	452	377	276
1948	240	511	465	346
1949	417	625	576	406
1950	197	710	465	473
1951	136	616	571	395
1952	285	717	631	451
1953	212	840	765	322
1954	241	987	829	695
1955	208	832	761	550
1956	228	943	866	657
1957	606	1,142	941	709
1958	421	1,482	1,193	840
1959	362	655	397	135

Source: AO Report, table C3 (1946–59). Nationally, tort actions made up somewhere between 20 and 30 percent of all private civil filings. This trend received repeated comment from the administrative director. See *AO Report* (1947), p. 30; (1948), p. 16; (1950), p. 110; (1954), p. 89; (1956), p. 129.

industrial accidents and hence a greater TIAB workload. The TIAB, however, remained small, inefficient, and overworked. Insurance companies continued to manipulate the TIAB, which resulted at least in those cases in which no prior settlement had been reached, in an almost "automatic" appeal by the worker to the courts, usually a state court, to overturn the TIAB's decision. Where the insurance company protecting the employer was a "foreign" corporation, and most companies providing workers' compensation coverage in Texas were out-of-state entities, these suits would then be removed to the Southern District.[71]

As during the war, most postwar TIAB appeals were settled before going to trial. Settlements were, in fact, the primary reasons litigants came to court. The court served as a forum in which to scare one's opponent into accepting a favorable compromise. As Thomas Weatherly, a tort attorney who handled many TIAB appeals, recalls, "this was the only way that you could get things done." Once a settlement had been reached, however, the court's role in such cases became routine and minimal. Checking the written settlement agreement to assure that its outcome was "fair, just and equitable, and to the best interests of all parties," the judge would file a consent decree implementing the settlement's provisions.[72]

When the two sides could not work out their differences and a trial was required, the court's ability to produce a decision likely to change business practices remained limited. The outcome in most TIAB trials depended on the answers to a very few factual questions. Was the worker actually on the job when injured? Did the injury result from job-related activities? How badly hurt was the worker and for how long incapacitated? What was the proper compensation for this injury as provided for by the Texas Workman's Compensation Act? At no time was the employer's responsibility a matter of controversy or even concern. As in most states, Texas' workers compensation law was "no fault." As long as employees were injured while on the job they were entitled to compensation. Even when the court held a trial, therefore, there was little opportunity for the judge to affect the region's business practices.[73]

Similar powerlessness was evident in the court's other insurance cases. Technically, the clarification of responsibility provided by interpleader and declaratory judgment petitions should have brought about major change in the region's business practices, as had been true in the 1930s, when the court's decisions in insurance matters helped that industry reorganize from the disaster of the depression. The economic situation in the 1950s, however, was different and the insurance industry less in need of protections and legal certainties provided by interpleader and declaratory judgments. When an insurance company litigated in the 1950s, it turned to the court as a forum in which to integrate the particular facts of the case at hand into an understood legal structure. The issue in contention was not whether the company had to pay, but to whom and how much. The goal in litigating was to arrive at this amount in as controlled a way as possible. As the actions of the federal courts in past cases were well known, the insurance companies were confident of the outcome.[74]

The generally small size of the average insurance claim of the 1950s also limited the effects of insurance cases on insurance company practices. The most common sources of insurance litigation, both nationally and in the Southern District, involved automobile accidents and house fires. While large awards were given on some occasions, most suits of this sort involved relatively small amounts, usually under ten thousand dollars and rarely over seventy-five thousand dollars. Hence, even if the court's judges or juries had imposed the maximum award possible, the impact on the industry would have been small.[75]

Not so with the third category of postwar tort action: personal injury suits. Though making up the smallest percentage of the court's tort case load,[76] personal injury suits were exceptions to the general pattern in tort cases. Personal injury suits allowed the judges directly to affect the region's economic structures. First, the size of personal injury awards was significantly larger than those in insurance and TIAB cases, and thus had the potential to change business practices. Second, personal injury cases were the tort action most likely to go to trial, thereby providing the court more opportunities to alter business practices. Last, these suits often involved issues that grew out of the everyday activities of area businesses, and the court's decisions could change the direction and extent of these practices.[77]

To be sure, the court proved unwilling to force drastic changes. Most decisions in personal injury matters favored defendants, "the plaintiff [taking] nothing from his suit." Where juries decided for the plaintiff, the judge often lowered the awards. For example, in mid-1952 a jury awarded C. F. Palmer $82,000 against the Texas and New Orleans Railroad. Judge Allred, however, lowered the award to $41,250.[78]

Even with personal injury suits, then, the impact of tort cases on Southeast Texas' economic structures and practices proved to be minimal. In the 1930s and 1940s the court's tort decisions had played a transformative role, reshaping business practices. By the 1950s the region's industries and insurance companies no longer needed such help. Healthy, confident, and in control of their own destinies, these companies viewed the court primarily as an alternate forum in which to integrate individual needs and concerns into preexisting structures and practices.

What then of the judges' private agenda? Almost as soon as the war was over, the Administrative Office commented negatively on the large numbers of private tort cases being filed in the federal courts: "It is the civil business, which, . . . occupies the greater part of the time of the ordinary judge," one *AO Report* announced. Suits of this sort "take two to threefold as much time on the part of the judge [to complete] as a Government case." As the number of private tort suits before the federal courts increased, the "burden [being placed] . . . upon the district judges" in their efforts to clear their dockets became heavier.[79]

In Houston the judges saw these reports and also the greater number of tort cases on the court's docket. Hannay and Kennerly in separate letters to the 1949 House Subcommittee on the Judiciary noted this increase and its unhappy implications. Not only did the court face more cases every year, but the time required to hear these cases was growing at an even faster rate. Worse yet, these tort actions involved small, boring issues that had little to do with the development of Southeast Texas or of the law. It did not take the judges long to appreciate, and resent, their growing powerlessness in this situation.[80]

As Thomas Weatherly recalls, however, the judges may have "disliked tort cases, but [they] tolerated them" because they had long emphasized the private docket. Kennerly, Hannay, and Allred had always afforded top priority to private civil matters. It was understandably difficult for them to change lifetime habits. Connally and Ingraham had not devoted so much toward this end, but they did support the older judges' general goal of promoting economic development. More important, there was very little the judges could do to change matters. As long as the amount in dispute was over three thousand dollars and diversity existed, these cases had to be placed on the court's docket. The judges, in other words, had to "take what they could get. They didn't like these cases, but they had to follow the law."[81]

By the mid-1950s the judges' frustration led to action. Not surprisingly, it was one of the newer judges, Ben Connally, who took the lead. At first informally and later as a member of the Judicial Conference, Connally began to push for a change in the laws governing the jurisdiction of the federal courts. In particular, he championed the exclusion of workers' compensation cases from the federal courts' jurisdiction, a change guaranteed to have an immediate impact on the docket of the Southern District. In addition, he joined with other federal judges in calling for an increase, from three thousand dollars to ten thousand dollars in the minimum for diversity jurisdiction and for a redefinition of citizenship to make corporations citizens of every state in which they did business. Combined, all three proposals aimed at shifting the burden posed by small tort matters to the state courts.[82]

Formally proposed in 1957 by the Judicial Conference, these jurisdictional reforms became law in August, 1958, with an immediate effect on the private civil case load of the federal courts. One year later, national filings of private civil cases were down 17 percent, in Texas, even more. The four Texas districts saw private civil filings decrease by 48 percent, most of this decline accounted for by the loss of over two thousand TIAB cases. The decline in the Southern District was even more extreme, with the private civil docket standing at just over 45 percent of its former size by 1959. These lower numbers, both in Texas and the Southern District, would continue for almost a decade until new federal statutes once again expanded the range of federal tort actions.[83]

None of the judges, least of all Connally, had abandoned their private agenda. In contract, patent, and real estate litigations before them, they continued to lavish the time and effort traditional in private civil cases.[84] The change was not in the judges, but in the needs of the region. A successful system of regional growth had been found, and the court's services in this regard were no longer necessary. While the effect of this shift in the 1950s was minimal, it would play an important part in allowing the coming transformation of the court's agenda to public matters.

V

Technically, the rise of civil rights suits following World War II was not a new phenomenon for the federal courts. Cases involving the judicial definition and protection of individual and group rights had always been part of the federal courts' docket. At certain times, such as during the 1790s, the Civil War and Reconstruction years, and World War I, cases of this sort had even become the dominant issue before these bodies. Yet for all this technical familiarity, the civil rights suits of the post–World War II years were something new and different.

The difference lay in the federal courts' response to these suits. Though many decisions affecting the rights of the individual had been made by the federal courts prior to 1945, with the exception of those made during the Reconstruction years, these decisions were largely negative in their effect and intent. Most aimed at illuminating limits placed on individuals by society, not in expanding protections society owed to individuals. Where suits were filed seeking federal protection of individual or group rights from government or private action, the federal courts proved reluctant to act, especially when such suits involved the rights of women, African Americans, and aliens.[85]

This negative attitude toward expanded civil rights protections changed after 1945. Led by the Supreme Court, the federal judicial system began to reorient its views on individual and corporate civil rights, extending the range of actions protected by the Constitution. Determining the duties society owed to the individual, rather than what the individual owed to society, became the new standard in civil rights. Cases seeking the expansion of minority rights began to receive positive responses from the federal courts. This positive response, in turn, generated still more suits involving even newer rights for the federal courts to protect. The result was a legal, social, and institutional revolution as expanded individual and group rights transformed the nation, the law, and the work load of the federal courts.[86]

This change was gradual. Not all federal judges approved of this revolutionary reorientation toward civil rights. Many, especially in the South, continued to oppose the shift well into the 1960s. Years of constant pressure from the Supreme Court and the Circuit Courts of Appeals would be needed before such correctives as desegregation become even a *de jure* reality; still more before they became de facto. In most districts, the process of change would not even begin until the late 1950s.[87]

For the district courts the positive expansion of individual and group civil rights was to be more a concern of the 1960s and 1970s than of the 1940s and 1950s. Where suits seeking the expansion of individual or corporate rights were filed prior to 1960, the district courts' responses remained generally traditional. Expanding individual and group rights was not yet seen to be a proper function of the federal courts. It was only at the Supreme Court and, to a lesser extent, the circuit court levels that attitudes significantly changed.

Still, changes did occur. The immediate postwar years witnessed important structural transformations in the judicial response to civil rights. In some instances, real gains were made, though many federal judges wished to ignore the issue.

The Southern District was no exception. Like other federal courts, it had heard a number of civil rights suits prior to 1945.[88] Most of these suits involved attempts by African American Texans to break the all-white Democratic party primary and were part of a series of legal challenges brought in both state and federal courts over a twenty-five-year period. The Southern District's response to these suits was essentially negative. Unless directed by explicit Supreme Court rulings to entertain such suits, the court's judges refused to hear them or ruled against the plaintiffs every time they came before the court. Even where the Supreme Court required lower court action, the judges still resisted, providing only the minimum actions required to fulfill this mandate.

African Americans had been effectively excluded from voting in the Texas Democratic primary since the passage of the 1903 Terrell Election Act. The first

Texas law to regulate primary elections, the Terrell Act granted all qualified voters in the state the right to vote in any party primary as long as they had successfully completed a prescribed "party test." Determining the exact content of this test, however, was left to the individual parties. The act further allowed any "county executive committee of the party holding any primary election" the right to "prescribe additional qualifications" for participating voters. With no guidelines to limit party action, qualifications for party membership were quickly adopted that effectively barred many Texas African Americans from voting in the Democratic primary. In 1923 the state legislature made this prohibition official, ordering "that in no event shall a negro be eligible to participate in a Democratic party primary."[89] Since the Texas Democratic party controlled state government, this ban on participation meant the effective disfranchisement of Texas African Americans. Voting in the general election was meaningless, for real choices were made in the Democratic primary.

Angered, Texas African Americans challenged the "white primary" in the courts. The first such effort was made by Houston journalist C. N. Love, who along with educator William Leonard Davis and business leaders James Grigsby, William Nickerson, Jr., Newman Dudley, Jr., and Perry Mack, filed suit in state district court on February 5, 1921, against Harris County Democratic party head James Griffith and numerous local election judges.

Charging that state laws prohibiting qualified African Americans from voting in the Democratic primary violated the Fourteenth and Fifteenth amendments, the plaintiffs sought an injunction preventing the defendants from disallowing the votes of Houston African Americans in the upcoming primary election. The defendants argued that the state law prohibiting African Americans from voting in the Democratic primary did not infringe the Fifteenth Amendment and that the plaintiffs' complaint, flawed for including arguments to this end, was inadequate to justify court jurisdiction. State District Judge Charles Ashe agreed and ordered the plaintiffs to submit a new complaint minus the offending sections. Love and his fellow plaintiffs refused. The Fifteenth Amendment was the basis of their case; to remove it would destroy their chances of victory. With no new complaint filed, Judge Ashe ordered Love's case thrown out of court.

Subsequently appealed to both the court of civil appeals and the Texas Supreme Court, the case was each time dismissed on the grounds that, as the election had already passed, no actual controversy existed. With no real controversy present, equity jurisdiction did not arise and the appeals courts had no case to rule on. Persisting, Love and his associates then brought the case to the United States Supreme Court on a writ of error, charging that the state appellate courts had erred in failing to rule on the case. Justice Holmes, writing for the majority, affirmed the state court's positions, however. As the cause of action had ceased to exist, Holmes wrote "there was no constitutional obligation to extend the remedy beyond what was prayed." Holmes did, however, hold out a ray of hope to Texas African Americans: "If the case [had] stood here as it stood before the court of first instance, it would [have] presented a grave question of constitutional law [which the court] should be astute to avoid hindrances in the way of taking it up."[90]

Encouraged by Holmes's dicta in the *Love* case, a second attempt to break the white primary was made in 1924 by El Paso physician L. A. Nixon. Nixon had recently been denied the right to vote in the Democratic primary by election judge C. C. Herndon, who cited the state's 1923 election law. Nixon brought suit in the Western District of Texas and the Fifth Circuit, but his cases were dismissed each time for the same reasons given in *Love et al. v. Griffith et al.*: the event that Nixon sought to avoid had already occurred and hence no actual controversy or pending harm existed for the court to prohibit. The case was then appealed to the Supreme Court, which, Holmes again writing for the majority, held the 1923 voting rights law an unconstitutional violation of the Fourteenth Amendment: "It seems . . . hard to imagine a more direct and obvious infringement of the Fourteenth Amendment. While states may do a good deal of classifying that is difficult to believe rational, there are limits [to this power], and it is too clear for extended argument that color cannot be made the basis of a statutory classification affecting the right" to vote in a primary election.[91]

Jubilation with the *Nixon* decision proved short-lived. Holmes's opinion dealt only with the legislature's explicit prohibition of African American voting. Following Holmes's decision, Governor Dan Moody called a special session of the state legislature to amend the primary voting law by deleting provisions explicitly barring African American voters. The Democratic party would again determine voter qualifications. Soon after the amended law was passed (June 7, 1927), the Democratic party executive committee resolved that "all white Democrats who are qualified voters under the Constitutions and laws of Texas . . . and none other, [will] be allowed to participate in the primary elections to be [subsequently] held."[92]

Once again barred from voting, a number of prominent African American Houstonians, led by James Grigsby and Owen DeWalt, set out to challenge the Texas Democratic party's ban. In July, 1928, they appeared before Judge Hutcheson and requested a temporary injunction against the executive committee of the Harris County Democratic party, prohibiting it from hindering qualified African American voters in the coming primary, in violation of the Fourteenth and Fifteenth amendments. Primaries existed under authority of the State of Texas, which made the party's actions "state action" under the constitution. In line with Holmes's dicta in *Nixon,* the plaintiffs contended, the court could not allow a ban on voting to continue.

Judge Hutcheson disagreed. The state executive committee resolution was "purely party action." Though Texas authorized the Democratic party to run its primaries, it was still a private, voluntary organization and could limit its membership as it chose. The ban on joining the Democratic party therefore posed no "invasion of [the plaintiffs'] legal rights." And, the judge concluded, as no legal rights were threatened, no decision on relief need be made. Hutcheson therefore denied the request for a restraining injunction.[93]

Hindered once more by a lower federal court, by 1930 Houston African Americans were ready to try again to challenge the white primary. Julius White, a Houston nightclub owner, sued J. B. "Shorty" Lubbock, Harris County Democratic party executive committee head, in state court seeking an injunction ordering Lubbock to ignore orders from the state executive committee to bar African Americans from voting. Concurrent with this suit, C. N. Love turned to the Southern District Court for a similar injunction. Citing *Grigsby v. Harris,* both the Texas Court of Civil Appeals and Judge Hutcheson refused the requested writ. As both judges saw matters, until the Supreme Court acted against the all-white primary, the law was settled.[94]

Soon after this, a second suit by El Paso's Dr. L. A. Nixon against election judge C. C. Herndon resulted in just such a Supreme Court opinion challenging the Texas white primary. Justice Cardozo spoke for the High Court. The Texas Democratic party was not a simply voluntary association in primary elections. Its organization and control of these elections derived directly from a "grant of power" from the state, and hence was a prohibited "state action" under the Fourteenth Amendment. As with Holmes's earlier opinion attacking the Texas white primary, however, Cardozo left a loophole through which the Texas Democrats could circumvent the High Court's ruling. Cardozo noted that "[w]hatever inherent power a state political party has to determine the content of its membership resides in the state convention." And, the justice pointed out, this body had never declared its "will to bar negroes of the state from admission to the party ranks."[95]

Texas Democrats quickly called a state convention that limited participation in the party to "all white citizens." Foiled in their efforts to fully break the white primary by this concession and resolution, Houston African Americans turned once more to the Southern District Court for relief, hoping that the court's new judge, Kennerly, would prove more open to their arguments than Hutcheson.

In part, this proved to be the case. Given Justice Cardozo's opinion in the second *Nixon* case, Kennerly ruled that "the powers exercised by the [state Democratic] convention in passing such a resolution [banning African American voters] were derived from the state of Texas" and hence prohibited by the Fourteenth Amendment. "Unlike Moses, who refused to be known as the son of Pharaoh's daughter, the Democratic Party in Texas has over a period of twenty-five years, chosen to be known as a child and agency of the state of Texas, abandoning its own inherent powers, and choosing to conduct its affairs under grants of power from the state."

Yet, despite this concession to the right of African Americans to vote in the Democratic primary, Kennerly ultimately proved no more willing to act than had Hutcheson and dismissed this case on the grounds that the court did not have "jurisdiction to entertain complainant's bill because of the nature of his prayer for relief." In effect, Kennerly explained, the plaintiffs were requesting "a mandamus against respondents to require [the] respondents . . . to allow [African Americans] to vote in such primary." While his court had "jurisdiction of the parties and the subject matter," the judge concluded, "[it had] no jurisdiction to grant [said] mandamus." Unable to provide a remedy, Kennerly was forced, as he put it, to dismiss the case.[96]

With their right to vote upheld but unprotected by Kennerly's decision, Houston African Americans were once again refused the ballot by election judges in the subsequent Democratic primary. They returned to the court again in 1932, but Kennerly once more refused to hear the case, citing both the past justifications for bigotry and the technicality that the plaintiffs' attorneys had given insufficient notice of the case to the defendants.[97]

This pattern continued for the remainder of the 1930s. Cases would be brought before the court, only to have the judge refuse to order injunctions after citing a number of procedural and occasionally substantive reasons for this opinion. In 1933, for example, Julius White and other prominent African American Houstonians sued the Houston Democratic party to uphold their right to vote in a primary election for city officials. Kennerly denied their plea on the grounds that in barring African Americans from voting city Democrats had been acting under an "inherent power of the party." As no state power was involved in city primaries, Kennerly asserted, their conduct was not governed by *Nixon v. Herndon* or even his opinion in *White v. Lubbock*. In 1938 Houston African Americans tried again, only to have Kennerly refuse to consider the case on the grounds that it offered no new arguments from those made in 1933.[98]

Only in the early 1940s would this trend begin to change. Following the Supreme Court's 1941 decision in *U.S. v. Classic*, that Article I, Section 4 of the U.S. Constitution gave Congress the power to regulate primary elections "where the primary is by law made an integral part of the election machinery," Houston doctor Lonnie Smith sued S. E. Allwright and James E. Luizza, election judges of the 48th precinct, for refusing to allow him to vote in a July, 1940, primary.

Smith's lawyer, NAACP chief counsel Thurgood Marshall, intended a direct attack on the Texas white primary. Few expected Judge Kennerly or the Fifth Circuit to rule in the plaintiff's favor, however. Nor were they disappointed in their expectations. Despite Marshall's arguments seeking to extend *U.S. v. Classic* to the Texas situation, neither Kennerly nor the judges of the Fifth Circuit agreed with this reading of the *Classic* rule. "In Louisiana," Kennerly noted, "the State Law . . . made the primary 'an integral part of the procedure of choice.' In Texas it has not."[99]

Marshall's arguments were aimed at the Supreme Court. In 1944 the High Court held that the Texas Democratic party's control of the state's primary system was evidence that it operated as an "agency of the state" and hence was prohibited by the Constitution from denying any citizen the right to vote on the basis of race alone. The fact that this ban reflected the wishes of party members was no valid excuse. "The party takes its character as a state agency from the duties imposed upon it by state statutes; the duties do not become matters of private law because they are performed by a political party." The Democratic party's exclusion of African Americans, therefore, was a violation that the courts could not allow. "The fusing by the Classic case of the primary and general elections into a single instrumentality for the choice of officers has [created]," the high court ruled, a definite prohibition as to "the permissibility under the Constitution of excluding Negroes from primaries."[100]

At first skeptical that *Smith v. Allwright* would have any greater impact than the two *Nixon* cases, Texas African Americans soon realized that they had won a major victory. In the summer of 1944, they voted in the Democratic primary for the first time without contest or conflict. The Texas white primary was dead.[101]

Victory, however, did not end their efforts to attack legal inequities, nor did it change the court's response to these suits. The judges' pattern of doing only the minimum required under the law continued unchecked in the post-1945 period. This fact became painfully clear in 1950, when Houston African Americans returned to the Southern District Court in hopes of ending the legal segregation on Houston's three municipal golf courses.

In common with most other southern cities, Houston maintained separate city parks for African Americans and Anglo Americans. Although the facilities for both were equal in theory, in actuality, those in the parks for Anglos were superior to those for African Americans. None of the city-operated golf courses were situated in African American–only parks, a fact that, in effect, prohibited Houston African Americans from playing golf on courses built and maintained by public resources. Bothered by this inequity, Houston African Americans sued the city and its officers for an injunction and a declaratory judgment to open the city golf courses to their use.

Plaintiffs argued that the city golf courses were an integral part of the park system; to separate them from other facilities in the city parks was illogical. They were as much a part of the experience of using the city parks as were ball diamonds or tennis courts. To "promulgate rules which will deny [this] form of recreational facility . . . to a citizen solely on account of race and color while furnishing such facility to white citizens" was a violation of the constitutional guarantee of equal protection of the law.

The city, conversely, denied that "any rights of the Plaintiffs guaranteed by the fourteenth Amendment" had been "infringe[d]" by the placement of the golf courses, nor that the city ordinance "providing for the separation of the races in public parks" was unconstitutional. It defended these positions by reminding the court that "the doctrine of *Plessy v. Ferguson* [had] not been overruled and that, as a result, segregated facilities were not prima facie unconstitutional." In addition, the city's lawyers continued, Houston had made every effort possible to "provide the most modern facilities" for segregated African American parks. While none of these parks had a golf course, many Anglo parks did not have the pools and gymnasiums of some African American parks. The absence of public golf courses on which African Americans could play was not in itself, therefore, inequitable.[102]

It was this last argument that was to prove the most telling to Judge Kennerly. Holding that "[i]t has long been established that the States may provide for the separation of the Negro race and the white race in certain public places and public institutions," Kennerly noted that "the action of the City of Houston in setting aside certain of its parks for the use of white people and certain others for the use of Negroes may be regarded as lawful *if* the facilities furnished or provided for each race are substantially equal" (emphasis added). This, the judge found, was in fact the case. "The stipulation [of facts] shows that the 4 parks used and to be used exclusively by the Negroes have substantially the same facilities and equipment as the 17 parks used exclusively by white people, except that 3 of the [Anglo] parks . . . have golf courses." In all other categories of facilities, "tennis courts, baseball diamonds, . . . playgrounds and apparatus, picnic grounds with tables and other equipment," the segregated African American parks were "equal to those used by the white people." To argue that they were not equal "solely because they ha[d] no golf courses . . . was not meritorious. . . . I do not think that the failure to provide golf courses in parks used by Negroes is either as a matter of law or fact a discrimination against the Negroes."[103]

The Fifth Circuit, however, disagreed. Unlike Kennerly, who refused to apply *Smith v. Allwright* beyond its narrow application to voting in primaries, the Fifth Circuit took its cue from this decision and overruled Kennerly. "This [case] is denying to a negro, because he is a negro, his individual, his personal rights as a citizen to use and enjoy a facility furnished at the public expense while permitting a white man, because he is white, to use and enjoy it," wrote Judge Hutcheson. To allow this was wrong. It was also unconstitutional. All citizens, Hutcheson argued, had a right to equal treatment under law, and the failure of the City of Houston to provide equal golf facilities to its African American citizens was a clear inequity.

This did not mean, however, that the Fifth Circuit sought the reversal of segregation as applied under *Plessy v. Ferguson*. The appeal court's decision rested on a very specific application of *Plessy*'s "separate but equal" doctrine. As the separate park facilities provided by Houston were not truly equal in that the only golf courses provided were limited to Anglo use, some remedial action was necessary. The Fifth Circuit's order, therefore, permitted the city to "preserv[e] segregation" in the use of the golf courses, as long as African Americans were given an equal opportunity to use these facilities.[104]

The case was sent back to Kennerly's docket and "equal but segregated use" was what the judge ordered. Quoting Judge Hutcheson's mandate, Kennerly allowed the city "'a reasonable opportunity to promptly prepare and put into effect regulations for the use of the municipal golf facilities, which while preserving segregation, will be in full and fair accord with [the equality under the law] principle.'" Ironically, the city chose to discontinue segregating its municipal golf courses. There were few African American golfers. Afraid that if they provided equal time to the city's few African American golfers the courses would be soon bankrupted, the city in late in 1954 opened the courses to all users.[105]

This was the civil rights situation in the Southern District when the Supreme Court decided *Brown v. Board of Education* in 1954. Personally, ideologically, and institutionally unwilling to extend the court's functions to encompass protections of political—as opposed to economic—rights and issues, the district court's judges had refused to help Texas African Americans break the bonds of segregation and racism. Only after the Supreme Court had literally ordered this did the district court change its views on the subject, and even then, it proved unwilling to extend this view to other civil rights issues.

This unwillingness to act was not surprising. Both Hutcheson and Kennerly were men of their time and place. Each accepted what today would be considered unjust actions, especially concerning questions of race. Both were southerners, and Hutcheson was the son of a Confederate soldier; thus the judges accepted segregation. Among civil rights activists Hutcheson had a bad reputation. They believed he viewed African Americans as if they were "a lower type of individual and an inferior race," and thus held "against Negroes repeatedly." Kennerly's reputation was almost as bad.[106]

More important, the institutional constraints limiting the judges' vision of their duties dictated this seemingly racist outcome. With the sole exception of the Civil War and Reconstruction years, for most of the nation's history the emphasis of the federal court system, and of the legal system as a whole, had been on expanding economic, not social or political, rights. While the judges' backgrounds made a negative vision of civil rights comfortable, it was a tradition whose origins predated the court itself.

It should not be surprising that the judges not only refused help to Texas African Americans prior to *Brown v. Board of Education,* but were slow to implement that landmark decision. They ordered desegregation to commence, but allowed community pressures and obstructionists to slow the desegregation process for over a decade.[107]

This reluctance to act was especially visible in the first and largest desegregation case to be heard in the district, that of the Houston Independent School District (HISD). Judge Ben Connally, who was assigned this case, was troubled by *Brown.* Circuit Judge John R. Brown, who was to become one of the "unlikely heroes" of the desegregation fight, recalled that "in his heart, Connally always felt that *Brown v. Board of Education* was wrong—that it made bad law." Connally was also perplexed by the whole issue, feeling that "most blacks, like most whites, preferred their own schools." Still, he "recognized the importance of establishing the right to attend the school of one's choice" and saw it as his duty under the Supreme Court's decision to desegregate the Houston schools.[108]

With a heavy heart, but a firm conviction that he had to act, the judge set out to achieve this result when the case of Delores Ross and two other African American children who had been refused permission to register in an all-Anglo school came before him in late May, 1957. Four months later, Judge Connally declared unconstitutional those portions of Texas law mandating segregated schools. He did not however, order immediate desegregation. "The [School] Board here does not rely upon the assertion that the present policy of segregation is lawful or is justified by Texas statute," the judge noted. Rather, "it is suggested that the public good flowing from an orderly and planned program of desegregation to be adopted and enforced by the Board, with Court intervention, warrants a temporary delay in the enforcement of the Constitutional rights of the two individuals primarily involved here." Such arguments, the judge concluded, were "cogent and weighty."

> It cannot be denied that the first intermingling of the races of the schools of the community is calculated to arouse tension and emotional upset. Customs and traditions in which the people of this land have been steeped for a century are not forgotten in a day. The layman does not readily understand that what on yesterday had been accepted law for a generation is no longer law today. The daily press and periodicals show that in many Texas cities where the local school authorities have placed in operation their own carefully devised plans for desegregation, the transition has been without incident. This is in sharp contrast to the situations presented in other sites where enforcement of court actions in similar cases has led to resentment, rioting and disorder.

Though the plaintiffs had argued that if desegregation were left to the school board no African American students would be admitted to Anglo schools, Connally was moved by the school board's arguments. "I am not as yet prepared to find that these public officials are so blind to their duty or devoid of responsibility as to abandon their obligation properly to administer the schools in a time of crisis. If it be true that the board desires to temper the impact of the *Brown* decision, I do not wish to deny them that opportunity." The judge thus granted the school board's motion and permitted it the time to implement its own desegregation plan. He did, however, warn the board that "a court of equity will not countenance inordinate delay or evasion where the enjoyment of a constitutional right is involved, though its recognition and enforcement be difficult and unpopular."[109]

Yet "countenanc[e] inordinate delay [or] evasion" was exactly what Connally subsequently did. As the plaintiffs had suggested, left to its own devices the school board was unwilling to implement real desegregation. Though the board initiated an "upgrading" program for African American teachers and administrators in the summer of 1958 and started test programs in two African American schools, no African American students were allowed to transfer to Anglo schools.[110]

Faced with rising complaints over the lack of progress, Connally ordered the board to report in mid-August, 1959, on specific steps taken toward desegregation. The board found this difficult to do, for while three desegregation plans had been created, none were approved. It was simply too hot a political topic, as past board president Mrs. Frank Dyer explained in a letter to the judge, for the board to choose between the three available options.[111]

With no plan before him, Connally had few options. As the judge explained in a letter to counsel, he was forced to infer "from the reply of the defendant Board . . . that the Board desired to avoid responsibility for adopting any plan [to desegregate the HISD], and was, in effect, stating to the Court that the Court could adopt and enforce any one of several plans which had been suggested by various interested parties." In the absence of an acceptable settlement initiating desegregation, the court would have to act. Still, Connally allowed the school board until June 1, 1960, to submit a specific desegregation plan. The board failed to come up with such a plan. By August, 1960, the judge had no choice but to order the implementation of a twelve-year "stairstep" plan in which one grade a year would be desegregated. One month later, twelve African American children moved to formerly all Anglo schools.[112]

It would be another decade, however, before more than token desegregation took place. Wherever possible, the school board sought to obstruct implementation. It required the signed permission of principals in the old as well as the new school, as well as permission from the director of attendance, census, and transfer, before a student could transfer. Board rules also prohibited members of a single family from attending different schools. As only one grade a year was desegregated, families with older children technically still bound by segregation rules were unable to transfer their younger children to desegregated schools.[113]

Connally was unwilling to go further. The Supreme Court's mandate had been fulfilled in a manner allowing for a "minimum of friction and discontent." By 1962 two grades had been "desegregated" and more were to follow in the years to come. This was a matter in which the judge took great pride. Despite the fact that few African Americans had actually been able to take advantage of the opportunity to attend desegregated schools, the judge saw little need for further action, a view visible in a 1962 contempt hearing in which Connally ruled that the HISD board's regulations did not unlawfully discriminate against African Americans: "While it is true that application of the [above] rule will perhaps prevent certain colored scholastics from attending the school of their choice, it does not necessarily follow that the rule thereby becomes invalid. Under the same circumstances, the rule also prevents white children from attending the school of their choice." Hence, "in the motions now before the Court [it is] the colored plaintiffs . . . [who] seek a different, and superior, treatment, by reasons of their race." This "the law does not grant them."[114]

With this decision, Connally's actions merged with those of Hutcheson and Kennerly thirty years earlier. The standards had changed, but the court's unwillingness to act beyond the bare minimum to enforce those standards remained the same. As with other aspects of its docket, it would be another decade before the court's judge's shifted their priorities to serving public issues. The 1950s had seen a start, but only a start, in this direction.

VI

The decade and a half following the end of World War II witnessed an important transformation in the work load of the Southern District Court. Extreme growth matched with the continuing maturation of the region's business sector made the Southern District's services as a defender of regional growth increasingly unessential; other institutions, both private and public, were providing the economic adjustment services once provided by the court. Cases directly affecting the region's economic structure were no longer being filed. As a result, the court found itself progressively powerless to make the sort of significant contributions to continued growth for which its private agenda was created. Concurrent with the decline in demand for its private services, the court faced an expansion in its public functions as expanded governmental regulations, statutes, and judicial decisions created new public duties for the court, duties that the judges could not ignore.

None of this was clear, however, when the court opened its first postwar term in 1946. Nor was it obvious as late as 1955. These changes were largely structural, laying the foundation for future transformations rather than demanding present changes. A flood of familiar public and private cases hid from the judges the changes affecting their court. Not until 1957 or 1958 did the first hints of the transformations occurring enter their consciousness as a changed private civil docket and the rise of civil rights suits made it impossible to ignore the changes reshaping the court's case load. Yet, even then, the judges sought to limit the changes in their priorities as much as possible for as long as possible.

With few calls for the court's private functions being heard and demands for its public role growing, further change was inevitable. Judge Hutcheson's 1944 declaration that "these are times when rules and standards are changing over night, when no one can speak with assurance for the persistence of any known rule of law, and when even the most devoted worshippers of the 'Glorious Uncertainty' of the law are thinking of deleting 'Glorious'" only became more perceptive and true with the passage of time. The 1950s were the end of an era. For sixty years—more if you count the actions of those courts preceding the Southern District—serving the needs of private economic development had stood as the golden rule of the Southern District's seven judges. Though the methods chosen to achieve this goal changed as the needs of the region changed, the goal remained constant and in control of the court's actions. In coming decades, however, new roles, new functions, would be forced on the court. A new age for the court, the region it served, and the nation was dawning.

Conclusion

On July 24, 1959, Judge Allred died while holding court in Corpus Christi. A few weeks later, President Eisenhower named Houston attorney T. Everton Kennerly as Allred's replacement. Son of the late Judge Thomas M. Kennerly and a former Republican candidate for the Senate, Everton Kennerly seemed destined to receive the vacant position. Though both of Texas' senators were Democrats, Kennerly was known to each and was deemed an acceptable choice. He even received the verbal assurances of Senator Lyndon Johnson that he would do "everything in his power" to further Kennerly's appointment. Kennerly's nomination, however, quickly bogged down in committee. Hoping to fill the position with a Democrat, Johnson secretly withheld his support for the Republican candidate until the results of the 1960 presidential election became known. Following John F. Kennedy's victory, Kennerly's name was withdrawn from consideration and that of Reynaldo G. Garza, a Hispanic lawyer from Brownsville, put in his place. On April 14, 1961, Garza was confirmed by the Senate and took his place on the Southern District Court bench.[1]

The choice of a Hispanic lawyer from Brownsville over a Houston corporate attorney symbolized the significant changes about to transform the functions of the Southern District Court. Since its creation in 1902 the court's primary goal was promoting the private economic development of Southeast Texas. From contract disagreements to equity receiverships, municipal bond restructuring to tort litigation, the court sought to resolve legal disputes in ways conducive to growth. The same goal also shaped its handling of government cases, where the court attempted to limit the negative effects of economic regulations and social reforms on private economic activities by negative decisions and limited, routine patterns of enforcement.

It was the ability to define and promote this private agenda that changed after 1960. A new legal culture was emerging in the 1960s, one in which "the concept of distributive justice . . . [demanded that] government under law . . . diminish economic risk taking and . . . heighten individual economic opportunity." Lawmakers under this concept had "an affirmative duty to provide for rights and liberties, not just to refrain from interfering with their enjoyment."

Courts, in turn, were to "restrain themselves in considering economic regulatory measures" that limited risk and expanded economic opportunity while "assertively . . . promot[ing] individual rights and liberties."[2]

Fusing the "social reformist impulse of Progressivism [with the] relativism and instrumentalism of legal realism . . . and the regulatory responsibility of the state associated with the New Deal," this liberal legal philosophy transormed the American legal system, and with it, the work load of the Southern District Court. Supreme Court directives seeking to foster racial and economic equality multiplied the court's duties to include providing remedies to social, economic, and political problems. Laws and programs aimed at expanding citizens' access to such necessities as adequate housing, job training, education, health and legal services did the same, only with greater specificity. Meanwhile, technological and scientific advances brought increased "social interdependence," dissolved the distinction between public and private affairs, and raised troulesome questions about where individual responsibility ended and public duties began.

These changes and othes placed new burdens on the court. In place of traditional actions involving private property, cases concerning civil and individual rights, personal safety, and the environment suddenly dominated the court's case load. These cases were larger, more complex, and ultimately limiting of the court's ability to enforce a private agenda. Unlike the public cases of old, these actions could not be ignored or handled routinely. Supported by Supreme Court directives and congressional mandates, these new cases demanded immediate action. Though the Southern District's judges were reluctant at first to change their priorities, the realities of a docket crowded with important public cases forced change. By the 1970s a public agenda stressing service to these new types of cases dominated the court's actions and priorities. Even the economic downturn of the 1980s could not change the dominance this public agenda had on the court's priorities.[3]

In other words, 1960 marked the end of an era for the Southern District Court. For sixty years its functions and priorities had remained constant. Despite the radical economic and social changes reshaping the region, the court consistently maintained a private orientation in setting its priorities by stressing private over public matters and seeking new and better ways to foster the economic development of Southeast Texas. The methods used to achieve these results may have varied between cases or over time, but the goal remained constant.

That the court's judges made this choice should not be surprising. This was a comfortable agenda for them. Men of conservative values and conservative legal training, they believed that the first duty of the federal courts was to protect and foster private property. The very origin of the federal courts, they beieved, lay in the nation's need for a national institution capable of fostering economic growth and protecting individual property rights. Without such an institution, economic chaos and the subsequent destruction of the nation was inevitable. Rapid economic growth, private ownership of property, and an

Judges of the U.S. District Court, Southern District of Texas, 1991. *Front row from left:* Judge Ricardo H. Hinojosa, Judge Filemon B. Vela, Judge Norman W. Black, Chief Judge James De Anda, Judge George P. Kazan, Judge Hayden W. Head, Jr., Judge Lynn N. Hughes. *Back row from left:* Judge Hugh Gibson, Judge Samuel B. Kent, Judge Melinda Furche Harmon, Judge Kenneth M. Hoyt, Judge David Hittner, Judge Simeon T. Lake III, Judge John D. Rainey, Senior Judge John V. Singleton. Photo by Alan Ross, courtesy U.S. District Court, Southern District of Texas

economically activist federal court, in other words, were good things. They were not only the foundation of Anglo-American law, but the basis of the nation's greatness and prosperity. The judges of the Southern District felt pride in their court's efforts toward these ends.[4]

What is surprising is the longevity this agenda had. Southeast Texas in 1960 was radically changed from the turn of the century. From an underdeveloped colony of northern and eastern economic interests, Southeast Texas had become one of the strongest, fastest-growing regional economies in the nation. Houston had grown from a city of under one hundred thousand to one of almost a million inhabitants. Agriculture, once the sole basis of the region's economy, was now joined by such industries as oil and gas, petrochemicals, shipping, and lumber. Yet, despite these and other changes, the court's priorities remained the same.

What makes this continuity even more impressive is that the private agenda was not the sole program being urged on the court in these years. In direct opposition to its private emphasis stood a public agenda stressing enforcement of federal social reforms and economic regulations. Of little consequence in 1900, with each passing decade this agenda grew in power and scope. In the 1920s Prohibition placed urgent demands on the court for action. Ten years later it was the economic reforms of the New Deal that generated public cases. The 1940s brought the Second World War and the dilemmas of the postwar economic conversions, while the 1950s had civil rights and the maturing regulatory state. None of these were minor problems, yet the court consistently refused to support national efforts aimed at their solution.

That the court could successfully ignore this public agenda for sixty years was the result of three factors. The first was the extensive control federal judges had over their docket. The Southern District Court, in the words of one Houston attorney, was an "exclusive club." The judges, in turn, were the supreme authority within this club.[5] If they wanted to hear a case first, it was heard first; if they wanted to ignore a case, it was ignored. Aside from the real, but limited, threat of being overturned on appeal, the only restriction on the judges' actions was the risk of impeachment. And, as few federal judges had ever been impeached successfully, this was a mild deterrent at best. Only the judges' sense of duty forced them to clear their public as well as private dockets. That same sense of duty, however, also stressed the importance of giving private matters priority.

The second factor was the wide support this agenda generated outside the court. A reactionary institution in the technical sense of the word, the court was powerless to effect change unless cases involving the region's economy were brought before it. Luckily, the region's business leaders, lawyers, and politicians also dreamed of economic greatness. More so than the judges, they stood to benefit from growth. It was their use of the court as a tool in which to create business certainty that provided the court with its opportunity to create and apply its private agenda. Without the help of the local business community, the court would have been impotent.

The support of other courts within the federal system also aided in the longevity of the private agenda. While individual reversals had little impact on the actions of a district judge, large numbers of reversals applied constantly toward a single doctrinal or substantive end could force a lower court judge to change his priorities. If nothing else, it negated the effect of the judge's decisions. As Melvin Urofsky has noted, however, "between the 1880s and 1937, property issues dominated the docket of the Supreme Court . . . [and] conservative judges" the High Court bench. The same can be said for the Fifth Circuit Court of Appeals. Like the Southern District's judges and the region's lawyers and business leaders, appellate judges also saw private property as the foundation of society and held growth to be an unqualified good. While this concurrence would begin to disappear after 1937, it would be another fifteen years before systematic efforts were made to force district court agendas to match national priorities. Prior to this time, few appellate judges questioned the Southern District's emphasis on private matters and thus left its agenda intact.

The court's successful emphasis on private development carried wide ramifications for the region. Booming business and investment growth carried social costs. "Houstonians paid a price for the low taxes and laissez-faire government associated with a good business climate," notes sociologist Joe Feagin. The choice of "private urban development without intelligent planning in the larger public interest" by the city's elite "create[d] huge social costs for city residents, . . . [with the] poorest Houstonians often bearing the heaviest burden." Among these costs were "major poverty, homelessness, minority displacement, subsidence, flooding, water pollution, toxic waste, sewage, and street maintenance problems."[6]

This choice had similar negative ramifications for the nation as a whole. For sixty years the court stood as a barrier to change that did not enhance private control of the economy. This arose not only from its negative decisions in public cases affecting private property, but from its positive but routine decisions in matters having little to do with economic matters. Whereas in the former decisions the court explicitly hindered economic changes Congress or the president felt necessary, in the latter, it merely stood in the way of change by ignoring the needs represented in favor of private matters.

Yet, if the court's actions had costs, they also had benefits. It is impossible to say with any certainty the exact impact the Southern District had in bringing about Southeast Texas' rapid development. It is likely that growth would have occurred even had the court not worked toward this end. Still, the fact that it did provide this service clearly had an effect on the actual path the region took toward maturity. Accessible, powerful, and interested in helping, the court provided a convenient forum in which to work out the details of growth. It provided a thread of continuity in a time of intense change, a friendly haven in which to seek shelter from unsettled business conditions and find answers to difficult problems. While today, thirty years after the start of the judicial revolution that would bring the end to this agenda, this may seem like a bad choice for the court to have made, in the context of the day, it was the only choice.

Appendix

COURT PERSONNEL

Judges of Southern District Court of Texas

Judge	*Dates of Service*
Waller T. Burns	April 22, 1902–November 17, 1917
Joseph C. Hutcheson, Jr.	April 6, 1918–July 25, 1931
Thomas M. Kennerly*	February 7, 1931–August 6, 1954
James V. Allred*	July 11, 1938–May 15, 1942; October 13, 1949–July 24, 1959
Allen B. Hannay*	August 12, 1942–June 6, 1975
Ben C. Connally*	October 13, 1949–December 2, 1975
Joe McDonald Ingraham	August 6, 1954–December 31, 1969
Reynaldo G. Garza*	April 14, 1961–August 1, 1979
James L. Noel, Jr.	October 5, 1961–December 15, 1976
John V. Singleton, Jr.*	July 22, 1966–April 1, 1988
Woodrow B. Seals	July 23, 1966–December 25, 1982
Carl O. Bue, Jr.	October 15, 1970–September 1, 1987
Owen D. Cox	December 1, 1970–March 20, 1981
Robert O'Conor, Jr.	April 15, 1975–September 3, 1984
Ross N. Sterling	May 7, 1976–January 14, 1988
Finis E. Cowan	June 14, 1977–July 30, 1979
James De Anda*	May 11, 1979–present
Norman W. Black	May 11, 1979–present
George E. Cire	May 11, 1979–May 5, 1985
George P. Kazen	May 11, 1979–present
Gabriele K. McDonald	May 11, 1979–August 14, 1988
Hugh Gibson	October 5, 1979–November 1, 1989
Filemon B. Vela	June 18, 1980–present
Hayden W. Head, Jr.	October 26, 1981–present
Ricardo H. Hinojosa	May 5, 1983–present
Lynn Hughes	December 17, 1985–present
David Hittner	June 9, 1986–present

*Chief Judge for part or all of the time

Judge	*Dates of Service*
Kenneth M. Hoyt	April 1, 1988–present
Simeon T. Lake III	August 12, 1988–present
Melinda Furche Harmon	May 22, 1989–present
John D. Rainey	May 14, 1990–present
Samuel B. Kent	October 1, 1990–present

U.S. Attorneys

Attorney	*Years of Service*
Lock McDaniel	1902–14
John E. Green, Jr.	1914–19
David E. Simmons	1919–22
Henry M. Holden	1922–34
Douglas W. McGregor	1934–44
Brian S. Odem	1944–54
Malcolm R. Wilkey	1954–58
William B. Butler	1958–61
Woodrow Seals	1961–66
Morton L. Susman	1966–69
Anthony J. P. Farris	1969–74
Edward B. McDonough, Jr.	1974–77
J. A. "Tony" Canales	1977–80
Daniel K. Hedges	1981–85
Henry K. Oncken	1985–90
Ronald Woods	1990–present

Clerks of the Court

Clerk	*Years of Service*
Christopher Dart	1902–13
L. C. Masterson	1913–40
Hal V. Watts	1940–51
V. Bailey Thomas	1951–79
Jesse E. Clark	1979–present

Notes

Abbreviations

Ad	Admiralty Cases
AO Report	*Annual Report of the Director of the Administrative Office of the United States Courts*
Atty. Gen. Report	*Annual Report of the Attorney General of the United States*
B	Bankruptcy Cases
Civ	Civil Cases
Cr	Criminal Cases
Eq	Equity Cases
Fed Cases	*Federal Cases*
F.	*Federal Reports*
F(2d)	*Federal Reports* (2d ed.)
L	Law Cases
RG	Record Group
S.W.	*Southwestern Reporter*
U.S.	*United States Reports*
U.S.C.	*United States Code*

Introduction

1. Max Farrand, ed., *The Records of the Federal Convention of 1787,* I:21, 124–27, 244–45, 292, 317; II:45–46, 136, 433; Charles Warren, "New Light on the History of the Federal Judiciary Act of 1789," *Harvard Law Review* 37 (Nov., 1927): 53, 131; "The Address and Reasons of Dissent of the Minority of the Convention of the State of Pennsylvania to Their Constituents," quoted in Richard Ellis, *The Jeffersonian Crisis: Courts and Politics in the Young Republic,* p. 11. On opposition in all thirteen states, see Dwight F. Henderson, *Courts for a New Nation,* pp. 5–19. See also Stanley Kutler, "A Sword for a Scabbard: Reflections on the Making of the Judiciary Act of 1789," *Nova Law Review* 14 (1989): 97–110; John P. Reid, "Another Origin of Judicial Review: The Constitutional Crisis of 1776 and the Need for a Dernier Judge," *New York University Law Review* 64 (Nov., 1989): 963–89.

2. Julius Goebel, Jr., *Antecedents and Beginnings to 1801,* p. 458.

3. District court jurisdiction was limited to seizures in pursuance of federal law, the enforcement of navigation and trade statutes, minor diversity of citizenship actions, and admiralty cases. In addition, district courts held criminal jurisdiction over crimes in which the punishment did not exceed one hundred dollars or imprisonment of six months. Circuit courts had limited appellate powers over the district courts' original jurisdiction over diversity of citizenship cases in which more than five hundred dollars was in dispute and in felony criminal cases ("Judiciary Act 1789," 1 *U.S. Statutes at Large*, p. 73). See also Erwin C. Surrency, "A History of the Federal Courts," *Missouri Law Review* 28 (Winter, 1963): 214–17. Local controls included "the placement of district court boundaries within a single state, the recruitment of judges from within the state in which the court was held, the enactment of legislation requiring district and circuit courts to follow state rules of practice, the use of state facilities, the practice of requiring Supreme Court justices to serve on the circuit courts, and the recruitment of Supreme Court justices from sectional divisions that corresponded to the jurisdictional boundaries of the circuits" (Kermit Hall, "The Civil War Era as a Crucible for Nationalizing the Lower Federal Courts," *Prologue* 7 [Fall, 1975]: 177). To this can be added the role of partisan politics and interregional tensions. See idem, *The Politics of Justice: Lower Federal Judicial Selection and the Second Party System, 1829–61*, and *The Magic Mirror: Law in American History*, p. 75.

4. See Morton Keller, "Powers and Rights: Two Centuries of American Constitutionalism," *Journal of American History* 74 (Dec., 1987): 676. Another trend in the literature is to document the growth of the federal court case load and efforts to control this growth. The best example of this is Felix Frankfurter and James Landis, *The Business of the Supreme Court: A Study in the Federal Judicial System*. See also Richard A. Posner, *The Federal Courts: Crisis and Reform*; J. Woodford Howard, Jr., *Courts of Appeals in the Federal Judicial System: A Study of the Second, Fifth and District of Columbia Circuits*. Other analysts apply a purely administrative approach and ignore the issue of the actions of lower federal courts. See, e.g., Peter Fish, *The Politics of Federal Judicial Administration*.

5. Mary K. Bonsteel Tachau, *Federal Courts in the Early Republic: Kentucky, 1789–1816*, pp. 191–92. For similar descriptions of federal courts during this period, see Ellis, *The Jeffersonian Crisis*; Stephen Presser, *Studies in the History of the United States Courts of the Third Circuit*, pp. 19–59; Jeffrey Morris, *Federal Justice in the Second Circuit: A History of the United States Courts in New York, Connecticut and Vermont, 1787–1987*, pp. 1–65.

6. Hall, "The Civil War Era," p. 177. See also idem, "Children of the Cabins: The Lower Federal Judiciary, Modernization and Political Culture, 1789–1899," *Northwestern University Law Review* 75 (Oct., 1980): 423–70, in which he notes that "the backgrounds of the lower federal judiciary belie assertions that modernization swept the political culture of the pre-twentieth century United States" (p. 464). See as well idem, "Social Backgrounds and Judicial Recruitment: A Nineteenth Century Perspective on the Lower Federal Judiciary," *Western Political Quarterly* 29 (June, 1976): 243–57.

7. Tony Freyer, *Forums of Order: The Federal Courts and Business in American History*, pp. xv, xviii. Federal judges' independence from local pressures is also discussed in ibid., p. 26. See also idem, *Harmony and Dissonance: The* Swift *and* Erie *Cases in American Federalism*.

8. Neither author explicitly argues against the other; the comparison is mine. In fact, Hall in *The Magic Mirror*, p. 229, draws on Freyer and in Hall and Eric W. Rise, *From Local Courts to National Tribunals*, argues a position similar to that presented here.

9. Ibid., p. 7. For a discussion of the tensions between public and private law, see Harry Scheiber, "Public Rights and the Rule of Law in American History," *California Law Review* 72 (Mar., 1984): 217–51, and idem, "American Constitutional History and the New Legal History: Complementary Themes in Two Modes," *Journal of American History* 68 (Sept., 1981): 337–50.

10. Freyer, *Harmony and Dissonance*, p. xii.

11. See Frankfurter and Landis, *Business of the Supreme Court*, pp. 4–55.

12. Harold M. Hyman, *A More Perfect Union: The Impact of the Civil War and Reconstruction on the Constitution*, pp. 224, 227.

13. William Wiecek, "The Reconstruction of Federal Judicial Power, 1863–1875," *American Journal of Legal History* 13 (Oct., 1969): 333–42. See also Stanley Kutler, *Judicial Power and Reconstruction Politics*, pp. 143–60.

14. This trend is described in detail in Freyer, *Forums of Order*, pp. 99–114, and idem, *Harmony and Dissonance*, pp. 45–100.

15. David Clark, "Adjudication to Administration: A Statistical Analysis of Federal District Courts in the Twentieth Century," *Southern California Law Review* 55 (Nov., 1981): 98.

16. Freyer, *Harmony and Dissonance*, pp. 17–44, xii, xiii.

17. *Congressional Record*, 2d sess., 1883, vol. 14, pt. 2:1245, 1248. For an extended discussion of these views, see Freyer, *Harmony and Dissonance*, pp. 75–100; idem, *Forums of Order*, pp. 121–36, 147–48.

18. *Congressional Record*, 2d sess., 1878, vol. 9, pt. 2:4000; 2d sess., 1880, vol. 10, pt. 1:681; 2d sess., 1883, vol. 14, pt. 2:1244; 1st sess., 1884, vol. 15, pt. 5:4879; 1st sess., 1892, vol. 23, pt. 2:1070; 2d sess., 1894, vol. 26, pt. 4:3048. Diversity cases are those in which a resident from one state sues a resident from another state in the federal courts simply on the basis of their different domicile. See Freyer, *Forums of Order*, pp. 19–35, 99–120. For an example of these bills, see ibid., 2d sess., 1883, vol. 14, pt. 2:1144. The Judiciary Act of 1887 came closest to accepting Culberson's plans by limiting the right of removal on the grounds of local prejudice. The bill was so badly written, however, that it had little impact on removal litigation. The circuit courts of appeals in 1891 also drew much of their form from Culberson's earlier proposals (Freyer, *Forums of Order*, p. 133).

19. *Central Law Journal* 18 (Apr., 1884): 281–82. William Meigs, "General Principles of Jurisprudence," *Central Law Journal* 24 (Dec., 1889): 465–70, 485–90. See also Charles Fairman, *Reconstruction and Reunion, 1864–88*, p. 938; Freyer, *Harmony and Dissonance*, pp. 101–22; idem, *Forums of Order*, pp. 142–60.

20. Daniel M. Chamberlain, *Constitutional History of the United States as Seen in the Development of American Law*, quoted in Freyer, *Harmony and Dissonance*, pp. 82–83. William Howard Taft, "Criticism of the Federal Judiciary," *American Law Review* 29 (Sept.–Oct., 1895): 651. For more examples of corporate business's views on state courts, see Thomas C. Cochran, *Railroad Leaders, 1845–1890; Business Mind in Action*, pp. 184–85; Edward Chase Kirkland, *Dream and Thought in the Business Community, 1860–1900*, pp. 135–36. On differences between state courts, see Freyer, *Forums of Order*, pp. 127–29.

21. Of course, a large part of corporate business's support for this uniformity was that in most cases, the decisions made were in their favor (Freyer, *Forums of Order*, p. 108). William Howard Taft, "Possible and Needed Reforms in the Administration of Justice in the Federal Courts," *Report of the American Bar Association* 45 (1922): 258–59; "Resolutions

and Statement of the Committee on Jurisprudence and Law Reform," *Report of the American Bar Association* 51 (1928): 435. See also Taft, "Criticism of the Federal Judiciary," p. 651.

22. This process is described in Frankfurter and Landis, *Business of the Supreme Court*, pp. 56–145, 187–216, 255–318; Freyer, *Forums of Order*, pp. 142–76. See also Clark, "Adjudication to Administration," pp. 118–29. Another attempt by Congress to clear federal court dockets was the creation of courts of specialized jurisdiction, such as the tax and customs courts. Their impact on most aspects of lower court dockets was minimal, however (Frankfurter and Landis, *Business of the Supreme Court*, pp. 146–86).

23. For an insightful discussion of the political context of this local debate in Texas, see Chandler Davidson, *Race and Class in Texas Politics*. See also George Green, *The Establishment in Texas Politics: The Primitive Years, 1938–1957*.

24. Since, even today, most federal judges are male, and for the period covered by this book all such judges were male, when speaking of judges in the general, this book will use the masculine pronoun.

25. John R. Brown, "Hail to the Chief: Hutcheson, the Judge," *Texas Law Review* 38 (Dec., 1959): 145.

26. Frankfurter and Landis, *Business of the Supreme Court*, p. 218. These efforts to standardize the actions of the lower federal courts began in the 1920s. They have begun to be successful only in the last twenty years or so (Henry P. Chandler, "Some Major Advances in the Federal Judicial System, 1922–1947," *Federal Rules Decisions* 31 [1963]: 307–517; Erwin Surrency, "Federal District Court Judges and the History of Their Courts," *Federal Rules Decisions* 40 [1967]: 139–310; Walter Murphy, "Chief Justice Taft and the Lower Court Bureaucracy: A Study in Judicial Administration," *Journal of Politics* 24 [Aug., 1962]: 453–76; Posner, *The Federal Courts*).

27. Alfred D. Chandler, *The Visible Hand: The Managerial Revolution in American Business*; Louis Galambos and Joseph Pratt, *The Rise of the Corporate Commonwealth: U.S. Business and Public Policy in the Twentieth Century*; Gabriel Kolko, *The Triumph of Conservatism: A Reinterpretation of American History, 1900–1915*. For business's preference for the federal courts, see Freyer, *Harmony and Dissonance*, and idem, *Forums of Order*. For views within Texas, see Joe R. Feagin, *Free Enterprise City: Houston in Political and Economic Perspective*; and Green, *The Establishment in Texas Politics*, pp. 3–10, 20.

28. Harold Platt, *City Building in the New South: The Growth of Public Services in Houston Texas, 1830–1915*, pp. 199–201; Douglass Smith, *The New Deal in the Urban South*.

29. For an example of this vision in one of the region's most well known business leaders, see Walter L. Buenger, "Between Community and Corporation: The Southern Roots of Jesse H. Jones and the Reconstruction Finance Corporation," *Journal of Southern History* 56 (Aug., 1990): 481–510.

30. Howard Zinn, *The Southern Mystique* p. 21. See also Green, *The Establishment in Texas Politics*, p. 17.

31. Feagin, *Free Enterprise City*, p. 272. For the political ramifications of these matters, see Davidson, *Race and Class in Texas Politics*.

32. A planned second volume will deal with the post-1960 period.

1. Federal Justice in a Frontier State: The Federal Courts in Nineteenth-Century Texas

1. 9 *U.S. Statutes at Large*, p. 1. See also Surrency, "Federal District Court Judges," pp. 285–88.

2. Tachau, *Federal Courts in the Early Republic.*

3. By the mid-1850s, the expansion of commercial agriculture had brought a new standard of wealth into the state: slaves. This is something that Texans actively sought; however, even in 1860 most of Texas remained a frontier. As a whole, Texas had fewer slaves than other southern states. Thus land remained a major definer of wealth into the post–Civil War era (T. R. Fehrenbach, *Lone Star: A History of Texas and the Texans,* p. 281). Randolph Campbell, "Planters and Plain Folk: Harrison County, Texas, as a Test Case, 1850–1860," *Journal of Southern History* 40 (Aug., 1974): 369–98, describes the growing importance of slaves as a definer of wealth. Harrison County, however, was one of the most developed counties in the state and as a result contained more slaves than any other county in the state throughout this period.

4. Fehrenbach, *Lone Star,* pp. 282–83. Reuben McKitrick, *The Public Land System of Texas, 1823–1910* pp. 20–23, describes this system.

5. The theory was that the oldest grant took precedence, but since many of these grants were later declared invalid, no title to land acquired through a grant was completely safe until a court had ruled on it. Fehrenbach, *Lone Star,* pp. 282–83, Wallace Hawkins, *The Case of John C. Watrous, United States Judge for Texas: A Political Story of High Crimes and Misdemeanors,* p. 25. Exactly the same problems were faced by the Kentucky District Court in the 1790s. See Tachau, *Federal Courts in the Early Republic,* pp. 167–90.

6. Fehrenbach, *Lone Star,* pp. 266–67.

7. Hawkins, *The Case of John C. Watrous,* p. 18; Hal, *The Politics of Justice,* pp. 68–70. This power is known as "senatorial courtesy" and operates to this day. See Robert A. Carp and Ronald Stidham, *The Federal Courts,* pp. 103–10.

8. Biographical information taken from Bicentennial Committee of the Judicial Conference of the United States, *Judges of the United States,* p. 518; Hawkins, *The Case of John C. Watrous,* pp. 1–13; Hall, *The Politics of Justice,* pp. 68–70.

9. Quoted in Hawkins, *The Case of John Watrous,* pp. 16, 18. Watrous's politics was also acceptable to all concerned. Polk, in his own words, wanted to "appoint some able lawyer, who is sound upon the constitutional questions, according to the Jeffersonian faith." Alabama senator Dixon H. Lewis, a friend of Watrous, assured the president that Watrous fit this category and noted how he was not only an able lawyer but an "orthodox Democrat of the state rights constitutional school" (James K. Polk to Sam Houston, Jan. 13, 1846; Dixon H. Lewis to James K. Polk, Feb. 26, 1846, both quoted in Hall, *The Politics of Justice,* p. 69).

10. During its eleven years of existence (1846–1857), the District Court of Texas heard 1,500 to 2,000 cases. In Galveston, 746 law cases, equally split between land and debt actions, 80 equity suits, again mostly involving land issues, and 600 to 700 admiralty cases were filed. A few criminal cases were also filed, most involving tax issues. The docket in Brownsville was similar in content, but much smaller in volume than that of Galveston. By 1857 the business of the court had grown to the point that a new western district was created (Hawkins, *The Case of John Watrous,* pp. 68, 103). See also *Reports of Committees of the House of Representatives,* 35th Cong., 1st sess., Rep. 540, pp. 355, 675, 685 (hereafter Report 540), and ibid., 36th Cong., 2d sess., Rep. 2, p. 258 (hereafter Report 2).

11. Mexican law required that grants be made to Mexican citizens, yet by the date of the Texas Revolution, much of this land was in the hands of American speculators. The opinion in *League v. Egery et al.,* 65 U.S., 264, describes the background of the littoral

and border grants. See also McKitrick, *The Public Land System of Texas,* p. 39.

12. Report 540, pp. 45–46 (testimony of Robert Hughes, Feb. 25, 1858). McKitrick, *The Public Land System of Texas,* p. 39. See *Goode v. McQueen's Heirs,* 3 Texas Reports, 241; *Edwards v. Davis,* 3 Texas Reports, 321; *Republic of Texas v. Frost Thorn,* 3 Texas Reports, 499; *Smith v. Power,* 23 Texas Reports, 30.

13. Hawkins, *The Case of John Watrous,* pp. 12–13, 21.

14. Watrous had the right to interpret state statute even in contrast to state court interpretations of the law by what was known as the "Swift Doctrine." In the 1842 case of *Swift v. Tyson* (16 Peters, 1) associate justice Joseph Story ruled that where state court interpretations of state statute law were "inconclusive," federal judges could use their own interpretations of that law to rule on cases. See Freyer, *Harmony and Dissonance.* Records for the early years of the court are incomplete. Few records exist from 1846 to 1852 and even fewer are extant from 1852 to 1865. The number of littoral and border cases decided by Watrous is drawn from testimony in Report 2, p. 173 (testimony of clerk of the court, James Love, May 28, 1860).

15. *Smith v. Power,* 23 Texas Reports, 30 (quote). See also *Smith v. Power,* 14 Texas Reports, 147; *League v. Egery et al.,* 65 U.S., 264; Hawkins, *The Case of John Watrous,* pp. 21–23. There is no way of telling exactly why Watrous changed his mind and accepted the Texas Supreme Court's views on the subject. No. doctrinal power existed to force him to so act. Perhaps the reasons were political or maybe the judge felt that the U.S. Supreme Court would back the state court's interpretation and not his and so he acted to put off being overturned.

16. First quote by Robert Hughes in Report 540, pp. 45–46; second quote by Senator Phil Cuney, quoted in Hawkins, *The Case of John Watrous,* p. 20.

17. *Hosner v. De Young,* 1 Texas Reports, 764; *League v. De Young,* 2 Texas Reports, 497 (affirmed, 51 U.S., 185); *Herman v. Phalen,* U.S. District Court, Southern District of Louisiana, decided June 30, 1847 (overturned, 55 U.S., 79).

18. Mussina and Spencer Memorials to the Congress to impeach Judge Watrous, reprinted in Hawkins, *The Case of John Watrous,* pp. 76–88. One of the more telling complaints in these memorials was that, in having to transfer the case to Louisiana, the case was decided by a "foreign" jury.

19. *Spencer v. Lapsley,* 60 U.S., 264; Hawkins, *The Case of John Watrous,* pp. 43–47. In the eleven years the Texas District Court existed, Watrous disqualified himself in eighteen cases, most of them involving land grant issues (ibid., p. 68).

20. See Report 540, pp. 45–46.

21. Hawkins, *The Case of John Watrous,* p. 20. A similar case involving a debt for slaves occurred in 1848: *Union Bank of Louisiana v. Stafford* (affirmed in *New Orleans Canal and Banking Co. v. Stafford,* 53 U.S., 343). The politically powerful individual in this case was lawyer William Alexander (Hawkins, *The Case of John Watrous,* p. 24).

22. Hawkins, *The Case of John Watrous,* pp. 20–21.

23. It was argued that the judge favored a few lawyers, all of whom represented big land speculators, and helped their cases to the detriment of other attorneys. They also questioned his use of and demeanor toward juries (ibid., pp. 29–30).

24. Ibid., pp. 24–28. Much of the documentary evidence from this investigation was reprinted in Report 2.

25. Ibid., p. 91. See also *Reports of Committees of the House of Representatives,* 34th Cong., 3d sess., Rep. 175. In an *ex parte* proceeding, the defendant is not present. Habeas corpus cases and other cases involving prisoners are usually *ex parte,* for example.

26. Hawkins, *The Case of John Watrous,* p. 91. See also Report 540.

27. Hawkins, *The Case of John Watrous,* p. 91. See also Report 2.

28. Fehrenbach, *Lone Star,* p. 275, notes that the federal government as a whole was distrusted by most Texans. "Texans tended to resent all national interference, even when there was a national consensus, in their own affairs, whether the matter was a question of boundaries, finances, or internal politics."

29. Ibid., pp. 279–324, and John Spratt, *The Road to Spindletop: Economic Change in Texas, 1875–1901,* pp. 3–18, describe conditions in Texas at this time.

30. Confederate Constitution, art. III, sec. 2; *Statutes at Large, Provisional Government of the Confederate States of America,* 1st sess., sec. 44. The Confederate Supreme Court never sat. See William Robinson, Jr., *Justice in Grey: A History of the Judicial System of the Confederate States of America.* The decision to combine law and equity was initiated by Texas and Louisiana, both of whose legal systems originated in the civil law (as opposed to the common law), where a distinction between law and equity was not made. The U.S. courts had made this distinction, and lawyers in both states had found the differences confusing. As a courtesy to these states, the Confederate Congress omitted any mention of law and equity as separate entities (Robinson, *Justice in Grey*).

31. Robinson, *Justice in Grey,* p. 51.

32. T. R. Havins, "Administration of the Sequestration Act in the Confederate District Court for the Western District of Texas, 1862–1865," *Southwestern Historical Quarterly* 43 (Jan., 1940): 281–322; Nowlin Randolph, "Judge William Pickney Hill Aids the Confederate War Effort," *Southwestern Historical Quarterly* 68 (July, 1964): 14–28.

33. This proved to be the case for the state as a whole. Throughout Texas, previous economic concerns such as railroad construction and trade were halted to better use resources for the war effort. See Ernest Wallace, *Texas in Turmoil,* and S. G. Reed, *A History of the Texas Railroads,* pp. 125–27.

34. The rest dealt with such war issues as admiralty prizes and treason. See Havins, "Administration," p. 304, who notes that the Western District heard 2,774 cases, all but 24 sequestration actions. No full counts exist for the Eastern District, but Judge Hill noted in August, 1862, that his court would likely hear 1,000 to 2,000 cases. Most of these were sequestration actions, though the ratio to other types of cases was not as high as in the Western District (Randolph, "Judge William Pickney Hill," p. 22).

35. Enemy aliens included all northerners as well as any southerners who supported the North. Europeans living or owning property in the South were enemy aliens or not, depending on their views about the war. U.S. War Department, *The War of the Rebellion: A Compilation of the Official Records of the Union and Confederate Armies,* ser. 4, III: 586–93. See also Brian Dirck, "The Confederate Sequestration Act: Its Origins and Provisions, 1861" (unpublished).

36. Havins, "Administration," pp. 306, 311; Randolph, "Judge William Pickney Hill," pp. 17–18. No records exist as to how much of this money was ever collected by the receivers. It is likely that the amount was far smaller than the total amount of debt.

37. Havins, "Administration," pp. 306, 311; Randolph, "Judge William Pickney Hill," pp. 17–18.

38. Wallace, *Texas in Turmoil,* pp. 70, 133–38. See also Walter L. Buenger, *Secession and the Union in Texas;* Havins, "Administration," p. 317. *In rem* means a suit against property, not a person. *In rem* suits are filed when the owner of a piece of property is not available for prosecution.

39. Randolph, "Judge William Pickney Hill," pp. 20–21.

40. For an example of this, see Morris, *Federal Justice in the Second Circuit,* pp. 60–65.

41. Havins, "Administration," pp. 321–22; Hawkins, *The Case of John Watrous,* pp. 57–59.

42. Robert Kaczorowski, *The Politics of Judicial Interpretation: The Federal Courts, Department of Justice and Civil Rights, 1866–1876,* pp. 49–78, describes the difficulties faced in enforcing civil rights under the thirteenth and fourteenth amendments prior to 1870. John Hope Franklin, "The Enforcement of the Civil Rights Act of 1875," *Prologue* 6 (Winter, 1974): 228–30, and Everette Swinney, "Enforcing the Fifteenth Amendment, 1870–1877," *Journal of Southern History* 28 (May, 1962): 206, note the failure of the attorney general's office to provide backing and support to U.S. attorneys enforcing the Enforcement Acts of 1870 and 1875. See also Ross Webb, "Benjamin H. Bristow: Civil Rights Champion, 1866–1872," *Civil War History* 15 (Mar., 1969): 39–53.

43. Judge Duval, a Unionist with ties to the Democratic party, supported these laws less than Judge Morrill did, however. See Carl Moneyhon, *Republicanism in Reconstruction Texas,* pp. 165–70. On Morrill, see *New York Times* (June 9, 1875). See also Franklin, "The Enforcement of the Civil Rights Act of 1875," pp. 231–32. In a sidelight to this episode, the editor of the *Galveston News* criticized Judge Morrill's decision. Angered, the judge ordered the marshal to bring the editor into court to show cause why he should not be held in contempt. The editor later apologized for his views.

44. Quoted in Swinney, "Enforcing the Fifteenth Amendment," p. 210. On the inadequacies of the state courts for enforcing these laws, see Moneyhon, *Republicanism in Reconstruction Texas,* pp. 51–55.

45. *Atty. Gen. Report* (1870–1900). There are no published case records before 1870, but Kaczorowski, *The Politics of Judicial Interpretation,* p. 50, notes that, except in a few districts such as Kentucky, few civil rights cases were filed prior to 1870. In the Eastern District, 15 cases were listed as criminal civil rights and 41 as enforcement cases. The rest were election law cases, which may or may not have involved African Americans. In the Western District, 34 were civil rights and enforcement cases; the remaining 56 were voting rights cases. This was out of a national total of more than 5,386 enforcement, civil rights, and voting rights cases.

In some circuit court cases, where the court included one district judge and a Supreme Court justice or circuit judge, the Texas courts began to limit removal powers and jurisdictions to state infractions only. In *Texas v. Gains,* 23 Fed Cases, 869 (1874), Justice Bradley ruled in a Western District Circuit Court case that, to plead successfully for removal, the defendant must "show deprivation of a right which is guaranteed by the civil rights act" and in which the deprivation was a result of the laws of Texas. Deprivation that resulted only from the "prejudice and enmity of the people," that was "private infringements of those rights" protected by the law, was not removable to federal court. See also *Le Grand v. U.S.,* 12 F., 577 (1882).

46. Harold Hyman and William Wiecek, *Equal Justice under Law: Constitutional Development, 1835–1875,* pp. 467–68; Christopher Meakin, "Congressional Control of Federal Court Jurisdiction and the Effect of Protection of Civil Rights" (M. A. thesis).

47. *U.S. v. Dodge,* 25 Fed Cases, 882. See also James Holmes, "From Railroads to Immigration: Texas Federal Courts in the Late Nineteenth Century" (unpublished), pp. 41–48.

48. *Ex parte Brown* (unpublished decision) quoted in *Ex parte Francois,* 9 Fed Cases, 699. In *Frasher v. State,* 3 Texas Reports, 163, the Texas Supreme Court ruled that the 1858 anti-miscegenation law was constitutional. The state decision "induce[d] [Duval]

to doubt the correctness of [his] first impression when acting in the case of *Ex parte Brown*." Though he still felt the law "unwise and unjust, . . . repugnant to the spirit of the Constitution," he did not declare it unconstitutional in this later case.

49. Larry Adams, "Economic Development in Texas during Reconstruction, 1865–1875" (Ph. D. diss.), p. 92; Wallace, *Texas in Turmoil*, pp. 125–32; Fehrenbach, *Lone Star*, p. 394.

50. Moneyhon, *Republicanism in Reconstruction Texas;* see also Adams, "Economic Development," pp. 196–204.

51. See James Baggett, "Origins of Early Texas Republican Party Leadership," *Journal of Southern History* 40 (Aug., 1974): 448. Additional biographical information on Texas' federal judges can be found in Bicentennial Committee of the Judicial Conference of the United States, *Judges of the United States*. It should be noted that federal judges were not the only Texans to support investment in Texas. Many Texans became associated with outside capital, serving northern investment interests and seeking to bring more capital into the state. Like the judges, they saw this capital as Texas' best means to develop. For one example, see Joe Pratt and Kenneth Lipartito, *Baker and Botts in the Development of Modern Houston*, chap. 1.

It is possible that some state courts were favorable to outside investors and corporations; however, little evidence exists to show this point. Most historians believe that southern and western state courts were antibusiness. See Freyer, *Forums of Order*, pp. 102–107.

The only other type of case that equaled the numbers of these economic actions were criminal internal revenue cases. For example, in the Eastern District, between 1870 and 1900 there were 7,568 internal revenue cases filed, most between 1873 and 1882. Arising from a failure to pay import and excise taxes, many of these cases were never prosecuted (*Atty. Gen. Report* [1870–1900]).

52. It is important to stress that the federal courts were only one of many groups that held this vision for Texas' future and worked actively for its creation. For examples of other groups attempting this change, see Pratt and Lipartito, *Baker and Botts*, esp. chaps. 1 and 2, and Walter L. Buenger and Joseph Pratt, *But Also Good Business: Texas Commerce Banks and the Financing of Houston and Texas, 1886–1986*.

53. Alfred Chandler, Jr., *The Railroads: The Nation's First Big Business*. On the importance of railroads in economic development, see Robert Fogel, *Railroads and American Economic Growth: Essays in Econometric History*, esp. chap. 4, "Railroads and the 'Take Off' Thesis: The American Case," pp. 111–46; and Chandler, *The Railroads*.

On Texas land grants to railroads see Seth McKay, "Texas and the Southern Pacific Railroad, 1848–1860," *Southwestern Historical Quarterly* 35 (July, 1931): 1–27, and Reed, *A History of the Texas Railroads*, pp. 129–86.

Many railroads were run by locals, however. See John Stover, *The Railroads of the South, 1865–1900: A Study in Finance and Control*, pp. 278–83.

54. M. M. Crane, "Recollections of the Establishment of the Texas Railroad Commission," *Southwestern Historical Quarterly* 50 (1947): 478.

55. Holmes, "From Railroads to Immigration," pp. 3–4, 16–18; Mizell Kennedy, "A Study of James Stephen Hogg, Attorney General and Governor" (M.A. thesis), pp. 69–80.

56. Crane, "Recollections of the Establishment of the Texas Railroad Commission," pp. 478–80.

57. The Northern District of Texas was created in 1879 (20 *U.S. Statutes at Large*, p. 320). *Texas Express Co. v. Houston and Texas Central RR Co.*, 6 F., 426.

58. *Mercantile Trust Co. v. Texas and Pacific RR Co. et al.; Farmers' Loan and Trust Co. v. International and G.N. RR Co. et al.; Mercantile Trust Co. v. St. Louis. S.W. RR Co. of Texas et al.; Farmers' Loan and Trust Co. v. Gulf. C and S.F. RR Co. et al.*, all at 51 F., 529.

59. The Eleventh Amendments prohibits federal suits against the states. *Reagan v. Farmer's Loan and Trust Co.* 154 U.S., 362 (1893).

60. Ibid.

61. On the history of railroads in the nineteenth century, see John Stover, *American Railroads* and idem, *The Railroads of the South.* See also Albro Martin, "Railroads and the Equity Receivership: An Essay on Institutional Change," *Journal of Economic History* 34 (Sept., 1974): 686, 702; Stover, *Railroads of the South*, pp. 254–55. Reed, *Texas Railroads*, pp. 190–434, gives a history of the Texas lines during this period.

62. In Texas, state judges were popularly elected. State judges who took a position in opposition to popular views faced the chance of losing their position in the next election. The same held true for other elected officials.

63. Martin, "Railroads and the Equity Receivership." For a more complete discussion of the equity receivership, see chapter 2 here. Quote is from *Forbes v. Memphis El Paso RR Co.*, 9 Fed Cases, 408.

64. Alexander Noyes, *Forty Years of American Finance*, pp. 276–77. See also Keith Bryant, Jr., and Henry Dethloff, *A History of American Business*, pp. 123–25.

65. Stover, *Railroads of the South*, pp. 280–81.

66. Pratt and Lipartito, *Baker and Botts and the Building of Modern Houston*, p. 10. The Texas and Pacific remained a separate line for a time (Reed, *Texas Railroads*, pp. 356–75).

67. Reed, *Texas Railroads*, p. 218.

68. Trustees were representatives of the shareholders and bondholders of the insolvent company. They, along with the receiver, worked out the reorganization plan. A master, or master in chancery, is a court-appointed official who, in equity and bankruptcy matters, stands in for the judge in ruling on technical or routine matters. The decisions of the master, however, are always appealable to the judge. On the appointing of receivers friendly to the railroads and northern creditors, see "Speech of the Governor before the Twenty-seventh Legislature," by Governor James Hogg, in Robert Cotner, ed., *Address and State Papers of James Stephen Hogg*, pp. 384–400.

69. Justice Bradley in *Forbes v. Memphis, El Paso RR. Co.*, 9 Fed Cases, 408 (1872). See also *Easton v. Houston and Texas Central RR Co.*, 38 F., 12 (1889).

70. Justice Bradley in *Cowdrey v. Railroad et al.*, 6 Fed Cases, 660 (1870).

71. *Missouri, Kansas and Texas RR Co. v. Scott*, 13 F., 793.

72. An intervenor is an interested party in a suit, separate from the plaintiff or defendant. In receivership suits, intervenors are usually other creditors of the failed business.

73. *Snow et al. v. Texas Trunk RR*, 16 F., 1 (quoted passage comes from Supreme Court's opinion in *Davis v. Gray*, 16 Wallace, 203).

74. see chap. 2 here.

75. For a complete picture of the new types of cases being filed in the late 1890s, see *Docket Books*, Circuit Court of the Eastern District of Texas, 1890–1902.

76. *House Report no. 577*, House Judiciary Committee, 57th Cong., 1st sess., Feb. 21, 1902 (hereafter *House Report no. 577*). This was for all three districts combined. See also *Congressional Record*, 57th Cong., 1st sess., vol. 35:2136–37.

77. *Congressional Record*, 57th Cong., 1st sess., vol. 35:2136–37.

78. *House Report no. 577.*

79. *Congressional Record*, 57th Cong., 1st sess., vol. 35:2357, 2135, 2163. See also 32

U.S. Statutes at Large, p. 65. The counties making up the new district were Polk, Trinity, Madison, Brazos, Grimes, Walker, San Jacinto, Montgomery, Harris, Chambers, Galveston, Brazoria, Fort Bend, Waller, Austin, Colorado, Lavaca, Wharton, Matagorda, Jackson, Victoria, Goliad, Calhoun, Refugio, Aransas, San Patricio, Nueces, Cameron, Hidalgo, Starr, Zapata, Webb, Dimmit, Lasalle, McMullen, and Duvall. In 1903 Dimmit was moved into the Western District. See *House Report no. 3016,* House Judiciary Committee, 57th Cong., 2d sess., Jan. 9, 1903. Only Houston was a new seat for a federal court in 1902. Galveston had been the first seat of the federal court in Texas, Brownsville had been made a seat in 1857, Laredo had been made a seat in 1899; Victoria was to be added in 1906 and Corpus Christi in 1912.

2. "Awhir with a Buoyant Business Progressiveness": The Progressive Era, 1902–17

1. M. G. Cunniff, "Texas and Texans," *World's Work* 11 (Mar., 1906): 7269–70, quoted in Dewey Grantham, *Southern Progressivism: The Reconciliation of Progress and Tradition,* p. 98. On Spindletop and the discovery of oil, see Spratt, *The Road to Spindletop;* pp. 277–86. Spratt contends that the oil gusher at Spindletop set off a chain reaction in the state's economy that led to the development of a more balanced economy. At the same time, he notes that the Texas economy in 1900 was ready for such an event. Edwin Caldwell, "Highlights of the Development of Manufacturing in Texas, 1900–1960," *Southwestern Historical Quarterly* 68 (Apr., 1965): 405–31, also notes that, while Texas traveled "the road to industrialization on the coat-tails of the oil and gas industry," the chain reaction oil set off had "many links" in it leading to modernization (pp. 406–407). See also Seth McKay and Odie Faulk, *Texas after Spindletop,* pp. 1–16.

2. On the growth of the Texas economy in the first years of the twentieth century, see Buenger and Pratt, *But Also Good Business,* pp. 40–41, and Platt, *City Building in the New South,* pp. 181–208. For the development of South Texas' economy, see Evan Anders, *Boss Rule in South Texas: The Progressive Era,* pp. 139–41, 146. Statistics of the Texas economy's growth can be found in Texas Commercial Secretaries and Business Men's Association, *Industrial Texas.*

3. Ralph Steen, *Twentieth Century Texas: An Economic and Social History,* pp. 94–95. See also Spratt, *The Road to Spindletop,* p. 283, and Grantham, *Southern Progressivism,* pp. 98–99.

4. Alwyn Barr, *Reconstruction to Reform: Texas Politics, 1876–1906.*

5. On the reforms of Governor James Hogg, see Robert Cotner, *James Stephen Hogg: A Biography,* pp. 320–52. On the rise and fall of oil booms, see Roger Olien and Diana Olien, *Oil Booms: Social Change in Five Texas Towns.*

6. Louis Rodrigues, ed., *Dynamics of Growth: An Economic Profile of Texas,* p. 16.

7. Barr, *Reconstruction to Reform;* Arthur Link, "The Wilson Movement in Texas, 1910–1912," *Southwestern Historical Quarterly* 48 (Oct., 1944): 167–85.

8. See Platt, *City Building in the New South;* Rodrigues, *Dynamics of Growth,* pp. 16–17; and Buenger and Pratt, *But Also Good Business,* pp. 40–41. For national efforts to this end, see Martin Sklar, *The Corporate Reconstruction of American Capitalism, 1890–1916: The Market, the Law and Politics,* pp. 1–42.

9. James Baker to President Roosevelt, Mar. 13, 1902. "Applications and Endorsements File," Record Group 60, National Archives, Washington, D.C., Box 862 (hereafter, Burns File, RG 60, NA-W, Box 862). See also Marilyn Sibley, *The Port of Houston: A History,* pp.

122–23. Biographical information can be found in Bicentennial Committee of the Judicial Conference of the United States, *Judges of the United States,* p. 69, and *Proceedings of the Texas Bar Association* 37 (July, 1918): pp. 344–46.

10. Thomas Dodd to President Roosevelt, Mar. 7, 1902; R. H. Ward to President Roosevelt, Mar. 20, 1902; Spencer Russell to President Roosevelt, Mar. 7, 1902; W. G. Sterrett to President Roosevelt, Mar. 18, 1902; O. B. Colquitt to President Roosevelt, Mar. 10, 1902; L. Meggett to President Roosevelt, Mar. 8, 1902; Joseph Sayers to President Roosevelt, Mar. 7, 1902, Burns file, RG 60, NA-W, Box 862.

11. On the "Lilly White" (segregationist) faction of the Texas Republican party, see Paul Casdorph, *A History of the Republican Party in Texas, 1865–1965,* pp. 70–97.

12. Burns to Lucy [?], Sept. 17, 1912, (Burns, *Letters,* vol. 5, no. 1, p. 94); Burns to Renie [?], Sept. 16, 1912 (ibid., no. 2, p. 92); Burns to W. P. Lockhart, Sept. 23, 1913 (ibid., no. 1, p. 341). See also Burns to W. G. Thomas, Feb. 9, 1913, in which Burns notes how Thomas's failure to pay back a loan "embarrass[ed]" him (ibid., no. 2, p. 186).

13. Burns to J. Tregoe, June 24, 1914 (ibid., p. 18).

14. Casdorph, *Republican Party in Texas,* pp. 49, 53. After McDaniel withdrew as U.S. attorney he continued to have an impact, serving as a special master in bankruptcy and equity matters. See *Brownsville Irrigation Company v. The Ohio and Texas Sugar Company,* Eq 20, Houston Division.

15. W. Ernest Thompson, "John E. Green, Jr." *Texas Bar Journal* 30 (Oct., 1967): 777–78; John E. Green, *John E. Green and His Forty Years in Houston,* pp. 123–25; *Houston City Directory,* 1913–15. The case was *The City of Houston v. Southern Telegraph and Telephone,* Eq 107 and 108, Houston Division.

16. On makeup of federal juries, see Burns to David Reid, Sept. 24, 1914 (Burns, *Letters,* vol. 5, no. 2, p. 70), in which Burns notes that "in matters of this character [the naming of a juror] the State Statute governs." See also Burns to Fox Campbell, Sept. 24, 1914 (ibid., p. 69), in which Burns notes that if a man is "neither a free holder nor a house-holder he is not a qualified Juror." On Texas' limiting of the franchise through the use of poll taxes, see Grantham, *Southern Progressivism,* pp. 10–11.

On the typical juror, see a letter from Burns to L. C. Rummel, Oct. 3, 1912 (Burns, *Letters,* vol. 5, no. 1, p. 104), in which Burns writes that "business men make very satisfactory Jurors, and for this reason I am anxious for you to attend."

17. Burns to L. C. Rummel, Oct. 3, 1912 (Burns, *Letters,* vol. 5, no. 1, p. 104); Burns to T. J. Davis, Feb. 2, 1915 (ibid., no. 2, p. 172). See also Burns to W. L. Hill, Sept. 23, 1915 (ibid., p. 275) and Burns to W. L. Dean, Oct. 3, 1912 (ibid., no. 1, p. 101).

18. Burns to W. L. Dean, Oct. 3, 1912 (ibid.); Burns to W. L. Hill, Sept. 23, 1915 (ibid., no. 2, p. 275); Burns to L. C. Rummel, Oct. 3, 1912 (ibid., no. 1, pp. 104–105); Burns to Ben Prause, Oct. 3, 1912 (ibid., p. 995).

19. Burns to W. L. Hill, Sept. 23, 1915 (ibid., no. 2, p. 275); Burns to Pardee, Mar. 9, 1915 (ibid., pp. 215–17).

20. Bankruptcy and equity are not the same action; however, they are very similar in content and effect. A bankruptcy court is an equity court and both actions are part of the federal courts' jurisdiction by virtue of the Constitution (art. I, sec. 8; art. III, sec. 2). Bankruptcy, however, requires a congressional statute to be put into force, while equity is an inherent part of the federal courts' jurisdiction. Thus there have been periods in which no federal bankruptcy statute existed but equity receiverships were instituted. Bankruptcy and equity also operate in a similar manner. The receivership function of

equity and the trusteeship function of bankruptcy are essentially the same. Following two decades of evolution, receiverships at the turn of the century had become a means by which either a creditor or the failing company itself could turn to the courts for protection of the company prior to reorganization or liquidation. Under the Bankruptcy Act of 1898 the same process was followed. Any debtor could request bankruptcy proceedings on an application of insolvency. Also, any creditor owed a debt four months past due could request an involuntary bankruptcy. In either case, the courts would appoint a trustee to watch over and, if necessary, to operate the estate of the bankrupt prior to liquidation. In 1933 these two procedures were combined in a new Bankruptcy Act (47 *U.S. Statutes at Large*, p. 1474). The main difference in the operation of bankruptcy and equity was one of scale: most bankruptcy cases involved individuals and small businesses; equity involved mostly large business.

On receiverships, see Charles Payne, "The General Administration of Equity Receiverships of Corporations," *Yale Law Journal* 31 (May, 1922): 685–701; Henry Swain, *Economic Aspects of Railroad Receiverships;* Martin, "Railroads and the Equity Receivership"; Warner Fuller, "The Background and Techniques of Equity and Bankruptcy Railroad Reorganizations–A Survey," *Law and Contemporary Problems* 7 (Summer, 1940): 375–92. On bankruptcy, see William Collier, *The Law and Practice in Bankruptcy under the National Bankruptcy Act of 1898;* Graydon Staring, "Bankruptcy: An Historical View," *Tulane Law Review* 59 (June, 1985): 1162; and Charles Warren, *Bankruptcy in United States History.*

21. William Cunningham, *American Railroads: Government Control and Reconstruction Policies,* pp. 19–20; Stover, *The Railroads of the South,* p. 254; idem, *American Railroads,* pp. 134–46.

22. *Farmers Loan and Trust Comany v. International and Great Northern Railroad et al.,* Eq 96, Circuit Court, Houston Division; *Central Trust Company of New York v. International and Great Northern Railroad,* Eq 49, Houston Division; Reed, *Texas Railroads,* pp. 325–27.

23. Reed, *Texas Railroads,* pp. 330–43. See also Burns to J. C. Houts, Apr. 19, 1915 (Burns, *Letters,* vol. 5, no. 2, p. 240); Burns to John Jones, Apr. 22, 1915 (ibid., p. 241). *St. Louis Frog and Switch Company v. St. Louis, Brownsville and Mexico Railroad,* Eq 36, Houston Division, was the case that initiated the St L, B & M receivership. On the condition of the line, see Burns to Cecil [?], July 8, 1913 (ibid., no. 1, p. 299), in which the judge notes that "the property is poor in purse and it will take rigid economy to meet current debts."

24. Burns to Southwestern Mercantile Agency, Apr. 19, 1915 (ibid., no. 2, p. 239). Other railroad receiverships include *Freeport Texas Company v. Houston and Brazos Valley Railroad,* Eq 77, Houston Division; *Mercantile Trust Company v. Houston and Brazos Valley Railroad,* Eq 88, Houston division.

25. Burns to Cecil [?], July 12, 1913 (ibid., no. 1, pp. 309, 299). Receiver's certificates were bonds authorized by the courts to raise money for the operation and improvement of railroads under receivership. Backed by the courts, these bonds took precedence over all other obligations of the railroad. If the road had to be liquidated to pay off its debts, these bonds were paid before those held by the original creditors. Hence, in issuing receiver's certificates, the courts were placing the needs of the public above those of the original creditors. See also Burns to Andrews, Ball and Streetman, attorneys at law, Feb. 27, 1912 (ibid., p. 48), and *St. Louis Frog and Switch Company v. St. Louis, Brownsville and Mexico Railroad,* Eq 36, Houston Division). The files in this case fill over fifteen storage

boxes. Most of these files are made up of reports and requests by the receiver to the court for the right to raise money through receiver's bonds or to improve the physical condition of the road. The majority of requests were approved by the court.

26. Burns to J. Tregoe, June 24, 1914 (ibid., no. 2, p. 18); Burns to Messrs. Graham, Jones, West and Dancy, attorneys at law, Feb. 12, 1914 (ibid., no. 1, pp. 398–402).

27. Burns to J. A. Herring, Feb. 23, 1915 (ibid., no. 2, pp. 202–204). The judge notes in this letter that "I conceive it my duty to inspect this property once each year while the same is being administered, and would regard failure so to do, as criminal negligence."

28. Reed, *Texas Railroads,* pp. 326, 342.

29. Burns to J. A. Herring, Feb. 23, 1915 (Burns, *Letters,* vol. 5, no. 2, p. 203). "Petition of Frank Andrews, Receiver of the St. Louis, Brownsville and Mexico Railroad," July 17, 1914; "Order of the Court in the Matter of the St. Louis, Brownsville and Mexico Railroad," July 17, 1914, in *St. Louis Frog and Switch Company v. St. Louis, Brownsville, and Mexico Railroad,* Eq 36, Houston Division.

30. Prior to the late 1890s, most federal receiverships were instituted only for railroads. Few other economic concerns were considered important enough, nor were they complex enough in their operations to require the protections and continuities of service provided by a receivership. By the late 1890s other business began meeting these criteria and were granted receivers. Even after the turn of the century, however, railroads made up most federal receiverships. Though not unique in expanding the receivership function beyond railroads, the court's actions were noticeable in this regard. On receiverships, see note 20, this chapter.

Brownsville Irrigation Company v. The Ohio and Texas Sugar Co., Eq 20, Brownsville Division; *Southwest National Bank of Commerce of Kansas City, Mo. v. The Glen Lumber Co.* Eq 50, Houston Division; *Bush and Witherspoon Co. v. The Garner Co. et al.,* Eq 67, Houston Division; *Mississippi Valley Trust Co. v. Hill Sugar Co.,* Eq 80, Houston Division; *Miller Pendleton v. Petroleum Production Co.,* Eq 30, Brownsville Division.

31. Anders, *Boss Rule,* p. 141. J. L. Allhands, *Gringo Builders,* pp. 173–85, describes the growth of private irrigation companies; pp. 81–103, 165–72 describe the impact of the St. Louis, Brownsville, and Mexico Railroad on the region.

32. On the background of the San Benito Land and Water Company, see Allhands, *Gringo Builders,* pp. 177–79.

33. Burns to Messrs. Graham, Jones, West, and Dancy, attorneys at law, Feb. 12, 1914 (Burns, *Letters,* vol. 5, no. 1, pp. 398–402). "Application by Receivers for authority to borrow $3,000," July 9, 1914; "Order granting receiver authority to borrow $3,000," July 9, 1914; "Order authorizing issuance of receiver's certificates," Mar. 3, 1916, in *St. Louis Trust Co. v. San Benito Land and Water Co.,* Eq 40, Houston Division. Burns to E. F. Rowson, July 6, 1915 (ibid., no. 2, p. 263); Burns to W. Swift, July 18, 1914 (ibid., p. 43); Burns to W. M. Yariger, Sept. 23, 1915 (ibid., pp. 278–79).

Robertson and Emert resigned as receivers on Mar. 14, 1914, and E. F. Rowson was appointed sole receiver on Mar. 20, 1914. He was granted the power to issue an additional $75,000 in receiver certificates. "Order accepting resignation of Fred Emert and S. A. Robertson as receivers and appointing receiver, and authorizing receiver's certificates and certain improvements," Mar. 20, 1914, *St. Louis Trust Co. v. San Benito Land and Water Co.,* Eq 40, Houston Division.

Selling a company in receivership back to its creditors in open auction was common. The result was to return the company back to its owners, reorganized and free and clear of all preexisting debts ("Confirmation Decree," Apr. 12, 1917, *St. Louis Trust Co. v. San Benito Land and Water Co.*, Eq 40, Houston Division).

34. *Proceedings of the Texas Bar Association* 37 (July, 1918): 344; David McComb, *Galveston: A History,* pp. 146–48.

35. For an example of one individual's difficulties with speculation, see Anders, *Boss Rule,* pp. 142–43, for the story of James Wells. Wells, an attorney and political leader in Cameron County, invested heavily in ranch- and farmland in South Texas throughout the early part of the century. Heavy debts, however, often forced him to sell his holdings at cut-rate prices or even at a loss to pay off creditors.

36. For example, see *New York Trust Co. v. Beaumont Tour Lake and Western Railroad,* Eq 38, Houston Division; *St. Louis Union Trust Co. v. San Benito Land and Water Co.*, Eq 40, Houston Division; *Central Trust Co. of New York v. International and Great Northern Railroad,* Eq 49, Houston Division. It is possible that many equity receiverships and involuntary bankruptcies were collusive and hence really voluntary efforts to seek federal protection.

Involuntary bankruptcy was also a method that in-state creditors could use. Details about the number of bankruptcy proceedings in the Southern District can be found in the *Atty. Gen. Report* (1903–17). For examples of involuntary bankruptcy, see *First State Bank of Aransas Pass v. John Bryett and Sons,* B 14, Corpus Christi Division; *H. D. Taylor and Sons et al., v. Lake Jackson Sugar Co.*, B 1044, Galveston Division; *Rousler and Hasslacher Chemical Co. et al., v. Texas Chemical Works,* B 1119, Galveston Division; *In re A. P. Hall,* B 38, Brownsville Division.

37. On the limits of involuntary bankruptcy, see Judge Burns's decisions in *In re Lake Jackson Sugar Co.*, 129 F., 640, and *In re Bay City Irrigation Co.*, 135 F., 850.

38. Prior to 1948 and the adoption of the Revised Rules of Civil Procedure, federal civil cases were split into equity and law categories. The law docket made no distinction between private and public cases; however, since these two types of actions served different functions in relation to the court's impact on the district, they will be split here.

Regarding suits to recover debt, see *Blum Hardware Co. v. George Paul,* L 13, Corpus Christi Division; *Gregorio de Savo v. C. Barreda,* L 194, Brownsville Division; *Philip Ringling v. City of Hempstead,* L 44, Houston Division (transferred to Western District of Texas —see Burns to Locke and Locke, attorneys at law, Feb. 25, 1913 [Burns, *Letters,* vol. 5, no. 1, pp. 192–93]); *American Lumber Co. v. Continental Lumber Co.*, L 118, Houston Division; *John Lucas and Co. v. Brown Fitzpatrick Co. et al.*, L 159, Houston Division; *Kissel Motor Car Co. v. J. L. Walker and J. M. West,* L 166, Houston Division.

Regarding suits to prove title, see *Houston Pasture Co. v. The Alice State Bank et al.*, L 8, Corpus Christi Division; *Carlota Villarreal et al. v. A. A. Browne et al.*, L 183, Brownsville Division; *Dudley Olott II et al. v. A. C. Winter et al.*, L 38, Houston Division; *B. F. Moore v. Foster Lumber Co.*, L 41, Houston Division; *Elizabeth Peebles v. Foster Lumber Co.*, L 60, Houston Division; *Foster Lumber Co. v. Ed Diamond et al.*, L 147, Houston Division.

Regarding damages, see *Mollie Nowell v. B. O. Johnson,* L 9, Corpus Christi Division; *Mrs. A. Sport et al., v. St. Louis, Brownsville, and Mexico Railroad et al.*, L 11, Corpus Christi Division; *East Branch et al. v. Texas City, Texas et al.*, L 584, Galveston Division; *T. L. L. Temple v. Cary Shaw et al.*, L 49, Houston Division; *Mrs. Alice Sheppard v. Trinity County Lumber Co.*, L 111, Houston Division; *T. Hofmann-Olson et al., v. W. E. Haskell and Co.*, L 135, Houston Division. Many admiralty cases served this same function. A large part of the court's admiralty docket involved personal injury actions, but much of it was libels to recover debts. See, for personal injury cases, *John Larsen v. British SS 'Jones'*, Ad 814, Galveston Division; *Samuel Browning v. SS 'Miramichi'*, Ad 816, Galveston Division; *Alex Thofson v. SS 'Rio Grande'*, Ad 854, Galveston Division.

Regarding unpaid freight charges, see *Gulf, Colorado, and San Francisco et al. v. H. L. Roberts and Co.*, L 527, Galveston Division; *San Antonio and Aransas Pass Railroad v. Moses Wellman et al.*, L 545, Galveston Division; *Gulf and Interstate Railroad v. East Texas Brown Ore Development Co. et al.*, L 573, Galveston Division; *Gulf, Colorado, and San Francisco v. George Bowles*, L 216, Houston Division.

39. Federal common law for commercial matters drew its source from the 1842 case of *Swift v. Tyson*. Until it was overturned in 1938 by *Erie R R Co. v. Tompkins*, federal courts held that they had the power to decide issues of commercial law irrespective of state court decisions. An example of how the *Swift* doctrine powers could be used in a manner having significant impact on the economy is found in the late nineteenth and early twentieth centuries, where the federal courts used their interpretations of the common law to protect large corporations from local discriminatory regulations. The result was to foster the economic growth and domination of the large multistate corporation in the twentieth century. See Freyer, *Forums of Order;* Presser, *Studies*, chaps. 3 and 4. In some instances equity cases also served this purpose as out-of-state corporations being sued in state courts removed the case to the federal courts under diversity jurisdiction as a means of finding a "friendlier" forum to hear their case. In the Southern District, see *Fred and Mary Johnson v. G. I. Turner*, Eq 45, Houston Division. See also Freyer, *Forums of Order.*

40. *Leyner Engineering Works v. Kempner*, 163 F., 605.

41. The court also tried to protect the interests of creditors in bankruptcy hearings by administering the estate of the bankrupt as economically as possible to assure for the maximum return to creditors. In all cases of bankruptcy, however, the court also tried to keep the needs of the bankrupt in mind as well (Burns to J. H. Tregoe, June 24, 1914 [Burns, *Letters*, vol. 5, no. 2, p. 18]; Burns to W. B. Lockhart, Nov. 20, 1912 [ibid., no. 1, p. 147]).

42. In addition to these four categories, two other types of action were prosecuted on the U.S. civil docket. The first were suits brought against jurors and criminal defendants who failed to arrive at court as ordered. The defaulting jurors were usually fined fifty dollars. Defaulting defendants forfeited their bonds and had a warrant for their arrest sent out. The second category contained Internal Revenue suits. For the Safety Appliance Act, see 27 *U.S. Statutes at Large*, p. 501. Regarding the Hours of Service Act, see 34 *U.S. Statutes at Large*, p. 1415.

43. 34 *U.S. Statutes at Large*, p. 768. See also George Mowry, *The Era of Theodore Roosevelt, 1900–1912*, pp. 207–208.

44. 34 *U.S. Statutes at Large*, p. 898; *U.S. v. James McCoy*, L 98, Brownsville Division; *U.S. v. Adolfo Garza*, L 101, Brownsville Division; *U.S. v. Taskpoislos Brothers et al.*, L 492, Galveston Division; *U.S. v. Paul Keller*, L 58, Laredo Division; *U.S. v. Mexican-American Soup Co. and Alfarcia Rodríquez*, L 102, Laredo Division. See also Elizabeth Harper and Roland Chase, *Immigration Laws of the United States*, pp. 6–7.

45. *U.S. v. Missouri, Kansas, and Texas Railroad*, L 496, Galveston Division; *U.S. v. Gulf, Colorado, and Santa Fe Railroad*, L 497, Galveston Division; *U.S. v. Gulf, Colorado, and Santa Fe Railroad*, L 606, Galveston Division.

46. For sentences in immigration cases, see *U.S. v. Danaso Guzmán*, Cr 1967, Brownsville Division (60 days or $60); *U.S. v. Enrique Ayola*, Cr 1968, Brownsville Division (same

sentence). Related to immigration suits were cases of illegal reentry into the United States after deportation. The sentence in these cases usually was time served and deportation. See *U.S. v. Petra Falson,* Cr 2018, Brownsville Division; *U.S. v. María García,* Cr 2063, Brownsville Division; *U.S. v. C. Gonzales,* Cr 559, Laredo Division.

47. On the importance of smuggling to the South Texas economy, see Don Coerver and Linda Hall, *Texas and the Mexican Revolution: A Study in State and National Border Policy, 1910–1920,* pp. 8, 42. As to the type of goods being smuggled, see condemnation cases in the *Law Dockets,* Brownsville and Laredo divisions, for example *U.S. v. One Sorel Stallion et al.,* L 152, Brownsville Division; *U.S. v. 201 Beef Hides,* L 159, Brownsville Division; *U.S. v. 46 Bulls and Yearling, 7 Heifers and One Steer Yearling,* L 170, Brownsville Division. See also *U.S. v. Espedian Salinas,* Cr 1889, Brownsville Division (smuggled 7 horses); *U.S. v. Jeff Mynatt,* Cr 1891, Brownsville Division (smuggled 2 gallons of mescal); *U.S. v. Cesario Treviño,* Cr 1898, Brownsville Division (smuggled 1 gallon of mescal), Burns to Attorney General, May 5, 1915 (Burns, *Letters,* vol. 5, no. 2, pp. 251–53).

48. See, for example, *U.S. v. Jesús Flores,* Cr 231, Laredo Division (15 days, Webb County jail); *U.S. v. Antonio García,* Cr 232, Laredo Division (10 days, Webb County jail); *U.S. v. C. Rodríguez,* Cr 298, Laredo Division (30 days, Webb County jail); *U.S. v. Refugio Rodríguez,* Cr 344, Laredo Division (5 months, Webb County jail, discharged at time served); *U.S. v. Jesús Ríos,* Cr 348, Laredo Division (30 days, Webb County jail, sentence suspended for good behavior); *U.S. v. Victoriana Rodríquez,* Cr 1897, Brownsville Division (30 days, Cameron County jail); *U.S. v. Jesús Olivárez,* Cr 1936, Brownsville Division (30 days, Cameron County jail). Title 34, sec. 5548, *U.S. Compiled Statutes, 1918* p. 881.

49. See *U.S. v. Juan Longacia,* Cr 2182, Brownsville Division (pleaded guilty, 30 days and $100 fine); *U.S. v. Abelardo Leiva,* Cr 2238, Brownsville Division (pleaded guilty, 30 days and $100 fine); *U.S. v. Juan Hinojosa,* Cr 11, Corpus Christi Division (dismissed on motion by U.S. attorney); *U.S. v. Eliza McCraw,* Cr 12, Corpus Christi Division (dismissed on evidence); *U.S. v. Charles Burrell,* Cr 2342, Galveston Division (found not guilty by jury); *U.S. v. E. Edwards,* Cr 2556, Galveston Division (20 days and $100 fine). Title 35, sec. 5966, *U.S. Compiled Statutes, 1918,* p. 936.

A related category of cases were Internal Revenue actions brought in regards to the selling of cigarettes not bearing proper Internal Revenue stamps. The court also took a lenient view of this crime, often giving the minimum sentence. On one occasion the judge even wrote the pardon attorney in Washington, arguing that "the penalty provided by Statute [was] altogether out of proportion to the offense charged." Rather than being forced by the statute to give a jail sentence for internal revenue crimes, Burns would have preferred simply to have given suspended sentences, as allowed in Texas under state statute (Burns to James Finch, July 9, 1913 (Burns, *Letters,* vol. 5, no. 1, p. 302).

50. Burns to Wm. Russell, Nov. 3, 1913 (Burns, *Letters,* vol. 5, no. 1, pp. 359–40); Burns to Manuel Tyerina, Feb. 22, 1915, (ibid., no. 2, p. 198); Burns to Emilio Tijerina, Feb. 9, 1915 (ibid., p. 184).

51. Burns to O. G. Brewster, June 20, 1912 (ibid., no. 1, p. 84); Burns to William Russell, Nov. 18, 1913 (ibid., p. 370); W. O. Staver, Mar. 12, 1912 (ibid., p. 67).

52. On the political nature of the customs service in Texas, and for examples of the often-partisan applications of federal laws by this service, see Anders, *Boss Rule,* pp. 5, 19, 27–29, 45–60, 114, 167–68, 198.

53. Burns to Hon. Joe H. Eagle, Apr. 24, 1914 (Burns, *Letters,* vol. 5, no. 2, pp. 16–17); Burns to William Russell, Nov. 18, 1913 (ibid., no. 1, p. 370).

54. See *U.S. v. Alex Lind,* Cr 2563, Galveston Division; *U.S. v. B. Busch, F. Reséndez*

and T. Galán, Cr 2583, Galveston Division; *U.S. v. Ben Lutz,* Cr 2591, Galveston Division; *U.S. v. Charles Martin,* Cr 35, Corpus Christi Division; Burns to Jack McCullar, July 26, 1915 (Burns, *Letters,* vol. 5, no. 2, pp. 272–73).

55. Prior to 1911 district courts had a more limited jurisdiction than they do today. Most significant cases were filed in the circuit courts (courts made up of a district judge and a circuit judge or supreme court justice). Only in admiralty matters did the district courts have a clear dominance. After 1911, however, the circuit courts were disbanded and all trial court jurisdictions were placed in the district courts.

56. Coerver and Hall, *Mexican Revolution,* p. 8.

57. Concerning Reyes, ibid., pp. 27–37; Charles Harris and Louis Sadler, "The 1911 Reyes Conspiracy: The Texas Side," *Southwestern Historical Quarterly*" 83 (Apr., 1980): 325–48; Vic Niemeyer, "Frustrated Invasion: The Revolutionary Attempt of General Bernardo Reyes from San Antonio in 1911," *Southwestern Historical Quarterly* 67 (Oct., 1963): 213–25.

58. *U.S. v. General Bernardo Reyes et al.,* Cr 552, 893, Laredo Division; *U.S. v. José Montenyo et al.,* Cr 2053, 2055, Brownsville Division; *U.S. v. Ishmael R. Retana et al.,* Cr 2060, Brownsville Division.

59. "An Act in Addition to the Act for the Punishment of Certain Crimes against the United States," June 5, 1794, sec. 5, 1 *U.S. Statutes at Large,* p. 381; "An Act to Codify, Revise and Amend the Penal Laws of the United States," Mar. 4, 1909, chap. 2, sec. 13, 35 *U.S. Statutes at Large,* p. 1089.

60. *Houston Post* (Jan. 3, 1912), p. 11; (Jan. 5, 1912), p. 8; (Jan. 6, 1912), p. 2; Harris and Sadler, "Reyes Conspiracy," p. 336.

61. *Houston Post* (Jan. 9, 1912), p. 1.

62. Ibid. (Jan. 11, 1912), p. 1; Harris and Sadler, "Reyes Conspiracy," p. 336; Coerver and Hall, *Mexican Revolution,* p. 36.

63. Early in the trial, the judge had sought to make sure that the defendants were comfortable in the Cameron County jail. On being told that they would like additional pillows, the judge ordered more pillows sent to the jail. Ultimately, Burns released the defendants on their own recognizance, allowing them to mix freely with witnesses and the public (see note 62).

64. See note 62 and Burns to José Sandoval, Jan. 19, 1912 (Burns, *Letters,* vol. 5, no. 1, p. 9); Burns to Judge McCormick, Feb. 12, 1912 (ibid., p. 44).

65. Burns to Amador Sánchez, Feb. 12, 1913 (ibid., p. 186); Burns to President, Oct. 4, 1912 (ibid., p. 117); Burns to Wickersham (pardon attorney), Feb. 12, 1913 (ibid., p. 188); Burns to President, July 14, 1914 (ibid., no. 2, p. 39).

66. Burns to José Sandoval, Jan. 19, 1912 (ibid., no. 1, p. 9).

3. Trade Not Treason: Public Law in War and Peace, 1918–33

1. On this point, see chap. 1 here. See also Clark, "Adjudication to Administration," pp. 65–114.

2. Freyer, *Harmony and Dissonance.*

3. Oliver Wendell Holmes to Harold Laski, Mar. 16, 1919, in Mark DeW. Howe, ed. *The Holmes-Laski Letters,* p. 190; Harry Scheiber, *The Wilson Administration and Civil Liberties, 1917–1921,* p. 43. See also Paul L. Murphy, *World War I and the Origin of Civil Liberties in the United States,* pp. 189–90, 198, 210–11, 216.

4. The high incidence of Espionage Act prosecutions in some judicial districts may be explained by this very point. The districts of Arizona (99 cases), Western Texas (89 cases), Western Washington (54 cases), and North Dakota (103 cases) all contained borders over which illegal trading could have been carried out. This possibility does not, however, explain the high incidence in districts not along the border (*Atty. Gen. Report* [1918] and [1919]).

5. In 1919, 444 criminal and 132 civil cases were filed (ibid., [1918], p. 231; [1919], p. 195). In 1919, of the 444 criminal cases filed, 247 were war actions (139 draft actions, 90 customs, and 18 espionage). An additional 156 unclassified cases included an unknown number arising from wartime conditions. In 1920 there were 579 new criminal cases filed. Of this number, 123 were draft cases, 158 were Prohibition actions, 91 were unclassified, 162 were customs, and the rest were in miscellaneous categories (ibid., [1919], p. 195; [1920], pp. 350–51).

6. There were 304 draft and 64 espionage cases out of the 483 criminal prosecutions in 1918. Most of the remaining cases involved illegal export of goods needed for the war effort and serving alcohol to a soldier or operating a house of ill repute within five miles of a military base (ibid., [1918], p. 231). See also John Whiteclay Chambers II, *To Raise an Army: The Draft Comes to Modern America*, pp. 110–11.

7. This "other manner" usually meant voluntary induction into the army (Chambers, *To Raise an Army*, pp. 110–15).

8. Ibid., pp. 211–12. The majority of resisters failed to register not only because they were in opposition to the wider society fighting the war but because they were intimidated by the bureaucratic complexity of the selective service system.

9. In 1915 and 1916, hundreds of South Texas Hispanics were killed in the backlash to the Plan of San Diego (an unsuccessful plot proposing an uprising of the Southwest's Hispanics, African Americans, and Indians against the region's Anglos) and bandit raids from Mexico. Few Hispanics were safe from vigilante violence during this reign of terror (Anders, *Boss Rule*, p. 227). See also Charles Harris and Louis Sadler, "The Plan of San Diego and the Mexican–United States War Crisis of 1916: A Reexamination," *Hispanic American Historical Review* 58 (Aug., 1978): 381–408; James Sandos, "The Plan of San Diego: War and Diplomacy on the Texas Border, 1915–1916," *Arizona and the West* 14 (Spring, 1972): 4–24.

10. James Ferguson to Woodrow Wilson, May 29, 1917 (quoted in Anders, *Boss Rule*, p. 235). George Kiser and Martha Kiser, eds., *Mexican Workers in the United States: Historical and Political Perspectives*, pp. 9–10; Mark Reisler, *By the Sweat of Their Brow*, pp. 24–48. The problem of the drafting of Mexican nationals continued throughout the war. Many draft boards refused to accept certificates of Mexican citizenship issued by Mexican consuls, requiring instead the deposition of three American witnesses or an inscription in the immigration records. At first the Justice Department backed up this policy, ruling that a certificate from the consul only "makes out a prima facie case of citizenship," which the draft boards could "go behind . . . [to find] evidence . . . to the effect that the persons certified [were] not in fact Mexican Citizens." By Oct., 1917, however, the department had changed its mind and ordered that "in order to avoid any differences between this country and Mexico . . . [that] except in very exceptional cases, all cases against such Mexican subjects should be dropped, as these men are exempt from the draft, and the situation seems to be one which may cause friction between this country and Mexico" (William Fitts, asst. attorney general, to J. L. Camp, U.S. attorney, Western District, Texas, Sept. 4, 1917; Attorney General to John Green, Oct. 1, 1917, RG 60, File 186233–168).

11. John Green to Attorney General, Dec. 11, 1918, RG 60, File 186233-168. Most South Texas Hispanics worked on ranches owned and operated by those running the local draft boards. They therefore depended on the goodwill of these officials for their livelihood. The failure of thousands of qualified Hispanics to register was an act of courage or desperation or based on the assumption that local bosses would not prosecute for failure to register. In some cases the failure to register was obviously the effect of ignorance of the meaning of the law. In any case, given the power of local political bosses, the failure of the registration drives was surprising unless we assume that the bosses themselves were against the drafting of Hispanics.

12. Anders, *Boss Rule,* pp. 235–36; D. Simmons to Attorney General, May 24, 1919, RG 60, File 186233–168.

13. Of 304 draft cases filed through late 1918, only 10 were docketed in the Houston and Galveston divisions: *Criminal Docket,* Houston Division, vol. 2; *Criminal Docket,* Galveston Division, vol. 4. In 1920 there were 388,675 "Mexicans" in Texas, 145,940 of whom were born in the United States. This group constituted 11.7 percent of the state's population. In the Southern District, Mexicans made up over 50 percent of the population. Hispanics numbered well over 60 percent in the district's southern half, where most of the cases originated, however (U.S. Bureau of the Census, *Fifteenth Census of the United States: 1930. Population,* vol. 11:941; George Coalson, *The Development of the Migratory Farm Labor System in Texas, 1900–1954,* pp. 12–15).

The four possible German American cases were in the Houston and Galveston divisions. No German-sounding names were found in Corpus Christi, despite a large German American population in that division (*Criminal Docket,* Houston Division, vol. 2; *Criminal Docket,* Galveston Division, vol. 4; *Criminal Docket,* Corpus Christi Division, vol. 1). Actions were taken against German nationals, however. See note 14 below. On Texans' fears of German American loyalty, see the letters between J. F. Carl, secretary of the Texas State Council of Defense, to Charles Breniman, division superintendent for Texas Department of Justice, *Texas War Records,* Box 2j358, Barker Library, Austin, Texas. See also Harold Hyman, *To Try Men's Souls: Loyalty Tests in American History,* pp. 267–97. As to the distribution of Germans in Southeast Texas, see Terry Jordan, "The German Settlement of Texas after 1865," *Southwestern Historical Quarterly* 73 (Oct., 1969): 193–212. It is unknown at this time whether the low number of African Americans indicted for failure to register was because most did register or because they were not prosecuted. In Houston at least, African Americans supported the war effort. On the African American community during the war, see James SoRelle, "The Darker Side of 'Heaven': The Black Community in Houston, Texas, 1917–1945," (Ph.D. diss.), chaps. 1 and 2; and Robert V. Haynes, *A Night of Violence: The Houston Riot of 1917.*

14. Simmons to Attorney General, May 24, 1919, RG 60, File 186233-168. The U.S. attorney also did not file in those cases in which it was obvious that the failure to register had occurred as the result of ignorance of the law; he simply allowed the individual to register for the draft. This was Department of Justice policy (Attorney General to Green, Sept. 25, 1917, RG 60, File 186233-168). The 5 to 10 percent not prosecuted usually had their cases dismissed because the defendant could not be found or because he had already been inducted into the army. "Not guilty" decisions were almost never given. In 1918, 287 draft cases were terminated: 27 were not prosecuted; 50 were guilty on pleas of not guilty; and 210 were guilty on pleas of guilty. Only 4 acquittals were filed. In 1919, of 145 cases terminated, 128 were convictions. Of this number, 124 were ended on pleas of guilty. In 1920, 112 draft cases were terminated, 102 of which were

on pleas of guilty and 10 of which were not prosecuted (*Atty. Gen. Report* [1918], p. 231; [1919], p. 195; [1920], p. 351).

15. By late 1918, following the signing of the Armistice, grand juries in Brownsville and Laredo began to refuse to indict Hispanics who had fled to Mexico to avoid the draft and who were now returning to Texas. "It is my information," wrote U.S. attorney John Green "that the Grand Jury took this action because they were of the opinion that the Mexicans probably ought not to be held as strictly accountable as American citizens of Anglo-Saxon blood and also because the labor situation in the border country is serious and these Mexican laborers are very much needed. In my opinion it is altogether probable that the Grand Jury was influenced fully as much by this latter consideration as by the former" (Green to Attorney General, Dec. 11, 1918, RG 60, File 186233-168).

16. "Espionage Act," 40 *U.S. Statutes at Large*, p. 217, Titles I–V, Title I, sec. 3; Titles XII, IX, and VII. Scheiber, *The Wilson Administration*, pp. 17–20, describes the passage of the Espionage Act. In addition to the Espionage Act, the U.S. attorney's office dealt administratively with enemy aliens (mostly German and Austrian nationals). The Southern District generated some 7,527 files in the Justice Department concerning enemy aliens. In most cases, after investigation and the posting of a bond by the alien and a sponsor, the individual concerned was released. A significant minority, however, were interned in U.S. military bases throughout the West. See Department of Justice, RG 60, File 9-16-12.

17. *Atty. Gen. Report (1918)*, p. 231; (1919), pp. 194–95. There is a discrepancy between the attorney general's report and the dockets of the Southern District. According to the dockets, there were 86 cases filed under the Espionage Act; the court's dockets show more. However, a number of these cases were ultimately dismissed without ever coming to trial, which may explain the discrepancy. The court's more than 86 cases put it sixth in the nation for this type of action. See Scheiber, *The Wilson Administration*, p. 43.

18. 40 *U.S. Statutes at Large*, p. 225. Forty-five of these cases were out of Brownsville and 31 from Laredo. There were none in the other divisions.

19. Hugh Robertson, U.S. attorney for the Western District of Texas, wrote that "most of the seizures which are made in this District are of goods in small quantities, such as lard in ten-pound buckets, sugar in ten-pound packages, the value of which when condemned and ordered sold, would of course, be wholly insufficient to pay the cost of the proceedings, and the persons from whom the goods are usually seized are Mexicans of the laboring classes, who are wholly insolvent." The same condition existed in the Southern District (Robertson to attorney general, Aug. 20, 1918, RG 60, File 187415-2-38).

20. *U.S. v. José Cisneros, Andrés Cisneros, and Isidoro Cornea*, Cr 2343, Brownsville Division. Ten of these cases were dismissed by the U.S. attorney.

21. *Atty. Gen. Report* (1918) p. 231; (1919), p. 195. Green to Attorney General, June 8, 1918; Green to Attorney General, July 23, 1918; Attorney General to Green, Aug. 1, 1918, RG 60, File 187415-2. For the similar problems of other districts along the Mexican border, see RG 60, File 187415-2. See esp. Robertson to Attorney General, Aug. 20, 1918. For Justice Department policy on this issue, see Circular Letter 70, June 14, 1918, and Circular Letter 841, June 3, 1918, RG 60, File 187415-2.

22. For passport cases, see *U.S. v. Israel Kolb*, Cr 886, Laredo Division; *U.S. v. Paul Abood*, Cr 887, Laredo Division; *U.S. v. Georges Zrike*, Cr 906, Laredo Division; and *U.S. v. Jim Ganga*, Cr 907, Laredo Division. For disloyalty cases, see *U.S. v. Guadalupe de los Santos, Jr.*, Cr 2297, Brownsville Division; *U.S. v. José Vega and Jesús Dintanilla*, Cr 2298, Brownsville Division; *U.S. v. Maurice Wand*, Cr 634, Houston Division; *U.S. v. W. Gainor*, Cr 639, Houston Division; and *U.S. v. Florentinio Rodríguez*, Cr 97, Corpus Christi Divi-

sion. See also RG 60, File 191866-3. For examples of Espionage Act cases in other districts, see Murphy, *World War I*, pp. 210–47.

23. Lewis Gould, *Progressives and Prohibitionists: Texas Democrats in the Wilson Era*, p. 224; Thomas Mackey, "Red Lights Out: A Legal History of Prostitution, Disorderly Houses, and Vice Districts, 1870–1917" (Ph.D. diss.). Another problem was race. A large segment of the troops training in Texas were African American. Confrontations between Anglo citizens and African American soldiers were common both in Texas and the South as a whole. In 1917 a race riot broke out between African American soldiers of the 24th Infantry stationed at Camp Logan near Houston and Anglo citizens. Sixteen Anglos, five of whom were policemen, were killed. The entire unit of African American soldiers was ultimately court-martialed. This and similar cases never became an issue for the federal courts, however.

24. Steen, *Twentieth Century Texas; Houston Post* (Jan. 22, 1961); Mackey, "Red Lights Out," pp. 238–59.

25. Brownsville had thirty-five cases filed; Houston had eighty-two; Corpus Christi, six; Laredo, twelve; and Galveston, eighteen. On alcohol cases, see RG 60, File 185818-63. A similar type of action on the civil law docket was RLD prosecutions for selling unlicensed liquor to soldiers outside of the five-mile limit. See *U.S. v. Hilario Rodríguez*, Cr 104, Corpus Christi Division (received thirty days); *U.S. v. G. Rodríguez*, Cr 105, Corpus Christi Division (received thirty days).

26. Brownsville had five of these cases; Houston had eighteen; Corpus Christi, two; Laredo, six; and Galveston, eleven. On prostitution cases, see RG 60, file 185818-90.

27. "Rising Flood" quote by Congressman Albert Johnson, head of the House Committee on Immigration in 1927, quoted in Carl Degler, *Out of Our Past: The Forces That Shaped Modern America*, p. 301. Congressman Johnson continued, stressing the dangers of America's "capacity to maintain our cherished institutions" in this situation. Volstead Act, 41 *U.S. Statutes at Large*, p. 305; Immigration Act, 42 *U.S. Statutes at Large*, p. 5. The Immigration Act of 1924, 43 *U.S. Statutes at Large*, p. 153, limited entrance to the United States for non-western Europeans even more. See Degler, *Out of Our Past*, pp. 299–303.

28. Civil filings increased from 17,511 in 1917 to 48,325 in 1930 (Clark, "Adjudication to Administration," p. 114).

29. On the rise in immigration cases in the early 1930s, see chap. 4. On Galveston's experience with Prohibition, see McComb, *Galveston*, pp. 159–63; *Galveston Daily News* (May 4, 1931, Feb. 14, 1932, Dec. 11, 1932, Dec. 23, 1924, Mar. 12, 1925, July 8, 1925, and Feb. 12, 1929).

30. Clark, "Adjudication to Administration," pp. 110–17. On national efforts to enforce Prohibition see Charles Merz, *The Dry Decade*, pp. 133–57; David McCullough, "Bone Dry? Prohibition New Mexico Style, 1918–1933," *New Mexico Historical Review* 63 (Jan., 1988): 25–42; and Rayman Solomon, "Regulating the Regulators: Prohibition Enforcement in the Seventh Circuit," pp. 81–96.

31. See *Criminal Docket Books*, Brownsville, Laredo, and Houston divisions, for examples of the speed with which Prohibition cases were handled. In most cases, only two entries were made: one noting the filing of the indictment, and the other listing the defendant's plea of guilty and the court's judgment and sentence. This pattern became so routine that rubber stamps listing this information were made to ease the court clerk's job.

32. Joseph C. Hutcheson, Jr., "The Local Jail," *American Bar Association Journal* 21 (Feb., 1935): 83.

33. For an example of Hutcheson's lenient view toward deserving Prohibition defendants, see *United States v. Echols,* 253 F., 826 (1918). For an example of a case in which the judge took a harder stance in a case over the Volstead Act, see *United States v. Smith,* 43 F(2d), 173 (1930); for immigration, see *United States ex rel. Louros v. Lindsey,* 51 F(2d), 303 (1931) and *United States ex rel. Dobra v. Lindsey,* 51 F(2d), 141 (1931).

Other judges in Texas and the South were not as lenient as Hutcheson. For example, Judge West, sitting in San Antonio and Del Rio, was reputed to be much harder on even first-time Prohibition defendants, giving maximum sentences on many occasions (William Whalen to Commissioner General of Immigration, Jan. 21, 1928, RG 60, File 23-47-51).

34. See note 33. See also Joseph Hutcheson, "The Local Jail," pp. 81–85, 88. For Hutcheson's views on probation (suspended sentence "upon good behavior"), see *United States v. Maisel,* 26 F(2d), 275 (1928). See Criminal Cases 3083–3183, *Criminal Docket Book,* Houston Division (July, 1928) and Criminal Cases 4259–4339, *Criminal Docket Book,* Brownsville Division (May, 1928). One of the reasons the judge was less willing to give probation in the southern divisions was that most of the defendants were Mexican and, as has always been the case, it was feared that they would simply flee to Mexico.

35. Horace Soule to Mrs. Mabel Willebrandt, asst. attorney general, June 23, 1925, RG 60, File 23-74-9-11; "Memorandum for Assistant Attorney General Willebrandt: Re, Power of Immigration Officers to Make Seizures under the National Prohibition Act," May 10, 1928; "Memorandum on Motion to Suppress Evidence," *U.S. v. Tom Mason,* L 1434, Laredo Division, Nov. 17, 1927; William Whalen to Commissioner General of Immigration, Dec. 5, 1927; C. A. Perkins to District Director of Immigration, Dec. 10, 1927; Mabel Willebrandt to Henry Holden, Dec. 13, 1927, RG 60, File 23-74-51; see also Henry Holden to Attorney General, Mar. 15, 1928, RG 60, File 23-74-51.

36. Unnamed journalist, quoted in Walter P. Armstrong, "Joseph C. Hutcheson, Jr.: Chief Judge, Fifth Circuit Court of Appeals," *American Bar Association Journal* 35 (June, 1949): 547.

37. All three cases are described in "Memorandum for Mrs. Willebrandt, Assistant Attorney General," July 29, 1924, RG 60, File 23-74-7. The maximum sentence under sec. 593 of the Tariff Act of 1922 was two years and five thousand dollars. On the generally "lawless conditions existing in Galveston" throughout the 1920s as a result of bootlegging, see RG 60, File 23-74-9, and McComb, *Galveston,* pp. 160–61.

38. *Houston Post* (Mar. 2, 1923, pp. 1, 2, Feb. 27, 1923, p. 4); see also Matthew Taylor, "Rise and Fall of the Ku Klux Klan in Houston, Texas, 1920–1923" (unpublished), pp. 1, 46–48.

39. *Houston Post* (Feb. 27, 1923), pp. 1, 4.

40. Immigration cases were an exception to this rule. With immigration, Hutcheson was more concerned with keeping illegal aliens out of Texas than with helping the mostly poor Mexican defendants before him. However, even here, Hutcheson was less likely than his successor, Thomas Kennerly, to require additional jail time for repeat offenders. See chap. 4.

41. Hutcheson realized that his "duty to these people did not end, but in fact really began, when, after conviction or plea of guilty, they came helpless under the power of the law." See Hutcheson, "The Local Jail," pp. 81–85, 83. Attempting to match the punishment to the crime is not necessarily a goal unique to Hutcheson. Most judges attempt in some manner to balance the punishment with the crime; however, Hutcheson is unusual in his vocalness on the subject.

In the May term of 1930 in Brownsville, Judge Hutcheson sentenced thirty-two Prohibition defendants to jail, nine were given fines, and thirty-one were sentenced to one to five years of probation. One year later, with Judge Kennerly on the bench, there were thirty-eight jail sentences for Prohibition violations, eleven cases in which fines were given, and only seventeen cases in which probation was granted.

42. Willebrandt to Hermon Soule, June 30, 1925; Willebrandt to Henry Holden, May 19, 1923, RG 60, File 23-74-0. Writing to all U.S. attorneys, Willebrandt wrote that "the injunction feature is a very effective weapon for wholesale elimination of places running contrary to the prohibition law. It should be made use of frequently by United States Attorneys" (Willebrant to Henry Holden, May 15, 1923, RG 60, File 23-010-1).

43. For example, in Houston on July 11, 1926, seventeen nuisance cases were filed. Of these, seven had the injunction dismissed, seven had the injunction perpetuated for one year, and three required the payment of a bond. On Apr. 12, 1929, seventeen cases were filed: eleven were dismissed on agreement with defendant to pay all costs; four had the injunctions made permanent; and two required payment of a bond. In Galveston in July and Aug., 1926, forty-seven abatement cases were filed: seven were dismissed; two had the injunctions made permanent; seven required the payment of bonds; and twenty-nine were dismissed as litigation had lasted longer than one year and the property had as a result been under lock for longer than the requested time (*Equity Docket Books*, Houston Division, vols. 2, 3, and 4; *Equity Docket Books*, Galveston Division, vols. 1 and 2). This was a common pattern throughout the state. Both the Western and the Eastern districts had the same policy toward owners (Randolph Bryant, U.S. attorney, Eastern District, Texas, to Attorney General, May 21, 1923; Wayne Borah, U.S. attorney, Eastern District, Texas, to Attorney General, Sept. 17, 1927, RG 60, File 23-010-1).

44. *U.S. v. One Fargo Truck*, 46 F(2d), 171; "Memorandum for Assistant Attorney General Youngquist and the Solicitor General," Dec. 24, 1931; Henry Holden to Attorney General, Dec. 9, 1931; Henry Holden to Attorney General, Dec. 18, 1931, RG 60, File 23-74-85.

45. Henry Holden, U.S. attorney, Southern District, Texas, to Attorney General, Feb. 7, 1933; D. Hardy, assistant to the attorney general, to Malcolm McCordale, assistant U.S. attorney, Apr. 7, 1933, RG 60, File 23-74-104. The attorney general reported these forfeiture cases under the same general heading as equity-nuisance cases ("Public Health and Safety"). For the nation as a whole, the attorney general did separate out data for "other Liquor Traffic Cases" but did not specify what these other cases were. For individual districts no separate category was given at all. In the case of the Southern District, this combining of cases may explain the large rise in the public health and safety category from 1930 to 1932. If this was the case, it adds to the uniqueness of the Southern District in handling equity-nuisance cases. For examples of Prohibition forfeiture cases in the Southern District, see the district's *Law Docket Books* for 1930–33; *Atty. Gen. Report* (1920–33). See also Roy McDonald, "Automobile Forfeitures and the Eighteenth Amendment," *Texas Law Review* 10 (Feb., 1932): 140–62.

4. Balancing Rights with Duties: Private Law during the Twenties

1. Francis May and Florence Escott, *Economic Statistics of Texas, 1900–1962; Atty. Gen. Report* (1920), p. 351, (1930), p. 194; Feagin, *Free Enterprise City*, pp. 8–9; Sibley, *The Port of Houston*. See also Robert Maxwell, *Texas Economic Growth, 1890 to World War II: From Frontier to Industrial Giant;* and Harold Platt, "Houston at the Crossroads: The Emergence of the Urban Center of the Southwest," *Journal of the West* 18 (July, 1979): 56.

2. Governor William Hobby, quoted in McKay and Faulk, *Texas after Spindletop,* pp. 98, 105. See also note 6 below. Feagin, *Free Enterprise City,* pp. 46–48; Mike Weingart et al., *Big Town, Big Money: The Business of Houston,* p. 28.

3. On the fight over Prohibition in Texas before 1920, see Gould, *Progressives and Prohibitionists.*

4. Nic Bohn, Sr., to G. J. Palmer, attorney general, Jan. 17, 1921, RG 60, File 23-74-4.

5. Hutcheson, "The Local Jail," pp. 81–85, 83.

6. Buenger and Pratt, *But Also Good Business,* pp. 12, 39. On the economic situation, see David McComb, *Houston: The Bayou City,* chap. 4; Spratt, *The Road to Spindletop;* Harold Platt, "Energy and Urban Growth: A Comparison of Houston and Chicago," *Southwestern Historical Quarterly* 91 (July, 1987): 1–18; McKay and Faulk, *Texas after Spindletop,* pp. 93–116; Dan E. Kilgore, "Corpus Christi: A Quarter Century of Development, 1900–1925," *Southwestern Historical Quarterly* 75 (Apr., 1972): 434–43. On the social and political situation, see Writers Program, Work Progress Administration, *Houston: A History and Guide,* p. 112; McComb, *Houston,* chap. 5; idem, *Galveston;* Evan Anders, "Boss Rule and Constituent Interests: South Texas Politics during the Progressive Era," *Southwestern Historical Quarterly* 84 (Jan., 1981): 269–92.

7. *Equity Docket Books,* Houston Division, vols. 2–4.

8. *Houston Post* (Jan. 1, 1961); Leon Jaworski, "Joseph C. Hutcheson, Jr.: A Lifetime of Judicial Service," *Texas Bar Journal* 24 (Dec., 1961): 1107–1108; interview, Joseph C. Hutcheson III (Mar. 3, 1988); "List of Applicants for the Position of United States District Judge, Southern District of Texas," in RG 60, "Applicants for Judge, Southern District Texas, 1917–1918 File," Box 861, National Archives, Washington, D.C.

9. *Interview* John R. Brown (Feb. 16, 1988); interview, Joe McDonald Ingraham (Feb. 4, 1988).

10. Joseph C. Hutcheson, Jr., "In Praise of Lawyers and Lawyering," *Insurance Council Journal* 21 (July, 1954): 241–42.

11. Joseph C. Hutcheson, Jr., "This Thing Called Law," *University of Chicago Law Review* 2 (Dec., 1934): 4; idem, "In Praise of Lawyers," pp. 241–42, quoting from *Duncan v. Alger,* 25 Texas Reports, 245.

12. Joseph C. Hutcheson, Jr., *Law as Liberator: The Principle of Democracy in America: The Spirit of Its Laws,* pp. 52, vi (quoting from John Locke).

13. Joseph Hutcheson, "Judging as Administration, Administration as Judging," *Texas Law Review* 21 (Nov., 1942): 1–2; idem, "The Judgement Intuitive: The Function of the 'Hunch' in Judicial Decision," *Cornell Law Quarterly* 14 (1929): 274–88. In arguing for the use and acknowledgment of the judicial hunch, Hutcheson was participating in the creation of the sociological jurisprudence movement, a forerunner to the legal realist movement. Sociological jurisprudence argued that judging was by its nature an illogical and idiosyncratic effort–that legal decisions, like all other forms of decisions, were made not in a rational process, but by an internal and irrational working out of the facts in the judge's mind. The role of the judge, however, was to attempt to construct a logical (if intuitive) method to create continuity to the past. This, in turn, made Hutcheson a partial or early legal realist. While his views on the method of judging merged with those of most realists, the substance of Hutcheson's decision had as much in common with nineteenth-century jurisprudence as with the realists. Like Cardozo, Hutcheson helped build the foundations for the realist movement, but disagreed with the arguments of a mature legal realism. See G. Edward White, *The American Judicial Tradition,* pp. 252, 270.

14. Frederic Maitland, *Equity: A Course of Lectures.*

15. *Galveston Electric Co. v. City of Galveston,* 272 F., 147. Discussion of the case is taken from Hutcheson's description in his decision. See also *Brush Electric Co. v. City of Galveston,* Eq 39, Galveston Division, and *Galveston Electric Co. v. City of Galveston,* Eq 40, Galveston Division.

16. See *Houston Post* (Feb. 12, 1921), p. 9.

17. *Galveston Electric Co. v. City of Galveston,* 272 F., 149, 164.

18. On the Supreme Court's use of "reasonableness" as a standard for judging rate regulations, see Clyde Jacobs, *Law Writers and the Courts: The Influence of Thomas Cooley, Christopher Tiedeman and John Dillion upon American Constitutional Law,* and Gabriel Kolko, *Railroads and Regulation, 1877–1916.*

19. *Galveston Electric Co. v. City of Galveston,* 272 F., 150, Hutcheson's italics; *San Diego Land Co. v. National City,* 174 U.S., 753.

20. *Galveston Electric Co. v. City of Galveston,* 272 F., 151; *Knoxville v. Knoxville Water Co.,* 212 U.S., 16. On the actions of the Supreme Court, see Jacobs, *Law Writers,* and Morton Keller, *Affairs of State.*

21. *Galveston Electric Co. v. City of Galveston,* 272 F., 153.

22. Part of the brief was quoting from *Knoxville v. Knoxville Water Co.,* 212 U.S., 18; *Galveston Electric Co. v. City of Galveston,* 272 F., 153–54.

23. On the fears of the brotherhood, see *Houston Post-Dispatch* (July 26, 1927), p. 2. On intimidation, see "Exhibit 'B,'" in U. S. Circuit Court of Appeals, Fifth Circuit, *Transcript of Record, #5406* (*Tx and NO Railroad, Co. v. Brotherhood of RW and SS Clerks*) (1928), pp. 48–73 (hereinafter, *Transcript of Record*).

The railroad felt it could not afford a ten cent per hour increase in wages. An increase of this magnitude, in the opinion of H. M. Lull, vice-president of the Texas and New Orleans, would have cost the railroad over $340,000 per year. The railroad also feared it would lose arbitration as it had in a recent arbitration case west of Texas (letter from H. M. Lull to A. D. McDonald, May 24, 1927, quoted in full in *Brotherhood of Railway and Steamship Clerks, etc. v. Texas and New Orleans Railroad Co.* 25 F(2d), 873 at 874. See also *Houston Post-Dispatch* (July 26, 1927), pp. 1, 2, on the impact of a positive decision for the union. The creation of the association, therefore, was meant to forestall the attempts at arbitration originated by the brotherhood. The railroad used intimidation, subsidization, and a bribe of $75,000 to gain enough signatures so as to reasonably recognize the association as the legitimate representative of the railroad's employees and thus to refuse to arbitrate with the brotherhood (letter from H. M. Lull to A. D. McDonald, May 24, 1927; *Transcript of Record*). It was at this point, in July of 1927, that the brotherhood filed suit in the Southern District Court of Texas.

24. 44 *U.S. Statutes at Large,* p. 577.

25. *Pennsylvania, etc., Federation v. Pennsylvania Railroad Co.,* 267 U.S., 203. This decision dealt with injunctive enforcement of a ruling of the now-defunct United States Railroad Labor Board. For the problems with this in the present case, see *Brotherhood of Railway and Steamship Clerks, etc. v. Texas and New Orleans RR Co.,* 33 F(2d), 16.

26. The railroad in its briefs and oral argument questioned the jurisdiction of the court on this issue on a number of grounds, from the constitutionality of the statute under which the injunction was asked for to the applicability of an equity hearing "for an abstract right, the enforcement of which would lead to no definite result" ("Argument for the Defendant," District Court of the U.S. for the Southern District of Texas, Houston Division, *Brotherhood of Railway and Steamship Clerks v. Texas and New Orleans R.R. Co.* in *Briefs: United States Supreme Court October Term,* 1929, no. 469. p. 2 (hereinafter *Briefs*);

see also discussion by Hutcheson in *Brotherhood of Railway and Steamship Clerks v. Texas and New Orleans RR Co.*, 25 F(2d), 873.

27. See Felix Frankfurter and Nathan Green, *The Labor Injunction*, esp. chap. 3; Alpheus T. Mason, "Organized Labor as Party Plaintiff in Injunction Cases," *Columbia Law Review* 30 (Apr., 1930): 466–87. On uses of injunctions against unions, see Gerald Eggert, *Railroad Labor Disputes: The Beginnings of Federal Strike Policy;* and Leon Fink, "Labor, Liberty, and the Law: Trade Unionism and the Problem of the American Constitutional Order," *Journal of American History* 79 (Dec., 1987): 904–25.

Sec. 20, Clayton Act, 30 *U.S. Statutes at Large*, p. 730 (the Clayton Act was passed in part to make additions to the Judicial Code), quoted in "Argument for the Defendant," *Briefs*. See also discussion by Hutcheson in *Brotherhood of Railway and Steamship Clerks v. Texas and New Orleans RR Co.*, 25 F(2d), 873 at 875.

28. Armstrong, "Joseph C. Hutcheson, Jr., pp. 546–50, 614–18. See also interview, Joseph C. Hutcheson III (Mar. 3, 1988), on the judge's social position and the tensions generated by this case. On the importance of the Southern Pacific in the region's economy, see Joseph Pratt and Kenneth Lipartito, *Baker and Botts and the Building of Modern Houston*, chaps. 2 and 3.

29. "Order for Temporary Injunction," *Transcript of Record*, p. 84. "Nothing in this injunction shall be considered authority to prevent any employee of the Railroad . . . from organizing as many unions as he wants to in any way he wants to" ("Opinion of the Court," *Transcript of Record*, pp. 77, 82).

30. *Houston Post-Dispatch* (July 30, 1927), p. 5.

31. *Brotherhood of Railway and Steamship Clerks, etc. v. Texas and New Orleans RR Co.*, 24 F(2d), 433.

32. *Brotherhood of Railway and Steamship Clerks v. Texas and New Orleans, RR Co.*, 24 F(2d), 426.

33. Ibid, pp. 432–34. See also *Houston Post-Dispatch* (Feb. 12, 1928), pp. 1, 2.

34. "Opinion of the Court," *Transcript of Record*, pp. 80, 432.

35. *Brotherhood of Railway and Steamship Clerks v. Texas and New Orleans RR Co.*, 25 F(2d), 875, 876.

36. The same three-judge court also heard a number of similar cases in the Southern District in 1933, though with a less exciting result, the point already having been made in *Constintin v. Smith*. See *Southern Drilling and Production Co. v. Lon Smith et al.*, Eq 576, Houston Division, and *Boxrollium Oil Co. v. Lon Smith et al.*, Eq 575, Houston Division. For background on this case, see Norman Nordhauser, *The Quest for Stability: Domestic Oil Regulation, 1917–1935*, chap. 6.

A three-judge court was a special court called to rule on issues of special constitutional importance. Consisting of two district court judges and a circuit court judge, the decisions of this court were appealable directly to the Supreme Court. On three-judge courts, see Joseph Hutcheson, "A Case for Three Judges," *Harvard Law Review* 47 (Mar., 1934): 795–826.

37. Quoted in Nordhauser, *Quest for Stability*, p. 89. On Sterling, see Robert Hardwicke, "Legal History of Conservation of Oil in Texas," p. 231.

38. *Constintin v. Smith*, 57 F(2d), 239–41.

39. Until the Texas legislature passed a law authorizing the Railroad Commission to prorate to control market demand (i.e., to limit production to control prices) in 1933, the federal courts ruled that proration for market demand was illegal under Texas law (*MacMillan v. Commission*, 51 F(2d), 400; *Henderson v. Commission*, 56 F(2d), 218). On

the judge's allowing the state militia to remain temporarily in the oil fields and his order limiting the amount of oil the plaintiffs could pump, see *Constintin v. Smith*, 57 F(2d), 242; Nordhauser, *Quest for Stability*, p. 90; and Hart, "Legal History of Conservation of Oil in Texas," p. 235.

In *Amazon Petroleum Corp. v. Commission*, 5 F. Supp., 693 [1934] the courts accepted the new law as authorizing proration for market conditions. See also David Prindle, *Petroleum Politics and the Texas Railroad Commission*, pp. 30–31. Lawrence Smith described the requirements of the *Constintin* decision in the *National Petroleum News* of Mar. 16, 1932, in the following humorous, but correct, manner:

> Governor Sterling, Adjutant General Sterling, General Wolters:
>
> Gentlemen:
>
> We, the undersigned, have looked carefully into the lawsuit brought against your by Messers. Constintin and Wrather. We find that you have overstepped the bounds of your authority in declaring and enforcing martial law on the wells of these plaintiffs.
>
> We are going to sign an injunction against you just as soon as the plaintiffs satisfy us that they intend to produce their wells in a manner that will not violate the conservation law of Texas. We are not quarreling with the principle of conservation; on the contrary, we think it is a fine thing. The legislature of the state, however, put this into the hands of the Railroad Commission and nothing in the law or the Constitution confers upon you the right to take charge.
>
> We have not been able to find from the testimony that there was any rioting, etc., which you advanced as the occasion for sending in your troops.
>
> Had there been, under the Constitution of the State, you would have been limited to sending in these guardsmen as aid to the local civil authorities.
>
> As for the assertions that this court cannot enjoin you, nerts, governor, nerts.
>
> Attached to this memorandum you will find 40 pages of instructive reasoning, giving decision of various courts, summary of the testimony and analysis of the argument, on all points which pertain to this cause.
>
> Hope you are enjoying good health and advising you in the future to keep your head down and your left arm straight, we are . . .
>
> P.S. Tell Gen. Wolters that the next time he goes in with his troops, he is, as far as we are concerned, a deputy sheriff. (Quoted in Hart, "Legal History of Conservation of Oil in Texas," p. 235)

40. The court averaged 33 admiralty cases per year during this decade. The most cases were filed in 1922, when 61 actions were started; the least were filed in 1923 and 1926, when 25 cases were filed. During this period, the total number of filings in the court rose from 724 in 1920 to 1,688 in 1929 (*Atty. Gen. Report* [1920–30]). On federal admiralty practice, see Erwin C. Surrency, *A History of the Federal Courts*, pp. 145–53.

41. Hutcheson, "The Judgement Intuitive," pp. 282–83.

42. *The Hornby Castle*, 26 F(2d), 387. For a general discussion of the negligence principle in tort law, see G. Edward White, *Tort Law in America*, pp. 60–114; see also F. L. Wiswall, Jr., *The Development of Admiralty Jurisdiction and Practice since 1800: An English Study with American Comparisons*.

43. An example of Hutcheson's use of the social justice standard in a commercial case took place in 1921. In 1917 Joseph Alexander had asked his agent, Jesse Martin, to deposit in the Security Bank and Trust Company of Wharton County a certain amount

of money. Martin did this, but placed the money under his own name to cover a debt he owed to the bank (the bank allowed this, although it knew that Martin was unlikely have such an amount of money at that time). When, in 1918, Alexander attempted to get the money from the bank, he found that the bank had appropriated the money deposited by Martin. Alexander then sued the bank for his money. In deciding this case, Hutcheson noted that "[n]o character of case better illustrates the principle of the equitable maxim, 'Ubi jus ibi remedium' [where there is an action there is a remedy] than that of tracing trust moneys misappropriated by banks with the connivance, or through the active agency, of a depositor." Since the bank had knowledge of Martin's financial position and the likelihood that the money was fraudulently acquired, the judge ruled that "the defendant [the bank] having been found in default ex maleficio, through a deliberate and knowing misappropriation of complainants' funds, this court will be slow to erect out of a transaction which admittedly failed to result . . . by which the bank could keep the fruits of its wrong" (*Alexander et al. v. Security Bank and Trust Co. et al.*, 273 F., 258).

44. *St. Louis and San Francisco Railway v. Republic Box Co.*, 12 F(2d), 441. It should be noted that Hutcheson's views of equitable justice had a part in this decision. "In addition, I am of the opinion that, there having been two routes over which the shipment could have moved, and the shipper having designated the route and the rate, the carrier was just as responsible for the loss to the shipper, and just as little entitled to recover the full legal rate from it" (p. 443).

45. Feagin, *Free Enterprise City*, p. 47.

5. Keeping the Law within Reasonable Limits: Public Law during the Depression

1. *Atty. Gen. Report* (1930), p. 286; (1931), p. 320; (1932), p. 326. *Congressional Record*, 72d Cong., 1st sess., p. 3238. Unemployment rose from 1.4 percent in mid-1930 to 4.4 percent by year-end (Diane Oxment, "The Port City of Galveston," p. 145). For the depression's effects on Texas in general, see other articles in Cotner, *Texas Cities and the Great Depression*.

2. For example, in Corpus Christi, ten thousand of the area's twenty thousand farms were put up for sale by the banks. Farther south the numbers were even greater. See Robert Caro, *The Years of Lyndon Johnson: The Path to Power*, pp. 242–44.

3. "The Sun Still Shines," *Cotton and Cotton Oil News* 30 (Nov. 18, 1929): 1. See also *Houston* 1 (Mar., 1930): 3; *Journal of the* [Texas] *House of Representatives*, 42d Legisl., reg. sess., 1931, pp. 85–89.

4. *Galveston Daily News* (Aug. 29, 1930); editorial in *Houston* 2 (Nov., 1931): 15; *Houston Post-Dispatch* (Jan. 22, 1931).

5. This was after the Houston Community Chest, a private relief organization, had raised $8,883 in 1931 and 1932, and the city had spent thousands more.

6. Lionel Patenaude, "The New Deal and Texas" (Ph.D. diss.), p. 305, notes that by 1934, "sentiment had crystallized into one main Channel–the government was practicing too much regulation." See also, pp. 290, 311; Buenger and Pratt, *But Also Good Business*, pp. 90–92; Helen Burns, *The American Banking Community and New Deal Banking Reforms, 1933–35*, pp. 53–74. An additional cause for declining support rested in the rebounding of the region's economy, especially around Houston, by late 1933. As one historian has put it: "Houston's experience involved less suffering than occurred in many other cities." This was also the case in Galveston and to a lesser extent in the Rio Grande

Valley. The personal and public crisis caused by the depression did, however, continue to have an impact throughout the remainder of the decade (William Montgomery, "The Depression in Houston, 1929–1933," and Oxment, "The Port City of Galveston," pp. 153–69, 135–51.

7. Interview, T. Everton Kennerly, Apr. 4, 1989; "Federal Judges in Texas," *Texas Bar Journal* 37 (May, 1974): 411; *Houston Post* (July 30, 1962); "Thomas M. Kennerly," *Texas Bar Journal* 21 (Feb. 23, 1958): 80, 108; "In Memoriam," Mrs. M. A. Miller, July 31, 1962 (Thomas M. Kennerly papers).

8. Other conservative Texans were in complete agreement with Judge Kennerly's views on these matters. "Businessmen felt that good business methods would sweep aside the ills that beset agriculture [and industry]. They reasoned that the permanent cure lay in 'improved quality production at lower cost, improved marketing especially in local markets, and lowered tariff burdens.'" They definitely did not accept "the economy of scarcity" (Patenaude, "The New Deal and Texas," p. 299, quoting from *Texas Business Review* [June 27, 1935]: 5).

9. "Traditional" also meant providing loans to the states and facilitating private efforts at reconstruction. Herbert Hoover deeply believed in the importance of such concepts as "individualism," "voluntarism," and a limited (though active) role for the federal government in economic regulatory affairs. His first response to the depression was to help others to help themselves. The large amount of money lent by the Reconstruction Finance Corporation to banks and by the Agriculture Department to farmers is an example of how far Hoover was willing to go to help others. He refused, however, to "put the nation on the dole" with direct federal relief measures. When it came to a direct federal response, Hoover expanded the role of the federal government only in those areas in which the federal government had traditionally acted (Robert McElvaine, *The Great Depression,* pp. 51–71).

10. *Atty. Gen. Reports* (1925–32).

11. Significant nativist sentiment existed in Texas. One Houston man wrote that "they are right here to take white labors place every time a job shows up . . . they do not let us work in Mexico and why should they be permitted to cut wages and take the bread out of our white childrens mouths" (quoted in George Kiser and David Silvermen, "Mexican Repatriation during the Great Depression," p. 49). Newspapers supported the reparation movement. The *Houston Post-Dispatch* wrote on October 12, 1931, that "the Departure of the Mexican eases the unemployment situation in Southern California perceptibly, and simplifies the relief problem no little." It suggested the same result would occur as Texas Mexicans were removed. Some of these repatriates were documented aliens who left because of bad economic times and local discrimination. Some were actually Americans–born on U.S. soil– but without adequate records to prove it. See Abraham Hoffman, *Unwanted Mexican Americans in the Great Depression: Repatriation Pressures, 1929–1939,* pp. 120, 174–75; Marilyn Rhinehart and Thomas Krenck, "'In the Shadow of Uncertainty: Texas Mexicans and Repatriation in Houston during the Great Depression," *Houston Review* 10 (1988): 21–33.

12. There were 5,855 cases filed in 1931 and 5,765 in 1932 (*Atty. Gen. Reports* [1929–32]). Deportations by the federal courts were joined by administrative deportations by the Labor Department. In fiscal year 1931 the Labor Department deported 7,116 Mexicans. An additional 7,500 or so chose voluntary departure over deportation. In fiscal 1932, 7,750 Mexicans were deported, with an additional 10,347 voluntarily leaving the country (Hoffman, *Unwanted Mexican Americans,* p. 125).

13. Immigration and Naturalization Service Records, RG 85, Files 55640-535 and 55652-917 (National Archives, Washington, D.C.); Rhinehart and Krenck, "'In the Shadow of Uncertainty,'" pp. 25–26; Abraham Hoffman, "Stimulus to Repatriation: The 1931 Federal Deportation Drive and the Los Angeles Mexican Community;" *Pacific Historical Review* 42 (May, 1973): 205–19.

14. Judge Kennerly "never did know what was going on in immigration cases, the defendants all spoke Spanish and the judge did not. He did all his work through an interpreter. In addition, most defendants pled guilty, and all he could do was send them across the border–after which they just came back and he saw them in the court again." Further, despite the presence of nativist sentiment in Texas, most politically powerful Texans, especially in the Rio Grande Valley, were in favor of an open border with Mexico. If nothing else, as the owners of farms and ranches that used mostly Hispanic labor, they benefited from an open border. While Judge Kennerly was a black-letter-law judge who followed the law's dictates, he also understood the role Mexican laborers played in the local economy (interview, T. Everton Kennerly, Apr. 4, 1989).

15. Susan Estabrook Kennedy, *The Banking Crisis of 1933*, p. 177. For a quick background on southern banking before and during the depression, see Emory Hawk, *Economic History of the South,* pp. 530–37.

16. Buenger and Pratt, *But Also Good Business,* pp. 90–92; Oxment, "The Port City of Galveston," p. 143. See also Buenger, "Between Community and Corporation."

17. Eq 50, 51, 52, 55, 56, 63, 70, 71, 72, 73, Equity Docket, Corpus Christi Division; Eq 548, 552, 572, 578, 619, 628, 640, Equity Dockets, Houston Division.

18. Prior to being appointed receiver, Meek was vice-president of the Security National Bank, Duncan, Oklahoma (1921–27), and manager of certain oil properties in Texas (1927–31). In 1935 he resigned as receiver to become president of the Citizens National Bank, Abilene. John Randle, another local banker was appointed by the comptroller of the currency to replace Meek (*Texian Who's Who,* I: 310). A capital stock assessment is the amount of the bank's debts a bank stockholder is liable for. The authority to call on the stockholder to pay this assessment was granted to the Office of the Comptroller by secs. 5151 and 5234 of the *Revised Statutes,* sec. 1c 156 (act of June 30, 1876), and sec. 23 (act approved Dec. 23, 1913–the Federal Reserve Act). George Barse, "A Summary of the Procedure and Principles Relating to the Liquidation of National Banks in Receivership," *Federal Bar Association Journal* 1 (Oct., 1932): 3–10, summarizes how a bank receivership worked and notes that "the sale of assets, or compromises of debts" had to be "'upon the order of a court of competent jurisdiction'" if "title [to] the assets sold, and . . . the compromise . . . obtained" was to transfer (p. 5).

19. On suits to collect capital assessments, see *Malcolm Meek, Receiver of the Public National Bank and Trust Co. of Houston v. Carter Stewart,* L 2495, Houston Division (plaintiff recovered $190,528 with 6 percent interest), and *Malcolm Meek, Receiver of the Public National Bank and Trust Co. of Houston v. J. Browne,* L 2512, Houston Division (plaintiff recovered $1,123 with 6 percent interest on compromise agreement). On applications to sell assets, see *In Re the Receivership of the City National Bank and Trust Co. of Corpus Christi,* Eq 50, Corpus Christi Division and *In Re the Receivership of the First National Bank of Mathis Texas,* Eq 56, Corpus Christi Division. On suits to recover loans, see *Malcolm Meek, Receiver of First National Bank of Corpus Christi v. M. K. Hunt et al.,* Eq 72, Corpus Christi Division (plaintiff recovered $7,414 with 10 percent interest).

20. McKay and Faulk, *Texas after Spindletop,* p. 125.

21. *Houston Press* (Jan. 5, 1932). See also Nordhauser, *The Quest for Stability,* p. 89;

James Hart, "Oil, the Courts, and the Railroad Commission," *Southwestern Historical Quarterly* 44 (Jan., 1941): 313; August W. Giebelhaus, *Business and Government in the Oil Industry: A Case Study of Sun Oil, 1876–1945*, pp. 199–207.

22. *People's Petroleum Producers v. Sterling et al.*, 60 F(2d), 1041. See also Hardwicke, "Legal History of Conservation," p. 238. Most of these cases were decided by a three-judge court that included Judge Kennerly.

23. The allowable production level was the maximum output allowed from all wells in a particular field. The flat-rate method of allocation meant limiting all wells to a similar number of barrels per day regardless of the potential output of individual wells.

24. See chap. 4 of this book. See also Prindle, *Petroleum Politics*, pp. 29–32; Nordhauser, *The Quest for Stability*, pp. 74–95; and Hart, "Oil, the Courts," pp. 316–26.

25. *Boxrollium Oil Co. v. Smith et al.*, 4 F. Supp., 624 (Equity 576, Houston Division); *W. W. Hawkins v. Smith et al.*, Eq 564, Houston Division; *Southern Drilling and Production Co. v. Smith et al.*, Eq 575, Houston Division; *Felson Oil Co. v. Smith et al.*, Eq 565, Houston Division (case dismissed on agreement); *H. M. Crighton v. Smith et al.*, Eq 580, Houston Division (case dismissed without prejudice).

26. Texas Railroad Commission, "Special Order Promulgating Certain Rules and Regulations for the Conroe or Strake Field, Montgomery County, Texas, and Allocating to the Various Wells Therein the Maximum Amount of Oil to be Produced from Said Wells," July 5, 1933, quoted in "Opinion of the Court," *Boxrollium Oil Co. v. Smith et al.*, Eq 576, Houston Division.

27. "Original Complaint," May 11, 1933, *Boxrollium Oil Co. v. Smith et al.*, Eq 576, Houston Division.

28. "Supplemental Complaint," July 21, 1933, *Boxrollium Oil Co. v. Smith et al.*, Eq 576, Houston Division. Oil, as a liquid, will flow toward a well when pumped. If one well is pumping excessive amounts of oil, it will literally draw oil currently lying under another piece of property. According to the legal doctrine of capture, there is nothing that a property owner can do to stop this "stealing" of oil except to pump the oil up as fast as possible. See Prindle, *Petroleum Politics*, pp. 29–32.

29. "Opinion of the Court," Aug. 8, 1933, *Boxrollium Oil Co. v. Smith et al.*, Eq 576, Houston Division.

30. In the Eastern District this standard was set in *Amazon Petroleum Corp. v. Commission*, 5 F. Supp., 693 (1934).

31. "Affidavit of C. F. Petet, Secretary of the Railroad Commission," in *J. H. McLeaish and Co. v. Binford et al.*, Eq 467, Houston Division. On general condition of the trucking industry, see William R. Childs, *Trucking and the Public Interest: The Emergence of Federal Regulation, 1914–1940*, pp. 65–100.

32. May and Escott, *Economic Statistics of Texas, 1900–1962*, pp. 11, 13.

33. "Affidavit of J. H. McLeaish," in *J. H. McLeaish and Co. v. Binford et al.*, Eq 467, Houston Division. See also Tuffly Ellis, *The Texas Cotton Compress Industry: A History*.

34. Ellis, *Texas Cotton Compress Industry*, pp. 125–31; Childs, *Trucking and the Public Interest*, pp. 74–75. See also "Stipulation of Evidence," in *J. H. McLeaish and Co. v. Binford et al.*, Eq 467, Houston Division.

35. "Affidavit of Carl Callaway" and "R. W. Franklin" in *J. H. McLeaish and Co. v. Binford et al.*, Eq 467, Houston Division. See also Ellis, *Texas Cotton Compress Industry*, p. 130.

36. Bill 628, *Acts of the 42nd Legislature of Texas (Vernon's Annotated P.C. Texas*, Art. 827c Sec. 1-5-6); Bill 336, *Acts of the 42nd Legislature of Texas (Vernon's Annotated P.C. Texas*, Art. 827a Sec. 1, etc.); Bill 335, *Acts of the 42nd Legislature of Texas (Vernon's Annotated*

P.C. *Texas*, Art. 9111b, Sec. 22b); Ellis, *Texas Cotton Compress Industry*, p. 130. See also briefs in *J. H. McLeaish and Co. v. Binford et al.*, Eq 467, Houston Division; *Sproles v. Binford et al.*, Eq 476, Houston Division; *J. H. Stephenson v. Binford et al.*, Eq 479, Houston Division.

37. All of the federal cases were filed in the Southern District: *J. H. McLeaish and Co. v. Binford et al.*, 52 F(2d), 151; *Sproles v. Binford et al.*, 56 F(2d), 189; *J. H. Stephenson v. Binford et al.*, 53 F(2d), 509. Binford was the sheriff of Harris County. His codefendants included the sheriffs in a dozen other counties, the members of the Railroad Commission, the governor, and the state attorney general. The state cases were finally settled in *Ex parte Sterling et al.*, 53 Southwestern Reporter (2d), 294; *Ex parte Phares et al.*, 53 Southwestern Reporter (2d), 297; *Anderson, Clayton and Co. et al. v. State of Texas et al.*, 122 Texas Reports, 530. Stephenson was an intervenor in *J. H. McLeaish and Co. v. Binford et al.*, 52 F(2d), 151 (Eq 478, Houston Division), which became a companion case to *J. H. Stephenson v. Binford et al.*, 53 F(2d), 509. Response to these laws within the trucking industry can be seen in Henry Spurr, "A New and Significant Test of the Right to Be Regulated," *Public Utilities Fortnightly* 9 (Feb. 18, 1932): 195–202, 284–89; and V. E. Phelps, "The Right to Regulate Contract Motor Carriers for Hire," *Public Utilities Fortnightly* 10 (Aug. 18, 1932): 202–11. For a view from outside the trucking industry, see Worth Allen, "Wanted–A Plan for Regulating the Highway Carriers," *Public Utilities Fortnightly* 10 (Mar. 31, 1932): 379–88. On trucking industry efforts to combat regulation generally, see Childs, *Trucking and the Public Interest*, pp. 73–82.

38. "Affidavit of J. H. McLeaish" and "Bill of Complaint" in *J. H. McLeaish and Co. v. Binford et al.*, Eq 467, Houston Division.

39. "Bill of Complaint" in *J. H. McLeaish and Co. v. Binford et al.*, Eq 467, Houston Division.

40. "Respondant's Answer" in *J. H. McLeaish and Co. v. Binford et al.*, Eq 467, Houston Division. This point as to whether trucks really *did* damage the state's roads became the center of the legal dispute. Larue Brown, attorney for the National Automobile Chamber of Commerce (NACC), noted that "important results [will] turn on assumptions by the trial court as to the effect of certain vehicles upon the highway, as to the location of 'common carrier receiving points' and as to other matters of fact which seem, to those familiar with the situation, utterly unsupported by the evidence" (quoted in Childs, *Trucking and the Public Interest*, pp. 74–75). Both the state and the truckers provided significant amounts of documentary and statistical evidence to support or contradict the claim of road deterioration.

41. *J. H. McLeaish and Co. v. Binford et al.*, 52 F(2d), 151. In another part of the decision Hutcheson wrote that, "since . . . such restrictions must have a due and just relation to the supposed mischief to be avoided, the injurious character of highway use, and may not be arbitrarily designed under the guise of reasonable regulations, to hamper and prohibit in a discriminatory way the business of those who use the highways, . . . plaintiffs may still have relief against the statute, if, though the basis of the classification is reasonable, the Legislature had used means having no just and fair relation to the mischief aimed at, means which, though by skillful bewording they do appear to regulate, in reality destroy."

42. *J. H. McLeaish and Co. v. Binford et al.*, 52 F(2d), 151 at 155–56.

43. Summaries of plaintiffs' arguments made in *Sproles v. Binford et al.*, 56 F(2d), 189; *J. H. Stephenson v. Binford et al.*, 53 F(2d), 509. See also briefs in *Sproles v. Binford et al.*, Eq 476, Houston Division; *J. H. Stephenson v. Binford et al.*, Eq 479, Houston Division.

44. "Brief in Behalf of Respondents" filed in *Sproles v. Binford,* Eq 476, Houston Division, pp. 120–25.

45. The preliminary injunction was made in *Sproles v. Binford et al.,* 52 F(2d), 730. The final decision was made in *Sproles v. Binford et al.,* 56 F(2d), 189. The first quote is from the former case, the second from the latter. The decision in this case was affirmed by the Supreme Court in *Sproles et al. v. Binford et al.,* 286 U.S., 374.

46. *J. H. Stephenson v. Binford et al.,* 53 F(2d), 509. In reaching this decision, Hutcheson drew on "Regulation of the Contract Motor Carrier under the Constitution," *Harvard Law Review* 44 (Feb., 1931): 530–71.

47. *J. H. Stephenson v. Binford et al.,* 53 F(2d), 509. The majority decision in this case was affirmed by the Supreme Court in *Stephenson et al. v. Binford et al.,* 287 U.S., 241.

48. *Sproles et al. v. Binford et al.,* 286 U.S., 394–95. Background to the Supreme Court's decision can be found in Childs, *Trucking and the Public Interest,* pp. 73–82.

49. With three consecutive Republican terms in the presidency prior to Roosevelt's entering the White House, the majority of judges in all nine of the judicial circuits were Republican. Most of these Republican judges were elderly (the average age was sixty) and conservative. Drawn from small town and city practices where they had served local and interstate businesses–exactly the type of litigant most affected by New Deal reforms–they held an anti-regulatory view of the law that originated in the late nineteenth century with Thomas Cooley's treatise *Constitutional Limitations.* Biographical data are taken from Harold Chase, *Biographical Dictionary of the Federal Judiciary.* See also Peter Irons, *The New Deal Lawyers,* pp. 13, 46; Thomas Cooley, *A Treatise on the Constitutional Limitations Which Rest upon the Legislative Power of the States of the American Union.*

50. Irons, *New Deal Lawyers,* pp. 203–209.

51. Ibid., pp. 12, 35, 133.

52. See, generally, ibid., pp. 17–110; Arthur Schlesinger, Jr., *The Coming of the New Deal,* pp. 87–178; Ellis Hawley, *The New Deal and the Problem of Monopoly: A Study in Economic Ambivalence.* For a different view of the NRA, see Donald Brand, *Corporatism and the Rule of Law: A Study of the National Recovery Administration.*

53. The NRA also began limiting the range of enforcement to large industries in general and to retail industries in cities and towns of over twenty-five hundred (Irons, *New Deal Lawyers,* p. 37).

54. Smith to Averell Harriman, Apr. 9, 1934, Memo File, Jan.–Apr., 1934, Box 45, Richberg Papers, Library of Congress (quoted in ibid., p. 39). Most defendants turned out to be small, locally well known manufacturers or distributors in peripheral industries. Peripheral industries were made up of mostly small, independent businesses in which either a core of major producers was nonexistent or was unable to control the industry. Oil, lumber, and the retail trades were peripheral industries in the 1930s. Along with litigation, most complaints to the NRA arose from these same businesses (Brand, *Corporatism and the Rule of Law,* pp. 150–74). Before the NRA was invalidated by the Supreme Court in the *Schechter* case in May, 1935, it had received 43,641 formal complaints and filed over 800 cases in the courts. Only 1 percent of the complaints were dealt with and 591 cases as of July, 1936, were dropped following *Schechter.* Most of these cases (566) were filed in 1935 and involved miscellaneous codes (401 cases). In all, the district courts decided 60 cases involving the NRA's constitutionality. Irons, *New Deal Lawyers,* pp. 5, 54–55; *Atty. Gen. Report* (1935); pp. 39–42, describe these cases and their disposition.

55. *Economy Dairy Co. v. Wallace* and *Beck v. Wallace,* 61 Wash. Law Reporter 633 (1933); *Nebbia v. New York,* 186 Northeastern Reporter 694 Court of Appeals, New York

1933), affirmed 291 U.S. 502 (1934); Irons, *New Deal Lawyers,* pp. 133–42. See also Schlesinger, *The Coming of the New Deal,* pp. 27–87.

56. *Atty. Gen. Report* (1935), p. 40, notes that seventy-four private suits challenging the NRA and parts of the AAA were filed in 1935. An additional six suits challenged the Oil Code of the NIRA. Pages 40–43 give examples of some of these private and public cases. Opposition to the NRA as a result of limited enforcement was especially prevalent in Texas. The head of the Dallas NRA office noted that "legislation providing for maximum hours, minimum wages, and simple trade practice procedures would have met 'with the approval of 95 percent of [the Texas] industries,' if the provisions of the various codes *could have been enforced*" (quoted in Patenaude, "The New Deal and Texas," p. 308, original emphasis).

57. The Justice Department did investigate 679 alleged NRA and 20 AAA violations, however. Most of the investigations were incomplete when the decision in *Schecter* came down and were dropped (Department of Justice, RG 60, Files 114–57-1 through 679 and 106-74-1 through 20. See also Department of Justice File 114-017 for reports by U.S. attorneys on status of NRA and AAA suits as of Dec., 1934).

58. Facts of the case taken from *Boggus Motor Co. v. Onderdonk et al.,* 9 F. Supp., 950. See also Department of Justice, RG 60, File 114-017-30.

59. In testimony before the court, Boggus stated that prior to the charges being brought against his company he had asked Mr. Onderdonk "just how long a fellow is going to have to tolerate some of the practices of some of the dealers and how long he is going to have to lose his business, . . . [before you reach] some definite decision on this code." Onderdonk evaded the question for a time and then showed a letter to Boggus from Hugh Johnson, director of the NRA. "This letter . . . was to the effect that he was to deal with labor and wages and to stay away from the fair practice part of the code, that is, the price fixing part of the code." Boggus responded, saying: "well . . . now we have appealed to you; we have sent numerous complaints here, there and yonder and you are the last word in this thing and you now tell me that there is not much that you can do about the fair practice part of this code. . . . If your hands are tied at present on that part [prices], they are tied as far as labor is concerned as far as I am concerned." Soon after the petition was drawn up, Boggus was charged with violations of the hours and wages sections of the code (quoted in n. 1, *Boggus Motor Co. v. Onderdonk et al.,* 9 F. Supp., 950).

60. Ibid. See also "Original Bill of Complaint" and "Respondant's Answer," *Boggus Motor Co. v. Onderdonk et al.,* Eq 269, Brownsville Division.

61. Carter Kelly had also filed suit against S. D. Bennett, U.S. attorney for the Eastern District of Texas, seeking to enjoin enforcement of the Lumber Code in that district. In order to prevent unnecessary duplication of effort, and since Judge Bryant had already ruled on the application for a temporary injunction against Bennett, Judge Kennerly requested that Judge Bryant also hear the case against McGregor. Bryant agreed and reached the decision in this case. Judge Kennerly, however, fully agreed with the outcome in this matter and, after the original decision was made, handled all further matters. Douglas McGregor to Attorney General, Nov. 8, 1934; Harold M. Stephens, assistant attorney general, to Douglas McGregor, Nov. 16, 1934; Charles Dunbar, attorney for Southern Pine Association, to William Pencks, assistant counsel, NRA, Dec. 22, 1934, all in Department of Justice, RG 60, File 114-160-43.

62. Leverett Lyons, ed., *The National Recovery Administration: An Analysis and Appraisal,* p. 142, Irons, *New Deal Lawyers,* pp. 75–76. See also "Amended Bill of Complaint," *Carter*

Kelly Lumber Co. v. McGregor, Eq 630, Houston Division, pp. 4–5. On the NRA and the lumber industry in general, see William Robbins, "The Great Experiment in Industrial Self-Government: The Lumber Industry and the National Recovery Administration," *Journal of Forest History* 25 (July, 1982): 125–43.

63. "Bill of Complaint," *Carter Kelly Lumber Co. v. McGregor,* Eq 630, Houston Division, pp. 4–5. See also Department of Justice, RG 60, File 114-160-43.

64. "Original Answer," *Carter Kelly Lumber Co. v. McGregor,* Eq 630, Houston Division.

65. "Memorandum for the Files," Feb. 26, 1935; H. Bruce to Douglas McGregor, Jan. 15, 1935; Douglas McGregor to Attorney General, Jan. 18, 1935; RG 60, File 114-160-43; "Final Order," Dec. 4, 1934 (by Judge Kennerly); "Order on Motion to Dissolve Permanent Injunction," Feb. 25, 1935, *Carter Kelly Lumber Co. v. McGregor,* Eq 630, Houston Division.

66. *Panama Refining Co. v. Ryan,* 293 U.S. 388. This case involved the "hot oil" provisions of the NIRA, sec. 9(c), which empowered the president to set oil prices. See Irons, *New Deal Lawyers,* chap. 3.

67. On the *Schecter* case and federal efforts to enforce the NIRA, see Irons, *New Deal Lawyers,* chap. 5.

68. *Wallace v. Smith,* Eq 278, Brownsville Division (11 F. Supp., 728); *U.S. v. U. Ray Brown,* Eq 281, Brownsville Division; *U.S. v. Donald Webb,* Eq 282, Brownsville Division; *U.S. v. P. J. Williams,* Eq 283, Brownsville Division; *U.S. v. W. E. Baden,* Eq 284, Brownsville Division; *Rio Valley Fruit and Vegetable Co.,* Eq 274, Brownsville Division. See also L. C. Masterson, clerk of the court to J. A. Mount, deputy clerk, Corpus Christi, May 22, 1935, in case file.

69. "Findings of Fact and Conclusions of Law under Equity Rule 70.5," "Stipulation," and "Motion to Dismiss Plaintiff's Application for a Temporary Injunction," *Wallace v. Smith,* Eq 278, Brownsville Division. See also Department of Justice, RG 60, File 106-14-8.

70. "Findings of Fact and Conclusions of Law under Equity Rule 70.5," and "Affidavit of M. H. Lowrie," *Wallace v. Smith,* Eq 278, Brownsville Division (quotes from affidavit).

71. "Findings of Fact and Conclusions of Law under Equity Rule 70.5," *Wallace v. Smith,* Eq 278, Brownsville Division.

72. *Wallace v. Smith,* 11 F. Supp., 728; "Findings of Fact and Conclusions of Law under Equity Rule 70.5," *Wallace v. Smith,* Eq 278, Brownsville Division. The five additional AAA cases were dropped on the motion of the U.S. attorney (L. C. Masterson, clerk of the court, to J. A. Mount, deputy clerk, Corpus Christi, May 22, 1935, in case file).

73. Other conservative Texans were in complete agreement with Judge Kennerly's views on these matters. "Businessmen felt that good business methods would sweep aside the ills that beset agriculture [and industry]. They reasoned that the permanent cure lay in 'improved quality production at lower cost, improved marketing especially in local markets, and lowered tariff burdens.'" They definitely did not accept "the economy of scarcity" (Patenaude, "The New Deal and Texas," p. 299, quoting from *Texas Business Review,* June 27, 1935:5).

74. Interview, T. Everton Kennerly, Apr. 4, 1989.

75. *Atty. Gen. Report* (1935), p. 199; (1936), p. 177; (1937), p. 187; (1938), p. 231; (1939), p. 214.

76. Emergency Farm Mortgage Act, 48 *U.S. Statutes at Large,* p. 31; Home Owners' Loan Act, 48 *U.S. Statutes at Large,* p. 128; Farm Credit Act, 48 *U.S. Statutes at Large,* p. 257; National Housing Act, 48 *U.S. Statutes at Large,* p. 1246.

77. *Atty. Gen. Report* (1937), p. 187; (1938), p. 231.

78. *U.S. v. H. L. and Fay Mae Martin,* L 2837, Houston Division; *U.S. v. Louis and Maggie*

Bruchart, L 2836, Houston Division. For more information on NHA loan foreclosures, see Justice Department File RG 60, 130-74-0.

79. William P. Hobby quoted in Patenaude, "The New Deal and Texas," p. 290; Francis Law, "New Deal Is Part of Changing World," *Texas Weekly* (Oct. 6, 1934): 8–9.

80. Quoted in Patenaude, "The New Deal and Texas," p. 311.

6. Regulation without Restriction: Private Law during the Depression

1. Green, *The Establishment in Texas Politics*, pp. 8–9. See also Feagin, *Free Enterprise City*.

2. Biographical information on Judge Kennerly is drawn from interview, T. Everton Kennerly, Apr. 4, 1989; interview, John R. Brown, Feb. 16, 1988; Thomas M. Kennerly, "The Pre-Trial Conference under the Federal Rules of Civil Procedure," *Texas Law Review* 18 (Feb., 1940): 190–96; "Federal Judges in Texas," p. 411; "Thomas M. Kennerly," p. 80; *Houston Post* (July 30, 1962).

3. Not all of these private suits were filed by failed businesses seeking the court's help in reorganizing their affairs. Also included were more mundane suits to try title, for debt, for interpleader, declaratory judgments, and so on, which had always been a part of the court's civil docket. The majority of these other suits, however, did involve businesses and individuals seeking to combat the depression's effects.

4. Also increasing, though not as much as equity receiverships, were cases for debt, personal injury, and title in lands. The petitions were for the appointment of ancillary receivers to reorganize or liquidate the insolvent company's holdings in the Southern District. This was done under the direction of a primary receiver appointed by the district court in which the case was first filed. In many cases the primary receiver was named ancillary receiver. See *T. H. Mastin and Co. v. Delta Land and Timer Co. et al.*, Eq 443, Houston Division (ancillary to suit pending in Western District of Missouri); *National Shareholders Corp. v. National Family Stores, Inc.*, Eq 485, Houston Division (ancillary to suit pending in Southern District of New York).

5. In the late nineteenth and early twentieth centuries, when most receiverships involved railroads and other public utilities whose insolvency came as the result of overcapitalization, most suits were initiated by a major creditor or investment company, often with the help of management. The intent was to use the protection of an equity receivership to reorganize and refinance the company at a more realistic level, and perhaps to combine the company with other similar concerns. After the receiver reorganized the company, the creditors involved in organizing the receivership would purchase the company at auction for a lower price (in essence taking their loss, since, as the creditors of the company, the profits of the sale came to them). Dissenting creditors would be paid off in cash. See chaps. 1 and 3 of this book. See also Edward Levi and James Moore, "Bankruptcy and Reorganization: A Survey of Changes," *University of Chicago Law Review* 5 (Dec. 1937): 1–40; Grenville Clark, "Reform in Bankruptcy Administration," *Harvard Law Review* 43 (June, 1930): 1189–1216.

6. These actions were often simply an alternate means of demanding the appointment of a receiver. Which equity plea was used to initiate a case depended on the plaintiff's tie to the company. Suits for accounting came mostly from stockholders while foreclosure suits were made primarily by bondholders and receiver suits by creditors. Such distinctions, however, were often ignored as all three requests were combined into a single suit.

7. Robert Maxwell and Robert Baker, *Sawdust Empire: The Texas Lumber Industry, 1830–1940*, pp. 98–103; John O. King, *The Early Years of the Houston Oil Company, 1901–1908*, p. 66; Mary Lasswell, *John Henry Kirby: Prince of the Pines* p. 194.

8. Most of the funding to organize this plan came from the Maryland Trust Company, which received as security shares of common stock in the oil company as well as a lien on the oil company's contract with Kirby to cut lumber on the lands purchased. In addition, Kirby provided $2.5 million in cash for immediate use in purchasing timberlands (Maxwell and Baker, *Sawdust Empire*, pp. 98–103; King, *Early Years*, p. 66; Lasswell, *John Henry Kirby*, p. 194.

9. *Maryland Trust Co. v. Houston Oil Co.*, Eq 54, Houston Division. One of the effects of the receivership was that Kirby's official ties to the Houston Oil Company were severed.

10. In addition, the Santa Fe was given a seat on the board of directors of the Kirby Lumber Company. Details of the early organization of the Kirby Lumber Company are taken from King, *The Early Years of the Houston Oil Company*, pp. 77–78, and "Brief in Support of the Interests of the Santa Fe Railroad," pp. 5–10 (filed before the Department of Justice in the case of *Southwestern Lumber Co. of New Jersey v. Kerr, Trustee in Bankruptcy for John Kirby*, 11 F. Supp., 253, in Department of Justice Records, RG 60, File 59-12-242).

11. Kirby actually did pay off part of the loans once. In 1922, faced with personal financial difficulties, he sold his stock in the lumber company to B. F. Bonner and J. W. Link (who used money acquired from the Santa Fe). Some of this money was used to pay off part of the Santa Fe loan and the rest to support Kirby's private finances. Two years later, using money acquired again from the Santa Fe ($2,201,305), Kirby repurchased his stock from Bonner and Link. This money was added to the Santa Fe loan agreement. In following years, two additional loans totaling $500,000 were made and added to the agreement. The total loan in 1934 was thus over $4,000,000 ("Brief in Support of the Interests of the Santa Fe Railroad," pp. 10–17, and *Southwestern Lumber Co. of New Jersey v. Kerr*, 11 F. Supp., 260. The larger amount included the accumulated interest as well as a number of smaller loans made in the 1920s.

12. Press release quoted in Lasswell, *John Henry Kirby*, p. 193; *In Re Kirby*, B 1717, Houston Division. Details of the Kirby bankruptcy, which lasted until Aug. 9, 1964, can be found in the John Henry Kirby Papers, Houston Metropolitan Research Center, Houston Public Library, Houston, Texas, Boxes 266–76, 379–84.

13. Quotes in Lasswell, *John Henry Kirby*, p. 193.

14. "Brief in Support of the . . . Santa Fe Railroad," p. 19; "Memorandum for Mr. Bell" by Mac Asbill, special assistant to the attorney general, Department of Justice Records, RG 60, File 59-12-242. The loan agreement gave the railroad the right to sell the stock if interest due remained unpaid for more than thirty days. Any profit from the sale beyond the amount of the loan would be returned to Kirby.

15. "Testimony of A. E. Kerr, Trustee of Kirby Estate," pp. 575–76, 582–84, 586–87; *Southwestern Lumber Co. of New Jersey v. Kerr*, Eq 608, Houston Division. See also John Henry Kirby Papers, Boxes 273–76. The bankruptcy petition listed the following assets: stocks, negotiable bonds, etc.–$8,311,299.65; debts due to open accounts–$1,987,388.52; unsecured amounts –$2,107,642.02; bills, promissory notes, and securities–$2,680,456.98; real estate–$6,118.98; and cash–$96.68 (quoted in Lasswell, *John Henry Kirby*, p. 192).

16. Kerr's objections to both the loan agreement and the sale of Kirby's stock is drawn from "Brief in Support of the . . . Santa Fe Railroad," pp. 19–23; "Memorandum for Mr. Bell," pp. 3–4; *Southwestern Lumber Co. of New Jersey v. Kerr*, 11 F. Supp., 260. That Kerr

held these objections prior to suit being filed can be seen in "Brief in Support of the . . . Santa Fe Railroad," p. 19.

17. "Brief in Support of the . . . Santa Fe Railroad," p. 19, "Bill of Complaint," *Southwestern Lumber Co. of New Jersey v. Kerr,* Eq 608, Houston Division. The Santa Fe petitioned for an immediate injunction allowing it to sell the stock. Kerr counterpetitioned for an injunction prohibiting the sale and seeking to have the debt found null and void. The court "regarded" it as its "duty . . . to fully exercise its equity powers to preserve the status quo of the subject-matter of the litigation" and placed the disputed stock under court protection subject to the final ruling of the court (*Southwestern Lumber Co. of New Jersey v. Kerr,* 11 F. Supp., 253).

18. Information on the financial standing of Kirby Lumber is taken from "Plaintiff's Original Bill of Complaint," pp. 3–4; *T. H. Mastin and Co. v. Kirby Lumber Company,* Eq 609, Houston Division.

19. "Plaintiff's Original Bill of Complaint," pp. 6–8.

20. "Answer of Western Improvement Company, to Second Supplemental and Amended Bill of Complaint of Whitney National Bank of New Orleans"; "Order Consolidating Cases 609 and 610 in Equity," *T. H. Mastin and Co. v. Kirby Lumber Co.,* Eq 609, Houston Division. This suit was originally filed as *Western Improvement Co. v. Kirby Lumber Co.,* Eq 610, Houston Division.

21. Though officially split in 1908, the Houston Oil Company and Kirby Lumber Company still worked closely together in exploiting the wealth of the East Texas timberlands. This provided Meachum with a familiarity with the lumber company's affairs (*National Cyclopaedia of American Biography,* vol. 43:433). See interview, T. Everton Kennerly, Apr. , 1989, on the ties between the Houston Oil Company and the Kirby Lumber Company. It is interesting to note that Meachum was also in this regard a confidant of Judge Kennerly, who was, prior to 1931, chief counsel for the oil company.

22. "Order Appointing Receiver," p. 3; *T. H. Mastin and Co. v. Kirby Lumber Co.,* Eq 609, Houston Division; Lasswell, *John Henry Kirby,* p. 198.

23. "Order Appointing Receiver," pp. 4–5; "Order with Reference to Receiver's Allowance"; "Order of Court Continuing Payments on Unpatented Lands"; "Order on Application of Receiver for Directions as to Insurance"; "Order as to Insurance"; *T. H. Mastin and Co. v. Kirby Lumber Co.,* Eq 609, Houston Division.

24. "Bill of Complaint," Eq 614; *Whitney National Bank of New Orleans v. Kirby Lumber Co. et al.,* Houston Division (later consolidated with *T. H. Mastin and Co. v. Kirby Lumber Co.,* Eq 614, Houston Division); *Southwestern Lumber Co. of New Jersey v. Kerr,* 11 F. Supp., 268.

25. Interview, T. Everton Kennerly, Apr. 4, 1989.

26. *Southwestern Lumber Co. of New Jersey v. Kerr,* 11 F. Supp., 261. In a memorial passed by the Texas House of Representatives following Kirby's death, it was noted how "Judge Kennerly, and Senator Keachum as Receiver, likewise felt that everybody's rights must be protected" (Texas House of Representatives, *Resolutions on the Life of John Henry Kirby,* passed Apr. 28, 1941, p. 41).

27. "Transcript of Hearing Held on March 23, 1935," p. 17, *T. H. Mastin and Co. v. Kirby Lumber Co.,* Eq 609, Houston Division.

28. See Kennerly's comments in decision in *Southwestern Lumber Co. of New Jersey v. Kerr,* 11 F. Supp., 261; Lasswell, *John Henry Kirby,* p. 198.

29. This did not mean that all creditors would receive the same amount of money or even the same percentage of their total debt. Some creditors—these included bond-

holders and major creditors—had what were known as superior liens on the property of the company. These loans (or investments) were protected by mortgages on the property of the company (agreements that, in the case of nonpayment, the property was transferred to the lender). Taxes were also considered superior to other liens. Common debts for services and materials were unsecured and were paid out of the remaining funds after the secured debts were paid off. What the court could do, however, was make sure that funds for paying off the unsecured creditors were made available and paid out equitably.

30. Quoted in Lasswell, *John Henry Kirby,* p. 198.

31. *Southwestern Lumber Co. of New Jersey v. Kerr,* 11 F. Supp., 260–61.

32. Ibid., pp. 267–68. See also "Testimony of John Henry Kirby," pp. 2–22, 646–97, *Southwestern Lumber Co. of New Jersey v. Kerr,* Eq 608, Houston Division.

33. *Southwestern Lumber Co. of New Jersey v. Kerr,* 11 F. Supp., 268. Ultimately, the Santa Fe never sold the stock, but purchased it itself, becoming majority owner of the Kirby Lumber Company.

34. Interview, T. Everton Kennerly, Apr. 4, 1989.

35. See letters from Burnham's attorney (unnamed) to Burnham, dated Aug. 2, and Sept. 4, 1928, in case file. See also D. H. Burnham to Miss Kate Scanlan, Nov. 21, 1928, also in case file; *D. H. Burnham v. Arcola Sugar Mills Co. et al.,* Eq 437, Houston Division.

36. See Payne, "The General Administration," p. 685.

37. Burnham argued that existing records showed that Scanlan was personally indebted to the company in the amount of $222,321 ("Original Complaint," *D. H. Burnham v. Arcola Sugar Mills Co. et al.,* Eq 437, Houston Division).

38. Ibid. See also "Final Opinion," *D. H. Burnham v. Arcola Sugar Mills Co. et al.,* Eq 437, Houston Division.

39. No copy of the brief was placed in the case file. Descriptions of the company's arguments are taken from Kennerly's discussion in his opinion: "Final Opinion," *D. H. Burnham v. Arcola Sugar Mills Co. et al.,* Eq 437, Houston Division.

40. Ibid. Arcola Sugar appealed to the Fifth Circuit. A three-judge panel of Judges Bryan, Foster, and Hutcheson, on Dec. 15, 1933, reversed and remanded Kennerly's decision as too extreme for the situation, though technically legal. "It may be assumed," Judge Bryan wrote for the panel, "that in a proper case he [Burnham] could maintain a suit to dissolve the corporation, and pending dissolution have a receiver appointed to preserve its assets. . . . But these are harsh measures which should not be resorted to except in extreme cases" (*Arcola Sugar Mills Co. v. D. H. Burnham,* decision placed in court file *D. H. Burnham v. Arcola Sugar Mills Co. et al.,* Eq 437, Houston Division. The case was subsequently dismissed on Jan. 23, 1935, at plaintiff's costs ("Order," *D. H. Burnham v. Arcola Sugar Mills Co. et al.,* Eq 437, Houston Division).

41. *In re Ainsworth,* 5 F. Supp., 523.

42. "Final Decree," "Supplement and Amendment to Decree," *Melvin L. Straus, Trustee v. Metropolitan Properties Corp. et al.,* Eq 567, Houston Division. In its "Decree" in *Bokay Corp. et al. v. Ladin Investment Co. et al.,* Eq 442, Houston Division, the court "retain[ed] jurisdiction over this cause for all purposes, and particularly for the purpose . . . of enforcing this Decree by the appointment of a receiver, removal of Directors, or in any manner that may be necessary for its enforcement." It should be noted that retaining jurisdiction in an equity case was not unique to Kennerly; Judge Hutcheson often did this in the 1920s. The difference lay in Kennerly's specific reasons for retaining jurisdiction.

43. See *D. H. Burnham v. Arcola Sugar Mills Co. et al.,* Eq 437, Houston Division; *Fidelity-*

Philadelphia Trust Co. and William Test, Trustee v. Houston Gas and Fuel Co., Eq 529, Houston Division; *Life Insurance Co. of Virginia v. San Benito Community Hotel et al.*, Eq 279, Brownsville Division.

44. Two types of oil and gas leases were common at this time. The first, known as a "mineral lease," was made between an oil company and an owner and gave the former the right to drill on the latter's land. In return, the owner usually received a 1/32 royalty on every barrel pumped. Often the lease required that drilling start by a certain date or that a cash fine be paid. The second type of lease, often called a "mineral deed," was between the owner and a second individual (usually, but not necessarily, an oil company) for the transfer of the owners' rights to a portion of the minerals or oil under the land. Often sold for a cash payment, such leases had no requirement for purchasers to attempt any drilling. They were merely purchasing a portion of the mineral wealth of the property. Later, if an oil company drilled on the land, the purchaser of the deed would be due a portion of the mineral wealth (usually a percentage of the 1/32 owner's royalty). For more information on mineral leases and mineral rights, see A. W. Walker, Jr., "The Nature of Property Interests Created by an Oil and Gas Lease in Texas," *Texas Law Review*, pt. I, 10 (Apr., 1932): 291–323, and pt. II, 11 (June, 1933): 399–454.

45. Roger Olien and Diana Olien, *Wildcatters: Texas Independent Oilmen*, pp. 56–58.

46. Ibid., pp. 76–77.

47. "Memorandum Opinion," *J. H. Bush and Wife v. Sun Oil Co. et al.*, Eq 582, Houston Division.

48. Ibid. These facts were the same for the other six cases filed: *J. Bush and Wife v. Sun Oil Co.*, Eq 582, Houston Division; *S. M. Raye and Wife v. Sun Oil Co.*, Eq 583, Houston Division; *C. Richardson and Wife v. Sun Oil Co.*, Eq 584, Houston Division; *E. Taylor and Wife v. Sun Oil Co.*, Eq 585, Houston Division; *J. Smith and Wife v. Sun Oil Co.*, Eq 586, Houston Division; and *R. Gary and Wife v. Sun Oil Co.*, Eq 587, Houston Division; *D. R. Bush and Wife v. Sun Oil Co.*, Eq 581, Houston Division (remanded to state court).

49. "Memorandum Opinion," "Order," *J. H. Bush and Wife v. Sun Oil Co.*, Eq 582, Houston Division. No efforts to sue Garvey were made in federal court. It is possible that such suits were filed in state court, but this is unknown. Whatever the outcome of any state suits that occurred, the mineral rights remained with Sun Oil.

50. *S. M. Raye and Wife v. Sun Oil Co.*, Eq 583, Houston Division ($300); *C. Richardson and Wife v. Sun Oil Co.*, Eq 584, Houston Division ($125); *E. Taylor and Wife v. Sun Oil Co.*, Eq 585, Houston Division ($160); *J. Smith and Wife v. Sun Oil Co.*, Eq 586, Houston Division ($100); *R. Gary and Wife v. Sun Oil Co.*, Eq 587, Houston Division ($160).

51. *Mary Williams v. F. M. Dooley, Hugh Gill, and Humble Oil Refining Co.*, Eq 642, Houston Division; *Katheryn Hines et al. v. A. P. Parks et al.*, Eq 624, Houston Division.

52. "Original Complaint," *Paul Kollatschny and Wife v. G. T. Blankenship et al.*, Case 6983, District Court of Austin County (removed to Eq 643, Houston Division). The same facts held for an additional fifteen cases, Eq 644–59, Houston Division.

53. "Decree," *Paul Kollatschny and Wife v. G. T. Blankenship et al.*, Eq 643, Houston Division.

54. Olien and Olien, *Wildcatters*, p. 76.

55. See *The Texas Co. v. S. P. Johnson et al.*, L 2497, Houston Division; *Shell Petroleum Corp. v. O. Pinckard et al.*, L 2532, Houston Division.

56. *W. Strickland et al. v. Humble Oil and Refining Co. et al.*, L 2829, Houston Division (this case was a consolidation of Law Cases 2880, 2881, and 2939).

57. This search for certainty started long before the depression. As early as the 1890s the insurance industry sought federal regulation, similar to that concerning nationally chartered banks, as a means of circumventing hostile state regulations. This drive failed, but efforts to create stability continued (Morton Keller, *The Life Insurance Enterprise, 1885–1910: A Study in the Limits of Corporate Power,* pp. 235–42).

58. *Chicago Fire and Marine Insurance Co. v. National Bond and Mortgage Corp. et al.,* Eq 440, Houston Division.

59. Note, "Developments in the Law: Declaratory Judgments, 1941–1949," *Harvard Law Review* 62 (Mar., 1949): 850.

60. *Black's Law Dictionary,* p. 953. See also Ralph Rogers, "Historical Origins of Interpleader," *Yale Law Journal* 51 (Apr., 1942): 942–50.

61. In 1932 Zachariah Chafee, Jr., noted how "the greater importance of the national sovereignty" of the federal courts made them "more ready to enjoin suits in another jurisdiction" than were state courts ("Interpleader in the United States Courts," *Yale Law Journal* 41 [June, 1932]: 1136). In 1936 he described how it had became a common practice in the federal courts to issue an injunction forbidding claimants in an interpleader suit from bringing any further proceedings directly against the insurance company during and after a suit (idem, "The Federal Interpleader Act of 1936," *Yale Law Journal* 45 [Apr., 1936]: 963–64).

62. The first act, passed in Feb., 1917 (39 *U.S. Statutes at Large,* p. 929) only included insurance companies. The May, 1926, act (43 *U.S. Statutes at Large,* p. 976) expanded those able to claim jurisdiction under this act. One of the most useful aspects of federal interpleader for the insurance industry was the requirement in the act that at the completion of a case the court "shall discharge the complainant from further liability; and shall make the injunction permanent and enter all such other orders and decrees as may be suitable and proper" (all quotes taken from the 1926 act, quoted in Chafee, "Interpleader in the United States Courts," pp. 1162–63). Chafee describes how interpleader suits operated in practice in "The Federal Interpleader Act of 1936," pp. 1161–80.

63. The National Bond and Mortgage Corporation and Henry Laithe were residents of Maryland; William Cameron and Company was a Texas concern. Thus diversity jurisdiction was allowed. "Bill of Interpleader," *Chicago Fire and Marine Insurance Co. v. National Bond and Mortgage Corp. et al.,* Eq 440, Houston Division.

64. "Final Decree," *Chicago Fire and Marine Insurance Co. v. National Bond and Mortgage Corp. et al.,* Eq 440, Houston Division.

65. Merkur then claimed the house as his homestead, which under Texas law could not be used to pay off creditors.

66. *National Liberty Insurance Co. of America v. Merkur et al.,* 29 F. Supp., 280.

67. 48 *U.S. Statutes at Large,* p. 955. Prior to 1933, the Supreme Court ruled that the Constitution's grant of power to the federal courts in Article III limited these courts to hearing only "cases" and "controversies" that the Supreme Court interpreted as requiring that a real conflict exist with actual harm or damages. If no damages existed or action was called for, the federal courts would be serving a nonjudicial function. In 1933, however, the Supreme Court agreed to hear and upheld a Tennessee declaratory judgment statute. With this concession, Congress passed the Federal Declaratory Judgment Act the next year. It was amended on Aug. 30, 1935. The Supreme Court upheld this amended act two years later in *Aetna Life Insurance Company v. Haworth,* 300 U.S., 227 (1937). Note, "Declaratory Judgements," pp. 790–93.

68. Most states allowed their courts to make declaratory judgments; however, the

reach of these judgments did not extend beyond the borders of the state in which they were made. The decision in a federal case was national in its reach and affected not only other federal courts but state courts as well (Note, "Declaratory Judgements," p. 791). Douglas McGregor, "The Federal Declaratory Judgment Act," *The Dallas Bar Speaks,* 66–79.

69. Note, "Declaratory Judgements," p. 850. See also note, "The Declaratory Judgment and the Insurance Contract," *Yale Law Journal* 46 (Dec., 1936): 286–99; Hutcheson, "Declaratory Judgments."

70. *Ohio Casualty Insurance Co. v. Plummer et al.,* 13 F. Supp., 169 (Eq 685, Houston Division) and *Commercial Casualty Insurance Co. v. Humphrey, et al.,* 13 F. Supp., 174 (Eq 689, Houston Division).

71. *Ohio Casualty Insurance Co. v. Plummer et al.,* 13 F. Supp., 169. "First Amended Bill of Complaint," *Ohio Casualty Insurance Co. v. Plummer et al.,* Eq 685, Houston Division.

72. Argument in the alternative occurs when a lawyer argues a number of points that are logically inconsistent. For example, "my client never saw the plaintiff's cat, never touched the plaintiff's cat, and when he returned the cat it was in perfect health." The idea is that if the first proposition is accepted the latter will be ignored, but if the first is deemed false, the later arguments will be used. Most bills of complaint and answers and briefs argue in this manner. As a trial progresses, those points deemed wrong are dropped in supplemental bills of complaint, answers, and briefs. "Defendant's Reply to First Amended Bill of Complaint," *Ohio Casualty Insurance Co. v. Plummer et al.,* Eq 685, Houston Division.

73. "First Amended Bill of Compaint," *Ohio Casualty Insurance Co. v. Plummer et al.,* Eq 685, Houston Division.

74. *Ohio Casualty Insurance Co. v. Plummer et al.,* 13 F. Supp., 173; Hutcheson, "Declaratory Judgments," p. 489. Though this case was not appealed, the direction of Kennerly's decision was upheld by the Fifth Circuit in *Gully v. Interstate National Gas Co.,* 82 F(2d), 145.

75. *Ohio Casualty Insurance Co. v. Plummer et al.,* 174.

76. "Brief for Plaintiff," pp. 2–4, *Commercial Casualty Insurance Co. v. Humphrey et al.,* Eq 689, Houston Division.

77. *Commercial Casualty Insurance Co. v. Humphrey et al.,* 13 F. Supp., 176, 178. See also "Brief for Respondent A. P. Pierce, Jr., Submitted Following Trial," *Commercial Casualty Insurance Co. v. Humphrey et al.,* Eq 689, Houston Division.

78. *Commercial Casualty Insurance Co. v. Humphrey et al.,* 13 F. Supp., 178.

79. See "Brief for Plaintiff," and "Brief for Respondent A. P. Pierce, Jr., Submitted Following Trial," *Commercial Casualty Insurance Co. v. Humphrey et al.,* Eq 689, Houston Division.

80. As late as Dec., 1937, the top twenty-six life insurance companies alone held 11.6 percent of the federal debt, 6.7 percent of the municipal and state debt, 17.4 percent of the railroad debt, 18.2 percent of the public utility debt, 11.7 percent of the industrial debt, 10.5 percent of all farm mortgages, and 13 percent of all urban mortgages, and this was less than they had held prior to 1930 (Sigmund Timberg, "Insurance and Interstate Commerce," *Yale Law Journal* 50 [Apr., 1941]: 959–62).

81. Henry Lehmann, "The Federal Municipal Bankruptcy Act," *Journal of Finance* 5 (Sept., 1950): 241.

82. A writ of mandamus is a court order to a government official to do his or her public duty. See ibid., p. 242; George H. Dession, "Municipal Debt Adjustment and the Supreme Court," *Yale Law Journal* 46 (Dec., 1936): 199–227.

83. Dissent in *Ashton et al. v. Cameron County Water Improvement District No. One,*

56 Supp., Ct. 900. Large investors also used legislative methods. As will be described below, large investors, municipal officials, and bondholders' protective committees lobbied for a national municipal bankruptcy act, subsequently passed in 1934, which would "take from minority creditors of a defaulting municipality or other local governmental unit their power to obstruct orderly debt readjustment" (Lehmann, "The Federal Municipal Bankruptcy Act," p. 242). It should be noted that not all insurance companies were in favor of this plan. Many liked the freedom of dissent from reorganization plans and objected to being forced into a plan they objected to (Dession, "Municipal Debt Adjustment and the Supreme Court," pp. 214–15).

84. "Bill of Complaint," *Frank Calvin et al. v. Hidalgo County Water Control and Improvement District No. 1 et al.*, Eq 256, Brownsville Division.

85. On the building craze of the 1920s and the subsequent financial difficulties of the 1930s, see John Huddleston, "Good Roads for Texas: A History of the Texas Highway Department, 1917–1947" (Ph.D. diss.), chaps. 5 and 6.

86. "Final Decree," *Frank Calvin et al. v. Hidalgo County Water Control and Improvement District No. 1 et al.*, Eq 256, Brownsville Division.

87. "Bill of Complaint," *Frank Calvin et al. v. Hidalgo County Water Control and Improvement District No. 1 et al.*, Eq 256, Brownsville Division.

88. "Final Decree," *Frank Calvin et al. v. Hidalgo County Water Control and Improvement District No. 1 et al.*, Eq 256, Brownsville Division.

89. *Bank Savings Life Insurance Co. et al. v. Road District No. 1 Hidalgo County et al.*, Eq 293, Brownsville Division (Eq 294–300 involved the *Bank Savings Life Insurance Co. v. Road Districts No. 2–8*). See also *Lincoln National Life Insurance Co. et al. v. Hidalgo County et al.*, Eq 265, Brownsville Division; *Sam Ramson, Jr. v. Hidalgo County et al.*, Eq 271, Brownsville Division.

90. *Pyramid Life Insurance Co. v. County of Hidalgo, Hidalgo Road District No. One et al.*, Eq 263, Brownsville Division; *Bank Savings Life Insurance Co. et al. v. Road District No. 1, Hidalgo County et al.*, Eq 293, Brownsville Division.

91. "Final Decree," *Frank Calvin et al. v. Hidalgo County Water Control and Improvement District No. 1 et al.*, Eq 256, Brownsville Division.

92. Under the act, insolvent municipalities could file for bankruptcy protection if they had the approval of bondholders owning 51 percent or more of the outstanding debt (30 percent in the case of irrigation or other types of taxing districts). Subsequently, it was necessary for the municipality to accept the plan officially and for an additional 24 percent of bondholders (totaling 75 percent of all outstanding loans) to accept the plan. If creditors holding 5 percent or more of outstanding claims objected to this plan and if the court subsequently felt that the plan was not equitable to all parties, it had the option of refusing it (48 *U.S. Statutes at Large*, p. 798; Lehmann, "The Federal Municipal Bankruptcy Act," p. 243; quote from Dession, "Municipal Debt Adjustment and the Supreme Court," p. 216).

93. Dession, "Municipal Debt Adjustment and the Supreme Court," p. 217, lists only eighty-eight petitioners under the National Municipal Bankruptcy Act as of 1936, of which twenty-four involved incorporated municipalities and the rest taxing districts such as road improvement districts. One of the largest cities to seek the protections of the act was Corpus Christi. On p. 218, Dession describes the application of the act by other district courts.

94. *In Re Cameron County Water Improvement District No. 1*, 9 F. Supp., 103 (quote from "Petition for Bankruptcy" taken from judge's decision). The plan called for the pay-

ing off of the existing bonds at 49.8 cents on the dollar, the funds to be supplied by the loan from the Reconstruction Finance Corporation at 4 percent (ibid., p. 104). See also Dession, "Municipal Debt Adjustment and the Supreme Court," p. 218.

95. Judge Kennerly went on to explain that "although the national government and the state governments exist within the same territorial limits, they are, each in their appropriate sphere, separate and independent, and it is indispensable to their preservation and safety that the sovereignty of each be preserved" (*In Re Cameron County Water Improvement District No. 1*, 9 F. Supp., 106).

96. *In Re Cameron County Water Improvement District No. 1*, 9 F. Supp., 104 (emphasis in original), 107.

97. Ibid., p. 107. Appealed to the Fifth Circuit Court of Appeals as *Cameron County Water Improvement District No. One v. Ashton et al.*, 81 F(2d), 905 (1936), the national Municipal Bankruptcy Act was held constitutional and the Southern District Court's decision was reversed. Appealed to the Supreme Court as *Ashton et al. v. Cameron County Water Improvement District No. One*, 298 U.S., 513 (1936), the Circuit Court's decision was itself overturned and the act once again declared unconstitutional.

98. *Bank Savings Life Insurance Co. et al. v. Road District No. 1 Hidalgo County et al.*, Eq 293, Brownsville Division (Eq 294–300 involved the *Bank Savings Life Insurance Co. v. Road Districts No. 2–8*). See also *Lincoln National Life Insurance Co. et al. v. Hidalgo County et al.*, Eq 265, Brownsville Division; *Security Benefit Asso. v. City of Mission et al.*, Eq 315, Brownsville Division; *Brown Crummer Investment Co. v. Starr County et al.*, Eq 317, Brownsville Division; *George McVey v. City of San Juan et al.*, Eq 327, Brownsville Division; *Sam Ramson, Jr. v. Hidalgo County et al.*, Eq 271, Brownsville Division. This last case was dismissed at plaintiff's costs in Sept., 1937.

7. Public Policies and Private Concerns: The Second World War

1. Richard Polenberg, *War and Society: The United States, 1941–1945*, pp. 5–36, 131–53; Harold G. Vatter, *The U.S. Economy in World War II* pp. 51–102.

2. The Southern District Court was not alone in providing these services. See Nathan Elliff, "The War in the Courts: A Review of the Lawyers' Wartime Work," *Federal Bar Journal* 7 (Oct., 1945): 75–85, for a general description of the wartime business of the federal courts.

3. These opportunities included tax incentives and direct investment in new factories, cost-plus contracts, and grants of immunity from antitrust laws, which removed many of business' greatest risks from expansion while promising significant profits (Polenberg, *War and Society*, pp. 12–13, 75, 90–91; Gerald D. Nash, *The American West Transformed: The Impact of the Second World War*, pp. 17–36. See also McKay and Faulk, *Texas after Spindletop*, pp. 184–86).

4. As even former president and conservative Herbert Hoover had to admit, "to win total war President Roosevelt must have many dictatorial economic powers. There must be no hesitation in giving them to him and upholding him in them" (*Addresses upon the American Road: World War II*, pp. 160–71). See *Civil Dockets*, Houston Division, 1941–45. T. Everton Kennerly, Judge Kennerly's son, recalls that generally there were few civil cases tried during the war. Most lawyers were in the service and any lawyer could get a continuance by saying "my opponent is in the service" (interview, T. Everton Kennerly, Apr. 4, 1989). This recollection is supported by *Caplen Oil Co. v. Humble Oil and*

Refining Co. et al., Civ 390, Houston Division, started in Sept., 1940, and not concluded until June, 1947. On May 28, 1942, this case was placed on the suspended docket after a letter was received from W. Clint Little, attorney for the plaintiff, that "he has been called into the Army." The case was returned to the active docket on Mar. 22, 1945, at which time a motion for trial was made.

5. None of the judges put their beliefs in print nor did they publicly explain why they acted as they did. This description of the judges' beliefs is drawn from interviews, secondary descriptions of their lives, private papers, and extrapolations from their actions while on the bench. On Allred, see letter from Judge D. S. Meredith to Allred, Mar. 4, 1939, Container 485, File 3, Allred Papers, University of Houston, and letter from J. Blake Timmons to President Harry Truman, July 21, 1949, "Allred File," Tom Connally Papers, Library of Congress, Washington, D.C. See also interview, Vince Tarlton, Mar. 18, 1988, and Pat Tidwell, "Allred's First Tenure on the Federal Bench, 1938–1942," (unpublished). On Hannay, see *Houston Post* (Nov. 12, 1972, Oct. 23, 27, 1983); *Victoria Advocate* (Oct. 24, 1983); Walter F. Hackney, "Giants of Houston: Allan Burroughs Hannay," *The Best of Houston* (Nov., 1965): 4–8, 13; and interview, Allen B. Hannay, June 5, 1969.

6. The Third Army, in charge of training operations throughout the South, was headquartered in San Antonio, Texas. The Army Air Corps' largest air facility, Randolph Field, was one of three army airfields in the same city (Seth S. McKay, *Texas and the Fair Deal, 1945–1952*, pp. 15–16; McKay and Faulk, *Texas after Spindletop*, pp. 184–86; Bureau of Yards and Docks, *Building the Navy's Bases in World War II: History of the Bureau of Yards and Docks and the Civil Engineer Corps, 1940–1946*, vol. 1:3–4, 229–38).

7. Condemnation is the process by which the government acquires private property for a public use. This taking, as it is called, can be made against the owner's specific wishes but must, under the Fifth Amendment, be exclusively for a public use, such as for a school, a military base, or a transportation system. The owner is guaranteed, again by the Fifth Amendment, a "just compensation" for the loss. The exact amount of that loss is determined by commissioners appointed by the court hearing the condemnation proceedings. Concerning the takings in the Southern District, see Bureau of Yards and Docks, *Building the Navy's Bases in World War II*, pp. 3–4, 229–38; McKay, *Texas and the Fair Deal*, p. 16.

8. The *AO Report* does not list the number of takings in the Southern District for 1940 and 1941; however, the dockets show fewer than thirty condemnations filed, most of these in the Corpus Christi and Galveston divisions. During the war, the Houston Division saw almost half of all filed condemnations. For the District as a whole there were eighteen filings in 1941 (most of these after Pearl Harbor), forty-six in 1942; ninety-five in 1943 (almost half of these for the San Jacinto Water Project); fifty-eight in 1944; thirty in 1945; and nine in 1946 (*AO Report*, table C3 [1941–46]. Like the *Atty. Gen. Report*, the *AO Reports* were for fiscal years running from July 1 of the preceding year to June 30 of the year reported). See *U.S. v. 10.26 Acres in Harris County*, Civ 883, Houston Division (synthetic rubber plant); *U.S. v. 9 Parcels of Land in Harris and Galveston Counties*, Civ 1005, Houston Division (butadiene plant); *U.S. v. .085 Acres in Harris County*, Civ 1026, Houston Division (butadiene plant); *U.S. v. 75 Acres in Harris County*, Civ 1270, Houston Division (manufacture and furnishing of triple and normal superphosphate). The Defense Plant Corporation built five synthetic rubber plants, seven oil-related plants, and two styrene plants in Southeast Texas (Jesse H. Jones, *Fifty Billion Dollars: My Thirteen Years with the RFC*, pp. 610–11). See also Polenberg, *War and Society*, pp. 17–18.

The project to improve the port of Houston was part of two large projects. One started just as the war began and sought to build dams and levees along Buffalo Bayou. The second was known as the San Jacinto Water Project. Involving forty-three separate suits in the Houston Division, it was an effort by the War Industries Board to control flooding along the San Jacinto River. For example, see *U.S. v. 2,877.37 Acres of Land in Harris County,* Civ 687, Houston Division (Buffalo Bayou); *U.S. v. 11 Parcels of Land in Harris County,* Civ 898, Houston Division (San Jacinto Water Project). The takings for oil pipelines were mostly associated with the construction of the Big Inch and the Little Big Inch. For examples of these takings, see *U.S. v. 3 Parcels of Land in Harris County,* Civ 1028, Houston Division; *U.S. v. 3 Parcels of Land in Harris County,* Civ 1033, Houston Division; *U.S. v. .4 Acres of Land in Harris County,* Civ 1568, Houston Division. On federal efforts to transport oil over land during World War II, see Gerald D. Nash, *United States Oil Policy, 1890–1964,* pp. 163–65; Polenberg, *War and Society,* p. 19; Jones, *Fifty Billion Dollars,* p. 343.

9. For the army, see act of Aug. 18, 1890 (26 *U.S. Statutes at Large,* p. 316) as amended by acts of Congress, Apr. 11, 1918 (40 *U.S. Statutes at Large,* pp. 241, 518); act of Aug. 12, 1935 (49 *U.S. Statutes at Large,* p. 611). For the navy, see act of June 15, 1940 (54 *U.S. Statutes at Large,* p. 375); act of June 11, 1940 (54 *U.S. Statutes at Large,* p. 313). For civilian takings, see act of Aug. 1, 1888 (25 *U.S. Statutes at Large,* p. 357); act of Jan. 22, 1932 (U.S.C, sec. 601–17); executive order 9217, issued on Aug. 7, 1942. Quote taken from "Petition in Condemnation," *U.S. v. 1875 Acres of Land, Situated in Brazos County and Charles Merka et al.,* Civ 824, Houston Division.

10. At the same time that the U.S. attorney filed the "Petition in Condemnation," a representative of the War Department would file a "Declaration of Taking," setting out in detail the facts mentioned in the petition. See "Petition in Condemnation," "Order of Possession," *U.S. v. 1875 Acres of Land, Situated in Brazos County and Charles Merka et al.,* Civ 824, Houston Division (both are dated Aug. 6, 1942). Quote is taken from "Order of Possession." See also *U.S. v. 2049.85 Acres in Nueces County and Eagle Lake Improvement Co. et al.,* Civ 87, Corpus Christi Division ("Petition for Condemnation" filed on June 25, 1940; "Order of Possession," filed on July 5, 1940); *U.S. v. 35,220 Acres of Land in Calhoun County and Matagorda County Texas, Lillie Culver et al.,* Civ 55, Galveston Division ("Petition for Condemnation," "Judgement on Declaration of Taking," and "Final Judgement on Declaration of Taking," filed on Jan. 10, 1941).

11. Under the law, where there was no applicable federal statute to set the procedures used in adjudging the value of a piece of condemned land, state statutes were used. In this case the court followed the procedures of the state of Texas on eminent domain (Title 52, Arts. 3264–271, *Vernon's Civil Statutes of Texas*). See Judge Kennerly's comments in *U.S. v. 250 Acres of Land in Nueces County et al.,* 43 F. Supp., 938. The three commissioners in Corpus Christi, for instance, heard all the cases involving the Naval Air Station. "Order Appointing Commissioners," *U.S. v. 250 Acres of Land in Nueces County et al.,* 43 F. Supp., 938. See also *U.S. v. 18,648 Acres of Land in Calhoun County, H. W. Hawes et al.,* Civ 22, Victoria Division (this case is half of *U.S. v. 35,220 Acres of Land in Calhoun County and Matagorda County Texas, Lillie Culver et al.,* Civ 55, Galveston Division, which was split on Jan. 10, 1941. The other half remained Civ 55, Galveston Division). Most commissioners received twenty-five dollars a day for their services. *U.S. v. 11 Parcels of Land in Harris County,* Civ 898, Houston Division, lists the compensation for the commissioners in this and nine additional cases.

12. The amount in the registry was based on the government's estimate of the cost of the land. Wire from Attorney General to Douglas McGregor, U.S. attorney, Southern District. Oct. 31, 1941, File 33-45-346-33, Department of Justice, Washington, D.C. (noted

in "Correspondence Slips," RG 60, National Archives, Washington, D.C.). Department of Justice Records after 1940 are still retained by the department and to date are not available. The Correspondence Slips, on file at the National Archives, were the department's primary method of indexing incoming and outgoing mail and note the contents of each letter.

13. The oil companies were seeking rights to drill for the oil under the condemned land (Attorney General to Douglas McGregor, U.S. attorney, Southern District, Dec. 11, 1940, File 33-45-341-0, Department of Justice, Washington, D.C.; wire, Attorney General to Douglas McGregor, U.S. attorney, Southern District, Jan. 9, 1941, File 33-45-0). See also letter from McGregor to Attorney General on Jan. 3, 1941, for copies of Orgel's *Valuation under Eminent Domain*, for use in connection with the Matagorda case, all noted in "Correspondence Slips," RG 60, National Archives, Washington, D.C.

14. Wire, Douglas McGregor to Attorney General, Mar. 18, 1941, File, 33-45-347-1, Department of Justice, Washington, D.C. (noted in "Correspondence Slips," RG 60, National Archives, Washington, D.C.).

15. The following discussion and quotes are taken from *U.S. v. 16.572 Acres of Land et al.*, 45 F. Supp., 23 (Civ 55, Galveston Division).

16. *U.S. v. 16.572 Acres of Land et al.*, 49 F. Supp., 555.

17. *U.S. v. 250 Acres of Land in Nueces County et al.* and *Same v. 245.7 Acres of Land in Nueces County et al.*, 43 F. Supp., 937 (Civ 166, Corpus Christi Division and Civ 171, Corpus Christi Division, respectively).

18. *U.S. v. 2,049.85 Acres of Land in Nueces County, Eagle Lake Improvement Co. et al.*, Civ 87, Corpus Christi Division; *U.S. v. 250 Acres of Land, etc.*, Civ 166, Corpus Christi Division; *U.S. v. 250 Acres of Land, etc.*, Civ 168, Corpus Christi Division; *U.S. v. 245.7 Acres of Land, etc.*, Civ 171, Corpus Christi Division; *U.S. v. 220 Acres of Land, etc.* (parcels A, D, and E), Civ 172, Corpus Christi Division.

17. For example, in *U.S. v. 250 Acres of Land in Nueces County*, Civ 166, Corpus Christi Division, the commissioners awarded a total compensation of $43,750, of which $4,125 was to go to holders of a mineral lease and the remainder to the landowner. The jury, however, awarded a total compensation of only $36,087.50, of which $35,000 was due the landowner ("Decision of the Commissioners," "Verdict of Jury," and "Final Judgment," in that case). These cases were heard by two judges. On May 15, 1942, Judge Allred resigned. His replacement, Judge Hannay was not approved until Aug. 12, 1942. The early stages of these cases were presided over by Judge William H. Atwell, of the Northern District, sitting in Corpus Christi to help Judge Kennerly cover the docket until Judge Hannay's nomination was approved.

20. *U.S. v. 2,049.85 Acres of Land in Nueces County, Eagle Lake Improvement Co. et al.*, 49 F. Supp., 21.

21. The case file in *U.S. v. 250 Acres of Land in Nueces County*, Civ 166, Corpus Christi Division, has copies oif proposed jury instructions. Each proposed instruction has the judge's signature and his decision whether to approve or deny the instruction. Given the similarity in the facts of the case, it is likely that the instructions in *U.S. v. 250 Acres of Land* were similar to those in this case.

22. *U.S. v. 2,877.37 Acres of Land in Harris County et al.* (tracts 46, 48, 49, 55), 52 F. Supp., 609. For other examples of this, see *U.S. v. 11 Parcels of Land in Harris County et al.* (parcels W-5 and W-6), Civ 898, Houston Division; *U.S. v. Certain Parcels of Land in Harris County et al.* (parcel W-8), Civ 1148, Houston Division; *U.S. v. 328.6 Acres of Land*

in Harris County et al. (parcels WR-2-A and WR-3-A), Civ 1150, Houston Division. These cases were decided together on Aug. 7, 1945.

23. Act of July 2, 1940, 54 *U.S. Statutes at Large*, p. 712; executive order no. 8839 (July 30, 1941); executive order no. 8982 (Dec. 17, 1941); act of June 30, 1942, 56 *U.S. Statutes at Large*, p. 463. The act of June 30, 1942, also provided statutory authority for the Board of Economic Warfare. List of items taken is drawn from cases filed in the Southern District. See *Civil Docket Books*, Laredo and Brownsville divisions.

24. In fiscal 1943, for example, there were 161 forfeiture proceedings across the nation, 76 in the Southern District (*AO Report*, table 6 [1944]; *Civil Dockets*, Brownsville and Laredo divisions). The *AO Report* does not list criminal violations of this act, though the dockets of the Southern District show that there were some prosecutions. However, most actions were civil *in rem* proceedings against goods in violation of the law and not criminal prosecutions against the exporter. The *AO Report*, table C2 (1943–46), lists just over 800 such violations from 1943. They went as follows: 1943–161 actions; 1944–153 actions; 1945–237 actions; 1946–265 actions. For the Southern District, see *Civil Docket Books*, Brownsville and Laredo divisions.

25. *U.S. v. 251 Ladies Dresses et al.*, 53 F. Supp., 772.

26. *U.S. v. 8 Automobiles: U.S. v. 2 Automobiles; U.S. v. 4 Automobiles*, 53 F. Supp., 775.

27. *U.S. v. 251 Ladies Dresses et al.*, 53 F. Supp., 772.

28. Ibid.; see also *U.S. v. 8 Automobiles; U.S. v. 2 Automobiles; U.S. v. 4 Automobiles*, 53 F. Supp., 775; *U.S. v. 7 Cartons of Wearing Apparel*, 53 F. Supp., 777.

29. *U.S. v. Rafael Nava Urrutia*, Cr 6740, Laredo Division; *U.S. v. One 1941 Chrysler Convertible Coupe and One 1940 Packard Coupe*, Civ 89, Laredo Division. Details of these cases are taken from "Findings of Fact and Conclusions of Law Prepared and Filed by the Trial Judge under Admiralty Rule 46½," *U.S. v. One 1941 Chrysler et al.* The implication in the judge's description of the case was that the criminal charge was brought because of Nava's failure to sign the statement prepared by the customs agent. This is supported by the small number of criminal indictments under this act, especially in comparison to the eight hundred civil cases filed. Both imply that if Nava had signed the statement, no criminal charges would have been filed against him. Civil actions against the two cars would have continued, however.

30. "Findings of Fact and Conclusions of Law Prepared and Filed by the Trial Judge under Admiralty Rule 46½," and "Final Judgement," *U.S. v. One. 1941 Chrysler Convertible Coupe and One 1940 Packard Coupe*, Civ 89, Laredo Division. The judge did, however, uphold the legality of the original seizer of the two cars and required Nava to pay all costs before the cars would be returned.

31. In many cases owners did not even contest the forfeiture proceedings. See *U.S. v. One Chevrolet Coupe*, Civ 63, Laredo Division; *U.S. v. M. A. Wiesel [Seven Boxes Stitching Wire]*, Civ 64, Laredo Division; *U.S. v. Electrical Supply Company*, Civ 65, Laredo Division; *U.S. v. 7500 Rounds 38 Special Ammunition*, Civ 66, Laredo Division; *U.S. v. Two Cylinder Heads for Dodge Truck Engine*, Civ 71, Laredo Division; *U.S. v. 24 Bags of Lithopone*, Civ 73, Laredo Division; *U.S. v. 100 Pounds Zinc Dust*, Civ 74, Laredo Division. See also *U.S. v. One Oldsmobile Sedan*, Civ 86, Laredo Division (car returned to owner); *U.S. v. 200 Pounds Ammonium Carbonate*, Civ 90, Laredo Division (returned to owner after payment of costs); *U.S. v. One 1941 Cadillac Coupe*, Civ 202, Brownsville Division (car returned to owner). The court kept its eyes open for such cases. In a procedure unique to the Southern District, Judge Kennerly had all cases in which the government requested authority to de-

tain seized property docketed as civil actions. While such requests for further detention were "strictly speaking, not a civil action," the judge felt that "this procedure enable[d] [him] to keep the run of the proceeding like any other case in Court and see to it that it is promptly disposed of." It also meant that he had first-hand knowledge of the case from its beginning and could catch any procedural errors on the part of customs officials (T. M. Kennerly to Hal V. Watts, clerk of the Southern District, June 17, 1942, filed in *U.S. v. M. A. Wiesel [Seven Boxes Stitching Wire]*, Civ 64, Laredo Division).

32. For the early history of the OPA, see Harvey C. Mansfield, *A Short History of the OPA*, pp. 7–36. On efforts to control prices and rents, see pp. 39–136. On rationing, see pp. 143–200. For judicial responses to price controls, see Robert A. Sprecher, "Price Control in the Courts," *Columbia Law Review* 44 (Jan., 1944): 34–64; and Paul L. Murphy, *The Constitution in Crisis Times, 1918–1969*, pp. 222–23. See also Polenberg, *War and Society*, pp. 31–35, 131.

33. Mansfield, *A Short History of the OPA*, pp. 255–57; Polenberg, *War and Society*, p. 131.

34. Also, an agreement with the Justice Department, worked out in Dec., 1941, prohibited the OPA from instituting criminal proceedings on its own. The "OPA could only certify facts which it believed to warrant criminal proceedings to the Department of Justice, which could act at its discretion." With civil suits, however, the OPA could bring suit in its own name, use its own lawyers, and settle cases out of court if it wished (Mansfield, *A Short History of the OPA*, pp. 262–63, 255–72).

35. Between 1943 and 1948 (at which time the government stopped prosecuting OPA violators) the court heard 825 civil OPA suits. Most were for injunctions. During the same period the court heard 109 criminal cases (*AO Report*, tables C2 and C3 [1943–48]). Defendants came from all sectors of the local economy. There were oil companies and steel manufacturers, wholesale distributors and retail establishments of all types. Especially common were merchants who sold necessities such as electrical appliances, clothing, used tools, and food. (Types of defendants are drawn from *Civil Docket Books*, Houston and Brownsville divisions.)

36. The number of injunction suits ended by consent decrees was well over 90 percent. See *Civil Docket Books*, Houston, Corpus Christi, Galveston, and Brownsville divisions (most OPA suits were filed in these four divisions). On efforts of the OPA to achieve out-of-court settlements, see Mansfield, *A Short History of the OPA*, pp. 262–69. Mansfield, it should be noted, only implies that injunction proceedings were used as a tool to force compromise decision. I have drawn this conclusion from the actions of the OPA in Southern District cases. See *Prentiss Brown, Administrator, OPA v. Joe D. Angel d.b.a. Do Drive Inn*, Civ 1116, Houston Division; *Chester Bowles, Administrator, OPA v. I. Weiner et al., d.b.a. Weiner's Stores*, Civ 1302, Houston Division; *Chester Bowles, Administrator, OPA v. Sidney Konig, d.b.a. American Iron and Metal Co.*, Civil Action 1372, Houston Division; *Prentiss Brown, Administrator, OPA v. Bessie Vines*, Civ 225, Brownsville Division; *Prentiss Brown, Administrator, OPA v. Anna Jeffers and Ray Jeffers*, Civ 218, Brownsville Division (agreed order of dismissal). In some cases, where no consent decree was agreed on, the court would deny the injunction. See *Leon Henderson, Administrator, OPA v. G. G. Conner, d.b.a. Houston Hide Company*, Civ 868, Houston Division. Judge Kennerly was careful to note in many of his decrees and memorandums that no questions "as to the Constitutional validity of the Act and Regulations promulgated thereunder" were made. His decrees in such cases were therefore always made under the assumption that the OPA's laws and regulations were "valid." He was not, however, deciding this fact ("Memorandum,"

Prentiss Brown, Administrator, OPA v. R. W. Moreland and Sadye Moreland, Civ 1125, Houston Division).

37. *Chester Bowles v. Joseph Epstein d.b.a. Capital Wholesale Drug and Liquor Co.,* Civ 1176, Houston Division. See also *Prentiss Brown v. Charles Divan, Inc.,* Civ 216, Brownsville Division. For an example of a damage case settled by agreement, see *Chester Bowles v. I. Westfeld, d.b.a. M. W. Fruit Co.,* Civ 251, Brownsville Division.

38. Cabell Phillips, *The 1940s: Decade of Triumph and Trouble,* pp. 71–74.

39. *Selective Service in Peacetime: First Report of the Director of Selective Service, 1940–41,* pp. 295–97; *Selective Service in Wartime: Second Report of the Director of Selective Service, 1941–1942,* p. 311. During the first year of the war, for instance, the Federal Bureau of Investigation examined 84,694 cases of delinquency. Of this number, 80,200 were subsequently closed without prosecution. Only 627 indictments were filed in the federal courts prior to Pearl Harbor. In all, only 2,847 were convicted during the first year of the war. Though this number rose in subsequent years the number never surpassed 8,000 – still a small percentage in relation to the total number of people in uniform. The breakdown was 3,360 in 1942; 7,893 in 1943; 6,718 in 1944; 4,301 in 1945; and 2,157 in 1946 (*Selective Service in Wartime,* p. 314; *AO Report,* table C2 [1942–46]. Note that the number of the first year of the war is taken from both the 1942 and the 1943 *AO Report*).

40. Douglas McGregor, U.S. attorney, Southern District, to Attorney General, Oct. 17, 1940, File 25-74-0, Department of Justice, Washington D.C. (noted in "Correspondence Slips," RG 60, National Archives, Washington, D.C.). The Correspondence Slips list 60 investigation files from the Southern District, Department of Justice files 25-74-1 through 25-74-60. There may have been additional files or investigations not noted on the Slips. The *AO Report* for 1941 does not list the number of draft cases filed for individual districts. The *AO Report* for 1942, table C3, lists 63 draft cases for the Southern District. This, however, includes the first six months of the war. Most of these cases were, in fact, filed after Dec. 7, 1941.

41. See *Criminal Docket Books* all divisions. This was a vastly different experience from the court's experience in WWI. Unlike during that conflict, the number of violations in the district remained lower than the national average; one section of the district did not dominate this category of filings, as did the Rio Grande Valley in World War I; and one segment of the population was not represented out of proportion to its numbers in the population, as had been Hispanics. On the court's experience in WWI, see chap. 3.

42. See for example, *U.S. v. Ray Harbush,* Cr 8233, Houston Division (not guilty on plea of not guilty); *U.S. v. John Heuson,* Cr 8309, Houston Division (not guilty on stipulation that defendant was above age for registering); *U.S. v. Martin Lavasich,* Cr 8356, Houston Division (Case dismissed after psychological testing).

43. See, for example, *U.S. v. Roy Fierney,* Cr 8310, Houston Division (thirty days); *U.S. v. Jon Danson,* Cr 8394, Houston Division (one year and one day, suspended for five years' good behavior, revoked on Sept. 29, 1942, and reduced to nine months); *U.S. v. Willie Brantley,* Cr 8398, Houston Division (one year and one day); *U.S. v. Luis Lema,* Cr 14140, Brownsville Division (ninety days); *U.S. v. Nincento Pardo,* Cr 14578, Brownsville Division (fifteen months); *U.S. v. Andrew Ray,* Cr 14898, Brownsville Division (one year and one day).

44. Unlike during the First World War, failure to report for induction was not considered desertion. Until a man was sworn into the military, any violations of the Selective Service law were the province of the federal district courts and not the military. On fugitive cases, see *U.S. v. Frank Abramovits,* Cr 8287, Houston Division (fifteen months, sus-

pended to five years' probation provided defendant was immediately inducted into military service); *U.S. v. Albert Johnson, Jr.*, Cr 8346, Houston Division (removed to District of Arizona); *U.S. v. Anthony Dudzinski*, Cr 8350, Houston Division (removed to Southern District of New York). On Southern District cases, see *U.S. v. Leo Sheehan*, Cr 8286, Houston Division (not guilty); *U.S. v. Eugene Kinderman*, Cr 8362, Houston Division (two years); *U.S. v. Frank Weis*, Cr 8450, Houston Division (two years); *U.S. v. Curtis Bratton*, Cr 8452, Houston Division (thirty days on plea of guilty); *U.S. v. Joseph Labus*, Cr 14250, Brownsville Division (three years); *U.S. v. José González*, Cr 14883, Brownsville Division (two years); *U.S. v. Juan Martínez*, Cr 14894, Brownsville Division (thirteen months).

45. *U.S. v. Rex Hall*, Cr 8230, Houston Division (eight months and defendant to be given the opportunity to fill out a questionnaire); *U.S. v. Winston Elroy*, Cr 8231, Houston Division (sixty days); *U.S. v. Foster Bowen*, Cr 8274, Houston Division (one hour in custody of U.S. marshal); *U.S. v. José Peneda*, Cr 8295, Houston Division (one hour in custody of U.S. marshal); *U.S. v. James Bradley*, Cr 8311, Houston Division (thirteen months); *U.S. v. Wilbert Hayes*, Cr 8333, Houston Division (ninety days suspended for five years good behavior, provided defendant followed all orders of draft board and sentence did not interfere with his induction into the army); *U.S. v. John Dye*, Cr 8336, Houston Division (ninety days suspended for five years, sentence not to interfere with induction); *U.S. v. Ramón Valladi*, Cr 14139, Brownsville Division (sixty days); *U.S. v. Hide Releford*, Cr 14251, Brownsville Division (two years suspended, thirty days conditional on defendant's being inducted into armed forces).

46. *Selective Service in Wartime*, p. 322; Julien Cornell, "Exemption from the Draft: A Study in Civil Liberties," *Yale Law Journal* 56 (Jan., 1947): 263–65.

47. First quote from "Demurrer to the Indictment," *U.S. v. Eugene John Kinderman*, Cr 8362, Houston Division. Second quote from "Demurrer to the Indictment," *U.S. v. Elton Julius Haberman*, Cr 8361, Houston Division. See also *U.S. v. Edgar Berger*, Cr 559, Victoria Division; *U.S. v. Grover Knocke*, Cr 560, Victoria Division; *U.S. v. Elmore Knocke*, Cr 561, Victoria Division; *U.S. v. Félix Lacina*, Cr 562, Victoria Division; *U.S. v. Henry Boehl*, Cr 565, Victoria Division.

48. "Oral Opinion," *U.S. v. Elton Julius Haberman*, Cr 8361, Houston Division. The judge did not go on to explain the reasons for his opinion; however, one explanation is provided by his son, T. Everton Kennerly, who recalls that his father, a religious man, had two grandsons in the army and did not think that anyone should get out of the service on such an excuse as this. This view also explains the judge's subsequent refusal to accept the defendant's views on the merits of the case (interview, T. Everton Kennerly, Apr. 4, 1989).

49. *U.S. v. Elton Julius Haberman*, Cr 8361, Houston Division. Only the constitutional argument was actually made in the demurrer; the validity argument was raised as part of the defense's position on the merits of the case.

50. Another constitutional issue involving Jehovah's Witnesses, though not in the Southern District, concerned saluting the flag. See *Minersville School District v. Gobitis*, 30 U.S. 586 (1940), in which the Supreme Court upheld a Pennsylvania law requiring children to salute the flag in school, despite the freedom of religion arguments of the Jehovah's Witnesses. Three years later in *West Virginia State Board of Education v. Barnette*, 319 U.S. 628, the Supreme Court reversed its position and overruled a similar West Virginia law under the clear-and-present-danger doctrine.

51. McKay, *Texas and the Fair Deal*, pp. 2, 5–15; McKay and Faulk, *Texas after Spindletop*, pp. 186–87. *Texas Almanac, 1945–1946*, pp. 262–63.

52. McKay, *Texas and the Fair Deal,* pp. 12–15; May and Escott, *Economic Statistics,* pp. 27–54; *Texas Almanac, 1945–1946,* p. 264. More traditional extractive industries, such as minerals and oil, also grew apace during the war. In 1940 mineral production was valued at $714,905,731; five years later it totaled $1,361,436,346. In 1941, 505,572,000 barrels of oil were produced; by 1945 the number produced was 754,710,000 (McKay, *Texas and the Fair Deal,* pp. 12–15). In addition, the construction industry entered a similar boom period largely caused by the increase in war-related activities (*Texas Almanac, 1945–1946,* p. 271).

53. Though some war industries, such as munitions, closed with the end of the war, most successfully made the transition to peacetime and continued to do business throughout the post-war era.

54. This was also a national trend. As plaintiff attorney Joseph Bear noted: "There were 19,000 amputations among service men during World War II, but more than 120,000 major amputations during the same period in our civilian population. Approximately 1,500 service men were blinded during the last war, but 60,000 civilians lost their sight during this period" ("Survey of the Legal Profession–Workmen's Compensation and the Lawyer," *Columbia Law Review* 51 [Dec., 1951]: 965).

55. Title 130, *Revised Civil Statutes of Texas,* 1925, and amendments; Sam Barton, *How Texas Cares for Her Injured Workers,* pp. 2, 4; *Protecting Texas Industries for Two Decades: A Brochure on the History and Operation of the Texas Employers Insurance Association,* pp. 12–13.

56. Barton, *How Texas Cares for Her Injured Workers,* p. 27. In most cases, failure to accept the board's decision resulted in immediate cessation of pre-award payments. It also precluded the worker from receiving any welfare payments (ibid., pp. 13–14).

57. In Barton's 1954 study of 1,000 compensation cases in the Texas workers' compensation system, 145 cases were appealed. Of this number the TIAB awarded no compensation in 50 cases. In 46 of these 50 cases, the board's denial was preceded by failure of the insurance company to pay preaward compensation. Eighty-eight of the 145 cases appealed (including the 50 noted above) were preceded by no preaward compensation (ibid., pp. 27–28). Barton goes on to describe the impact of the Texas compensation system as follows: "Under such conditions the Industrial Accident Board scarcely can be said to administer the compensation law. It merely processes the administrative decision of the employers and insurance companies, who are the real administrators of the [Workers' Compensation] Acts, in uncontested cases. In the contested cases, lawyers and judges take over administration" (ibid., p. 27).

58. *Texas Almanac, 1945–1946,* p. 279.

59. On elapsed time in workers' compensation cases in state courts, see Barton, *How Texas Cares for Her Injured Workers,* pp. 33, 44. For federal courts, see *Civil Docket Books,* Houston Division (1940–45).

60. Walter F. Dodd, *Administration of Workmen's Compensation,* pp. 346–47, 358–60.

61. *Atty. Gen. Report* (1930–39); *AO Reports,* tables C2 and C3 (1940–45). A few appeals from the TIAB were made prior to 1940. See, for example, *New York Indemnity Co. v. Rasmusson et al.,* 1 F. Supp., 156 (1932). The court also heard a second type of workers' compensation case. The Longshoremen's and Harbor Workers' Compensation Act of 1924 (LHWC) created a federal workers' compensation system for those workers engaged in maritime pursuits. Organized much like state compensation statutes, the LHWC was administered by commissioners appointed by the president and was subject to appeal in the district courts under their admiralty and equity jurisdictions. The court heard from a few dozen up to fifty LHWC appeals a year from the late 1920s on. For examples, see

Southern Stevedoring Co., Inc. v. G. Sheppard, Deputy Commissioner for the 8th Compensation District of the United States, Eq 425, Houston Division; *Boyd-Campbell Co., Inc v. G. Sheppard,* Eq 436, Houston Division.

62. For examples, see *Vera Fletcher Averett et al. v. Zurich General Accident and Liability Insurance Co.,* Civ 52, Galveston Division (failed to prove that accident occurred in course of employment); *Preston Yates v. Indemnity Insurance Co. of North America,* Civ 208, Galveston Division (failed to prove that accident occurred in course of employment); *Mrs. Vera Wisnoskie et al. v. The Travelers Insurance Co.,* Civ 896, Houston Division (failed to prove that accident occurred in course of employment); *Albert Foster v. Maryland Casualty Co.,* Civ 1580, Houston Division (failure to prove that claim was filed within six months); *Curtis Darett v. Liberty Mutual Insurance Co.,* Civ 1244, Houston Division (inadequate award from TIAB); *Employers' Liability Assurance Corp. v. E. G. Walker,* Civ 260, Houston Division (appeal of excessive TIAB award).

63. Statistics on out-of-court settlements are drawn from cases filed between 1940 and 1945. The maximum statutory return on a compensation claim was arrived at by multiplying the weekly maximum payment of twenty dollars by the maximum number of weeks compensation could be provided (401). Insight into the motives of litigants and their attorneys is derived from interview, Thomas B. Weatherly, Sept. 6 and 7, 1990. Weatherly was a plaintiff's lawyer in tort matters in the 1950s for the Houston law firm of Vinson and Elkins.

64. See "Final Judgement," *Preston Yates v. Indemnity Insurance Co. of North America et al.,* Civ 1035, Houston Division.

65. Interview, Thomas B. Weatherly, Sept. 6 and 7, 1990; Barton, *How Texas Cares for Her Injured Workers,* p. 44. For an example of the court's actions, see *Mrs. Pearl King, et al. v. Glens Falls Indemnity Co.,* Civ 328, Houston Division.

8. The More Things Change: Public and Private Law in the Post–World War II Era, 1946–60

1. *Texas Almanac, 1945–1946* pp. 255, 264–65; *Texas Almanac, 1947–1948,* p. 273; *U.S. News and World Report* (Nov. 23, 1956), pp. 70–72; McKay, *Texas and the Fair Deal,* pp. 1–14; McKay and Faulk, *Texas after Spindletop,* pp. 209–14.

2. *U.S. News and World Report* (Nov. 23, 1956), p. 89. On earlier boom periods, see chaps. 2, 4, 5, and 6. On the costs of growth for Texas, see Feagin, *Free Enterprise City,* pp. 40–42, 271–73. Feagin points out such costs as "major poverty, homelessness, minority displacement, subsidence, flooding, water pollution, toxic waste, sewage, and street maintenance problems" and argues that Houston elites ignored these costs as long as they did not limit business expansion (p. 272).

3. Joseph Pratt, *The Growth of a Refining Region;* "Texas Comes of Age," *Time* (Apr. 7, 1947), p. 88. See also Feagin, *Free Enterprise City,* pp. 65–72.

4. Galambos and Pratt, *The Rise of the Corporate Commonwealth,* pp. 129–31, 155–83.

5. Ibid., pp. 129–54, describes the redefinition of the public sector's views of business interests and that sector's willingness to serve business interests through its regulatory efforts. Feagin, *Free Enterprise City,* pp. 149–73, describes how this process worked in Southeast Texas.

6. Clark, "Adjudication to Administration," pp. 124–28, comments on the abundance

of private diversity suits in all eighty-four federal district courts and describes this period as a sort of "golden age" of diversity.

7. 63 *U.S. Statutes at Large,* p. 493 (creation of two new positions); 68 *U.S. Statutes at Large,* p. 8 (law making second judgeship added in 1949 permanent). On the pressing need for additional judges in 1949, see testimony of Congressmen John Lyle and Lloyd Bentsen, "Authorizing the Appointment of Additional Circuit and District Judges for the U.S. Courts," in House, *Hearings, Subcommittee no. 3, of the Committee on the Judiciary,* 81st Cong., 1st sess., pp. 16–26 and 26–30, respectively. For 1954 see Report of Will Shafroth, chief, Division of Procedural Studies and Statistics, AO Office, in "Omnibus Judgeship Bill," House, *Report no. 1005 of the Committee of the Judiciary,* 83d Cong., 1st sess., pp. 169–71.

8. There is an interesting story behind the Connally and Allred nominations. According to the newspapers of the time, it was Senator Tom Connally who recommended the nomination of Allred to the president, while Senator Lyndon Johnson recommended Ben Connally. Vince Tarlton, who was to become Judge Allred's permanent law clerk and whose father was, for a time, in the running for one of these judgeships, tells a different story. According to Tarlton, it was Johnson who recommended both Allred and Connally (though he talked Tom Connally into taking the credit for the Allred nomination). This served two purposes for Johnson. One, it tainted Senator Connally's reputation with the charge of nepotism, since even with Johnson taking credit for naming Ben Connally to the position, it looked liked Senator Connally was using his position as senator to benefit his son. (Senator Connally's letter files, in fact, show that this charge was often leveled, as every letter sent in response to congratulations for his son's appointment stressed how the senator had not taken any part in the nominating process – see "Connally Nomination, General File" and "Tom Connally Scrapbook, August 1949–December 1949," Boxes 513 and 618, respectively, Tom Connally Papers). Second, this nomination removed two potential Johnson competitors for future political office: Allred and Ben Connally (interview, Vince Tarlton, Mar. 18, 1988).

9. On Allred, see chap. 7; on Connally, see *Houston Post* (July 16, 1974); "Memorial to Judge Ben C. Connally," in "Ben C. Connally, Personnel File," Records of the Clerk, Southern District of Texas, RG 21, Houston, Texas; Blake Timmons to President Harry Truman, Sept. 24, 1949; Leon Jaworski, president, Houston Bar Association, to Senator Tom Connally, Sept. 24, 1949; and Wright Matthews to Tom Goosh, Sept. 23, 1949, in "Lawyers, Judges and State Politics File," Box 513, Tom Connally Papers. See also numerous newspaper clippings in "Connally Nomination, General File" and "Tom Connally Scrapbook, August 1949–December 1949," Boxes 513 and 618, respectively, Tom Connally Papers. On Ingraham, see numerous newspaper clippings in "Ingraham Scrapbook"; "Transcript of Court Proceedings, August 30, 1954" (Ingraham's swearing in to bench), and interview, Joe McDonald Ingraham, Nov. 9, 1972, and May 21, 1973, all in Joe McDonald Ingraham Papers. Also, interview, Joe McDonald Ingraham, Feb. 4, 1988.

10. On Allred, see Claude E. Carter to Senator Pat McCarran, head, Senate Judiciary Committee, Sept. 23, 1949," Allred File," Box 512 Tom Connally Papers. On Connally, see *Houston Post* (July 16, 1974); "Memorial to Judge Ben C. Connally," in "Ben C. Connally, Personnel File," Records of the Clerk, Southern District of Texas, RG 21, Houston, Texas; Leon Jaworski, president, Houston Bar Association, to Senator Tom Connally, Sept. 24, 1949, and Wright Matthews to Tom Goosh, Sept. 23, 1949, in "Lawyers, Judges and State Politics File," Box 513, Tom Connally Papers. The comment on being a "lawyer's

judge" is taken from Frank Read and Lucy McGough, *Let Them Be Judged: The Judicial Integration of the Deep South,* p. 104. On Ingraham, see interview, Joe McDonald Ingraham, Feb. 4, 1988. Each of the trio was considered, at some point in his career, a political liberal. Their liberalism, however, had a specific meaning in Texas, where liberals accepted primacy of private property and the dominance of the corporate business system. What made them liberals was their acceptance of government action in those areas not materially affecting the state's economic sectors, such as basic aid to the poor or probusiness government regulations. Where government action threatened private property rights or hindered growth, they quickly sided with the state's conservative majority in opposing such actions. On the solidarity of the Southern District's bench, see interview, Joe McDonald Ingraham, Feb. 4, 1988, and interview, Woodrow Seals, Mar. 2, 1988, where both judges note the basic collegiality of the Southern District Bench in the 1950s as exemplified by the weekly lunch in which all the judges met and discussed in general terms the business of the court and the basics of their jurisprudence. On the conservative tone of Texas politics during this period, see Green, *The Establishment in Texas Politics;* pp. 11–21; and McKay and Faulk, *Texas after Spindletop,* p. 216, where each notes how many Texas liberals, such as Ralph Yarborough, took to describing themselves as "Liberal-Conservatives." A "liberal-conservative," Yarborough supporter and later judge of the Southern District Woodrow Seals explains, is someone who "wants to keep and safeguard and protect all those institutions found to be good" but who is willing to "change[e] institutions when they need to change" (interview, Woodrow Seals, Mar. 2, 1988). Of course, differences could and did exist as to what institutions were deemed in need of change. On the acceptance of the corporate system in the 1950s by liberals, see Allen J. Matusow, *The Unraveling of America: A History of Liberalism in the 1960s,* pp. 32–33.

11. Vatter, *The U.S. Economy in World War II,* p. 169.

12. On the changing views of the Supreme Court and the Fifth Circuit Court of Appeals, see Melvin Urofsky, *The Continuity of Change: The Supreme Court and Individual Liberties, 1953–1986,* pp. 24–26; Murphy, *The Constitution in Crisis Times, 1918–1969,* chaps. 6 and 7; and Harvey C. Couch, *A History of the Fifth Circuit, 1891–1981,* pp. 75–104.

13. 52 *U.S. Statutes at Large,* p. 1060.

14. *Tennessee Coal Co. v. Muscoda Local,* 32 U.S., 590; *Anderson v. Mt. Clemens Pottery Co.,* 328 U.S., 680. A third such decision came in *Jewell Ridge Coal Corp. v. Local 6167,* 325 U.S., 161, reached in 1945. The Supreme Court reiterated its position on coal miners, holding once again that, "[as] the Fair Labor Standards Act was not designed to codify or perpetuate those customs and contracts which follow an employer to claim all of an employee's time while compensating him only for a part of it," work in a mine began the instant a miner entered the mineshaft and not when drilling began. See also Johanna M. D'Amico, "'Working Time' and the Portal-to-Portal Act of 1947," *Federal Bar Journal* 9 (July, 1948): 375–78; and E. Merrick Dodd, "The Supreme Court and Fair Labor Standards, 1941–1945," *Harvard Law Review* 59 (Feb., 1946): 350–64.

15. D'Amico, "Portal-to-Portal Act of 1947," p. 378. See also "Plaintiff's Original Petition," *G. H. Cansler et al. v. Shell Oil Co. et al.,* Civ. 2468, Houston Division; *C. C. Putman and J. Tyler, as Agents and Representatives of Certain Employees of Defendant v. General American Tank Storage Co.,* Civ. 2400, Houston Division; *Frank A. Hardesty, District Director of U.S. Steelworkers of America et al., v. Hughes Tool Co.,* Civ. 2456, Houston Division; *James Story and J. Kirtley et al. v. Todd-Houston Shipbuilding Co.,* Civ. 2458, Houston Division; *A. H. Brown et al., v. Houston Pipe Line Co.,* Civ 2459, Houston Division; *Robert Jones, President of Local 333, Oil Workers International Union et al. v. Humble Oil and Refining*

Co., Civ. 2467, Houston Division; *G. H. Cousler, President of Local 367, Oil Workers International Union et al. v. Shell Oil Co. and Shell Chemical Corp.*, Civ. 2468, Houston Division; *C. E. McGinnis et al. v. Hobbs Manufacturing Co.*, Civ. 2481, Houston Division; *George Warner et al., v. Todd-Houston Shipbuilding Corp.*, Civ. 2482, Houston Division.

16. See "Defendant's Answer" in cases listed in note 15.

17. In a Dec. 10, 1940, case, Judge Allred had in fact held that the FLSA should be "liberally construed" and granted overtime compensation to a Houston night watchman (*Lefevers v. General Export Iron and Metal Co.*, 36 F. Supp., 838). How Kennerly and Hannay would have ruled, however, is unknown.

18. *Congressional Record*, 80th Cong., 1st sess., vol. 93:538–39, 1002–04, 2083–84, 2192–98, A290–94, A513, A840, A927–28, A1230–31.

19. 61 *U.S. Statutes at Large*, p. 84. See also D'Amico, "Portal-to-Portal Act of 1947," pp. 378–82, and Virginia Cook, "The Administration of the Fair Labor Standards Act with Special Reference to Enforcement" (Ph.D. diss.). See also "Brief in Support of Motion of Defendant to Dismiss the Complaint," *Frank Hardesty, et al. v. Federal Steel Products Co.*, Civ. 2461, Houston Division.

20. This had been held constitutional since the 1869 case of *Ex parte McCardle*, 7 Wallace, 506.

21. See *James Story et al. v. Todd-Houston Shipbuilding Corp.*, Civ 2458, Houston Division. On decisions of other district courts, see *Burfeind v. Eagle-Picher Company of Texas*, decided May 21, 1947, Northern District of Texas; *Boehle v. Electrometallurgical Co.*, decided June 9, 1947, District of Oregon; and *Freeman Cochran et al. v. St. Paul and Tacoma Lumber Co.*, decided May 26, 1947, Western District of Washington, Southern Division (all citations taken from "Brief in Support of Motion of Defendant to Dismiss the Complaint," *Frank Hardesty et al. v. Federal Steel Products Co.*, Civ. 2461, Houston Division). Prior to these cases the court faced an FLSA overtime suit in *Lefevers v. General Export Iron and Metal Co.*, Civ 82, Corpus Christi Division. See also D'Amico, "Portal-to-Portal Act of 1947," p. 381. Thereafter, suits under the FLSA became the sole province of the Justice Department, which brought a small number of actions to enforce the minimum wage and contract provisions of the Act (Cook, "The Administration of the Fair Labor Standards Act," pp. 585–623).

22. Harold Vatter, *The U.S. Economy in the 1950s: An Economic History*, p. 49; Richard O. Davies, *Housing Reform during the Truman Administration*, pp. 40–41.

23. "Yes, it was a fine building boom," Wyatt noted, "except nobody much was bothering to build any homes that veterans could afford" (Wilson Wyatt, Speech to the Twenty-eighth American Legion Convention, Oct. 3, 1946, San Francisco [quoted in Davies, *Housing Reform*, p. 43]).

24. Davies, *Housing Reform*, pp. 43–58. See also Phillips, *The 1940*, pp. 276–78; Nathanael Keith, *Politics and the Housing Crisis since 1930*, pp. 58–67; Susan Hartmann, *Truman and the 80th Congress*, pp. 94–95, 103–104, 129, 149–50.

25. Davies, *Housing Reform*, pp. 8, 43–58, 117–18, 135. Often these federally insured loans went bad. Suit would then be brought by the government for the unpaid portion of the loan. For examples on suits under NHA, see *U.S. v. Able Jas Guidry et al.*, Civ 2484, Houston Division; *U.S. v. Edward Detuttle and Wife*, Civ 2494, Houston Division; *U.S. v. I. Robinson*, Civ 2917, Houston Division; *U.S. v. Sam Washington*, Civ 5415, Houston Division; *U.S. v. Frank Pinabeau*, Civ 5605, Houston Division; *U.S. v. William Beard*, Civ 6496, Houston Division.

26. This transfer of authority was made official in the Housing and Rent Act of 1947,

continued in the Housing Act of 1948, and set for termination on December 31, 1950, in the Housing Act of 1949 (Davies, *Housing Reform*, pp. 54, 65–66, 105–106, 121–22; Tighe Woods, "The Administration of a Law: Federal Rent Control," *Notre Dame Lawyer* 25 (Spring, 1950): 416–18). For a detailed description of the various housing acts, see Nathan Siegel, "Recent Decisions Construing Federal Rent Control Legislation," *Syracuse Law Review* 1 (Fall, 1949): 207–46.

27. Fiscal 1946 ran from July 1, 1945, through June 30, 1946. This meant that in fiscal 1947, the OPA was in charge of enforcement for the first five months and the OHE enforced the rents thereafter (*AO Report* [1946–50]).

28. In 1946, for instance, 28,282 civil suits were filed while only 2,520 criminal actions were. In 1947, 31,094 civil and 1465 criminal cases were filed; in 1948, 15,169 civil and 234 criminal; in 1949, 3,566 civil and 33 criminal (ibid.).

29. Compromise settlements included a large number of the dismissed cases, with the defendants' promise not to violate the law in the future being required before the government moved to dismiss the case. Nationally, most rent control cases were, in fact, settled to the government's satisfaction. In 1946, for instance, of 28,458 price and rent cases completed, 19,543 were ended by consent decrees in which the defendant was enjoined from future violations and/or damages and restitution was ordered, 1,087 were ended by a judicial decision (most, once again, in favor of the government), and 1,136 finished with default judgments against defendants who had not appeared in court. At the same time, 6,180 cases were dismissed by consent of all parties while 296 cases were dismissed for lack of prosecution. In 1947, the comparable numbers were 17,668 actions completed, 4,977 of which were consent judgments; 891 judicial decisions; 835 default judgments; 9,991 consent dismissals; and 776 judicial dismissals. Similarly, in 1948 there were 9,334 cases completed, 1,312 of which were consent judgments; 1,175 judicial judgments; 1,007 default judgments against the defendants; 5,209 consent dismissals; and 476 court dismissals (*AO Report*, table C4 [1946–48]).

30. These numbers are approximate because 372 of these suits were filed by the OPA and, as a result, a percentage of them involved commodities other than rents. Examination of the Houston Division's civil dockets (most OPA suits were filed in Houston) shows, however, that most of the OPA suits involved rents, especially the 269 OPA suits filed in fiscal 1947 (*AO Report* [1945–50]). All of the civil cases sought injunctions enjoining landlords from charging rents in excess of the legal limit. Most in addition requested restitution of excess rents for the tenants and damage awards totaling double the amount of the overcharge (*Civil Docket Books*, Houston Division, 1945–50).

31. In most instances the defendant was charged the costs of litigation, which in itself was a form of sanction. The high number of dismissals can be seen in the *Civil Docket Books* of the court, especially for the Houston Division, where more than half of these suits were filed. For examples, see *Philip Fleming, Administrator, Office of Temporary Controls, OPA, and Frank Creedon, Housing Expediter v. Florence Cameron*, Civ 2713, Houston Divison (case dismissed, defendant to pay costs); *Fleming et al. v. P. S. Quinn et al.*, Civ 2714, Houston Division (case dismissed on motion of OPA, defendant to pay costs); *Fleming et al. v. Orlen Chevalier*, Civ 2717, Houston Division (case dismissed on stipulation); *Fleming et al. v. Tille Katy Maxon et al.*, Civ 2720, Houston Division (case dismissed on motion of OHE, defendant to pay costs); *Fleming et al. v. Florencio Urdiablo*, Civ 2727, Houston Division (case dismissed on motion of OHE, no costs); *Fleming et al. v. Tony Baimonti, Jr.*, Civ 2735, Houston Division (case dismissed on motion of OHE, defendant to pay costs); *Frank Creedon v. Budson Steede et al.*, Civ 2774, Houston Division

(case dismissed on motion of OHE, defendant to pay costs); *Creedon v. Will Hooper,* Civ 2777, Houston Division (case dismissed, no costs to defendant); *Creedon v. Raymond Tuttle,* Civ 2790, Houston Division (case dismissed, defendant to pay costs).

32. The suit was originally titled *Philip Fleming, Administrator Office of Temporary Controls v. Carrie Haydell.* Woods's name was substituted for Fleming's following the OHE's acceptance of authority over housing controls in Nov., 1946. See also "Complaint," and "Findings of Fact and Conclusions of Law," *Tighe E. Woods, Housing Expediter v. Carrie Haydell et al.,* Civ 2722, Houston Division.

33. "Defendant's Answer and Exception to Plaintiff's Original and Amended Petitions," *Tighe E. Woods, Housing Expediter v. Carrie Haydell et al.,* Civ 2722, Houston Division.

34. "Plaintiff's Trial Brief," *Tighe E. Woods, Housing Expediter v. Carrie Haydell et al.,* Civ 2722, Houston Division.

35. The case was remanded for further proceedings in accordance with the circuit court's decision. Judge Kennerly subsequently ordered the payment of damages in favor of the government for $2,222.75 (*Woods v. Haydell et al.,* 178 F[2d], 914; "Judgement," *Tighe E. Woods, Housing Expediter v. Carrie Haydell et al.,* Civ 2722, Houston Division).

36. *Fleming v. Tate,* Civ 2719, Houston Division. Kennerly's decision was overturned in *Woods v. Tate,* 171 F(2d), 511. The appeals court held that a change in ownership did not invalidate a government order setting maximum rents. Further, it was the new owner's "duty to consult with the proper OPA authorities" for information as to what was the proper rent, so that "rent exacted from her tenant would not be at variance with the regulations. Not having done so, for aught the records reveal, she was legally chargeable with knowledge of the order establishing her maximum rent." *Woods v. Selber et al.,* 171 F(2d), 900.

37. For example, see the appeals in *Woods v. Turk,* 171 F(2d), 244; *Woods v. Willis,* 171 F(2d), 289; *Woods v. Stewart,* 171 F(2d), 544; *Woods v. Winters,* 171 F(2d), 759.

38. "Pluperfect Hell," *Time* (Apr. 28, 1947), pp. 22–24; "Why," *New Republic* (Apr. 28, 1947), p. 8; *Newsweek* (Apr. 28, 1947), pp. 29–32; *Galveston Daily News* (Apr. 17–29, 1947); *Houston Post* (Apr. 17–29, 1947); *Houston Chronicle* (Apr. 17–29, 1947). See also Ernst Behrendt, "What Really Happened at Texas City," *Popular Science* 166 (Apr., 1955): 268, 272; McComb, *Galveston;* pp. 193–95; Elizabeth Wheaton, *Texas City Remembers.* Further details can be found in "Texas City Disaster," *Hearings,* Senate Judiciary Committee, 83d Cong., 2d sess., Aug. 6–7, 1954, and "Texas City Disaster," *Hearings,* House Judiciary Committee, 83d Cong., 1st sess., Nov. 16–18, 1953.

39. Thomas Paterson, "The Quest for Peace and Prosperity: International Trade, Communism, and the Marshall Plan," p. 92; Phillips, *The 1940s,* p. 274; *Texas Almanac, 1945–1946,* p. 255. See also *Dalehite v. U.S.,* 346 U.S., 18–21.

40. On European famine and the Marshall Plan, see Paterson, "The Quest for Peace and Prosperity," pp. 78–105; Allen Matusow, *Farm Policies and Politics in the Truman Administration,* pp. 145–69. On the importance of fertilizer, see Opinion in *In Re Texas City Disaster Litigation,* 197 F(2d), 777.

41. *In Re Texas City Disaster Litigation,* 197 F(2d), 777; *Dalehite v. U.S.,* 346 U.S., 18–21.

42. Behrendt, "What Really Happened at Texas City," pp. 268, 272; interview, John R. Brown, Feb. 16, 1988. See also "Original Complaints," filed in *Texas City Consolidated Disaster Cases,* Galveston Division, and newspaper accounts of the disaster in *Houston Post, Houston Chronicle,* and *Galveston News,* Apr. 17–29, 1947.

43. *Texas City Consolidated Disaster Cases Docket,* Galveston Division. For examples of suits filed, see *Alice Bonewits et al. v. U.S.,* Civ 666, Galveston Division (wrongful death

and property damages for $9,500,553); *James I. Flagg and Texas Employers Insurance Co. v. U.S.*, Civ 688, Galveston Division (damages for personal injury totaling $75,000); *Humble Oil and Refining Co. v. U.S.*, Civ 691, Galveston Division (property damages for $345,099); *Monsanto Chemical Co. v. U.S.*, Civ 694, Galveston Division (property damages for $50 million); *Hartford Accident and Indem. Co. v. U.S.*, Civ 714, Galveston Division (property damages for $6,561); *Republic Oil Refining Co. v. U.S.*, Civ 757, Galveston Division (property damages and loss of personnel for $6.5 million); *M. J. Braddy et al., v. U.S.*, Civ 790, Galveston Division (property damages for $348,381); *Texas Employers Insurance Co. v. U.S.*, Civ 808, Galveston Division (damages for personal injury and wrongful death totaling $338,000).

44. *Dalehite v. U.S.*, 346 U.S., 24–30; comment, "The Federal Tort Claims Act," *Yale Law Journal* 56 (Feb., 1947): 534–35; note, "The Federal Tort Claims Act," *Mississippi Law Journal* 20 (May, 1949): 354–57; Jules E. Angoff, "The Federal Tort Claims Act: A General View," *Boston University Law Review* 37 (Fall, 1957): 387–88.

45. 60 *U.S. Statutes at Large*, p. 842. The act was amended on Aug. 1, 1947, 61 *U.S. Statutes at Large*, p. 722, and revised once again in 1948, at which time its provisions were codified under the title "Judicial Code and Judiciary," 62 *U.S. Statutes at Large*, p. 897. See also *In Re Texas City Disaster Litigation*, 197 F(2d), 777. Analysis of the act can be found in E. L. Fisher, "The Federal Tort Claims Act after Five Years," *Mercer Law Review* 3 (Spring, 1952): 263–77; note, "Federal Tort Claims Act," *Mississippi Law Journal* 20 (May, 1949): 355–72; and comment, "The Federal Tort Claims Act," *Yale Law Journal* 56 (Feb., 1947): 357–63.

46. "Order of Consolidation," "Order Appointing Working Committee of Attorneys," and "Statement of Fact and Conclusions of Law," *Consolidated Texas City Disaster Cases*, Galveston Division.

47. John R. Brown, who was one of the seven plaintiff's lawyers, recalls how both sets of attorneys crossed the country on a special train collecting evidence (interview, John R. Brown, Feb. 16, 1988). Kennerly actually asked the counsels for the plaintiffs and the defense to indicate what findings of fact and conclusions of law they felt should be made (*In Re Texas City Disaster Litigation*, 197 F[2d], 774).

48. "Consolidated Pleading" *Dalehite v. U.S.*, Civ 787, Galveston Division (quote from "Findings of Fact and Conclusions of Law," as quoted in *In Re Texas City Disaster Litigation*, 197 F[2d], 772–73). The text of Judge Kennerly's "Findings of Fact and Conclusions of Law" has not been found. The case files for the Texas City disaster cases mass over one hundred linear feet and over twenty thousand separate documents. Within this mass lie the twenty to fifty pages of Judge Kennerly's opinion. Despite my best efforts and those of the staff of the National Archives Southwest Region, it has proven impossible to find the text. However, both the Fifth Circuit's and the Supreme Court's decisions quote extensively from Judge Kennerly's statement of the case. All quotes and paraphrases come from these two sources as noted.

49. "Defendant's Answer," *Dalehite v. U.S.*, Civ 787, Galveston Division, and *In Re Texas City Disaster Litigation*, 197 F(2d), 772–73.

50. This insight into the motivations of Judge Kennerly is taken primarily from an interview with John R. Brown, one of the seven plaintiffs' attorneys and later a federal circuit judge himself. Brown, who knew the judge both professionally and personally, stresses that, ultimately, it was the human question, the needs of the plaintiffs, that shaped Kennerly's decision (interview, John R. Brown, Feb. 16, 1988). This opinion has been reinforced by conversations with Judge Ingraham, who replaced Kennerly on the bench,

and Judges Singleton and Seals. Though none of these men spoke intentionally on the Texas City disaster cases, their descriptions of Judge Kennerly and his personality support Judge Brown's opinion (interview, Joe McDonald Ingraham, Feb. 4, 1988; interview, John V. Singleton, Mar. 14, 1988, and interview, Woodrow Seals, (Mar. 2, 1988). So too do the descriptions given by T. Everton Kennerly, the judge's son (interview, T. Everton Kennerly, Apr. 4, 1989). Kennerly did not defend his opinion that the FTCA granted jurisdiction in this case, he simply asserted this fact as an obvious result of the government's negligence. In essence, his decision depended on the legal maxim of where there was a wrong a remedy had to exist. ("Findings of Fact and Conclusions of Law," *Dalehite v. U.S.*, Civ 787, Galveston Division).

51. "Findings of Fact and Conclusions of Law," *Dalehite v. U.S.*, Civ 787, Galveston Division (quoted in *Dalehite v. U.S.*, 346 U.S., 45–47). The description of Judge Kennerly's views is also taken in part from Judge Hutcheson's dissent in *In Re Texas City Disaster Litigation*, 197 F(2d), 786.

52. *In Re Texas City Disaster Litigation*, 197 F(2d), 774.

53. Ibid., pp. 774–75.

54. Ibid., pp. 776, 778.

55. *Dalehite v. U.S.*, 346 U.S., 24–42.

56. This is exactly what the plaintiffs did, procuring in Aug., 1954, passage of a special "compassionate responsibility" bill compensating the victims of the Texas City disaster. The bill, however, allowed for a maximum payment of only $25,000 per claimant (*Public Law No. 387*, 84th Cong., 1st sess.). See also "A report to Accompany H.R. 9785, a bill to provide a method for compensating claims for damages sustained as the result of the explosions at Texas City, Texas," *Report No. 2024*, House Judiciary Committee, 83d Cong., 2d sess.; "Texas City Disaster," *Hearings*, Senate Judiciary Committee, 83d Cong., 2d sess., Aug. 6–7, 1954; and "Texas City Disaster," *Hearings*, House Judiciary Committee, 83d Cong., 1st sess., Nov. 16–18, 1953.

57. *Dalehite v. U.S.*, 346 U.S., pp. 47–60.

58. Angoff, "The Federal Tort Claims Act," p. 389.

59. It is interesting to note that on the Fifth Circuit, it was Judge Hutcheson, the former Southern District judge, who most disliked and fought the growing acceptance of expanded government powers, in particular as related to the National Labor Relations Board. See John M. Spivack, "Race, Civil Rights, and the United States Court of Appeals for the Fifth Judicial Circuit" (Ph.D. diss.), p. 255.

60. Most of these suspended sentences were for five years and depended on the defendant's not returning to the United States for the duration of probation. On sentencing patterns in the Southern District and the high number of guilty pleas in immigration cases, see *Criminal Docket Books*, Brownsville and Laredo division. See also Bruce S. Meador, "Wetback Labor in the Lower Rio Grande Valley" (M.A. thesis), p. 12. Nor, it should be noted, was there much demand for this limited role to change. Criminal immigration laws had been in existence since the first years of the century. Enforcement of these laws had become so common and so traditional a part of the region's experience that the negative effects of this enforcement were accepted as a normal part of doing business. Rather than try to modify administration of the law at the federal court level, Texans preferred to use informal, mostly political, methods to circumvent local enforcement. The goal was to keep illegal immigrant laborers from being arrested in the first place; by the time illegal aliens reached a judge's bench, everyone agreed that they would have to be deported. Thus, even if the court judges could have hindered federal immigration

policy in some manner, it is unlikely they would have done so (Juan Ramón García, *Operation Wetback: The Mass Deportation of Mexican Undocumented Workers in 1954*, p. 207. See also Coalson, *Migratory Farm Labor System*, p. 81; Arthur Corwin, "A Story of Ad Hoc Exemptions: American Immigration Policy toward Mexico," p. 151). On Texans' attitudes toward immigration law enforcement in general, see García, *Operation Wetback*, pp. 206–207; Meador, "Wetback Labor in the Lower Rio Grande Valley," pp. 15–17; and Coalson, *Migratory Farm Labor System in Texas*, pp. 79–81.

61. García, *Operation Wetback*, pp. 157–79, 236; Corwin, "A Study of Ad Hoc Exemptions," pp. 151–52; Otey Scruggs, "Texas and the Bracero Program, 1942–1947," pp. 85–95. On conditions in South Texas for Mexican immigrants, see Ozzie Simmons, *Anglo-Americans and Mexican Americans in South Texas*.

62. Corwin, "A Study of Ad Hoc Exemptions," pp. 152–53. Ellis Hawley, "The Politics of the Mexican Labor Issue, 1950–1965," pp. 101–109, describes the debates over the bracero program and the issue of Mexican labor from the perspective of the farm bloc supporting extensive use of Mexican labor.

63. 66 *U.S. Statutes at Large*, p. 26; García, *Operation Wetback*, pp. 157–79, 236; Corwin, "A Study of Ad Hoc Exemptions," pp. 152–53.

64. García, *Operation Wetback*, p. 212. What differentiated one illegal immigrant from another in formal deportation proceedings depended on the immigrant's history. Meador, "Wetback Labor in the Lower Rio Grande Valley," pp. 11–12, notes that those formally charged in federal court were repeat offenders who had already been "voluntarily returned" (administratively deported) several times and thus had used up their free ride back to Mexico. Also, those who "were guilty of some crime, other than illegal entry, while in this country" were formally charged. The gain in formally charging an illegal was that it "prevent[ed] his applying for official permission to re-enter [the United States] for two years," as well as potentially leading to his serving of jail time. The cost in formally charging an illegal was administrative; it took time and resources to charge and maintain a deportee in jail prior to court hearing, resources that many in the Immigration Service felt were wasted, given the likelihood that the defendant would receive a suspended sentence and be deported. This also explains the small number of illegals formally charged as opposed to being administratively deported.

65. Meador, "Wetback Labor in the Lower Rio Grande Valley," p. 12.

66. *AO Report*, table D3 (1950–60).

67. Thomas Kennerly to Hon. John E. Lyle, Mar. 7, 1949; Allan Hannay to Hon. John E. Lyle, Mar. 8, 1949; and "Statement of Hon. Lloyd M. Bentsen," in House, *Hearings of Subcommittee #3 of the Committee of the Judiciary*, 81st Cong., 1st sess., pp. 25 and 27.

68. Meador, "Wetback Labor in the Lower Rio Grande Valley," p. 12. See also García, *Operation Wetback*, pp. 234–40, on decline in federal enforcement after 1955.

69. See *AO Report*, table C3 (1946–59).

70. In some instances the court's ability to set high awards was further limited by state statutes providing for "fault-free" compensation in workers' compensation matters. This limited the court's ability not only to determine the respective negligence of the parties, but also to determine the maximum amount of compensation. On the operation of Texas workers' compensation laws, see Title 130, *Revised Civil Statutes of Texas*, 1924, and amendments. See also Barton, *How Texas Cares for Her Injured Workers*. On the high number of settled tort cases, see *AO Report* (1947), p. 92, which notes that 63 percent of all private civil cases were ended by a consent decree or a consent dismissal, and (1952), p. 83, which notes how only one in six tort cases went to trial. See also (1954),

p. 111, which notes how 80 percent of all insurance cases, 78 percent of all auto personal injury, and 72 percent of all other personal injury cases were settled by agreement. (This ratio of trials to settled cases was larger than existed for public cases, where the number of trials was closer to one in nine–ibid. [1949], p. 84).

71. This large number of TIAB appeals was unique to the Texas federal courts. Most states strictly limited appeals from their industrial accident boards. Texas, however, allowed for a full court hearing of all disputed TIAB awards. These hearings, in turn, were completely new proceedings, not administrative appeals of the TIAB's decision. The Administrative Office estimated that over half of all federal workers' compensation cases were filed in Texas (*AO Report* [1959], p. 80). On the postwar boom and its effect on Texas' industrial, transportation, and construction industries, see *Texas Almanac, 1946–1960.* On TIAB following the war, see Barton, *How Texas Cares for Her Injured Workers,* p. 27. The comment on the "automatic" nature of appeals from the TIAB is taken from a telephone interview with long-time plaintiff tort attorney Thomas B. Weatherly of the firm of Vinson and Elkins. (Vinson and Elkins, in common with other large Houston law firms such as Baker and Botts and Butler and Binion, represented the insurance companies in these cases. See *Civil Docket Books,* Houston Division, 1945–55). Weatherly explains that plaintiff attorneys sought removal to the federal courts whenever diversity existed because they "felt they could get a better deal" in the federal courts and because these courts were "more expeditious." In retrospect, Weatherly figures that, while the federal courts were more expeditious, plaintiffs received no better deal there than they did in state; they merely thought they did (interview, Thomas B. Weatherly, Sept. 6 and 7, 1990).

72. Interview, Thomas B. Weatherly, Sept. 6 and 7, 1990. For examples of this process in TIAB cases, see *D. T. Gill v. Liberty Mutual Insurance,* Civ 2030, Houston Division; *Charles Appen v. Anchor Casualty Co.,* Civ 2185, Houston Division; *Horace Jones v. Liberty Mutual Insurance,* Civ 2747, Houston Division; *Herman Gregory v. Travelers Insurance Co.,* Civ 2746, Houston Division; *William Eason v. Liberty Mutual Insurance,* Civ 4805, Houston Division; *Charles Butler v. National Auto and Casualty Insurance Co.,* Civ 4825, Houston Division; *Coy Gathright v. Fireman's Fund Indemnity Co.,* Civ 7510, Houston Division; *Ralph Rubin v. Liberty Mutual Insurance,* Civ 8074, Houston Division.

73. Interview, Thomas B. Weatherly, Sept. 6 and 7, 1990. See *Travelers Insurance Co. v. Dickson,* 66 F. Supp., 72; *Chancey v. Associated Indemnity Corp.,* 99 F. Supp., 298; *Employers Mutual Liability Insurance Co. v. Konvicka,* 99 F. Supp., 433; *Burst v. Newark Fire Insurance Co.,* 100 F. Supp., 751.

74. On insurance suits in the 1930s, see chap. 6. On reasons for the defendant's removal to federal court, see interview, Thomas B. Weatherly, Sept. 6 and 7, 1990.

75. See *William Smith v. Saint Paul Fire and Marine Insurance Co.,* Civ 2056, Houston Division (suit on fire insurance for $9,000; plaintiff recovered $6,100); *Insurance Underwriters, Inc. v. Sam Milkie,* Civ 2479, Houston Division (suit to recover premiums due on insurance policy for $4,664; case dismissed); *Texas Radio Manufacturing Corp. v. Indiana Remembrance Mutual Insurance Co. of Indianapolis,* Civ 2769, Houston Division (suit on fire insurance for $13,742; case dismissed).

76. This was in contrast to the national trend, where personal injury cases made up the majority of tort cases (*AO Report* [1957], pp. 86–87).

77. While most personal injury cases arose from automobile accidents (*AO Report* [1957], p. 87), many of these and other cases involved issues relating to area business and their economic actions. For example, in *W. M. Parker and Gulf Brewing Co. v. Jefferson*

Lake Sulfur Co., Civ 4047, Houston Division, the injury sued over grew out of an auto accident near the sulfur company's place of business and raised questions as to the safety procedures of the company. Or, again, *Mrs. J. R. Randolph v. Sears, Roebuck and Co. and Southwestern Bell*, Civ 4775, Houston Division, involved the safety features of a telephone. *Mrs. Jessie Mildred Williams et al. v. Warren Petroleum Corp. et al.*, Civ 4780, Houston Division, raised questions about the safety procedures on an oil drill. The list continues. Of course, as will be noted below, none of this is to say that the court's decision in these cases actually had any effect on business practices.

78. *C. F. Palmer v. Texas and New Orleans RR*, Civ 6728, Houston Division.

79. *AO Report* (1952), p. 77; (1955), p. 105; (1949), p. 44.

80. The copies used for this study were in fact once Judge Hannay's and are now on file in the United States Courthouse Library in Houston. Interview, Thomas B. Weatherly, Sept. 6 and 7, 1990; Thomas Kennerly to Hon. John E. Lyle, Mar. 7, 1949; and Allan Hannay to Hon. John E. Lyle, Mar. 8, 1949, in House, *Hearings of Subcommittee #3 of the Committee of the Judiciary*, 81st Cong., 1st sess., pp. 25 and 27. The growing frustration of the federal bench as a whole in these matters can be seen in a speech by Bolthia J. Laws, chief judge, U.S. District Court for the District of Columbia, to the Insurance Law Section of the American Bar Association: "Do the Judicial Systems As They Now Function Meet Today's Needs?" *Proceedings of the Insurance Section of the American Bar Association* (Sept. 15–17, 1952): 16–28. See also an earlier speech to the Insurance Section by Judge Hutcheson, reprinted in Joseph C. Hutcheson, "Law and Fact in Insurance Cases," *Texas Law Review* 23 (Dec., 1944): 1–17.

81. Interview, Thomas B. Weatherly, Sept. 6 and 7, 1990.

82. A body made up of the chief justice of the United States, the chief judges of the Circuit Courts of Appeals, and selected district court judges, the Judicial Conference oversees the administration of the federal court system and makes proposals to Congress as to the budget and jurisdiction of the federal courts. See Fish, *The Politics of Federal Judicial Administration*. 72 *U.S. Statutes at Large*, p. 415; "Connally Fact Sheet," in "Ben C. Connally, Personnel File," Records of the Clerk, Southern District of Texas, RG 21, Houston, Texas; interview, Thomas B. Weatherly, Sept. 6 and 7, 1990. On the Judicial Conference's proposals, see *Annual Report of the Proceedings of the Judicial Conference of the United States* (1957), pp. 4–7, (1958), pp. 5–6. See also *AO Report* (1958), pp. 83–84, (1959), p. 80. For Congress's response, see *Congressional Record*, 85th Cong., 2d sess., pp. 12689–90. On the Supreme Court's reception of this change, see *Horton v. Liberty Mutual Insurance Co.*, 367 U.S., 348, 356.

83. *AO Report* (1959), pp. 80, 83–84. On future trends, see ibid., table C1 (1960–68).

84. See *Standard Accident Insurance Co. v. Texas Water Supply Corp. et al.*, Civ 2463, Houston Division (suit for debt); *Galban Lobo Co. v. Imperial Sugar Co.*, Civ 2464, Houston Division (suit for breach of contract); *Ned Gill Building Corp. v. Continental Oil Co., and Ramada Clubs et al.*, Civ 4807, Houston Division (suit for declaratory judgment on rents and to settle relationship between defendants); *Jess Allen v. Chrysler Corp.*, Civ 5928, Houston Division (recovery of damages arising from failure of defendant to meet requirements of contractual agreement); *Standard Pipe Supply Co. v. Standard Pipe Co. and Standard Pipe and Supply Co.*, Civ 6038, Houston Division (suit on trademark and use of name of company).

85. Prior to the late 1950s (with the exception, of course, of the Civil War and Reconstruction eras), most civil rights suits were criminal actions brought by the government against individuals who in turn based their defense on the Bill of Rights. The major

exception to this, as will be noted below, was suits filed by African Americans seeking to end Jim Crow segregation. These suits, however, almost always failed until the 1950s (John Braeman, *Before the Civil Rights Revolution: The Old Court and Individual Rights* p. viii).

86. This process is described for the Supreme Court in Urofsky, *The Continuity of Change.*

87. See J. W. Peltason, *58 Lonely Men: Southern Federal Judges and School Desegregation.*

88. The court also heard a small number of civil rights–type cases during World War I, the 1920s, and World War II. Brought in regard to federal penal statutes, these cases caused little controversy. On the whole, they involved few deeply held rights or interests. Most defendants were innocent of the charges. In those cases in which this was not the case, most accepted their punishment with few objections. (The one exception was draft cases in WWII.) The court response to these civil rights cases, therefore, was mostly routine and had minimal impact on the civil rights question. For similar problems in World War I and with Prohibition, see chap. 3; for World War II, see chap. 7.

89. *General Laws of the State of Texas* (1903,) pp. 148–52; *General Laws of the State of Texas* (1923), pp. 74–75. Much of the following discussion is drawn from Robert Hainsworth, "The Negro and the Texas Primaries," *Journal of Negro History* 18 (Oct., 1933): 426–27; Darlene Clark Hines, *Black Victory: The Rise and Fall of the White Primary in Texas;* Sorelle, "The Darker Side of 'Heaven,'" pp. 169–73; and Chandler Davidson, "Negro Politics and the Rise of the Civil Rights Movement in Houston, Texas" (Ph.D. diss.).

90. *Love et al. v. Griffith et al.*, 236 S.W., 239 (Tx Ct. App., 1922); *Love et al. v. Griffith et al.*, 266 U.S., 45, 32 (1924). See also Sorelle, "The Darker Side of 'Heaven,'" pp. 173–76.

91. *Nixon v. Herndon et al.*, 273 U.S., 536. See also Sorelle, "The Darker Side of 'Heaven,'" pp. 176–77; and Hines, *Black Victory,* chap. 6.

92. Quoted in Hainsworth, "The Negro and the Texas Primaries," p. 428. See also Sorelle, "The Darker Side of 'Heaven,'" pp. 177–78.

93. *Grigsby v. Harris,* 27 F(2d) 942. In Aug., 1928, Hutcheson denied a request from the plaintiffs in this case for permission to appeal directly to the Supreme Court (*Grigsby v. Harris,* 27 F[2d] 945). See RG 60, File 72-100-5 for Justice Department's file on this case. See also Sorelle, "The Darker Side of 'Heaven,'" pp. 179–80.

94. *White v. Lubbock et al.*, 30 S.W. 2(d), 722 (cites *Love* case). This case was not appealed because of the upcoming decision in *Nixon v. Condon.*

95. *Nixon v. Herndon et al.*, 286 U.S., 73.

96. *White v. County Democratic Executive Committee of Harris County et al.*, 60 F2(d), 973.

97. *White et al. v. County Democratic Executive Committee of Harris County et al.*, Eq 523, Houston Division. A similar result occurred in *W. Drake v. State Democratic Executive Committee,* 2 F. Supp., 486 (Eq 524, Houston Division) and *Love v. George Thorpe, Election Judge of Precinct no. 24 et al.*, Eq 527, Houston Division, both of which were subsequently filed for runoff elections.

98. *White et al. v. Executive Committee of the Democratic Party of Houston,* Eq 538, Houston Division. The judge also justified his decision under authority of a 1934 Supreme Court case, *Grovey v. Townsend* (295 U.S., 45), in which the High Court backed off its opposition to the Texas white primary and ruled that the Texas State Democratic party's ban on African American voting was inherently a power of party and not "state action" and thus in violation of the Fourteenth Amendment (*C. Richardson et al., v. Executive Committee of the Democratic Party for the City of Houston,* discussed in Sorelle, "The Darker Side of 'Heaven'").

99. *Smith v. Allwright et al.*, Civ. 645, Houston Division. A transcript of the oral proceedings filed with the district court case also shows Marshall's attempt to link *U.S. v. Classic* to the Texas situation.

100. *Smith v. Allwright,* 321 U.S., 639. See also Robert Cushman, "The Texas 'White Primary' Case—*Smith v. Allwright,*" *Cornell Law Quarterly* 30 (Sept., 1944): 73–76.

101. Sorelle, "The Darker Side of 'Heaven,'" p. 213.

102. "Plaintiffs' Brief,' pp. 5–6, and "Defendants' Brief," pp. 21, 23–24 *Beal et al. v. Holcombe et al.*, Civ 5407, Houston Division.

103. *Beal et al. v. Holcombe et al.*, 103 F. Supp., 218.

104. *Beal v. Holcombe,* 193 F(2d), 384, 387 (the Supreme Court subsequently refused to hear the case when appealed by the city, *Beal v. Holcombe,* 347 U.S., 974).

105. "Final Judgement" and "Correspondence, etc. with Respect to Final Decree," *Beal et al. v. Holcombe et al.*, Civ 5407, Houston Division.

106. Quoted in Hines, *Black Victory,* pp. 115, 217.

107. On both the federal courts' and the American legal system's traditional emphasis on economic issues, see Charles McCurdy, "Justice Field and the Jurisprudence of Government-Business Relations: Some Parameters of Laissez-Faire Constitutionalism, 1863–1897," *Journal of American History* 61 (Mar., 1975): 970–1005; Michael Les Benedict, "Laissez-Faire and Liberty: A Re-Evaluation of the Meaning and Origins of Laissez-Faire Constitutionalism," *Law and History Review* 3 (Fall, 1985): 293–331; Murphy, *The Constitution in Crisis Times, 1918–1969.* It should be noted that Hutcheson, while on the Fifth Circuit bench, did accept and uphold the Supreme Court's decision in *Brown v. Board of Education* requiring desegregation. However, he was often "disturbed by the activism—judicial and otherwise—bred by racial unrest" (Couch, *A History of the Fifth Circuit,* p. 114; see also Spivack, "Race, Civil Rights, and the United States Court of Appeals for the Fifth Judicial Circuit," p. 255).

108. Interview, John R. Brown, Feb. 16, 1988; Read and McGough, *Let Them Be Judged,* p. 104.

109. *Ross et al. v. Houston Independent School District,* Civ 10444, Houston Division. A transcript of Judge Connally's opinion was printed in the *Houston Post* (Oct. 16, 1957), p. 10.

110. Read and McGough, *Let Them Be Judged,* p. 101.

111. Ibid., p. 103.

112. *Ross et al. v. Houston Independent School District,* Civ 10444, Houston Division.

113. See *Ross v. Dyer,* 203 F. Supp., 124 (1962).

114. Ibid. This decision was reversed in part by the Fifth Circuit, which objected to the requiring of all children of the same family to attend the same school. Similarly, the Fifth Circuit gave warning that the requirement of signatures for transfer was acceptable only in the short term, as part of the transition from segregated to desegregated schools (*Ross v. Dyer,* 312 F(2d), 191).

Conclusion

1. Interview, T. Everton Kennerly, Apr. 4, 1989.
2. Hall, *The Magic Mirror;* p. 284.
3. Ibid., p. 287. See also Urofsky, *The Continuity of Change,* pp. 24–26.
4. This description of the judges' conservative beliefs is my own, drawn from the

material presented in this book. For a more general discussion of this conservative philosophy, see Benedict, "Laissez-Faire and Liberty."

5. Interview, Jeff Crain, Sept. 18, 1990.

6. Feagin, *Free Enterprise City,* p. 272. Of course, it should be kept in mind that Houston was not the only city to make these decisions and face these costs.

Bibliography

Court Records

U.S. District Court, Southern District of Texas, RG 21, National Archives, Southwest Region, Fort Worth

Civil Case Files
Brownsville Division, nos. 1–1541 (1938–62)
Corpus Christi Division, nos. 1–2168 (1938–62)
Galveston Division, nos. 1–2941 (1938–62)
Houston Division, nos. 1–9900 (1938–57)
Laredo Division, nos. 1–846 (1938–62)
Victoria Division, nos. 1–502 (1938–52)

Civil Docket Books
Brownsville Division, vols. 1–4 (1938–54)
Corpus Christi Division, vols. 1–6 (1938–54)
Galveston Division, vols. 1–17 (1938–55)
Houston Division, vols. 1–31 (1938–54)
Laredo Division, vols. 1–5 (1938–71)
Victoria Division, vols. 1–2 (1938–55)

Criminal Case Files
Brownsville Division, nos. 1833–42687 (1905–69
Corpus Christi Division, nos. 1–6432 (1913–62)
Galveston Division, nos. 1–6220 (1866–1955)
Houston Division, nos. 103–13705 (1908–60)
Laredo Division, nos. 1–18402 (1899–1962)
Victoria Division, nos. 1–533 (1908–38)

Criminal Docket Books
Brownsville Division, vols. 1–74 (1907–54)
Corpus Christi Division, vols. 1–12 (1913–54)
Galveston Division, vols. 1–11 (1866–1955)

Houston Division, vols. 1–25 (1908–54)
Laredo Division, vols. 1–34 (1899–1969)
Victoria Division, vols. 1–2 (1907–55)

Equity Case Files
Brownsville Division, nos. 1–358 (1912–38)
Corpus Christi Division, nos. 1–108 (1913–38)
Galveston Division, nos. 30–282 (1916–38)
Houston Division, nos. 1–797 (1908–38)
Laredo Division, nos. 2–50 (1912–38)
Victoria Division, nos. 1–27 (1916–38)

Equity Docket Books
Brownsville Division, vols. 1–2 (1912–38)
Corpus Christi Division, vols. 1–2 (1912–38)
Galveston Division, vols. 1–3 (1909–38)
Houston Division, vols. 1–8 (1908–38)
Laredo Division, vol. 1 (1912–38)
Victoria Division, vol. 1 (1916–38)

Law Case Files
Brownsville Division, nos. 94–1049 (1910–38)
Corpus Christi Division, nos. 1–416 (1913–38)
Galveston Division, nos. 1–1331 (1867–1938)
Houston Division, nos. 1–3113 (1908–38)
Laredo Division, nos. 1–525 (1889–1938)
Victoria Division, nos. 1–109 (1911–38)

Law Docket Books
Brownsville Division, vols. 1–7 (1907–38)
Corpus Christi Division, vols. 1–4 (1913–38)
Galveston Division, vols. 1–8 (1867–1938)
Houston Division, vols. 1–18 (1908–38)
Laredo Division, vols. 1–4 (1907–38)
Victoria Division, vol. 1 (1910–38)

Docket of Consolidated Texas City Disaster Cases (1947–50)

U.S. District Court, Southern District of Texas, RG 21, Houston Division, Houston

Civil Docket Books, Houston Division, vols. 32– (1955–60)
Criminal Docket Books, Houston Division, vols. 26– (1955–60)

U.S. Circuit Court, Southern District of Texas, RG 21, National Archives, Southwest Region, Fort Worth

Equity Case Files
Galveston Division, nos. 1–513 (1867–1911)
Houston Division, nos. 1–149 (1907–11)

Equity Docket Books
Galveston Division, vols. 1–2 (1867–1911)
Houston Division, vol. 1 (1907–11)

Public Records

Annual Report of the Attorney General of the United States (1870–1939).
Annual Report of the Director of the Administrative Office of the United States Courts (1940–60).
Annual Report of the Proceedings of the Judicial Conference of the United States (1945–60).
Confederate Constitution, Article III, Section 2. *Statutes at Large, Provisional Government of the Confederate States of America.*
Congressional Globe.
Congressional Record.
Department of Justice Records, RG 60, National Archives, Washington, D.C.
Federal Cases.
Federal Reports.
Federal Reports (2d ed.).
Federal Supplement.
General Laws of the State of Texas (1903).
General Laws of the State of Texas (1923).
Journal of the [Texas] House of Representatives, 42d Legislature, regular session, 1931.
Northeastern Reporter.
Records of the Clerk, Southern District of Texas, RG 21, Houston.
Revised Civil Statutes of Texas.
Selective Service in Peacetime: First Report of the Director of Selective Service, 1940–41. Washington, D.C.: U.S. Government Printing Office, 1942.
Selective Service in Wartime: Second Report of the Director of Selective Service, 1941–1942. Washington, D.C.: U.S. Government Printing Office, 1943.
Southwestern Reporter.
Texas House of Representatives. *Resolutions on the Life of John Henry Kirby.* Passed April 28, 1941.
Texas Reports.
Texas War Records, Barker Texas History Center, University of Texas, Austin.
U.S. Bureau of the Census. *Fifteenth Census of the United States: 1930. Population.* Vol. 11. Washington, D.C.: U.S. Government Printing Office, 1933.
U.S. Compiled Statutes, 1918. St. Paul, Minn.: West Publishing, 1918.

U.S. House of Representatives. "Authorizing the Appointment of Additional Circuit and District Judges for the U.S. Courts." *Hearings of Subcommittee No. 3 of the House Judiciary Committee,* 81st Congress, 1st session.

———. "Omnibus Judgeship Bill." *Report No. 1005 of the House Judiciary Committee,* 83d Congress, 1st session.

———. *Report No. 2 of the House Judiciary Committee,* 36th Congress, 2d session.

———. *Report No. 175 of the House Judiciary Committee,* 34th Congress, 3d session.

———. *Report No. 540 of the House Judiciary Committee,* 35th Congress, 1st session.

———. *Report No. 577 of the House Judiciary Committee,* 57th Congress, 1st session.

———. "A Report to Accompany H.R. 9785, a Bill to Provide a Method for Compensating Claims for Damages Sustained as the Result of the Explosions at Texas City, Texas." *Report No. 2024 of the House Judiciary Committee,* 83d Congress, 2d session.

———. "Texas City Disaster." *Hearings of the House Judiciary Committee,* 83d Congress, 1st session.

U.S. Reports.

U.S. Senate. "Texas City Disaster." *Hearings of the Senate Judiciary Committee,* 83d Congress, 2d session.

U.S. Statutes at Large.

U.S. War Department. *The War of the Rebellion: A Compilation of the Official Records of the Union and Confederate Armies.* Washington, D.C.: 1880–91.

Vernon's Civil Statutes of Texas.

Private Papers

Allred, James V., Papers, University of Houston, Houston, Texas

Burns, Waller T., Papers, held by Waller T. Burns III, Austin, Texas

Connally, Tom, Papers, Library of Congress, Washington, D.C.

Hannay, Allen B., Papers, held by clerk of the U.S. District Court, Southern District of Texas, Houston

Hutcheson, Joseph C., Jr., Papers, held by Joseph C. Hutcheson, III, Houston, Texas

Ingraham, Joe McDonald, Papers, Houston Metropolitan Research Center, Houston Public Library, Houston, Texas

Kennerly, Thomas M., Papers, held by T. Everton Kennerly, Houston, Texas

Kirby, John Henry, Papers, Houston Metropolitan Research Center, Houston Public Library, Houston, Texas

Selected Federal and State Cases

Note: Published legal cases are normally cited by the title of the case followed by the volume and title of the reporter (usually abbreviated) it can be found in. This is then followed by the first page the decision appears on. For example: *John Doe v. U.S.*, 33 F 222, means that the case of *John Doe v. the United States* can be found in volume 33 of the *Federal Reporter* starting on page 222. All subsequent citations to that decision will either repeat this information or, where a specific passage is being addressed, list the page where that passage can be found. Thus, if a direct quote is taken from a published decision, the page listed in the citation will be the one the quote came from, not the first page. In some cases, however, such as when a case is mentioned for the first time by quoting from it, the citation will include two page designations, the first denoting the first page of the decision and the second the page quoted from.

The following is a selected list of some of the more important federal and state cases cited in this book. Cases were included on this list merely as a guide to the more typical cases filed within the court. All cases used in this study are fully cited in the notes.

Alexander et al. v. Security Bank and Trust Co. et al., 273 F. 258.

Amazon Petroleum Corp. v. Commission, F. Supp., 693.

Anderson v. Mt. Clemens Pottery Co., 328 U.S., 680.

Beal et al. v. Holcombe, Civ. 5407, Houston Division.

Blum Hardware Co. v. George Paul, L 13, Corpus Christi Division.

Boggus Motor Co. v. Onderdonk et al., 9 F. Supp., 950.

Boxrollium Oil Co. v. Smith et al., 4 F. Supp., 624.

Boxrollium Oil Co. v. Smith, Eq 576, Houston Division.

Brotherhood of Railway and Steamship Clerks, etc. v. Texas and New Orleans RR Co., 24 F., 426.

Brotherhood of Railway and Steamship Clerks, etc. v. Texas and New Orleans RR Co., 25 F., 873.

Brotherhood of Railway and Steamship Clerks, etc. v. Texas and New Orleans RR Co., 33 F., 16.

Brownsville Irrigation Co. v. The Ohio and Texas Sugar Co., Eq 20, Houston Division.

Burst v. Newark Fire Insurance Co., 100 F. Supp., 751.

C. C. Putman and J. Tyler et al. v. General American Tank Storage Co., Civ 2400, Houston Division.

C. F. Palmer v. Texas and New Orleans RR, Civ 6728, Houston Division.

Cameron County Water Improvement District No. 1 v. Ashton et al., 81 F(2d), 905.

Carter Kelly Lumber Co. v. McGregor, Eq 630, Houston Division.

Central Trust Company of New York v. International and Great Northern RR, Eq 49, Houston Division.

Chancey v. Associated Indemnity Corp., 90 F. Supp., 298.

Charles Appen v. Anchor Casualty Co., Civ 2185, Houston Division.

Chicago Fire and Marine Insurance Co. v. National Bond and Mortgage Corp. et al., Eq 440, Houston Division.

Commercial Casualty Insurance Co. v. Humphrey et al., Eq 689, Houston Division.

Constintin v. Smith, 57 F(2d), 277.

Cowdrey v. Railroad et al., 6 Fed Cases, 660.
Creedon v. Budson Steede et al., Civ 2774, Houston Division.
D. H. Burnham v. Arcola Sugar Mills Co. et al., Eq 437, Houston Division.
D. T. Gill v. Liberty Mutual Insurance, Civ 2030, Houston Division.
Dalehite v. U.S., 346 U.S., 18.
Dalehite v. U.S., Civ 787, Galveston Division.
Employers Mutual Liability Insurance Co. v. Konvicka, 99 F. Supp., 433.
Erie RR Co. v. Tompkins, 304 U.S., 64.
Ex Parte Francois, 9 Fed Cases, 699.
Farmers Loan and Trust Co. v. International and Great Northern RR et al., Eq 96, Houston Division.
Fleming et al. v. Florence Cameron, Civ 2713, Houston Division.
Fleming et al. v. P. S. Quinn et al., Civ 2714, Houston Division.
Forbes v. Memphis El Paso RR Co., Fed Cases, 408.
Frank A Hardesty et al. v. Federal Steel Products Co., Civ 2461, Houston Division.
Frank A Hardesty et al. v. Hughes Tool Co., Civ 2456, Houston Division.
Frank Calvin et al. v. Hidalgo County Water Control and Improvement District No. 1 et al., Eq 256, Brownsville Division.
Galveston Electric Co. v. City of Galveston, 272 F., 147.
Grigsby v. Harris, 27 F(2d), 942.
Grovey v. Townsend, 295 U.S., 45.
Henderson v. Commission, 56 F(2d), 218.
Houston Pasture Co. v. The Alice State Bank et al., L 8, Corpus Christi Division.
In Re Cameron County Water Improvement District No. 1, 9 F. Supp., 103.
In Re Kirby, Bankruptcy Case 1717, Houston Division.
In Re Lake Jackson Sugar Co., 129 F. 640.
In Re Texas City Disaster Litigation, 197 F(2d), 774.
Insurance Underwriters, Inc. v. Sam Milkie, Civ 2479, Houston Division.
J. H. Bush and Wife v. Sun Oil Co., Eq 582, Houston Division.
J. H. McLeaish and Co. v. Binford et al., 52 F(2d), 151.
J. H. McLeaish and Co. v. Binford et al., Eq 467, Houston Division.
J. H. Stephenson v. Binford et al., 53 F(2d), 509.
J. H. Stephenson v. Binford et al., Eq 479, Houston Division.
James Story and J. Kirtley et al. v. Todd-Houston Shipbuilding Co., Civ 2458, Houston Division.
Jewell Ridge Coal Corp. v. Local 6167, 325 U.S., 161.
Knoxville v. Knoxville Water Co., 212 U.S., 16.
Lefevers v. General Export Iron and Metal Co., 36 F. Supp., 838.
Leon Henderson v. G. G. Conner dba Houston Hide Co., Civ 868, Houston Division.
Leyner Engineering Works v. Kempner, 123 F., 605.
Love et al. v. Griffith et al., 236 S.W., 239.
Love et al. v. Griffith et al., 266 U.S., 45.
Love v. George Thorpe, Election Judge of Precinct No. 24, et al., Eq 527, Houston Division.

MacMillan v. Commission, 51 F(2d), 400.

Malcolm Meek, Receiver v. Carter Stewart, L 2495, Houston Division.

Maryland Trust Co. v. Houston Oil Co., Eq 54, Houston Division.

Melvin L. Struas v. Metropolitan Properties Corp. et al., Eq 567, Houston Division.

Mercantile Trust Co. v. Texas and Pacific RR Co. et al., 51 F. 529.

Missouri, Kansas and Texas RR Co. v. Scott, 13 F. 793.

Mollie Nowell v. B. O. Johnson, L 9, Corpus Christi Division.

Mr. J. R. Randolph v. Sears, Roebuck and Co. and Southwestern Bell, Civ 4775, Houston Division.

Mr. S. Sport et al. v. St. Louis, Brownsville and Mexico RR et al., L 11, Corpus Christi Division.

National Liberty Insurance Co. of America v. Merkur et al., 29 F. Supp., 280.

Nebbia v. New York, 186, *Northeastern Reporter,* 694.

Nixon v. Herndon et al., 273 U.S., 536.

Nixon v. Herndon et al., 286 U.S., 73.

Ohio Casualty Insurance Co. v. Plummer et al., 13 F. Supp., 169.

Panama Refining Co. v. Ryan, 293 U.S., 388.

Paul Killatschny and Wife v. G. T. Blankenship et al., Eq 643, Houston Division.

People's Petroleum Producers v. Sterling et al., 60 F(2d), 1041.

Plessy v. Ferguson, 163 U.S. 537.

Prentiss Brown v. Joe D. Angel dba Weiner's Stores, Civ 1302, Houston Division.

Reagan v. Farmer's Loan and Trust Co., 154 U.S. 362.

Ross et al. v. Houston Independent School District, Civ 10444, Houston Division.

Ross v. Dyer, 203 F. Supp., 124.

Ross v. Dyer, 312 F(2d), 191.

San Diego Land Co. v. National City, 174 U.S., 753.

Smith v. Allwright, 321 U.S., 639.

Snow et al. v. Texas Trunk RR, 16 F., 1.

Southwestern Lumber Co. of New Jersey v. Kerr, 11 F. Supp., 260.

Spencer v. Lapsley, 60 U.S., 264.

Sproles v. Binford et al., 56 F(2d), 189.

Sproles v. Binford et al., Eq 476, Houston Division.

St. Louis and San Francisco RR v. Republic Box Co., 12 F(2d), 441.

St. Louis Frog and Switch Co. v. St. Louis, Brownsville and Mexico RR, Eq 36, Houston Division.

St. Louis Trust Co. v. San Benito Land and Water Co., Eq 40, Houston Division.

Swift v. Tyson, 16 Peters, 1.

T. H. Mastin and Co. v. Delta Land and Timber Co. et al., Eq 443, Houston Division.

Tennessee Coal Co. v. Muscoda Local, 321 U.S., 590.

Texas Express Co. v. Houston and Texas Central RR Co., 6 F., 426.

The Hornby Castle, 26 F(2d), 387.

Tighe E. Woods, Housing Expediter v. Carrie Haydell et al., Civ 2722, Houston Division.

Travelers Insurance Co. v. Dickson, 66 F. Supp., 72.
U.S. v. Able Guidry et al., Civ 2484, Houston Division.
U.S. v. Eugene John Kniderman, Cr 8352, Houston Division.
U.S. v. General Bernardo Reyes et al., Cr 552, 893, Laredo Division.
U.S. v. Israel Kolb, Cr 886, Laredo Division.
U.S. v. José Cisneros, Andrés Cisneros, and Isidoro Cornea, Cr 2343, Brownsville Division.
U.S. v. José Montenyo et al., Cr 2053, 2055, Brownsville Division.
U.S. v. One Sorrel Stallion et al., L 152, Brownsville Division.
U.S. v. Rafael Urrutia, Cr 6740, Houston Division.
U.S. v. 1.26 Acres in Harris County, Civ 883, Houston Division.
U.S. v. 8 Automobiles et al., 53 F. Supp., 775.
U.S. v. 16.275 Acres of Land et al., 45 F. Supp., 23.
U.S. v. 250 Acres of Land in Nueces County et al., 43 F. Supp., 938.
U.S. v. 251 Ladies Dresses et al., 53 F. Supp., 772.
U.S. v. 2049.85 Acres in Nueces County and Eagle Lake Improvement Co. et al., Civ 87, Corpus Christi Division.
U.S. v. Adolfo Garza, L 101, Brownsville Division.
U.S. v. Danaso Guzmán, Cr 1967, Brownsville Division.
U.S. v. Dodge, 25 Fed cases, 882.
U.S. v. Echols, 253 F. 826.
U.S. v. Edward Detuttle and Wife, Civ 2494, Houston Division.
U.S. v. Elton Julius Haberman, Cr 8361, Houston Division.
U.S. v. Enrique Ayola, Cr 1968, Brownsville Division.
U.S. v. Smith, 43 F(2d), 173.
Vera Fletcher Averett v. Zurich General Accident and Liability Insurance Co., Civ 52, Galveston Division.
Vera Wisnoskie et al. v. The Travelers Insurance Co., Civ 896, Houston Division.
W. Drake v. State Democratic Executive Committee, 2 F. Supp., 486.
W. M. Parker and Gulf Brewing Co. v. Jefferson Lake Sulfur Co., Civ 4047, Houston Division.
W. Strickland v. Humble Oil and Refining Co., L 2829, Houston Division.
Wallace v. Smith, 11 F. Supp., 728.
Wallace v. Smith, Eq 278, Brownsville Division.
White et al. v. County Democratic Executive Committee of Harris County et al., Eq 523, Houston Division.
White v. County Democratic Executive Committee of Harris County et al., 60 F(2d), 973.
White v. Lubbock et al., 30 S.W. (2d), 722.
William Smith v. St. Paul Fire and Marine Insurance Co., Civ 2056, Houston Division.
Woods v. Selber et al., 171 F(2d), 900.
Woods v. Tate, 171 F(2d), 511.
Woods v. Tate, Civ 2719, Houston Division.

Secondary Sources

Allen, Worth, "Wanted–A Plan for Regulating the Highway Carriers." *Public Utilities Fortnightly* 10 (March 31, 1932): 379–88.

Allhands, J. L. *Gringo Builders*. Iowa City: Privately printed, n.d.

Anders, Evan. "Boss Rule and Constituent Interests: South Texas Politics during the Progressive Era." *Southwestern Historical Quarterly* 84 (January, 1981): 269–92.

———. *Boss Rule in South Texas: The Progressive Era*. Austin: University of Texas Press, 1982.

Angoff, Jules E. "The Federal Tort Claims Act: A General View." *Boston University Law Review* 37 (Fall, 1957): 387–403.

Armstrong, Walter P. "Joseph C. Hutcheson, Jr.: Chief Judge, Fifth Circuit Court of Appeals." *American Bar Association Journal* 35 (June, 1949): 546–48.

Baggett, James. "Origins of Early Texas Republican Party Leadership." *Journal of Southern History* 40 (August, 1974): 441–54.

Barr, Alwyn. *Reconstruction to Reform: Texas Politics, 1876–1906*. Austin: University of Texas Press, 1971.

Barse, George. "A Summary of the Procedure and Principles Relating to the Liquidation of National Banks in Receivership." *Federal Bar Association Journal* 1 (October, 1932): 3–10.

Barton, Sam. *How Texas Cares for Her Injured Workers*. Denton: North Texas State College, 1956.

Bear, Joseph, "Survey of the Legal Profession–Workmen's Compensation and the Lawyer," *Columbia Law Review* 51 (December, 1951), 965–76.

Behrendt, Ernst. "What Really Happened at Texas City." *Popular Science* 166 (April, 1955): 268, 272.

Benedict, Michael Les. "Laissez-Faire and Liberty: A Re-Evaluation of the Meaning and Origins of Laissez-Faire Constitutionalism." *Law and History Review* 3 (Fall, 1985): 293–331.

Bicentennial Committee of the Judicial Conference of the United States. *Judges of the United States*, 2d ed. Washington, D.C.: U.S. Government Printing Office, 1983.

Black's Law Dictionary, 4th ed. St. Paul, Minn.: West Publishing, 1951.

Braeman, John. *Before the Civil Rights Revolution: The Old Court and Individual Rights*. New York: Greenwood Press, 1988.

Brand, Donald. *Corporatism and the Rule of Law: A Study of the National Recovery Administration*. Ithaca, N.Y.: Cornell University Press, 1988.

Brown, John R. "Hail to the Chief: Hutcheson, the Judge." *Texas Law Review* 38 (December, 1959): 140–46.

Bryant, Keith, Jr., and Henry Dethloff. *A History of American Business*. Englewood Cliffs, N.J.: Prentice-Hall, 1983.

Buenger, Walter L. "Between Community and Corporation: The Southern Roots of Jesse H. Jones and the Reconstruction Finance Corporation." *Journal of Southern History* 56 (August, 1990): 481–510.

———. *Secession and the Union in Texas.* Austin: University of Texas Press, 1984.

Buenger, Walter, and Joseph Pratt. *But Also Good Business: Texas Commerce Banks and the Financing of Houston and Texas, 1886–1986.* College Station: Texas A&M University Press, 1986.

Bureau of Yards and Docks. *Building the Navy's Bases in World War II: A History of the Bureau of Yards and Docks and the Civil Engineer Corps, 1940–1946.* Vols. I and II. Washington, D.C.: U.S. Government Printing Office, 1947.

Burns, Helen. *The American Banking Community and New Deal Banking Reforms, 1933–35.* Westport, Conn.: Greenwood Press, 1974.

Caldwell, Edwin. "Highlights of the Development of Manufacturing in Texas, 1900–1960." *Southwestern Historical Quarterly* 68 (April, 1965): 405–31.

Campbell, Randolph. "Planters and Plain Folk: Harrison County, Texas as a Test Case, 1850–60." *Journal of Southern History* 40 (August, 1974): 369–98.

Caro, Robert. *The Years of Lyndon Johnson: The Path to Power.* New York: Vintage, 1981.

Carp, Robert A., and Ronald Stidham. *The Federal Courts.* Washington, D.C.: C Q Press, 1985.

Casdorph, Paul. *A History of the Republican Party in Texas, 1865–1965.* Austin, Tex.: Pemberton Press, 1965.

Central Law Journal 18 (April, 1884): 281–82.

Chafee, Zachariah, Jr. "The Federal Interpleader Act of 1936." *Yale Law Journal* 45 (April, 1936): 1161–80.

———. "Interpleader in the United States Courts." *Yale Law Journal* 41 (June, 1932): 1134–71.

Chamberlain, Daniel M. *Constitutional History of the United States as Seen in the Development of American Law.* New York: G. Putnam's Sons, 1889.

Chambers, John Whiteclay. *To Raise an Army: The Draft Comes to Modern America.* New York: Free Press, 1987.

Chandler, Alfred, Jr. *The Railroads: The Nation's First Big Business.* New York: Harcourt, Brace and World, 1965.

———. *The Visible Hand: The Managerial Revolution in American Business.* Cambridge, Mass.: Belknap Press, 1977.

Chandler, Henry P. "Some Major Advances in the Federal Judicial System, 1922–1947." *Federal Rules Decisions* 31 (1963): 307–517.

Chase, Harold. *Biographical Dictionary of the Federal Judiciary.* Detroit: Gale Research Co., 1976.

Childs, William R. *Trucking and the Public Interest: The Emergence of Federal Regulation, 1914–1940.* Knoxville: University of Tennessee Press, 1985.

Clark, David. "Adjudication to Administration: A Statistical Analysis of Federal District Courts in the Twentieth Century." *Southern California Law Review* 55 (November, 1981): 65–152.

Clark, Greenville. "Reform in Bankruptcy Administration." *Harvard Law Review* 43 (June, 1930): 1189–1216.

Coalson, George. *The Development of the Migratory Farm Labor System in Texas, 1900–1954*. San Francisco: R&E Research Associates, 1977.

Cochran, Thomas C. *Railroad Leaders, 1845–1890: Business Mind in Action*. Cambridge: Harvard University Press, 1953.

Coerver, Don, and Linda Hall. *Texas and the Mexican Revolution: A Study in State and National Border Policy, 1910–1920*. San Antonio, Tex.: Trinity University Press, 1984.

Collier, William. *The Law and Practice in Bankruptcy under the National Bankruptcy Act of 1898*. 13th ed., 4 vols. Albany: M. Bender, 1923.

Comment, "The Federal Tort Claims Act." *Yale Law Journal* 56 (February, 1947): 534–61.

Cooley, Thomas. *A Treatise on the Constitutional Limitations Which Rest upon the Legislative Power of the States of the American Union*. Boston: Little, Brown and Co., 1968.

Cornell, Julien. "Exemption from the Draft: A Study in Civil Liberties." *Yale Law Journal* 56 (January, 1947): 263–65.

Corwin, Arthur. "A Story of Ad Hoc Exemptions: American Immigration Policy toward Mexico." In Arthur Corwin, ed., *Immigrants—and Immigrants: Perspectives on Mexican Labor Migration to the United States*, pp. 136–75. Westport, Conn.: Greenwood Press, 1978.

Cotner, Robert. *James Stephen Hogg: A Biography*. Austin: University of Texas Press, 1959.

Cotner, Robert, ed. *Address and State Papers of James Stephen Hogg*. Austin: University of Texas Press, 1951.

Cotner, Robert, et al., eds. *Texas Cities and the Great Depression*. Austin: Texas Memorial Museum, 1973.

Couch, Harvey. *A History of the Fifth Circuit, 1891–1981*. Washington, D.C.: Bicentennial Committee of the Judicial Conference of the United States, 1983.

Crane, M. M. "Recollections of the Establishment of the Texas Railroad Commission." *Southwestern Historical Quarterly* 50, no. 4 (1947): 478–86.

Cunniff, M. G. "Texas and Texans." *Worlds Work* 11 (March, 1906): 7269–70.

Cunningham, William. *American Railroads: Government Control and Reconstruction Policies*. Chicago: A. W. Shaw, 1922.

Cushman, Robert. "The Texas 'White Primary' Case—*Smith v. Allwright*," *Cornell Law Quarterly* 30 (September, 1944): 66–76.

D'Amico, Johanna M. "'Working Time' and the Portal-to-Portal Act of 1947." *Federal Bar Journal* 9 (July, 1948): 375–90.

Davidson, Chandler. *Race and Class in Texas Politics*. Princeton: Princeton University Press, 1990.

Davies, Richard O. *Housing Reform during the Truman Administration*. Columbia: University of Missouri Press, 1966.

"The Declaratory Judgment and the Insurance Contract." *Yale Law Journal* 46 (December, 1936): 286–99.

Degler, Carl. *Out of Our Past: The Forces That Shaped Modern America*. New York: Harper & Row, 1970.

Dession, George H. "Municipal Debt Adjustment and the Supreme Court." *Yale Law Journal* 46 (December, 1936): 199–227.

"Developments in the Law: Declaratory Judgements, 1941–1949." *Harvard Law Review* 62 (March, 1949): 787–833.

Dodd, E. Merrick. "The Supreme Court and Fair Labor Standards, 1941–1945." *Harvard Law Review* 59 (February, 1946): 321–73.

Dodd, Walter F. *Administration of Workmen's Compensation*. New York: Commonwealth Fund, 1936.

Eggert, Gerald. *Railroad Labor Disputes: The Beginnings of Federal Strike Policy*. Ann Arbor: University of Michigan Press, 1967.

Elliff, Nathan. "The War in the Courts: A Review of the Lawyers' Wartime Work," *Federal Bar Journal* 7 (October, 1945): 75–85.

Ellis, Richard. *The Jeffersonian Crisis: Courts and Politics in the Young Republic*. New York: W. W. Norton, 1971.

Ellis, Tuffly. *The Texas Cotton Compress Industry: A History*. Dallas: Privately printed, 1962.

Fairman, Charles. *Reconstruction and Reunion, 1864–88*. New York: Macmillan, 1971.

Farrand, Max, ed. *The Records of the Federal Convention of 1787*. 4 vols. New Haven: Yale University Press, 1911.

Feagin, Joe. *Free Enterprise City: Houston in Political and Economic Perspective*. New Brunswick: Rutgers University Press, 1988.

"Federal Judges in Texas." *Texas Bar Journal* 37 (May, 1974): 411.

Fehrenbach, R. *Lone Star: A History of Texas and the Texans*. New York: Macmillan, 1968.

Fink, Leon. "Labor, Liberty, and the Law: Trade Unionism and the Problem of the American Constitutional Order." *Journal of American History* 79 (December, 1987): 904–25.

Fish, Peter. *The Politics of Federal Judicial Administration*. Princeton, N.J.: Princeton University Press, 1973.

Fisher, E. L. "The Federal Tort Claims Act after Five Years." *Mercer Law Review* 3 (Spring, 1952): 253–77.

Fogel, Robert. *Railroads and American Economic Growth: Essays in Econometric History*. Baltimore: Johns Hopkins University Press, 1964.

Frankfurter, Felix, and Nathan Green. *The Labor Injunction*. New York: Macmillan, 1930.

Frankfurter, Felix, and James Landis. *The Business of the Supreme Court: A Study in the Federal Judicial System*. New York: Macmillan, 1927.

Franklin, John Hope. "The Enforcement of the Civil Rights Act of 1875." *Prologue* 6 (Winter, 1974): 225–35.

Freyer, Tony. *Forums of Order: The Federal Courts and Business in American History.* Greenwich, Conn.: Jai Press, 1979.

———. *Harmony and Dissonance: The* Swift *and* Erie *Cases in American Federalism.* New York: New York University Press, 1981.

Fuller, Warner. "The Background and Techniques of Equity and Bankruptcy Railroad Reorganizations—A Survey." *Law and Contemporary Problems* 7 (Summer, 1940): 375–92.

Galambos, Louis, and Joseph Pratt. *The Rise of the Corporate Commonwealth: U.S. Business and Public Policy in the Twentieth Century.* New York: Basic Books, 1988.

García, Juan Ramón. *Operation Wetback: The Mass Deportation of Mexican Undocumented Workers in 1954.* Westport, Conn.: Greenwood Press, 1980.

Gaston, Paul. *The New South Creed: A Study in Myth Making.* New York: Knopf, 1970.

Giebelhaus, August W. *Business and Government in the Oil Industry: A Case Study of Sun Oil, 1876–1945.* Greenwich, Conn.: Jai Press, 1980.

Goebel, Julius, Jr. *Antecedents and Beginnings to 1801.* New York: Macmillan, 1971.

Gould, Lewis. *Progressives and Prohibitionists: Texas Democrats in the Wilson Era.* Austin: University of Texas Press, 1973.

Grantham, Dewey. *Southern Progressivism: The Reconciliation of Progress and Tradition.* Knoxville: University of Tennessee Press, 1983.

Green, George N. *The Establishment in Texas Politics: The Primitive Years, 1938–1957.* Norman: University of Oklahoma Press, 1979.

Green, John E. *John E. Green and His Forty Years in Houston.* Houston: Dealy-Adey-Elgin, 1928.

"The Growth of Texas Is Unlimited: An Interview with Governor of Texas, Allan Shivers." *U.S. News and World Report* (November 23, 1956), pp. 88–89.

Hackney, Walter F. "Giants of Houston: Allan Burroughs Hannay." *The Best of Houston* (November, 1965): 4–8, 13.

Hainsworth, Robert. "The Negro and the Texas Primaries." *Journal of Negro History* 18 (October, 1933): 426–50.

Hall, Kermit. "Children of the Cabins": The Lower Federal Judiciary, Modernization and Political Culture, 1789–1899." *Northwestern University Law Review* 75 (October, 1980): 423–70.

———. "The Civil War Era as a Crucible for Nationalizing the Lower Federal Courts." *Prologue* 7 (Fall, 1975): 177–86.

———. *The Magic Mirror: Law in American History.* New York: Oxford University Press, 1989.

———. *The Politics of Justice: Lower Federal Judicial Selection and the Second Party System, 1829–61.* Lincoln: University of Nebraska Press, 1979.

———. "Social Backgrounds and Judicial Recruitment: Nineteenth Century Perspective on the Lower Federal Judiciary." *Western Political Quarterly* 29 (June, 1976): 243–57.

Hall, Kermit, and Eric W. Rise. *From Local Courts to National Tribunals: The Federal District Courts of Florida, 1821–1990.* Brooklyn: Carlson Publishing, 1991.

Hardwicke, Robert. "Legal History of Conservation of Oil in Texas." In American Bar Association, *Legal History of Conservation of Oil and Gas,* pp. 214–68. Chicago: 1938.

Harper, Elizabeth, and Roland Chase. *Immigration Laws of the United States.* 3d edition. Indianapolis: Bobbs-Merrill 1975.

Harris, Charles, and Louis Sadler. "The 1911 Reyes Conspiracy: The Texas Side." *Southwestern Historical Quarterly* 83 (April, 1980): 325–48.

———. "The Plan of San Diego and the Mexican–United States War Crisis of 1916: A Reexamination." *Hispanic American Historical Review* 58 (August, 1978): 381–408.

Hart, James. "Oil, the Courts, and the Railroad Commission." *Southwestern Historical Quarterly* 44 (January, 1941): 303–20.

Hartmann, Susan. *Truman and 80th Congress.* Columbia: University of Missouri Press, 1971.

Havins, T. R. "Administration of the Sequestration Act in the Confederate District Court for the Western District of Texas, 1862–1865." *Southwestern Historical Quarterly* 43 (January, 1940): 288–322.

Hawk, Emory. *Economic History of the South.* New York: Prentice-Hall, 1934.

Hawkins, Wallace. *The Case of John C. Watrous, United States Judge for Texas: A Political Story of High Crimes and Misdemeanors.* Dallas: University Press in Dallas, 1950.

Hawley, Ellis. *The New Deal and the Problem of Monopoly: A Study in Economic Ambivalence.* Princeton, N.J.: Princeton University Press, 1966.

———. "The Politics of the Mexican Labor Issue, 1950–65." In George Kiser and Martha Kiser, eds., *Mexican Workers in the United States: Historical and Political Perspectives,* pp. 101–109. Albuquerque: University of New Mexico Press, 1979.

Haynes, Robert V. *A Night of Violence: The Houston Riot of 1917.* Baton Rouge: Louisiana State University Press, 1976.

Henderson, Dwight F. *Courts for a New Nation.* Washington, D.C.: Public Affairs Press, 1971.

Hines, Darlene Clark. *Black Victory: The Rise and Fall of the White Primary in Texas.* Millwood, N.Y.: KTO Press, 1979.

Hoffman, Abraham. "Stimulus to Repatriation: The 1931 Federal Deportation Drive and the Los Angeles Mexican Community." *Pacific Historical Review* 42 (May, 1973): 205–19.

———. *Unwanted Mexican Americans in the Great Depression: Repatriation Pressures, 1929–1939.* Tucson: University of Arizona Press, 1974.

Hoover, Herbert. *Addresses upon the American Road: World War II.* New York: D. Van Nostrand, 1946.

Houston 1 (March, 1930): 3.

Howard, J. Woodford. *Courts of Appeals in the Federal Judicial System: A Study of the Second, Fifth and District of Columbia Circuits.* Princeton, N.J.: Princeton University Press, 1981.

Howe, Mark DeW., ed. *The Holmes-Laski Letters.* Cambridge: Harvard University Press, 1953.

Hutcheson, Joseph C., Jr. "A Case for Three Judges." *Harvard Law Review* 47 (March, 1934): 795–826.

———. "Declaratory Judgments as Applied to the Insurance Business." *Mississippi Law Journal* 14 (May, 1942): 484–94.

———. "In Praise of Lawyers and Lawyering." *Insurance Counsel Journal* 21 (July, 1954).

———. "The Judgement Intuitive: The Function of the 'Hunch' in Judicial Decision." *Cornell Law Quarterly* 14 (1929): 274–88.

———. "Judging as Administration, Administration as Judging." *Texas Law Review* 21 (November, 1942).

———. "Law and Fact in Insurance Cases." *Texas Law Review* 23 (December, 1944): 1–17.

———. *Law as Liberator: The Principle of Democracy in America: The Spirit of Its Laws.* Chicago: Foundation Press, 1937.

———. "The Local Jail." *American Bar Association Journal* 21 (February, 1935): 81–85, 88.

———. "This Thing Called Law." *University of Chicago Law Review* 2 (December, 1934).

Hyman, Harold. *A More Perfect Union: The Impact of the Civil War and Reconstruction on the Constitution.* Boston: Houghton Mifflin, 1975.

———. *To Try Men's Souls: Loyalty Tests in American History.* Berkeley and Los Angeles: University of California Press, 1960.

Hyman, Harold, and William Wiecek. *Equal Justice under Law: Constitutional Development, 1835–1875.* Cambridge, Mass.: Harper & Row, 1982.

Irons, Peter. *The New Deal Lawyers.* Princeton, N.J.: Princeton University Press, 1982.

Jacobs, Clyde. *Law Writers and the Courts: The Influence of Thomas Cooley, Christopher Tiedman and John Dillon upon American Constitutional Law.* Berkeley and Los Angeles: University of California Press, 1954.

Jaworski, Leon. "Joseph C. Hutcheson, Jr.: A Lifetime of Judicial Service." *Texas Bar Journal* 24 (December, 1961): 1107–1108.

Jones, Jesse H. *Fifty Billion Dollars: My Thirteen Years with the RFC.* New York: Macmillan, 1951.

Jordan, Terry. "The German Settlement of Texas after 1865." *Southwestern Historical Quarterly* 73 (October, 1969): 193–212.

Kaczorowski, Robert. *The Politics of Judicial Interpretation: The Federal Courts, Department of Justice and Civil Rights, 1866–1876.* New York: Oceana, 1985.

Keith, Nathanael. *Politics and the Housing Crisis since 1930.* New York: Universe Books, 1973.

Keller, Morton. *Affairs of State.* Cambridge, Mass.: Belknap Press, 1977.

———. *The Life Insurance Enterprise, 1885–1910; A Study in the Limits of Corporate Power.* Cambridge, Mass.: Belknap Press, 1963.

———. "Powers and Rights: Two Centuries of American Constitutionalism." *Journal of American History* 74 (December, 1987): 675–94.

Kelly, Alfred, Winfred Harbison, and Herman Belz. *The American Constitution: Its Origins and Development.* 6th ed. New York: W. W. Norton, 1983.

Kennedy, Susan Estabrook. *The Banking Crisis of 1933.* Lexington: University Press of Kentucky, 1973.

Kennerly, Thomas M. "The Pre-Trial Conference under the Federal Rules of Civil Procedure." *Texas Law Review* 18 (February, 1940): 190–96.

Kilgore, Dan E. "Corpus Christi: A Quarter Century of Development, 1900–1925." *Southwestern Historical Quarterly* 74 (April, 1972): 434–43.

King, John O. *The Early Years of the Houston Oil Company, 1901–1908. Texas Gulf Coast Historical Publications,* vol. 3, no. 1. Houston, 1959.

Kirkland, Edward Chase. *Dream and Thought in the Business Community, 1860–1900.* Ithaca, N.Y.: Cornell University Press, 1956.

Kiser, George, and Martha Kiser, eds. *Mexican Workers in the United States: Historical and Political Perspectives.* Albuquerque: University of New Mexico Press, 1979.

Kolko, Gabriel. *Railroads and Regulations, 1877–1916.* New York: W. W. Norton, 1965.

———. *The Triumph of Conservatism: A Reinterpretation of American History, 1900–1915.* Chicago: Quadrangle Books, 1963.

Kutler, Stanley. *Judicial Power and Reconstruction Politics.* Chicago: University of Chicago Press, 1968.

———. "A Sword for a Scabbard: Reflections on the Making of the Judiciary Act of 1789." *Nova Law Review* 14 (1989): 97–110.

Lasswell, Mary. *John Henry Kirby: Prince of the Pines.* Austin, Tex.: Encino Press, 1967.

Law, Francis. "New Deal Is Part of Changing World." *Texas Weekly* (October 6, 1934): 8–9.

Laws, Bolitha J. "Do the Judicial Systems as They Now Function Meet Today's Needs?" *Proceedings of the Insurance Section of the American Bar Association* (September 15–17, 1952): 16–28.

Levi, Edward, and James Moore. "Bankruptcy and Reorganization: A Survey of Changes." *University of Chicago Law Review* 5 (December, 1937): 1–40.

Link, Arthur. "The Wilson Movement in Texas, 1910–1912." *Southwestern Historical Quarterly* 48 (October, 1944): 167–85.

Lyons, Leverett, ed. *The National Recovery Administration: An Analysis and Appraisal.* Washington, D.C.: Government Printing Office, 1935.

McComb, David. *Galveston: A History.* Austin: University of Texas Press, 1986.

———. *Houston: The Bayou City.* Austin: University of Texas Press, 1969.

McCullough, David. "Bone Dry? Prohibition New Mexico Style, 1918–1933." *New Mexico Historical Review* 63 (January, 1988): 25–42.

McCurdy, Charles. "Justice Field and the Jurisprudence of Government-Business Relations: Some Parameters of Laissez-Faire Constitutionalism, 1863–1897." *Journal of American History* 61 (March, 1975): 970–1005.

McDonald, Roy. "Automobile Forfeitures and the Eighteenth Amendment." *Texas Law Review* 10 (February, 1932): 140–62.

McElvaine, Robert. *The Great Depression.* New York: Times Books, 1984.

McGregor, Douglas. "The Federal Declaratory Judgment Act." In *The Dallas Bar Speaks,* pp. 66–79. Dallas: 1939.

McKay, Seth. *Texas and the Fair Deal, 1945–1952.* San Antonio, Tex.: Naylor, 1954.

———. "Texas and the Southern Pacific Railroad, 1848–1860." *Southwestern Historical Quarterly* 35 (July, 1931): 1–27.

McKay, Seth, and Odie Faulk, *Texas after Spindletop.* Austin, Tex.: Steck-Vaughn, 1965.

McKitrick, Reuben. *The Public Land System of Texas, 1823–1910. Bulletin of the University of Wisconsin,* no. 405. Madison: 1918.

Maitland, Frederic. *Equity: A Course of Lectures.* Cambridge: At the University Press, 1909 [rev. ed., 1969].

Mansfield, Harvey C. *A Short History of the OPA.* Washington, D.C.: U.S. Government Printing Office, 1947.

Martin, Albro. "Railroads and the Equity Receivership: An Essay on Institutional Change." *Journal of Economic History* 34 (September, 1974): 685–709.

Mason, Alpheus T. "Organized Labor as Party Plaintiff in Injunction Cases." *Columbia Law Review* 30 (April, 1930): 466–87.

Matusow, Allen J. *Farm Policies and Politics in the Truman Administration.* Cambridge: Harvard University Press, 1967.

———. *The Unraveling of America: A History of Liberalism in the 1960s.* New York: Harper and Row, 1984.

Maxwell, Robert. *Texas Economic Growth, 1890 to World War II: From Frontier to Industrial Giant.* Boston: American Press, 1981.

Maxwell, Robert, and Robert Baker. *Sawdust Empire: The Texas Lumber Industry, 1830–1940.* College Station: Texas A&M University Press, 1983.

May, Francis, and Florence Escott. *Economic Statistics of Texas, 1900–1962.* Austin: *Historical Quarterly* 35 (July, 1931): 1–27.

Meigs, William. "General Principles of Jurisprudence." *Central Law Journal* 24 (December, 1889): 465–90.

Merz, Charles. *The Dry Decade.* Garden City, N.Y.: Doubleday, Doran, 1931.

Moneyhon, Carl. *Republicanism in Reconstruction Texas.* Austin: University of Texas Press, 1980.

Morris, Jeffrey. *Federal Justice in the Second Circuit: A History of the United States Courts in New York, Connecticut and Vermont, 1787–1987.* Washington, D.C.: Second Circuit Historical Committee, 1987.

Mowry, George. *The Era of Theodore Roosevelt, 1900–1912.* New York: Harper, 1958.

Murphy, Paul L. *The Constitution in Crisis Times, 1918–1969.* New York: Harper & Row, 1972.

———. *World War I and the Origin of Civil Liberties in the United States.* New York: Norton, 1979.

Murphy, Walter. "Chief Justice Taft and the Lower Court Bureaucracy: A Study in Judicial Administration." *Journal of Politics* 24 (August, 1962): 453–76.

Nash, Gerald. *The American West Transformed: The Impact of the Second World War.* Bloomington: Indiana University Press, 1985.

———. *United States Oil Policy, 1890–1964.* Pittsburgh: University of Pittsburgh Press, 1968.

National Cyclopaedia of American Biography. New York: James T. White, 1961.

Niemeyer, Vic. "Frustrated Invasion: The Revolutionary Attempt of General Bernardo Reyes from San Antonio in 1911." *Southwestern Historical Quarterly* 67 (October, 1963): 213–25.

Nordhauser, Norman. *The Quest for Stability: Domestic Oil Regulation, 1917–1935.* New York: Garland, 1979.

Note, "The Declaratory Judgment and the Insurance Contract." *Yale Law Journal* 46 (December, 1936): 286–99.

Note, "Developments in the Law of Declaratory Judgements, 1941–1949." *Harvard Law Review* 62 (March, 1949): 787–883.

Note, "The Federal Tort Claims Act." *Mississippi Law Journal* 20 (May, 1949): 354–72.

Noyes, Alexander. *Forty Years of American Finance.* New York: G. Putnam's Sons, 1909.

Olien, Roger, and Diana Olien. *Oil Booms: Social Change in Five Texas Towns.* Lincoln: University of Nebraska Press, 1982.

———. *Wildcatters: Texas Independent Oilmen.* Austin: Texas Monthly Press, 1984.

Oxment, Diane. "The Port City of Galveston." In Robert Cotner et al., eds. *Texas Cities and the Great Depression.* pp. 135–54. Miscellaneous Papers, no. 3, Texas Memorial Museum. Austin: 1973.

Paterson, Thomas. "The Quest for Peace and Prosperity: International Trade, Communism, and the Marshall Plan." In Barton Bernstein, ed., *Politics and Policies of the Truman Administration,* pp. 78–112. Chicago: Quadrangle Books, 1970.

Payne, Charles. "The General Administration of Equity Receiverships of Corporations." *Yale Law Journal* 31 (May, 1922): 685–701.

Peltason, J. W. *58 Lonely Men: Southern Federal Judges and School Desegregation.* Urbana: University of Illinois Press, 1961.

Phelps, V. E. "The Right to Regulate Contract Motor Carriers for Hire." *Public Utility Fortnightly* 10 (August 18, 1932): 202–11.

Phillips, Cabell. *The 1940s: Decade of Triumph and Trouble.* New York: Macmillan, 1975.

Platt, Harold. *City Building in the New South: The Growth of Public Services in Houston, Texas, 1830–1915.* Philadelphia: Temple University Press, 1983.

———. "Energy and Urban Growth: A Comparison of Houston and Chicago." *Southwestern Historical Quarterly* 91 (July, 1987): 1–18.

———. "Houston at the Crossroads: The Emergence of the Urban Center of the Southwest." *Journal of the West* 18 (July, 1979): 51–61.

"Pluperfect Hell." *Time*, April 28, 1947, pp. 22–24.

Polenberg, Richard. *War and Society: The United States, 1941–1945*. New York: J. B. Lippincott, 1972.

Posner, Richard A. *The Federal Courts: Crisis and Reform*. Cambridge: Harvard University Press, 1985.

Pratt, Joseph. *The Growth of a Refining Region*. Greenwich, Conn.: Jai Press, 1980.

Pratt, Joseph, and Kenneth Liparto. *Baker and Botts in the Development of Modern Houston*. Austin: University of Texas Press, 1991.

Presser, Stephen. *Studies in the History of the United States Courts of the Third Circuit*. Washington, D.C.: Bicentennial Committee of the Judicial Conference of the United States, 1983.

Prindle, David. *Petroleum Politics and the Texas Railroad Commission*. Austin: University of Texas Press, 1981.

Protecting Texas Industries for Two Decades: A Brochure on the History and Operation of the Texas Employers Insurance Association. Dallas: Privately printed, 1934.

Randolph, Nowlin. "Judge William Pinckney Hill Aids the Confederate War Effort." *Southwestern Historical Quarterly* 68 (July, 1964): 14–28.

Read, Frank, and Lucy McGough. *Let Them Be Judged: The Judicial Integration of the Deep South*. Metuchen, N.J.: Scarecrow Press, 1978.

Reed, S. G. *A History of the Texas Railroads*. Houston: St. Clair, 1941.

Reid, John P. "Another Origin of Judicial Review: The Constitutional Crisis of 1776 and the Need for a Dernier Judge." *New York University Law Review* 64 (November, 1989): 963–89.

Reisler, Mark. *By the Sweat of Their Brow*. Westport, Conn.: Greenwood Press, 1976:

"Resolutions and Statement of the Committee on Jurisprudence and Law Reform." *Report of the American Bar Association* 51 (1928): 435.

Rhinehart, Marilyn, and Thomas Krenck. "'In the Shadow of Uncertainty': Texas Mexicans and Repatriation in Houston during the Great Depression." *Houston Review* 10 (1988): 21–33.

Robbins, William. "The Great Experiment in Industrial Self-Government: The Lumber Industry and the National Recovery Administration." *Journal of Forest History* 25 (July, 1981): 125–43.

Robinson, William, Jr. *Justice in Grey: A History of the Judicial System of the Confederate States of America*. Cambridge: Harvard University Press, 1941.

Rodrigues, Louis, ed. *Dynamics of Growth: An Economic Profile of Texas*. Austin, Tex.: Madrona Press, 1978.

Rogers, Ralph. "Historical Origins of Interpleader." *Yale Law Journal* 51 (April, 1942): 942–50.

Sandos, James. "The Plan of San Diego: War and Diplomacy on the Texas Border, 1915–1916." *Arizona and the West* 14 (Spring, 1972): 4–24.

Scheiber, Harry, "American Constitutional History and the New Legal History:

Complementary Themes in Two Modes." *Journal of American History* 68 (September, 1981): 337–50.

———. "Public Rights and the Rule of Law in American History." *California Law Review* 72 (March, 1984): 217–51.

———. *The Wilson Administration and Civil Liberties, 1917–1921.* Ithaca, N.Y.: Cornell University Press, 1960.

Schlesinger, Arthur, Jr. *The Coming of the New Deal.* Cambridge, Mass.: Riverside Press, 1959.

Scruggs, Otey. "Texas and the Bracero Program, 1942–1947." In George Kiser and Martha Kiser, eds., *Mexican Workers in the United States: Historical and Political Perspectives,* pp. 85–96. Albuquerque: University of New Mexico Press, 1979.

Siegel, Nathan. "Recent Decisions Construing Federal Rent Control Legislation." *Syracuse Law Review* 1 (Fall, 1949): 207–46.

Sibley, Marilyn. *The Port of Houston: A History.* Austin: University of Texas Press, 1968.

Simmons, Ozzie. *Anglo-Americans and Mexican Americans in South Texas.* New York: Arno Press, 1974.

Sklar, Martin. *The Corporate Reconstruction of American Capitalism, 1890–1916: The Market, the Law and Politics.* Cambridge: Cambridge University Press, 1988.

Smith, Douglas. *The New Deal in the Urban South.* Baton Rouge: Louisiana State University Press, 1988.

Solomon, Rayman. "Regulating the Regulators: Prohibition Enforcement in the Seventh Circuit." In David Kyvig, ed. *Law, Alcohol, and Order: Perspectives on National Prohibition,* pp. 81–96. Westport, Conn.: Greenwood Press, 1985.

Spratt, John. *The Road to Spindletop: Economic Change in Texas, 1875–1901.* Dallas: Southern Methodist University Press, 1955.

Sprecher, Robert A. "Price Control in the Courts." *Columbia Law Review* 44 (January, 1944): 34–64.

Spurr, Henry. "A New and Significant Test of the Right to Be Regulated." *Public Utilities Fortnightly* 9 (February 18, 1932): 207–19.

Staring, Graydon. "Bankruptcy: An Historical View." *Tulane Law Review* 59 (June, 1985).

Steen, Ralph. *Twentieth Century Texas: An Economic and Social History.* Austin: Steck, 1942.

Stover, John. *American Railroads.* Chicago: University of Chicago Press, 1961.

———. *The Railroads of the South, 1865–1900: A Study in Finance and Control.* Chapel Hill: University of North Carolina Press, 1955.

"The Sun Still Shines." *Cotton and Cotton Oil News* 30 (November 18, 1929): 1.

Surrency, Erwin. "Federal District Court Judges and the History of Their Courts." *Federal Rules Decisions* 40 (1967): 139–310.

———. "A History of the Federal Courts." *Missouri Law Review* 28 (Winter, 1963): 214–44.

———. *A History of the Federal Courts.* New York: Oceana Publications, 1987.

Swain, Henry. *Economic Aspects of Railroad Receiverships.* Vol. 3, no. 2, *Proceedings of the American Economic Association.* New York: Macmillan, 1898.

Swinney, Everette. "Enforcing the Fifteenth Amendment, 1870–1877." *Journal of Southern History* 28 (May, 1962): 202–18.

Tachau, Mary K. Bonsteel. *Federal Courts in the Early Republic: Kentucky, 1789–1816.* Princeton: Princeton University Press, 1978.

Taft, William Howard. "Criticism of the Federal Judiciary." *American Law Review* 29 (September–October, 1895): 643–74.

———. "Possible and Needed Reforms in the Administration of Justice in the Federal Courts." *Report of the American Bar Association.* 45 (1922): 258–59.

Texas Almanac. Dallas: Dallas Morning News, 1945–60.

"Texas Comes of Age." *Time,* April 7, 1947, p. 88.

Texas Commercial Secretaries and Business Men's Association. *Industrial Texas.* Fort Worth: 1913.

Texas Employer's Insurance Association. *Protecting Texas Industries for Two Decades: A Brochure on the History and Operation of the Texas Employers Insurance Association.* Dallas: May, 1934.

Texian Who's Who. Dallas: Texian Co., 1937.

"Thomas M. Kennerly." *Texas Bar Journal* 21 (February 23, 1958): 80, 100.

Thompson, W. Ernest. "John E. Green, Jr." *Texas Bar Journal* 30 (October, 1967): 777–78.

Timberg, Sigmund. "Insurance and Interstate Commerce." *Yale Law Journal* 50 (April, 1941): 959–62.

Urofsky, Melvin. *The Continuity of Change: The Supreme Court and Individual Liberties, 1953–1986.* Belmont, Calif.: Wadsworth, 1990.

Vatter, Harold G. *The U.S. Economy in the 1950s: An Economic History.* New York: W. W. Norton, 1963.

———. *The U.S. Economy in World War II.* New York: Columbia University Press, 1985.

Walker, A. W., Jr. "The Nature of Property Interests Created by an Oil and Gas Lease in Texas." *Texas Law Review* 10 (April, 1932): 291–323; 11 (June, 1933): 399–454.

Wallace, Ernest. *Texas in Turmoil.* Austin: Steck-Vaughn, 1965.

"Waller T. Burns." *Proceedings of the Texas Bar Association* 37 (July, 1918): 344–46.

Warren, Charles. *Bankruptcy in United States History.* Cambridge: Harvard University Press, 1935.

———. "New Light on the History of the Federal Judiciary Act of 1789." *Harvard Law Review* 37 (November, 1927): 47–132.

Webb, Ross. "Benjamin H. Bristow: Civil Rights Champion, 1866–1872." *Civil War History* 15 (March, 1969): 39–53.

Weingart, Mike, et al. *Big Town, Big Money: The Business of Houston.* Houston: Cordovan Press, 1973.

Wheaton, Elizabeth. *Texas City Remembers.* San Antonio, Tex.: Naylor, 1948.

White, G. Edward. *The American Judicial Tradition.* Oxford: Oxford University Press, 1976.

———. *Tort Law in America.* New York: Oxford University Press, 1980.

"Why." *New Republic,* April 28, 1947, p. 8.

"Why Texas Is Thriving." *U.S. News and World Report,* November 23, 1956, pp. 70–86.

Wiecek, William. "The Reconstruction of Federal Judicial Power, 1863–1875." *American Journal of Legal History* 13 (October, 1969): 333–59.

Wiswall, F. L., Jr. *The Development of Admiralty Jurisdiction and Practice since 1800: An English Study with American Comparisons.* Cambridge: At the University Press, 1970.

Woods, Tighe. "The Administration of a Law: Federal Rent Control." *Notre Dame Lawyer* 25 (Spring, 1950): 407–37.

Woodward, C. Vann. *Origins of the New South, 1877–1913.* Baton Rouge: Louisiana State University Press, 1951.

Writers Program, Works Progress Administration. *Houston: A History and Guide.* Houston: 1942.

Zinn, Howard. *The Southern Mystique.* New York: Knopf, 1974.

Theses, Dissertations, and Unpublished Manuscripts

Adams, Larry, "Economic Development in Texas during Reconstruction, 1865–1875." Ph.D. dissertation, North Texas State University, 1980.

Cook, Virginia. "The Administration of the Fair Labor Standards Act with Special Reference to Enforcement." Ph.D. dissertation, Columbia University, 1953.

Davidson, Chandler. "Negro Politics and the Rise of the Civil Rights Movement in Houston, Texas." Ph.D. dissertation, Princeton University, 1968.

Dirck, Brian. "The Confederate Sequestration Act: Its Origins and Provisions, 1861." Manuscript, Houston, Texas, October 21, 1988.

Holmes, James. "From Railroads to Immigration: Texas Federal Courts in the Late Nineteenth Century." Manuscript, Houston, Texas, April 26, 1989.

Huddleston, John. "Good Roads for Texas: A History of the Texas Highway Department, 1917–1947." Ph.D. dissertation, Texas A&M University, 1981.

Kennedy, Mizell. "A Study of James Stephen Hogg, Attorney General and Governor." M.A. thesis, University of Texas, 1919.

Mackey, Thomas. "Red Lights Out: A Legal History of Prostitution, Disorderly Houses, and Vice Districts, 1870–1917." Ph.D. dissertation, Rice University, 1984.

Meador, Bruce S. "Wetback Labor in the Lower Rio Grande Valley." M.A. thesis, University of Texas, 1951.

Meakin, Christopher. "Congressional Control of Federal Court Jurisdiction and the Effect of Protection of Civil Rights." M.A. thesis, Rice University, 1988.

Patenaude, Lionel V. "The New Deal and Texas." Ph.D. dissertation, University of Texas, 1953.

Spivack, John M. "Race, Civil Rights, and the United States Court of Appeals for the Fifth Judicial Circuit." Ph.D. dissertation, University of Florida, 1978.

Sorelle, James. "The Darker Side of 'Heaven': The Black Community in Houston, Texas, 1917–1945," Ph.D. dissertation, Kent State University, 1980.

Taylor, Matthew. "Rise and Fall of the Ku Klux Klan in Houston, Texas, 1920–1923." Manuscript, Houston, Texas, 1987.

Tidwell, Pat. "Allred's First Tenure on the Federal Bench, 1938–1942," Manuscript, December 15, 1987.

Interviews

With the Author

Brown, Judge John R., February 16, 1988, Houston Texas.

Bue, Judge Carl. February 18, 1988, Houston, Texas.

Crain, Jeff. September 18, 1990, Houston, Texas.

Hutcheson III, Joseph C. March 3, 1988, Houston, Texas.

Ingraham, Judge Joe McDonald. February 4, 1988, Houston, Texas.

Kennerly, T. Everton. April 4, 1989.

Noel, Judge James L., Jr. February 12, 1988, Houston, Texas.

Seals, Judge Woodrow. March 2, 1988, Houston, Texas.

Singleton, Judge John V. March 14, 1988, Houston, Texas.

Tarlton, Vince. March 18, 1988, Houston, Texas.

Weatherly, Thomas B. September 6 and 7, 1990, Houston, Texas (telephone).

With David McComb (on file in Ingraham Papers)

Hannay, Judge Allen B. June 5, 1969.

With MacLyn Burg (on file in Ingraham Papers)

Ingraham, Judge Joe McDonald. November 9, 1972, and May 21, 1973.

With John Spivack (used with permission)

Smith, Allen. August 15, 1977, Columbia, Missouri.

Index

Justice Lies in the District was composed into type on a Compugraphic digital phototypesetter in ten point Berkeley Old Style with two points of spacing between the lines. Berkeley Old Style was also selected for display. The book was designed by Jim Billingsley, typeset by Metricomp, Inc., printed offset by Thomson-Shore, Inc., and bound by John H. Dekker & Sons, Inc. The paper on which this book is printed carries acid-free characteristics for an effective life of at least three hundred years.

TEXAS A&M UNIVERSITY PRESS
COLLEGE STATION